Guide to Ghana

THE BRADT STORY

In 1974, my former husband George Bradt and I spent three days sitting on a river barge in Bolivia writing our first guide for like-minded travellers: *Backpacking along Ancient Ways in Peru and Bolivia*. The 'little yellow book', as it became known, is now in its sixth edition and continues to sell to travellers throughout the world. Since 1980, with the establishment of Bradt Publications, I have continued to publish guides for the discerning traveller, covering more than 100 countries and all six continents, and winning the 1997 *Sunday Times* Small Publisher of the Year Award. *Guide to Ghana* is the 142nd Bradt title to be published.

The company continues to develop new titles and new series, but in the forefront of my mind there remains our original ethos – responsible travel with an emphasis on the culture and natural history of the region. I hope that you will get the most out of your trip, and perhaps have the opportunity to give something in return.

Travel guides are by their nature continuously evolving. If you experience anything which you would like to share with us, or if you have any amendments to make to this guide, please write; all your letters are read and passed on to the author. Most importantly, do remember to travel with an open mind and to respect the customs of your hosts – it will add immeasurably to your enjoyment.

Happy travelling!

Hilary Bradt

Hilary Bradt

41 Nortoft Road, Chalfont St Peter, Bucks SL9 0LA, England
Tel/fax: 01494 873478 Email: bradtpublications@compuserve.com

Guide to
Ghana

Philip Briggs

Bradt Publications, UK
The Globe Pequot Press Inc, USA

Published in 1998 by Bradt Publications,
19 High Street, Chalfont St Peter, Bucks SL9 9QE, England
Published in the USA by The Globe Pequot Press Inc, 246 Goose Lane,
PO Box 480, Guilford, Connecticut 06475-0480

Reprinted with amendments 1999
2nd reprint with amendments 2000

The author and publishers have made every effort to ensure the accuracy of the information
in this book at the time of going to press. However, they cannot accept any
responsibility for any loss, injury or inconvenience resulting from
the use of information contained in this guide.

ISBN 1 898323 69 0

British Library Cataloguing in Publication Data

A catalogue record for this book is available from the British Library

Library of Congress Cataloging-in-Publication Data

Briggs, Philip
    Guide to Ghana / Philip Briggs.
        p. cm.
    Includes bibliographical references and index.
    ISBN 1-898323-69-0
    1. Ghana—Guidebooks. I. Title.
DT510.2.B76 1998
916.6704'5—dc21   98-27865
                                                        CIP

Photographs   Ariadne Van Zandbergen
Front cover 19th century Wa-Na's palace,
built in west Sudanese mosque style
Back cover Kente cloth
Illustrations   Annabel Milne
Maps   Steve Munns
Inside back cover Mountain High Maps™ ©1995 Digital Wisdom Inc

Typeset from the author's disc by Wakewing, High Wycombe HP13 7QA
Printed and bound in Great Britain by The Guernsey Press Co Ltd

ABOUT THE AUTHOR

Philip Briggs is a travel writer and tour leader specialising in East and southern Africa. Born in Britain and raised in South Africa, he started travelling in East Africa in 1986 and has since spent the equivalent of five years exploring the highways and back roads of the subcontinent. His first book *Guide to South Africa*, now in its third edition, was published by Bradt in 1991. Since then Philip has written several other titles for Bradt: *Guide to Tanzania*, *Guide to Uganda*, *Guide to Ethiopia*, *Guide to Malawi*, *Guide to Mozambique* and *East & Southern Africa: The Backpackers Manual*. He is also the author of the *Visitors' Guide to Kenya and East Africa* (Southern Books) and a frequent contributor to several British and South African periodicals.

Ariadne Van Zandbergen, who took the photographs for this book and contributed to the research, is a freelance photographer and tour guide. Born and raised in Belgium, she travelled through Africa from Morocco to South Africa in 1994/5 and is now resident in Johannesburg. She has visited 20 African countries and her photographs have appeared in several books, magazines, newspapers, maps, periodicals and pamphlets.

ABOUT THE 2000 REPRINT

This reprint of Guide to Ghana has been put together at short notice so that the book doesn't go out of print before a fully updated second edition is published. It is not by any means a new edition, but I have used the opportunity to update what I can and incorporate the most essential snippets of information sent in by readers. Many thanks to all those who have written or emailed with their thoughts and suggestions; what I haven't been able to fit into this reprint will be incorporated into the second edition, when all correspondents will be acknowledged by name – so keep the letters rolling...

Please note that the prices quoted in this guide are unaltered from the original 1998 print. This is for the simple reason that giving the odd current price alongside others gathered two years ago would make it difficult for readers to compare the relative cost of different hotels or restaurants. In US dollar terms, most prices quoted in this guide will have increased only slightly, or not at all, since 1998. See the section on *Prices* on pages 55–6 for further details.

Based on readers' letters, I'm pleased to report that travel conditions in Ghana remain much as they were in early 1998. Better still, of perhaps 40 letters and emails received, every one has been overwhelmingly positive about the country. By the sound of it, Ghana is still a great country to travel in; we look forward to returning there soon to research a fresh edition!

CONTENTS

VIII

ACKNOWLEDGEMENTS

Many thanks to my wife, Ariadne, for her company throughout Ghana, for supplying all the photographs used in this guide, and for tolerating my frequently unsuccessful attempts to remain good humoured during the nine weeks I had to write this book. I probably owe Tricia Hayne at Bradt Publications a substantial vote of thanks on the tolerance front too.

Ariadne and I are both deeply indebted to John Awuah of Ghana Airways in South Africa, without whose generous support and assistance this book would never have got off the ground. Thanks, too, to Bernard Antoine of the Accra Novotel, Peter Fenwick of Labadi Beach Hotel, Frances Sey of the Shangrila Hotel, and Bertha de Graft-Johnson of the Golden Tulip.

Finally, my gratitude to those who contributed information, notably Don Evans of the Peace Corps in Accra, plus Michele Beasley and Donna Broughton, volunteers at Liate Wote and Somanya respectively, but also the many travellers and Ghanaians who knowingly or unknowingly helped with my research, and most especially Nicole Linnenbank for posting me reliable details about her off-the-beaten-track travels in northern Volta Region

WEBSITES

Three websites worth checking out before you travel to Ghana are www.africaonline.com.gh (general tourist information), www.ncrc.org.gh (currently under development but potentially a highly worthwhile resource for information about ecotourist and community development tourist sites) and www.wildlife.gov.gh (details of national parks).

Introduction

As travel destinations go, Ghana is difficult to flaw. When a few years back somebody coined the phrase 'Africa for Beginners' to describe Malawi, that most laid-back of southern African countries, they might as easily have been talking about Ghana today. Doubly so. Not only can Ghana, like Malawi, be recommended without reservation to even the most nervous of first-time independent travellers for being as amiable, affordable and hassle-free as practically any country on the African continent; just as important, Ghana boasts a travel circuit so varied and compact that it might almost be seen as offering a microcosmic first taste of Africa.

The southern part of Ghana is much as you'd expect of West Africa, all lush jungle, banana plantations and bone-white beaches, albeit with a unique dimension in the form of the string of 500-year old European forts and castles that line the former Gold Coast. But the real surprises begin as you travel further north, for instance to the game-rich savannah of Mole National Park, a setting that evokes East Africa more than West Africa, or to the deeply Muslim Burkina Faso border region, where both mood and architecture have unexpected overtones of North Africa.

For English-speaking travellers, Ghana must certainly be regarded as the obvious first port of call in West Africa. Of only five anglophile countries in the region, it's the only one that really caters to independent travellers – granted, not necessarily a major commendation from a shortlist which also includes such potential 'holiday' venues as Liberia, Nigeria and Sierra Leone. Fairer to say that you're unlikely to meet an English speaker who's travelled in West Africa in recent years and has anything negative to say about Ghana by comparison with its more expensive (and generally less well-equipped) francophone neighbours.

What Ghana does *not* have is one drop-dead, big-name attraction, the sort of place that friends who've visited will say you simply *have* to see once in your lifetime. Zimbabwe has Victoria Falls, Tanzania has Kilimanjaro, South Africa has Cape Town, Ethiopia its rock-hewn churches. The closest thing Ghana has to offer in the unmissability stakes is the above-mentioned castles, not quite the pyramids in terms of impact, I grant you, but nevertheless a unique and chilling memorial to an episode as sickening as any in the recorded history of Africa, the cruel trade in human life that resulted in several millions of Africans being displaced to a life of bondage in the plantations of the Americas and the Caribbean.

If Ghana lacks one truly great tourist attraction, then it is equally true that during the two rapidly paced months we spent researching this guide, barely a day went by without at least one memorable highlight, be it swimming below one of the gorgeous waterfalls of the eastern highlands, the thrill of getting closer on foot to a wild elephant than I ever have in East Africa, climbing to the roof of one of the surreal mosques that dot the northwest, taking a dugout canoe through papyrus swamps to the stilted village of Mzulezu, or watching colourful mona monkeys play between the houses of Baobeng village.

Ghana is a perfect travel destination, not least because it is so mercifully free of the trappings associated with mass tourism. Nowhere in the country are you made to feel part of some tourist treadmill, and – even if it has become something of a cliché for me to say so in the introduction to my guides – Ghana really *is* endowed with some remarkably exciting off-the-beaten-track possibilities. There are, for instance, at least five national parks and reserves ideally suited for equipped independent travellers, yet which currently go months on end without seeing a visitor. It is my hope that, by documenting for the first time the practicalities that surround visiting many of these places, I will encourage adventurous travellers to start realising the enormous potential for exploration that lies beyond Ghana's few relatively well-established tourist trails.

There has been much talk in the last couple of years of an African renaissance and, regardless of what one thinks of such generalisations, it is Ghana along with Uganda that is most frequently cited as being at the forefront of this movement. Trailblazing of this sort is not a new role for Ghana – the former Gold Coast was the first country in Africa to have extended contact with Europeans, one of the first to be formally colonised, and in 1957 it became the first to be granted independence in the post-war era. Less prestigiously, Ghana also became one of the first African countries to slide into post-independence chaos and, while it never plummeted to the depths reached by, say, Liberia or Rwanda, the modern visitor will find it difficult to reconcile accounts of Ghana ten years ago with the vibrant country they see today.

Ghana is indeed steeped in history and tradition, more tangibly so than most countries I have visited. Yet it is also, emphatically, a country building towards a brighter future – and this paradox, above all, makes it one of Africa's most rewarding and exciting travel destinations. As Ghanaians are so fond of saying, '*Akwaaba!*' – 'Welcome!' Ghana will not disappoint.

Part One

PRACTICAL INFORMATION

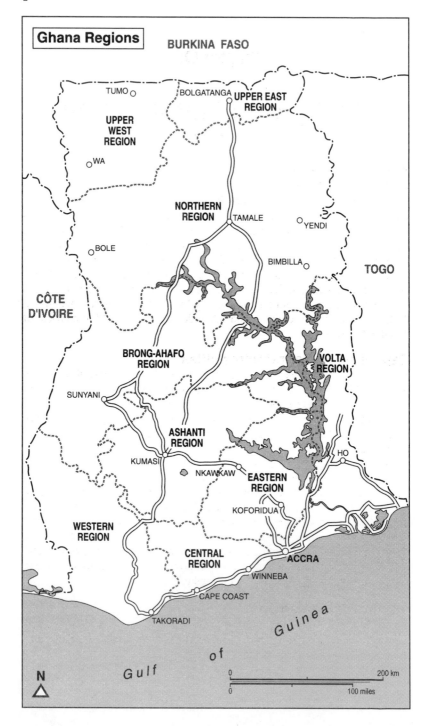

Ghana Regions

BURKINA FASO

TUMO

BOLGATANGA UPPER EAST REGION

UPPER WEST REGION

WA

NORTHERN REGION TAMALE

YENDI

BOLE

BIMBILLA

TOGO

CÔTE D'IVOIRE

BRONG-AHAFO REGION

VOLTA REGION

SUNYANI

ASHANTI REGION

KUMASI

NKAWKAW

HO

EASTERN REGION

KOFORIDUA

WESTERN REGION

CENTRAL REGION

ACCRA

WINNEBA

CAPE COAST

TAKORADI

Guinea

Gulf of

N

0 200 km

0 100 miles

Chapter One

Background Information

FACTS AND FIGURES
Location and size

The Republic of Ghana (formerly the Gold Coast) lies on the Gulf of Guinea on the western coast of tropical Africa. Ghana extends for a maximum of 672km from north to south between latitudes 4.5°N and 11°N, and for 536km east to west between longitudes 3°W and 1°E. It is bordered to the west by Côte d'Ivoire (Ivory Coast), to the north by Burkina Faso, to the west by Togo and to the south by the Atlantic Ocean. With a total land area of 239,460km² (similar to that of Great Britain or the state of Oregon in the USA), Ghana is not a large country by African standards, occupying 30th place between Guinea and Uganda among the 47 countries of mainland Africa.

Capital and other principal cities

The capital of Ghana is Accra, situated on the Atlantic coast about 25km west of the Greenwich Meridian. Population estimates for Accra vary greatly, but the current population certainly exceeds one million and is in all probability far closer to two million. The second largest city in the country is Kumasi, the former capital of the Ashanti Empire and modern capital of the synonymous administrative region, with a population of between half and one million people, depending on which figures you believe.

Various sources quote such wildly different population figures for other large towns in Ghana that it is impossible to rank them by size, at least with any great conviction. However, based on the divergent sources and my own impressions, I would regard the ten largest towns in Ghana, in approximate descending order of population, to be Accra, Kumasi, Tamale, Tema, Takoradi (excluding Sekondi), Cape Coast, Koforidua, Sunyani, Obuasi and Ho. Other towns with a population of around 50,000 or more include Winneba, Bolgatanga, Wa, Tafu and Bawku.

Administrative regions

Ghana is divided into ten administrative regions, all of which to some degree have borders dating from the earliest days of colonialism. Several of the regions also have names that date from the earliest colonial times in a manner that can create some confusion to new arrivals to the country. The Western, Central and Eastern regions as delineated by the British administration before the annexation of Ashanti in 1902 still go by those names, even though Eastern Region today lies to the west of Volta Region, and Central Region lies nowhere near the centre of modern Ghana but on its southern coast. Likewise, the original Northern Region as delineated by the colonial authorities has since been split in such a manner that Northern Region lies to the south of Upper East and Upper West regions. It is worth being aware of this, because the regions have a high profile in Ghana today, and when most Ghanaians speak of 'eastern', 'central' or 'northern' they mean the administrative region rather than the most easterly, central or northerly part of the country.

The ten modern administrative regions of Ghana are as follows:

	Km²	Population*	Capital	Other large towns
Ashanti	24,390	3,000,000	Kumasi	Obuasi, Tafo, Mampong
Brong-Ahafo	39,557	1,800,000	Sunyani	Techiman, Wenchi, Kintampo
Central Dumkwa	9,826	1,500,000	Cape Coast	Elmina, Winneba,
Eastern	19,223	2,200,000	Koforidua	Akim Oda, Nkawkaw, Akosombo
Greater Accra	3,245	2,500,000	Accra	Tema, Ada, Dodowa, Ashaiman
Northern	70,384	1,800,000	Tamale	Yendi, Bimbilla, Nalerigu
Upper East	8,842	1,100,000	Bolgatanga	Navrongo, Bawku, Zebilla
Upper West	18,476	800,000	Wa	Jiripa, Tumu, Lawra
Volta Keta	20,334	1,800,000	Ho	Hohoe, Aflao, Kpando,

Estimated by multiplying the regional population as recorded in the 1984 census by the percentage growth for that region recorded between 1970 and 1984, a calculation which should come close to the 1998 figure assuming the absence of other changing variables.

Time
Bisected by the Greenwich Meridian, Ghana is on GMT, which means that British visitors will remain in the same time zone as at home (except during daylight saving).

Flag
The national flag consists of three horizontal stripes – red, yellow and green from top to bottom – with a black star in the middle of the yellow stripe. The red band represents the blood of the nation's freedom fighters, the yellow its mineral wealth and the green its forest. The black star represents the lodestar of the emancipation of the black man.

Population
The population of Ghana as of July 1990 was estimated at 15 million, but with an annual growth rate of roughly 3.2% it is likely to exceed 17 million in 1998. The majority of the population is concentrated in the southern and central parts of the country, largely for climatic reasons, with Greater Accra Region the most densely populated. The northern three regions, despite

---

EDUCATION AND THE 'TREE' SCHOOL
Dorothy Williamson
Near the fishing village of Nyanyano west of Accra, there is a school with over 500
pupils. Not so extraordinary, except that this school was the inspiration of just one
man. Four years ago, Dave Mustill came across a group of children sitting under
a tree, singing. It was an ordinary school day, but during the heavy rains, school
was cancelled. Struck by the unfairness of the situation, Dave set about giving
these children a roof over their heads – and so was born 'The Lord is My
Shepherd Educational Centre'.

In a country where only 60% of children receive any formal education, these
children are among the lucky ones. Their fees of around £1 a week, the norm in
Ghana, include their tuition, meals and transport – it takes two buses an hour and
a half to bus all the children to and from school! Already the school has a hall,
modern classrooms and a library, while there are plans to train older children in
hairdressing, dressmaking and carpentry, giving them a viable trade and raising
money from sale of their work to boost funds. And, most important of all, school
doesn't stop when it rains.

For further information about the school, or to contribute to its fund, contact
Dave Mustill, 61 Malden Hill Gardens, New Malden KT3 4HX, England, tel: 0181
949 2864. Cheques should be made out to 'Ghana School Project'.

---

covering more than 40% of the national surface area, support only 25% of
Ghana's population.

Language

English is the official national language, and it is widely spoken as a result
of the country's long links with Britain and an unusually high standard of
education from colonial times to the present day. A total of at least 75
African languages and dialects are spoken in Ghana, generally divided into
the Akan, Mole-Dagbani, Ewe and Ga language groups. Twi is the main
Akan tongue, first language to roughly half the population, including both
the Ashanti and Fante, and widely spoken elsewhere in central and southern
parts of the country.

Religion

Freedom of religion is a constitutional right in Ghana and, while no official
figures seem to be available, it is thought that about 60% of Ghanaians are
Christian and at least 25% Muslim. Minority religions include Hinduism,
Buddhism, Judaism, Bahai and various traditional faiths. Although Islam is
a minority religion on a national level, it is the predominant faith in the
north, having reached West Africa via the trans-Sahara trade routes as early
as the eighth century AD. It has been practised in what is now northern
Ghana for at least 500 years, probably longer.

Christianity dominates in the southern and central parts of the country.
Catholicism was first introduced at the coast by the Portuguese in the late
fifteenth century (the first public mass was said at Elmina in January 1482),
but its influence dwindled after the Portuguese withdrew in 1637.
Christianity in modern Ghana dates mostly to the latter half of the
nineteenth century. Catholicism, now the most widespread and popular

TRADITIONAL FESTIVALS

A notable feature of Ghanaian society, and one that is of great interest to travellers, is the enormous number of local festivals that take place in various parts of the country throughout the year. Few travellers are likely to deliberately select the dates of their trip to Ghana to coincide with any one particular festival, but it's certainly worth taking note of any festivals that will take place while you are in Ghana and making the effort to be in the right place at the right time, bearing in mind that accommodation may be in relatively short supply in some areas during the most important festivals.

If you are visiting Ghana in early May, do try to get to Winneba for the first weekend of the month in time for the renowned **Aboakyir** deer-hunting festival, one of the most ancient in the country, described in detail in the section on Winneba (page 116).

Most other festivals in coastal parts of Ghana take place during the European autumn. The most important annual festival in Greater Accra region, celebrated in the capital as well as in other Ga towns such as Prampram, is **Homowo**, which literally means 'mocking hunger'. It takes place in August and September, the months that normally yield the largest harvest of fish and grain. A similar festival, called **Damba**, takes place in the Northern Region, centred around Tamale, during the same months. The most important festival on the Fante calendar is the colourful **Oguaa Fetu Afahye** (the last word literally means 'adorning of new clothes'), on the first Saturday of September, when local chiefs and asafo companies dressed in full traditional regalia lead processions through the streets of Cape Coast. The main festival in Anomabu is the five-day long **Bontungu**, in which a variety of drumming and dancing rituals are held to bring God's blessing for the forthcoming year.

In Elmina, the **Bakatue** festival takes place a bit earlier in the year, on the first Tuesday of July, the beginning of a new fishing season. Characterised by a variety of processions and competitions, this festival is said to pre-date the arrival of the Portuguese at Elmina 500 years ago, making it one of the most ancient in Ghana.

denomination, was reintroduced to the south with the establishment of a French mission at Elmina in 1880 and it arrived in the north in 1906, when the White Fathers opened a mission in Navrongo. The Presbyterian Church reached Ghana in 1828, with the foundation of a Swiss mission at Danish Osu Castle. After initial setbacks as several missionaries were claimed by malaria, Presbyterianism spread into much of what is now Eastern Region in the 1840s. The separate Ewe Presbyterian Church, established by German missionaries in the 1850s, has had its stronghold in what is now Volta Region for almost 150 years. The Methodist Church, formerly the Wesleyan Mission, is almost as widespread as Catholicism – it was established around British castles in the 1830s and spread largely through the pioneering work of the Reverend Thomas Birch Freeman, who served in the Gold Coast and Ashanti from 1838 to 1890. In addition to denominations familiar to most Europeans, a large number of American churches have been established in Ghana; most significantly the AME Zion Church, which spread out of Keta from 1896, as well as more recent ones. Roughly 60% of the present population of Ghana is Christian, though Christian slogans and music are so prevalent that you might easily think that should be 150%!

Despite Ghana being the most flagrantly Christian country that I've ever visited – exasperatingly so at times, at least for a crusty old rationalist such

In Volta Region, the whole of September is given over to the **Yam Festival**, and two other important festivals take place during November. In Anloga near Keta on the first Saturday of the month, **Hogbetsotso** or the 'Exodus' Festival commemorates the escape of the Ewe people from a tyrannical ruler in what is now Togo. It is marked by processions of traditionally dressed chiefs as well as lively drumming and dancing (note that a similar festival called the **Godigbeza** takes place in nearby Aflao every April). Later in November, the **Agamutsa Waterfall Festival** in Wli traditional area is also characterised by dancing, drumming and colourful costumes.

There is a small festival in Kumasi and other parts of Ashanti twice during each of the nine 42-day cycles or *adae* into which their annual calendar is divided. It is difficult to give dates for these, since they change from year to year (as astute mathematicians will realise, 9 times 42 does not equal 365), but basically the festival days fall on every sixth Sunday and then the 17th day after that, always a Wednesday. The most important annual festival in Ashanti is **Odwira**, a week-long affair that climaxes on Friday with a procession through town to the palace. The Odwira generally takes place during the ninth adae of the calendar, which falls in September. Among the most lively celebrations are those in Kumasi, Akwapim, Akrapong, Akuapem and Akwamu.

Visitors to northern Ghana might want to note the following festival dates:

January 22	Kpini Kyiu Festival	Wa
March 7	Kyiu Sung Festival	Upper East and West Regions
May 14	Don Festival	Wa, Bawku, Bolgatanga
June 11	Dzimbi Festival	Upper East and West Regions
November 1–12	Daa Festival	Tongo
November 9	Sabre Dance Festival	Lawra
November 15	Kobina Festival	Lawra
November 28	Boarim Festival	Tongo
December 1	Fao Festival	Navrongo

as myself – various traditional beliefs and customs have also retained an unusually high profile in the country. It's difficult to establish whether this is essentially a case of Christians and traditionalists existing alongside each other, or whether it's simply that a significant number of Ghanaians somehow manage to adhere to what appear to be two contradictory systems of belief. Either way, it makes for an interesting if occasionally bemusing cocktail of faiths to the outsider.

A HISTORICAL BACKGROUND

Before entering any historical discussion, it should be stressed that Ghana, like the other modern states of West Africa, is fundamentally a European creation of the late nineteenth century. For this reason it would be thoroughly misleading to write about Ghana as if it were a meaningful entity prior to the colonial era. True, as long ago as AD1700 the coast of modern-day Ghana stood firmly at the epicentre of European maritime trade out of West Africa, while the Ashanti Empire gave political and social cohesion to much of the area between the coastal belt and the Black Volta. But even as recently as 1860, few would have foreseen the eventual existence of a political state with borders approximating to those of present-day Ghana. The modern state of Ghana began to take a recognisable shape only in 1873 as the British Gold Coast colony. Even then, what are now central and northern Ghana were annexed to the colony only in 1902, while the interior to the east of what is now Lake Volta, part of German Togoland before World War I, was formally mandated to Britain by the League of Nations only in 1919.

Bearing the above in mind, I have started this history with a section offering a broad overview of West African history prior to 1500. In the sections that follow this, which focus more specifically on modern-day Ghana, I refer to the coastal belt of what is now Ghana prior to colonisation as the Gold Coast; to the interior south of the Black Volta as Ashanti; and to the interior north of the Black Volta as the northern regions (in colonial times this area was in fact called Northern Region, though it has since been divided into three administrative regions: Northern, Upper East and Upper West). Following this logic, I refer to Ghana in colonial times as the Gold Coast colony, and reserve use of the name Ghana to describe the country after it gained independence in 1957. To preclude confusion between the modern state of Ghana and the ancient state from which its name is taken, the latter is referred to as Ancient Ghana. For the sake of consistency, the term 'Ancient Mali' has been used to refer to another vanished West African empire that was to bequeath its name to a modern state.

West Africa before 1500

The northwestern 'bulge' of Africa can be divided into four economic units prior to 1500. The most northerly of these is the Mediterranean coastal belt of North Africa, an area which has had direct links with the other Mediterranean civilisations since ancient times, and which assimilated the influence of Islamic invaders as early as the eighth century AD, barely a century after the religion was founded. To the south of this lies the Sahara Desert, almost as large as Europe, yet devoid of permanent human settlement since time immemorial. South of the Sahara is the Sahel, an ever-expanding belt of dry savannah, thinly populated except where it's crossed by large rivers such as the Niger, Senegal and Volta. And further south still, there is the belt of moister savannah and forest that terminates at the Atlantic coast, the area we normally think of when we refer to West as opposed to North Africa, and the area to which the modern state of Ghana belongs.

Prior to the arrival of the Portuguese on the Gold Coast in the late fifteenth century, there had existed for centuries a trade relationship between these four regions. Merchant caravans would cross the Sahara from north to south, bringing with them salt, fine cloth and other luxury items which they would trade for goods such as gold, ivory and kola nuts. It is difficult to ascertain exactly when this epoch of trade started, but the available physical evidence would appear to show that a trade route across the Sahara similar to the modern one has existed since before 500BC. It can probably be assumed, too, that the spread of iron-age technology into the Sahel and areas further south before 600BC was influenced by trade routes which, for all we know, may have existed in some form or other for several millennia.

The specifics of this trade and of the societies south of the Sahel are difficult to determine prior to the eighth century AD. Some scholars suggest that there was a substantial increase in trade at around this time, based on the rather unconvincing argument that the first written record of the area south of the Sahel dates to AD773. It is just as likely that the reason no earlier records exist is linked to the rapid increase in written documentation in northwest Africa following the introduction of the Islamic faith in the eighth century AD. What is clear from this first written reference to the Sahel is firstly that its Arabic writer regarded it to be the 'Land of Gold' and secondly that it had long supported a powerful centralised trading empire which effectively acted as the 'middleman' between areas south of the Sahel and north of the Sahara.

This empire was the ancient state of Ghana, which – somewhat confusingly – lay completely to the north of its modern namesake (Nkrumah's choice of the name Ghana in 1957 was symbolic, as the former Gold Coast was the first African colony to gain independence from a European power, though it is also the case that many of modern Ghana's main groupings claim descent from ancient Ghana). Ancient Ghana was founded by Mande-speakers at some time between AD300 and AD700; at its peak it spread for roughly 300km from north to south and 500km east to west between the rivers Niger and Senegal. The capital of ancient Ghana at Kumbi Saleh (now a ruined city in southern Mauritania less than 100km from the Mali border) supported a population of roughly 15,000 and its emperor was able to muster an army numbering 200,000.

In AD992, ancient Ghana was at the height of its powers, and its leadership decided to cement the hold on the trade routes out of the southern Sahara by capturing the important terminus of Awdaghast, 300km northwest of Kumbi Saleh. In the long term, this proved to be the downfall of the state, as the displaced Berbers of Awdaghast consolidated under a somewhat fanatical religious movement known as the Almoravids (meaning 'the people of the hermitage') and waged a holy *jihad* culminating in the capture of Kumbi Saleh in the year 1076. The Almoravids held the ancient Ghanaian capital for little more than a decade, but their brief tenure appears to have been the catalyst that caused the vast empire to fissure into several smaller and less powerful states, a situation that evidently persisted throughout the twelfth century.

The beginning of the thirteenth century saw the emergence of a clear successor to ancient Ghana in the omnipotence stakes, and this was the ancient Mali empire founded by the Mandinka people of Kangaba. Accounts of the early days of this empire tend to be somewhat vague, but so far as anybody can ascertain the Mandinka had by 1205 taken over large parts of what had formerly been ancient Ghana. In 1230, the leadership of Mali was assumed by Munsa Sundiata, an inspirational expansionist who had doubled the area of Mali by the time of his death in 1255. In 1240, Sundiata captured Kumbi Saleh, and relocated the capital 300km northeast to Walata on the fringe of the Sahara; a location that evidently proved unsatisfactory, since all later accounts place the capital of Mali at Niani in the vicinity of the Guinea and Côte d'Ivoire border.

You might reasonably wonder what bearing all the above has on modern Ghana. The best answer, in the broadest sense, is simply that it puts paid to the common misconception that this part of Africa was some sort of stagnant backwater prior to the arrival of Europeans. More specifically, the area that lies within the modern state of Ghana played a palpable role in the trade patterns of this era – it was, indeed, the empires of the Sahel that controlled the southern end of the Saharan caravan routes, but it was through a more localised trade system involving the people of the moist savannah and rainforest region that they obtained most of their trade goods. Centuries ago, Ghana was the major supplier of kola nuts to the empires of the Sahel, as well as an important source of ivory. Of more lasting significance, the rainforest belt of modern Ghana was in medieval times, as it would be in the era of coastal trade and remains today, one of the region's richest sources of gold – the gold that not only lay at the heart of the trade route across the Sahara to Morocco, but would later be one of the factors that caused the Portuguese to set sail in search of a trade route to sub-Saharan Africa.

Another lasting effect of the cross-Sahara trade was the spread of Islam into West Africa. It is not certain when or how deeply Islam first took hold in the region, but the writings of the Arab Al-Bakri in 1067 testify to the presence of a permanent Islamic community situated roughly 10km from Kumbi Saleh. While it is clear from this that the rulers of ancient Ghana were not converts, the fact that this community boasted 12 mosques suggests it was reasonably significant.

The rulers of ancient Mali almost certainly *were* Muslim converts right from the empire's earliest days. As early as 1200, Mansa Uli of ancient Mali undertook a pilgrimage to Mecca. More famous was the pilgrimage of Mansa Musa in 1324–6, when the empire would have been at its economic prime. Contemporary records state that Musa gave away so many gifts of gold that the market for the metal was seriously undermined for some time after. His visit also put ancient Mali on the world map in the most literal sense; the West African empire first appeared by name on an Arabic map drawn up in 1339. And it is well documented that Musa returned home with several Islamic scholars who did much to entrench the exotic religion among the common people of ancient Mali, and were responsible for designing the mud-and-stick style of mosque construction that visitors to modern Ghana will see in places like Larabanga and Wa.

Islam was the state religion of the Songhai Empire, centred to the north of what is now Burkina Faso. One of several small empires that were ruled by the Mansa of ancient Mali following the collapse of ancient Ghana, Songhai was revived in the mid-fifteenth century by a leader called Sunni Ali, from his capital at the Niger River port of Gao, and it replaced ancient Mali as the dominant Sahelian state from roughly 1464. One of the most powerful of Songhai rulers, Askia Mohommed, made the pilgrimage to Mecca in the 1490s, after which Islam was forced on the commoners of the empire. The Songhai Empire collapsed in 1591, following an attack on Gao by an army from Morocco. This event is generally seen as signalling the beginning of what many historians refer to as the West African interior's 'Dark Age', a 300-year period of economic stagnation attributable less to any one single attack than to the reorientation of trade patterns that followed the arrival of Portugal at the Gold Coast in 1471.

Ghana before 1500

On the basis of archaeological evidence, it has been established that modern-day Ghana was inhabited by humans 300,000 years ago, though current knowledge of human movements prior to this would suggest that the country has been occupied for millions of years. The earliest people to inhabit the region were hunter-gatherers, of whom little of concrete can be said. It has yet to be determined when agriculture and pastoralism were adopted in the area, but this could have been as early as around 5000BC. Certainly by 2000BC both exotic creatures such as cattle and indigenous ones such as guinea fowl were being raised in domesticity, while archaeological findings near Kintampo demonstrate that substantial villages had been established at this time – a sure indication that hunter-gathering was no longer the predominant lifestyle in what are now Ashanti and Brong-Ahafo Regions. From around AD1000, it appears that an increased trend towards urbanisation was under way, with population centres of more than 2,000 people forming in the central and northern parts of what is now Ghana, presumably as a result of an economy that depended increasingly on trade with the great empires of the Sahel.

Oral tradition suggests that most modern Ghanaian population groups migrated to their present homeland from elsewhere in West Africa. The traditions widely agree that these migrants moved into territory occupied by the Guan, who are still regarded by other Ghanaians to be the true aboriginals of the country, though they are now assimilated into more recently arrived groups, with the exception of a few isolated Guan pockets at places such as Adakrom, Winneba and Efutu. It is difficult to tell whether these migration traditions reflect the influx of an entire group of people who would presumably have gained territory through conquest, or whether they relate to a small group of migrants who formed a ruling class over the existing occupants of an area. What does seem reasonably certain is that the modern country's broad pattern of population had taken a recognisable shape by the late fifteenth century, when the Portuguese arrived at the coast.

The people of modern Ghana are generally divided into four main regional groupings, each of which shares a similar language and culture. The Mole-Dagbani of the northern region were possibly the first to establish their approximate modern territory; tradition has it that they migrated from the Lake Chad region in the thirteenth century, settling briefly at Pusiga (on the modern border with Togo) before establishing the Mamprusi kingdom at Gambaga. Other northern chieftaincies such as Dagomba, Nanumba and Mossi are traditionally regarded to be offshoots of the Mamprusi, and even today secession disputes in most parts of the region are referred to the Chief of Gambaga (known as the 'Nayiri'), quite possibly the oldest extant chieftaincy in modern Ghana. The only significant exception to the above generalisations regarding the people of the northern region is the Gonja Kingdom, which is traditionally said to have been founded by Mande migrants from ancient Mali in the early sixteenth century.

As a result of its proximity to the ancient empires of the Sahel, the northern region has enjoyed a strong Islamic influence for centuries, though exactly when and how this exotic religion reached the area is a matter of conjecture – some sources place its arrival as early as the thirteenth century, while others date it to the seventeenth. This discrepancy in dates might be accounted for by a long delay between the establishment of the first Islamic settlements in the northern regions and a more widespread acceptance of the religion. It has been suggested that the large-scale influx of Islamic ideas into present-day Ghana was blocked for centuries by a powerful anti-Islamic kingdom in what is now Burkino Faso, but this would not have prevented Islamic traders from establishing their own settlements along the main trade routes through the region. The mud-and-stick mosques found in several villages in the northwest of modern Ghana almost certainly pinpoint some of the country's earliest Islamic settlements but, since the antiquity of these mosques is open to debate, it is difficult to draw any firm conclusions about when Islam first reached these villages.

The area to the east of Lake Volta is inhabited by the Ewe, fifteenth-century migrants from eastern Nigeria. Ewe society is the least centralised of any in modern Ghana; each of the roughly 130 small Ewe chieftaincies is entirely autonomous (in other words there is no paramount chief), though the larger Anglo Kingdom based around the port of Keta is something of an exception. The other important grouping of the east is the Ga-Adangbe, which consists of the Ga people of the Accra coastal plain and the Adangbe of Ada and Somanya. The Ga and Adangba have practically identical languages and they share several customs such as ritual circumcision and a defined order of child-naming, though over the centuries they have adopted a great many customs from the neighbouring Akan. Like the Ewe, the Ga-Adangbe are originally from eastern Nigeria, and it is more than probable that the Ga had settled the Accra area and gelled into a cohesive state by the time the Portuguese arrived.

The most significant population group in modern Ghana, territorially and numerically, is the Akan (see box *Akan culture* on pages 120–1). The Akans comprise more than half the country's population and inhabit five of its ten administrative regions: Western, Central, Eastern, Ashanti and Brong-Ahafo. Although every Akan village has its own chief, political centralisation into larger kingdoms has been a recurrent feature of Akan history, from the fourteenth-century Bono Kingdom of Techiman to more recent entities such as Denkyira, Ashanti and Fante. Superficially, oral traditions relating to the origin of the Akan vary greatly from one society to another, but in essence they tend to run along one of two basic themes: a migration from somewhere further north, or a sudden emergence from the sky or a hole in the ground or somewhere equally improbable. There does, however, appear to be a reasonable degree of consensus among historians that the Akan migrated to modern-day Ghana from the Sahel. Since most traditions claim Bono as the Cradle of the Akan, and Bono was firmly established as a gold-mining and trading empire under King Akumfi Ameyaw I (1328–63), any migration must have occurred before the end of the thirteenth century. On this evidence, it seems reasonable to assume that the Akan migrated to their modern territory as a result of the dissolution of ancient Ghana. It strikes me that those

Akan societies lacking a migration tradition could be older groupings which adopted Akan culture either through long periods of association with or colonisation by one of the larger Akan empires.

The Gold Coast 1471–1665

In 1415, Portugal captured the Moroccan port of Ceuta, one first small step in an era of naval exploration that would result in the circumnavigation of Africa before the end of the fifteenth century. The motives that lay behind the Portuguese Crown backing such a venture were manifold. Portugal believed that by sailing south around Africa they would be able to wrest control of the lucrative eastern spice trade and, although the Portuguese had no idea just how large an obstacle Africa would prove to be, they were ultimately correct in this. Religion, too, was an important factor, in that the Portuguese crown was eager to forge links with the Christian kingdom of Prester John (a legend referred to in many medieval writings, probably based on rumours emanating from Christian Ethiopia) and to spread Christianity to areas lying beyond the Islamic lands north of the Sahara. Finally, through having a foothold in Morocco, Portugal was keenly aware of the quantity of gold being transported across the Sahara, and recognised that finding a sea route to the source of the gold would be a more realistic goal than trying to take direct control of the Arabic caravan routes through the Sahara.

In 1471, the Portuguese arrived at the village then known as Edina (now called Elmina after the Portuguese *De Costa da el Mina de Ouro* – 'the Coast of Gold Mines' – a phrase which would also give rise to the moniker 'Gold Coast') and entered into trade with a powerful chief whose name is recorded as Caramansa. Eleven years later, with a written lease from Caramansa, the Portuguese built the castle of St George on a rocky outcrop next to Elmina. Architecturally reminiscent of the castles built by the Crusaders, St George was separated from the village by a dry moat and its strongest bastion faced inland, suggesting that the Portuguese perceived their greatest threat of attack to come not from the sea but from the interior. St George was the first of several forts and lodges established by the Portuguese – in 1515 and 1523 respectively they built forts at Axim and Shama, close to the mouths of the rivers Ankobra and Pra (both of which flowed from parts of the interior rich in gold), and later in the sixteenth century they constructed a short-lived trading lodge in what is now downtown Accra.

Elmina, however, was to remain the centre of the Portuguese gold trade throughout their 150-year tenure on the Gold Coast. The fact that Portugal found such bountiful gold at Elmina was no mere coincidence. On the contrary, Elmina's importance as a salt-production centre gave Portugal effortless access to a trade route established at least a century before its arrival, connecting Elmina to the Akan gold mines near what are now Tarkwa and Oduasi via the empire of Eguafo. Gold was far and away the most important export from the West African coast at this time – £100,000 worth annually throughout the sixteenth century, or roughly 10% of the world supply – but surviving Portuguese ledgers show that there was also a thriving trade in ivory, cotton and animal hides, while major imports included metal pots and bowls, beads, leatherware, alcoholic spirits and guns. Odd as it may seem with hindsight, the Portuguese also imported to Elmina a quantity of slaves, captured or bought in Benin during the period 1486 to 1506, and at São Tomé after 1506.

Some readers may wonder why Ghana (as opposed to, say, Senegal or Liberia) became the centre of European activities in West Africa. First and foremost, this is because Ghana is the only West African country with a coast that lies close to significant gold deposits. But this alone doesn't really explain why all but two of the roughly 60 forts and trading lodges built on the Gulf of Guinea were sited in what is now Ghana – especially as many of these forts were built to service the slave trade rather than the gold trade. Just as important as the presence of gold inland was the physical nature of the Gold Coast. Studded with large rocky outcrops rather than mangrove swamps and sprawling shallow lagoons, Ghana boasts a great many good natural harbours, easily approached by ship, but also easily guarded and protected, with ample local material for constructing fortified buildings.

It is also interesting to note that Portugal's tenure on the Gold Coast was in no respect colonialism as we think of it today. The Portuguese had no jurisdiction beyond their forts, which were built with the permission of the local chiefs on land that was formally leased for the purpose. The Portuguese did make a concerted effort to spread Christianity, but even this was restricted to the immediate vicinity of the forts. They made no serious attempt to venture inland, nor to capture the Akan gold mines, but instead traded with the local chiefs and merchants on an even footing. And, it should be noted, what is true of Portugal is largely true of the European powers that followed. The arrival of the Portuguese ushered in an era of trade that lasted more than three centuries. Only when describing events from the mid-nineteenth century onwards is it valid to talk in terms of colonists.

The level of Portuguese trade out of the Gold Coast had probably peaked as early as 1530, its decline thereafter a result largely of the increasingly widespread Portuguese global 'empire' that spread from Goa, Malindi and Mozambique in the Indian Ocean to South America and the Caribbean. Nevertheless, Portuguese dominance of the Gold Coast was not substantially threatened in the sixteenth century, though nor did it go entirely unchallenged. The first English ships reached the west coast of Africa in roughly 1530, and in 1542 a French ship landed at Dixcove where it purchased 28kg of gold. From the 1550s, non-Portuguese ships were an increasingly common sight off the coast – in 1553, Captain Thomas Wyndham returned with a stash of gold which he sold for £10,000, and a few years later the coast was visited by Francis Drake as part of his successful attempt to circumnavigate the globe. The Dutch, by comparison, were latecomers, and when their first ship did arrive on the Gold Coast, blown off course en route to Brazil in 1593, its captain was imprisoned – though he still managed to return home with a healthy amount of gold.

That the Dutch were the first to seriously challenge Portugal's monopoly on the Gold Coast is often attributed to the tension that already existed between these two countries in Europe. In reality, economics was probably the greater factor. The first Dutch attack on Elmina was an unsuccessful naval bombardment in 1596. From that time on, between 10 and 20 privately owned Dutch ships visited the Gold Coast annually. The Portuguese responded to this influx of new traders first by attacking Dutch ships whenever possible, and secondly by punishing brutally any African caught dealing with a rival European power. The offender's ears would be cut off for a first infringement; a second offence was rewarded with execution. Possibly as a result of this cruel policy, the chief of the Asubu sent two ambassadors to Holland requesting that a fort be erected at his capital 20km east of Elmina at Moree. In 1612, the Dutch did just this, shipping skilled artisans and the requisite materials direct from Holland so that the fort would be built too quickly for the Portuguese to mount an attack during its construction.

With a secure foothold at Moree, the Dutch were positioned to mount a concerted attack on Portugal's Gold Coast possessions, especially after 1621 when the powerfully backed West India Company (WIC) was formed in Amsterdam. By 1622, some 40 Dutch ships were assigned to the Gold Coast trade. Then, in 1630, what was in effect a Dutch navy took to the Atlantic, capturing several Portuguese possessions in the West Indies and Brazil before turning its attention on the West African coast. After an aborted naval attack, Elmina fell in 1637, bombarded from the nearest hill. Shama followed in the same year, and Axim was captured by Dutch boats in 1642, effectively ending Portugal's influence in this part of the world (though Portugal would remain a major player for centuries to come in the Indian Ocean and on the coast of what is now Angola).

The Dutch capture of Portugal's Gold Coast possessions signalled the beginning of a period of intense rivalry for dominance between several European powers, some of which had little lasting impact on what is now Ghana. The Swedes, for instance, occupied Fort Corolusbourg, which they built at Cape Coast in 1653, for a mere eleven years. The Brandenburgers built Fort Grossfriedrichsberg as Pokesu (Prince's Town) in 1683, only to vacate it in 1717. Even the French, later to become so powerful in West Africa, had little influence on the Gold Coast, never occupying any one place for longer than a decade.

A more important rival to Dutch dominance was Denmark, though on the whole the Dutch tolerated the Danish presence in a tacit alliance against stronger powers. Aside from their rather obscure outpost at Keta, the Danes restricted their activities on the Gold Coast to Osu in modern-day Accra. The Danish castle at Osu grew to be one of the most impressive on the Gold Coast, and the Danes occupied it almost continuously from 1642 to 1850, when it was sold to Britain. The most significant interruption in the Danish occupation of Osu occurred in 1681–3, when the castle was captured and occupied by Portugal; part of a rather desperate last bid at recapturing some of the Gold Coast trade.

The first British 'West Africa Company', formed in 1618, met with little success – its efforts at occupying the Gold Coast climaxed in 1640 with the construction at Kormantin of a small trading lodge that burnt down shortly after it was built, possibly with the assistance of a Dutch saboteur. More successful was the snappily titled 'Company of Royal Adventurers of English Trading to Africa', established in 1660 with a royal charter and the hearty backing of the Duke of York (later King James II, and – take note trivia lovers – rewarded for his efforts in backing the 'Adventurers' by being not only the James of Accra's Jamestown, but the York of the USA's New York, known as New Amsterdam until it was captured from the Dutch by his charges).

In 1665, the British company launched a concerted attack on Holland's West African possessions, capturing the forts at Takoradi, Shama, Moree and Anomabu, as well as Fort Carolusbourg at Cape Coast, which the Dutch had occupied since 1664. The British Company was unable to hold on to all of its newly captured forts, so it concentrated its efforts on ensuring that Fort Carolusbourg was impregnable, converting the modest fort into a castle covering roughly three-quarters of the area it does today. The British company had its foothold on the Gold Coast, one that was strengthened with its transformation to the wealthily backed Royal Africa Company in 1672, and by the end of the century Britain had become, if anything, more economically powerful than its more established rival. The reason for this is perfectly simple: instead of trading in gold, Britain decided to enter an altogether more lucrative arena of trade. The British capture of Cape Coast in 1665 can be seen as the critical point in the process that would, by 1700, cause a Dutch official to bemoan that 'the Gold Coast had changed into a virtual Slave Coast'.

The Slave Coast 1665–1807

However convenient it might be to see the trade in slaves as an abomination introduced to Africa by Europeans, there is no escaping the reality that a slave trade was in existence from the very earliest days of the trans-Sahara caravans, when people captured in the sub-Sahelian region were transported across the desert to be sold into domestic bondage in North Africa and parts of Europe. Nor can it be denied that a slave class has formed a part of practically every centralised African society on record, at least until modern times. And while it is true that in many past African societies slaves have had the opportunity to the climb the social ladder, it is also true that in many such societies slaves were treated as sub-human, and cruelly sacrificed to mark special occasions or entreat deities.

None of which makes Africa in any way unusual, since slavery in name or in kind has been a feature of most ancient societies until this century. It is merely worth noting that the slave trade out of the Gold Coast emerged in an environment where not only slavery but also trading in slaves were established practices, just as it should be noted that the Europeans who conducted this trade came from societies where it was customary to hold public executions for crimes as paltry as stock theft, and to burn alive witches and other perceived heretics on a stake. Viewed from the lofty moral heights of the late twentieth century, there is a certain uncomfortable irony in the realisation that the very earliest form of slave trade entered into by Europeans on the Gold Coast involved not the export of slaves but their import, as captives bought by Portuguese merchants from African sellers in Benin were sold to African buyers in Elmina.

Nevertheless, the trans-Atlantic slave trade is a singular event in human history, not simply because it operated on an unprecedented scale but also because it was so ruthlessly well-organised, and so shattering and wide-ranging in its effects. Before the arrival of Europeans, slaves were generally incidental captives of inter-tribal war, relatively few in number, and in most cases able to integrate themselves into the society that enslaved them. By the time the trans-Atlantic slave trade hit its peak, it would be an understatement to say that the capture of slaves had been transformed into the *raison d'être* for war; closer to the mark perhaps to say that the entire West African interior had deteriorated into a hunting ground wherein slave raiders with firearms attacked village after comparatively defenceless village, trading their booty at the coastal forts for yet more firepower. It is estimated that between 12 and 20 million Africans were transported across the Atlantic between the late seventeenth century and early nineteenth, a five-week trip in conditions so cramped and unhygienic that it was not unusual for a boat to lose half its human cargo in passage. It is impossible to tell how many more people – those who were too young or too old or too weak to be saleable – died in the course of the raids.

Most of us are familiar with the fate of the victims of these raids. Rather less well documented is the devastating affect that the slave trade had on African society. It has been noted, for instance, that many traditional industries were lost to the Gold Coast interior – iron-smelting and gold-mining are good examples – as the product of these industries became increasingly worthless by comparison with slaves, and their practitioners were taken in to bondage. Worse still was the arms race that built up between neighbouring groups, as in the seventeenth century Britain alone supplied around 100,000 guns annually to West Africa – and it is not difficult to see how this situation forced even the most unwilling of chiefs into finding slaves to trade for the firearms they needed to protect themselves. For two centuries, Africa lost a high proportion of its most able-bodied men and women to the slave trade. In return, it received items that were at best of no lasting value – alcoholic spirits and tobacco – and at worst entirely destructive.

In the sixteenth and seventeenth centuries, the Gold Coast was spared the worst of this. Both Portugal and later Holland made it policy not to buy slaves at the Gold Coast – not for any moral reason, but because they believed (correctly as it turned out) that the slave trade would interfere with the gold trade. Instead they concentrated their slaving efforts further south, along the stretch of coast between modern-day Nigeria and Angola. This was to change towards the end of the seventeenth century, firstly because the recently arrived British had difficulty breaking into the Dutch-controlled gold trade, and secondly as a result of the rise of the Akwamu empire, which at its peak controlled a 350km stretch of coast east of Accra crossing into what is now Togo, but at no point had access to the gold mines at Akan. The British and to a lesser extent the Danes started trading in slaves from around 1665, a situation that was rapidly exploited by the Akwamu, and the floodgates were opened in 1698 when the RAC forsook their monopoly on British trade, allowing any British boat to trade freely, provided a 10% custom was paid to the company. This policy was a failure in so far as few of the so-called 'ten-percenters' actually paid the required levy, but it did ensure that the market for slaves expanded exponentially from 1698 onwards, with Anomabu in particular becoming a major centre for 'free trade'.

In the late seventeenth century, two empires dominated the interior immediately north of the coast. These were Akwamu, already mentioned above, and a much older Akan empire called Denkyira, the region's main repository of gold-working skills and the centre of the gold trade to the coast. In 1701, Denkyira was conquered by the recently established Ashanti Empire of Kumasi, creating what was perhaps the most radical power shift in the Ghanaian interior since Portugal had first arrived at the coast. One result of Denkyira's defeat was that the lease papers for Elmina Castle passed into the hands of the Ashanti, who were far more interested in empire-building and trading slaves for guns than they were in such pastoral pursuits as scratching around for gold. Another was that the flow of gold to the coast, already stemmed by the emergent slave trade, dried up to such an extent that in 1703 the governor of Elmina formally requested that Amsterdam allow him to abandon the gold trade in favour of slaves.

The threat posed by the rampant Ashanti, whose king was courted by both the major European powers almost as soon as he conquered Denkyira, appears to have been pivotal in the expansion of the Fante state in the early eighteenth century. Based in the area around Mankessim and Anomabu, the Fante were in 1700 the most powerful and wealthy of perhaps 20 small Akan kingdoms running along the coast west of Accra, all of which were linked by a common culture and used to having a degree of control over trade with the Dutch and English, both of whose headquarters lay in this part of the country. Between 1707 and 1720, the Fante gradually exerted control over all these groups, including the Oguaa of Cape Coast and Edina of Elmina, using a combination of force and coercion as it became obvious to all that unity was their best weapon against an Ashanti attack. Ashanti, meanwhile, grew in power with almost every passing year, capturing Akwamu in 1730, Brong-Ahafo in 1744–45, and much of what are now Burkino Faso and the northern regions of Ghana in 1445–50. By the end of this period of expansion, Ashanti was probably bigger than Ghana is today, and along with Fante it was by far the most dominant power in what is now Ghana. Unexpectedly, perhaps, the two empires maintained a relatively peaceful co-existence, motivated partly by the recognition that a tacit alliance was the best way to exclude other kingdoms from the lucrative coastal trade, but also enforced to a degree by the British and Dutch, on whom they relied for weapons.

The slave trade out of the Gold Coast continued unabated throughout the eighteenth century. Roughly 5,000 slaves passed annually through each of the main British trading posts, Cape Coast and Anomabu, and were stored in cold, dark dungeons that are chilling to visit today. The Dutch tried in vain to revive the flagging gold trade in 1702 by building a new fort they named 'Good Hope' at Senya Beraku; ten years later the fort was extended to include slave dungeons. Ashanti prospered, as Kumasi lay at the heart of all three major trade routes to the coast west of Accra; and, although it was forbidden for an Ashanti to enslave another Ashanti, their frequent military expeditions and slave raids ensured the flow of human cargo to the coast never abated.

As the eighteenth century drew to a close, the anti-slave lobby became an increasingly powerful voice in Europe, a result not only of the strengthening liberal attitudes that emerged following the industrial revolution, but also of a greater public awareness as to how the trade slave actually operated following several publications on the subject. In 1804, Denmark abolished the slave trade, followed by Britain in 1807, the USA in 1808, and Holland, France, Portugal and Spain between 1814 and 1817. Also in 1817, several of the above nations signed a Reciprocal Search Treaty, which in effect allowed Britain to search boats captained by people of other nationalities. The slave trade was subdued by this, but it was by no means halted – it became common practice among slavers to throw all their human cargo overboard at the approach of a British naval patrol. Britain soon recognised that it would take nothing less than the abolition of slavery to end the trade, and it banned slavery throughout its colonies in 1833, followed by France in 1848, the USA in 1865 (after a bloody civil war dominated by the issue) and finally Brazil in 1888.

The build-up to colonialism 1806–1902

By 1800, Britain was the major European trading power on the Gold Coast and, although the Danes were to retain a presence there until 1850 and the Dutch until 1872, developments in the nineteenth century, in hindsight though perhaps not at the time, show a clear trend towards British colonisation. So far as the interior was concerned, a clear pattern had emerged by 1800 wherein various Fante chieftaincies acted as middlemen between the Ashanti and British traders. This arrangement suited the British, who believed that if Ashanti were to take full control of the interior it would be able to dictate terms of trade to Britain. It suited the Fante too, since without the tacit backing of Britain they would never have had the military prowess to resist an Ashanti invasion. The arrangement was, however, less agreeable to the Ashanti, who lost out substantially by having to deal through the Fante. Nevertheless, a few minor skirmishes aside, Fante and Ashanti had a reasonably healthy relationship in the second half of the eighteenth century, several times combining forces against upstart states to ensure they retained their joint trade monopoly.

The relationship between the European occupants of the forts and the surrounding chieftaincies changed little in essence between the construction of St George in 1482 and 1820. Theirs was a commercial not a colonial relationship: European control barely extended beyond the forts, and even those chieftaincies closest to the forts remained autonomous political units, though inevitably they were offered a degree of protection by their well-armed European neighbours. This long-standing balance was to waver in the first decade of the nineteenth century, partly as a result of Britain's wish to curb the slave trade at its Ashanti roots from 1807 onwards, no less because of escalating tension between Fante and Ashanti following a military skirmish between these states in 1806.

There are two main reasons why the Ashanti attacked Fante in 1806. The first is that Fante, always more a federation of disparate states than a cohesive empire, had been weakened by internal disputes such as the wars between Oguaa and Komenda in 1788, Anomabu and Mankessim in 1789, Oguaa and Anomabu in 1802 and Komenda and Shama in 1805. The second was the escalation of a long-standing dispute over trade with Elmina Castle. Ashanti had held the lease to the castle since 1701, for which reason they believed they had the right to trade with its Dutch occupants directly, but the Fante regularly blocked Ashanti access to Elmina in the late eighteenth century, and even attacked the town on a number of occasions. The above points noted, it was inevitable that sooner or later the vast Ashanti empire would decide to take direct control of the coast, and the remarkable thing is that they waited so long to try.

Between 1806 and 1874, there were nine military clashes between Ashanti and Fante, and three more were averted at the last moment. Up until 1820, these clashes were wholly internal affairs, resulting in one or other of the two dozen or so Fante states being conquered by Ashanti. The Fante, however, refused to recognise Ashanti's traditional rights of conquest, and tension between the two states meant that trade of all forms ground to a virtual halt. In this the Fante were supported by the British, not only because Britain favoured dealing with several small competitive states over an Ashanti monolith, but also because it was eager to end the slave raids in which the Ashanti still indulged. To this end, the British parliament placed all the Gold Coast forts formerly run by its companies under the Crown government in 1821. Three years later, Britain for the first time gave military support to the Fante, in a battle at the Adaamso River which ended in an Ashanti victory – one contemporary account claims that the wounded British governor was beheaded by his Ashanti counterpart, and that his head was taken to Kumasi as a trophy. In 1826, Britain and Ashanti clashed again at Akatamanso, to the north of Accra: a battle that ended in a resounding British victory. It would be three decades before another major clash took place between these powers.

By 1828, the British government was prepared to withdraw entirely from the Gold Coast, due to the high cost of maintaining the forts and the massive drop in trade following a decade of instability. In the end, however, it bowed to pressure from British merchants and the beleaguered Fante, selling the forts to a company called the London Committee of Merchants. In 1830, a new governor was installed, Gordon Maclean, who more than any other person would lay the foundation of future British rule. In 1831, Maclean pressed the humbled Ashanti into signing a tripartite treaty which required them to refrain from any further attacks on their southern neighbours. As a sign of good faith, the Ashanti left a large sum of gold with Maclean, to be returned after six years, as well as two Ashanti princes to be educated in Europe. Six years after the treaty was signed, Maclean returned the gold, and in 1841 the princes went back to Kumasi in order to help establish a Methodist mission there, creating a new atmosphere of trust between Ashanti and the British. In addition to his role as peacemaker, Maclean made great efforts to end the slave trade; and he turned around the Gold Coast economy, ushering in a new era of 'legitimate trade' as the value of exports leapt by 275% during the first decade of his governorship, and imports by more than 300%. This remarkably successful administration ended in 1843, when the British government decided to claim back the Gold Coast forts and to install its own governor. Many of Maclean's achievements were formalised with the so-called 'Bond of 1844', a sort of proto-protectorateship over several Fante states, in exchange for which the chiefs had to pledge allegiance to the Queen of England and give up practices regarded to be barbaric, such as human sacrifices and panyarring (the seizure of a debtor's relatives, to be sold into slavery if the debt wasn't met within a specified period). Maclean himself died in 1847, and was buried in the courtyard of Cape Coast Castle. It is said that the chiefs of southern states mourned his passing for months afterwards.

The two decades that followed the Maclean administration were relatively uneventful. In 1850, the year in which the governances of Sierra Leone and the Gold Coast were finally separated, Britain bought the forts at Keta and Osu from Denmark. It is doubtful that the British saw much use for these forts at the time of their purchase, but didn't want them falling into French or Dutch hands, and perhaps hoped to have more success than Denmark in curbing the clandestine slave trade running out of Keta. (As it turned out, Osu Castle would become the seat of government in 1876, a position it has retained to this day.) In 1852, the British authorities introduced a poll tax system which sparked a series of riots and battles (most famously the violent Anglo-Krobo confrontation that took place on Krobo Mountain) without ever raising a great deal of revenue – it was abandoned in 1861.

The year 1863 saw renewed tension between the British and Ashanti, caused by the former's refusal to hand over refugees from Ashanti justice. In 1864, the two armies clashed once again. The battle went the way of the Ashanti, largely because so many British troops died in an outbreak of fever or dysentery brought on by unusually heavy rain. It also signalled the beginning of a rush of events that would conspire to make the period 1867–74 of unparalleled decisiveness in the history of the Gold Coast.

The rush started in 1867, when Britain and Holland arrived at the mutual conclusion that every aspect of their increasingly unprofitable administrations would be improved were Britain to control a continuous strip of coast east of Cape Coast and the Dutch a strip of coast to the west of Elmina. The two countries signed the so-called 'Fort Exchange Treaty', much to the consternation of several Fante states, long allied to a nearby British fort and now suddenly forced to live alongside the Dutch, whom they regarded as foes due to their involvement with the Ashanti who still held the lease to Elmina fort. King Aggrey of Cape Coast led a protest against the treaty, and was arrested by the British and exiled to Sierra Leone. The arrest of Aggrey, along with widespread dissatisfaction with the new status quo, triggered the formation of the Fante Confederation. Founded at Mankessim in 1868, this was the first formal alliance incorporating all the Fante states from Axim to just east of Accra, and although it was to prove short-lived the movement had some success in preventing the Dutch from occupying forts they had traded with Britain. In 1871, Britain arrested the confederation leaders and imprisoned them for a month. In the following year, Holland finally limped away from the Gold Coast, selling its remaining possessions to Britain. In 1873, the Fante Confederation disbanded, having lost direction after the Dutch evacuation of the coast – and in any case riddled with leadership squabbles. By this stage, the British parliament was of the opinion that it would have to take one of two approaches to the governing of the increasingly fractious Gold Coast: in its own words, a 'very evil choice' between following the Dutch and withdrawing completely, or pursuing an active policy of territorial expansion and colonisation. On 24 July 1874, Britain formally declared the Gold Coast a Crown colony.

The withdrawal of Holland from Elmina proved to be the trigger of the notorious Anglo-Ashanti War of 1873–74. Fearing that Britain wouldn't honour the ancient lease, the Ashanti occupied Elmina in 1873. Britain responded with a naval bombardment that flattened the old town to the west of the castle, leaving around 20,000 people without a home. In 1874, British troops entered Ashanti for the first time, defeating its army at Bekwai and – after the Ashanti king refused to accept their initial terms of treaty – burning Kumasi to the ground. The treaty of Fomena, signed in Adanse towards the end of 1874, forced the Ashanti to renounce all claims on territories lying to the south of their core state, most of all Elmina. At the same time, several vassal states to the north (for instance Gonja, Bono and Dagomba) took advantage of the defeat to assert their independence from Ashanti, and so an empire that had once been larger than modern Ghana was reduced to an area similar in size to present-day Ashanti Region.

In its earliest incarnation, the Gold Coast colony was a fraction of the size of modern Ghana, with an identical coastline but barely extending more than 50km inland. So it might have remained were it not for the so-called 'Scramble for Africa', initiated in the late 1870s when Belgium and France entered into a race for control of the Congo. By 1888, most of the modern states of Africa had more or less taken shape, though not Ghana, presumably because its most interesting asset, the Gold Coast, had been British long before the scramble started. By the 1890s, however, both France and Germany were eying the interior of what is now Ghana. As a result of this, Britain extended its borders to cover the whole of the modern Western and Central Province in 1893, while the northern border was settled with France in 1898 and the eastern border with Germany agreed in 1899 (though the latter was to move further east exactly 20 years later when the League of Nations divided German Togoland between Britain and France).

In the 1890s, Britain's attention turned once again to Ashanti, which it was desperate not to let fall into German or French hands. In 1891, British

Protectorateship was offered to Ashanti, and soundly rejected by the recently installed King Prempreh I. Britain decided it would have to install a British resident in Kumasi to prevent the French from doing the same, and so it was that in 1896 a British military expedition (whose numbers, incidentally, included the future Lord Baden Powell, just in case you ever wonder why the Scout movement regularly comes up as a topic of small talk with students in this part of the country!) entered Kumasi without firing a shot. Prempreh, along with many other members of the royal family, was arrested and imprisoned in Elmina Castle before being exiled to Sierra Leone and later the Seychelles. Britain then demanded that the remaining Ashanti elders in Kumasi hand over the Golden Stool (not so much the symbol of the king as its embodiment, handed down from generation to generation), a request that had been anticipated to the extent that they had a fake stool ready to hand to Britain (the fake is now on display in the Prempreh II Museum in Kumasi).

In 1900, the Ashanti rose one last time against British colonisation in the war named after its main instigator, Yaa Asanatwaa, the Queen Mother of Ejisu. After heavy loss of life on both sides, Ashanti was defeated again in 1901 and yet another contingent of dignitaries, Yaa Asantewaa among them, was imprisoned and exiled to the Seychelles. On 1 January 1902, Ashanti was formally annexed to the British Gold Coast colony, along with the territories that today make up Ghana's three northern regions.

Gold Coast colony 1902–57

The Gold Coast, like most other British colonies in Africa, was run along the system of indirect rule, a sharp contrast to the French and Portuguese systems whereby African colonies were – in theory if not in practice – run as an extension of the so-called 'mother' country. The basic principle underlying indirect rule, as patented by Lord Lugard first in Uganda and later in Nigeria, was that traditional chiefs would continue to rule locally as before, but under the supervision of the colonial administration. The motivations for adopting this system were twofold. Firstly, Britain believed that the Gold Coast would be better served in the long run if it developed a system of government rooted in its own traditions rather than one imposed entirely from outside. More to the point, perhaps, the lack of funding and shortage of European manpower created by Britain's insistence that all colonies should be economically self-sufficient would have made it impossible for most colonial governors to rule in any other manner. Indirect rule was, in the words of the eminent Ghanaian historian Adu Boahen, 'in reality, the most indirect way of ruling directly'. It was also, doubtless, the cheapest.

The core problem with indirect rule as it was administered in the Gold Coast is that it undermined the very institution it was nominally designed to protect. A traditional chief in pre-colonial Ghana was not, as might be supposed, a hereditarily determined autocrat, but an appointee of the council of elders. And the elders who appointed a chief had not only a right to veto any ruling he made, but the customary right to remove him from the stool.

Prior to the colonial era, then, the authority of the chief was rooted in the council of elders over whom he presided. Under Britain, the authority of the chief came from the colonial administration, a situation that was bound to become a problem the moment that the administration tried to enforce an unpopular ruling through the chief.

The first steps towards indirect rule took place in 1883, when all chiefs in the Gold Coast (then only a fraction of what is now Ghana) were required to apply for recognition by the colonial administration. The policy took a more formal shape with the formation of so-called 'Native Authorities', comprising a paramount chief and his main sub-chiefs; an institution which, to its credit, paved the way for the modern regional and district councils of Ghana. In reality, Britain often tried to appoint a chief who was wholly unacceptable to his subjects. The clearest example of this occurred in Ashanti, where King Prempreh I and many other important chiefs were held in exile from 1896 until 1924, while the British authorities attempted to gain recognition for a dummy king of their choosing. Even when Prempreh I was returned to the stool in 1926, it was as King of Kumasi rather than King of Ashanti. Only in 1935 did Britain come full circle and restore the Ashanti Confederacy Council which it had abolished following the Yaa Asantewaa War in 1901, at the same time allowing the recently stooled King Prempreh II to assume his full traditional role.

Resistance to colonial rule emerged as early as 1897, when the Aboriginal Rights Protection Society successfully blocked a bill that would have made all physically unoccupied territory in the colony the property of the colonial administration. It appeared in a more orchestrated form in the wake of World War I with the formation of the National Congress of British West Africa (NCBWA) by the Gold Coast barrister, Casely Hayford. The formation of the NCBWA is widely seen as the begining of a formal split between educated nationalists, who were excluded from government under the system of indirect rule, and the uneducated and generally conservative traditional chiefs who gained from it. The inaugural meeting of the NCBWA took place in Accra in 1920, bringing together a total of 20 nationalist delegates from the Gambia, Nigeria, Sierra Leone and of course the Gold Coast. The delegates drew up a list of demands; notably that the government should provide equal job opportunities for Africans and Europeans with equivalent qualifications, that at least half of the legislative council in all countries should be freely elected, and that the colonial administration should cease interfering in the selection and removal of traditional chiefs. An NCBWA delegation was sent to London to present these demands to the Colonial Secretary, but was refused an appointment. Nevertheless, a great many changes along the lines suggested by the organisation had been set in place by the time of Casely Hayford's death in 1930, by which time the organisation was close to disintegration.

It was World War II, however, that proved decisive in ending the colonial era in the Gold Coast as elsewhere in Africa. In the Gold Coast specifically, at least 65,000 African conscripts were shipped to fight the war in Europe, where they were exposed on a daily basis to the democratic and anti-imperialistic ideals of the Allied Forces. The Atlantic Charter signed by Roosevelt and Churchill stated categorically that the signatories would 'respect the right of all peoples to choose the form of government under which they will live'. Churchill would later retract the statement insofar as colonies were concerned, but the American government affirmed that by all people they meant *all* people. When these African servicemen returned home after the war, they had high hopes of benefiting from the democratic ideals for which they had been obliged to fight. Instead, in at least 50,000 cases in the Gold Coast alone, the ex-servicemen returned home to unemployment, not to say a capital city whose population had increased threefold as a result of short-lived employment opportunities created by the European war.

In the Gold Coast more than any other British colony, the immediate post-war period saw events move with remarkable speed and purpose. In 1946, Governor Burns responded to the mood of the time with a new constitution that allowed 18 of the 30 seats in the colony's Legislative Council to be elected, 13 by the Provincial Council of Chiefs of the southern Regions and Ashanti, and five by the small number of registered African voters in Accra, Cape Coast and Sekondi. In 1947, the United Gold Coast Convention (UGCC), formed by Dr Danquah, demanded 'self-government within the shortest possible time' and objected to the new constitution on the valid grounds that the Provisional Council of Chiefs was seen as a stooge organisation by most commoners, that the electoral roll in the abovementioned cities was laughably unrepresentative, and that the Northern Region had no vote at all. November 1947 saw the return from 12 years in the USA and UK of the nationalist and pan-Africanist Dr Kwame Nkrumah, invited home by Danquah to act as Secretary General to the UGCC.

On 28 February 1948, colonial officers opened fire on a peaceful march organised by ex-servicemen to deliver a petition to the governor. Three marchers were killed, including the leader of the ex-servicemen, and another 12 died in the rioting that followed. This event proved decisive in the history of modern Africa. The Gold Coast was Britain's 'model colony', the most prosperous, educated and organised of them all, and the administration reasoned that if this could happen in the Gold Coast, then colonialism in Africa was surely doomed. Even before 28 February 1948, Britain had generally seen self-government as the end goal for its colonies, but it had been thinking ahead to a time decades, perhaps even centuries away. After 28 February, that time span changed to one of years.

In the short term, however, the colonial administration put the UGCC leadership in jail, hoping that would help quieten things down. On his release in July 1949, Nkrumah formed the new and more radical Convention People's Party (CPP) – motto 'self government now'! – and set about organising a series of strikes and boycotts that peaked in January 1950, with the aim of making the colony ungovernable. Nkrumah was once again thrown in jail, but the colonial administration backed down by installing a new constitution that allowed 36 seats in the government to be elected by the African population. In the 1951 election, the CPP won 33 of the seats, and Nkrumah was released to enter government. In March 1952, Nkrumah became the Gold Coast's first African prime minister. He then set about writing a new constitution which gave the Gold Coast virtual self-government after the 1954 election in which the CPP won 79 out of 104 seats. Nkrumah then lobbied for full independence from Britain, but this was held up while the UN resolved the so-called 'Ewe Question' (a legacy of the split of the Ewe homeland when the former German Togoland was divided between Britain and France by the League of Nations in 1919) with a referendum that went in favour of the British section becoming part of independent Ghana. In the election of July 1956, the CPP won 74 out of 104 seats on a pro-Independence ticket. Britain had no choice but to acquiesce to popular demand, and so on 6 March 1957 the former Gold Coast colony became independent Ghana. It was the first African colony to be granted independence in the post-war era, and its name was adopted from the most ancient of West African empires; in the words of Nkrumah, 'as an inspiration for the future'.

Ghana (1957 to the present day)

Ghana's pioneering status as the first independent former colony in Africa is pivotal to understanding much of what occurred in the country under Nkrumah, who evidently perceived himself as a spokesman not merely for his country, but for the far broader goal of liberating Africa from colonial rule. It is for this reason that the grassroots development of agriculture and the mining era were often ignored in favour of frittering away the country's financial reserves on a variety of grand schemes and empty gestures. Nkrumah's role as an African statesman cannot be denied – he was, for instance, the prime mover behind the formation of the Organisation of African Unity (OAU) in 1963, and he frequently gave generous financial support to other newly independent countries. But nor can one ignore a level of economic mismanagement and wastefulness that resulted in Ghana having accumulated a foreign debt of US$1 billion by 1966, despite having had foreign reserves ten times greater than its foreign debt at the time of independence. Characteristic of the Nkrumah era was the construction of an enormously expensive OAU Headquarters in Accra, one that was never to be used after the OAU decided to base itself in Ethiopia instead.

The Nkrumah government did have several far-reaching successes, for instance the vast improvement in the country's transport network between 1957 and 1966 – notably the laying of the 'new' Kumasi–Tamale road and surfacing of several other major trunk routes, and the construction of Akosombo Dam and a deepwater harbour at Tema. Another success was the expansion of an education system that already ranked among the best in Africa, resulting in a fivefold to twentyfold increase in enrolment at every level from primary school to university. And if Nkrumah's biggest failings were in the development of the crucial agricultural sector, then the 60% drop in the externally determined cocoa price during his rule must be cited as an important mitigating factor. It is also the case that post-independence Ghana was something of a victim of the cold war mentality – Nkrumah's espoused policy of African socialism, not to say his strong diplomatic ties with the

Eastern Bloc, made him an increasingly unpopular figure in the West, so that many Western governments were unwilling to provide Ghana with the support they might otherwise have given.

On the political front, the Nkrumah regime followed a path which, in hindsight, feels naggingly familiar. In July 1958, the Preventative Detention Act was passed in response to the formation of the opposition United Party under the leadership of Dr Kofi Busia, allowing for the detention without trial of perceived political opponennts for a period of up to five years. In July 1960, following a national referendum, Ghana was decreed a republic with Nkrumah elected as executive president. Shortly after the presidential election, Nkrumah's main opponent for the presidency, J B Danquah, was placed in detention, where he would eventually die, as would another former ally of Nkrumah's, Obetsebi Lamptey. It is estimated that by this time the jails of Ghana held some 3,000 political detaineees, a number that would increase dramatically following the attempted assassination of the president in 1962. It was this harsh repression of criticism, combined with the elavated status given to the Presidential Guard of the normal military, that would result in Nkrumah's downfall. On February 24 1966, while the president was away in Hanoi, control of the country was assumed by the military. Nkrumah never returned home, and he died of cancer in exile in 1972.

Between 1966 and 1969, Ghana was ruled by the military National Liberation Council under the leadership first of Lieutenent General Joseph Ankra, and later (and more briefly) Brigadier Akwasi Afrifa. This regime did much to restore democracy by releasing all political detainees and allowing a reasonable degree of free speech and a free press. It also restored Ghana's credibility in the West by breaking ties with the Eastern Bloc and initiating a widespread policy of privatisation. In May 1969, in line with a freshly drawn-up Bill of Rights, political parties were legalised. The election held a few months later was won by the Progress Party (PP) under Dr Kofi Busia, recently returned to the country after having fled to exile in 1959.

Busia's most notable contribution to the country was a remarkable drive towards rural improvement, for instance by building several new clinics and hospitals, drilling boreholes, and installing electricity in many places. By and large, the Busia regime maintained a policy of free speech and a free press, but these democratic ideals were undermined somewhat by their inconsistent application – at one point, for instance, Busia made it a criminal offence to mention Nkrumah by name, a response to the increasing lionisation of the former president. Busia's biggest failings were on the economic front and, although much of this can be blamed on a legacy of mismanagement left by former regimes, it would be an economic decision – the devaluation of the cedi by 44% – that triggered the coup which removed him from power on 13 January 1972.

The six-year presidency of General Ignatius Acheampong started out well enough, but all the initial grand talk of economic self-reliance and democracy soon deteriorated into a more familiar scenario. Acheampong's gross economic mismanagement and stubborn refusal to take advice

MUSIC

West Africa is well-known for its vibrant and largely self-contained music scene, and for many years Ghana was perhaps the leading innovator when it came to styles that combined traditional African sounds with foreign influences. More recently, Ghana has by and large relinquished its status as innovator to its francophone neighbours; nevertheless, a practically incessant backdrop of music remains a notable feature of travelling in urban parts of the country, and visitors will find themselves exposed to a rich variety of unfamiliar sounds.

The most popular music to have emerged out of Ghana is highlife, a term that covers a broad spectrum of homegrown styles fusing traditional percussive beats with various European, American and even Caribbean influences. Highlife, developed in the 1920s along the ports of what was then the Gold Coast, was first recorded in the late 1930s, reaching a popular peak in the period 1950–70. Its leading practitioners included E T Mensah, the African Brothers International Band, and more recently Alex Konadu and Koo Mino's Adadam Band.

Less easy to hear are the myriad traditional musical styles that hark from all around the country, generally drum-based in the south, more reliant on fiddles and other string instruments in the far north. It is in the north, though, that you are most likely to hear the peculiar 'talking drum', an instrument associated with the Sahel, as well as colourfully robed ensembles of Dagomba drummers (one of which we encountered by chance at a funeral in Bolgatanga).

Within Ghana, locally recorded music is largely drowned out by a plethora of exotica, not only the familiar contemporary Western hits, but also vibrant guitar music from the Congo and other parts of francophone Africa, as well as reggae – the South African reggae singer Lucky Dube is quite possibly the most popular recording artist in the country. Traditional Ghanaian music is most likely to be encountered by chance, at a street funeral or similar public festival, though in the north you could ask whether there is a specific day when music will be performed for the chief. The Academy of African Music and Arts on Kokrobite Beach near Accra is regarded to be one of the best places in West Africa to hear and learn about traditional and contemporary Ghanaian music.

Cassettes of popular Ghanaian recording artists – admittedly not always of the highest quality sound-wise – can be bought for next to nothing in lorry parks and markets in most substantial towns. The selection can be daunting; perhaps the simplest way to go about choosing a few cassettes as mementos of your trip is to make a habit, when you hear something you like in a bar or on a tro-tro, of asking somebody what's playing.

The most useful practical handbook to exploring Ghanaian and other contemporary and traditional African music forms is the Rough Guide's comprehensive tome *World Music*. In London, Stern's African Record Centre in Covent Garden (tel: 0171 387 5550) boasts an extensive catalogue of African recordings. Good starting points include E T Mensah's *All for You*, effectively a 'greatest hits' package, and various artists' compilations (*Akomko, Giants of Danceband Highlife, I've Found my Love* and *The Guitar and the Gun*), several of which are available on CD. For a broader overview of contemporary African music try Stern's *Guide to Contemporary African Music*, or the informatively packaged three-CD compilation *Africa Never Stands Still*, both available through Stern's.

regarding the freeing of the exchange rate resulted in an annual inflation rate of 130%, prompting an economic collapse that was exacerbated by two severe droughts during the early years of the regime. The repression of political activity continued with the mass detention of perceived political opponents. Meanwhile, the national coffers were drained by the regime, nepotism was rampant, and the level of corruption soared so high it caused one prominent Ghanaian to coin the term kleptocracy – rule by thieves. Amid an increasing level of civil unrest and widespread cries for a return to civilian rule, the military sacked Acheampong in 1978, and installed in his place Lieutenent General Akuffo. The ensuing months saw the unveling of a new constitution, as well as a lift on the six-year-old ban on political parties, and an election date was set for 1979.

On 4 June 1979, exactly two weeks before the scheduled election date, power was seized in a coup led by Flight Lieutenant Jerry Rawlings, a 32- year-old Ghanaian of mixed Scottish descent. Rawlings vowed that the election would go ahead, but that before power was transferred to the victor it was essential to purge corruption from the military and civil service. In the bout of bloodletting that followed, a great many civil servants were removed from office, tax offenders were forced to pay their debts, and several high ranking members of the military were executed publicly by firing squad, among them three former heads of state: Afrifa, Acheampong and Akuffo. Remarkably, on 24 September, a week ahead of schedule, civilian rule was restored when Rawlings handed power to the newly elected People's National Party under President Hilla Limann. The initial popularity of this government, however, was soon offset by the country's continued economic slide, and within a year the new government had become as corrupt as any before it.

On 31 December 1981, Ghana suffered its fourth coup in fifteen years, as power was seized once again by the popular figure of Jerry Rawlings. The constitution was abolished, parliament was dissolved, political parties were banned, and a number of prominent figures were jailed, President Limann among them. Rawlings installed a Provisional National Defence Council comprising three civilians and four military men, and at a local level he replaced councils with People's Defence Committees (later called Committees for the Defence of the Revolution). The next few years were marked by two clear trends. The first was unprecedented economic growth (a result of Rawlings' massive devaluation of the cedi), large-scale paring down of the civil service, privatisation of several state assets, and improved payments at the grassroots of the crucial cocoa industry. The second trend was one of repeated political instability, including several attempted coups and the unravelling of alleged assassination conspiracies against Rawlings, as well as a great many strikes and protests.

Things came to a head in 1989, when universities nationwide were closed for four months after protests and rioting, and Rawlings had introduced severe press restrictions. An attempted coup against the government was foiled in September, and a few months later one of its instigators was found hanged in his cell, prompting an international outcry led by Amnesty International as well as providing a rallying point for the many Ghanaians who wanted a return to civilian rule. In December 1990, Rawlings announced that a new constitution would be put in place within a year – it would in fact be enacted in April 1991 following a 92% approval among the 44% of the population who turned out for the national referendum. In May 1991, Rawlings endorsed the implementation of a multi-party system; the next month he passed amnesty on all political detainees, and six opposition groups were granted legal status. The most important of these were Dr Limann's People's National Convention (PNC) and Dr Boahen's New Patriotic Party (NPP), while Rawlings announced that he would retire from the military as per the new constitution and stood as president for the National Democratic Congress (NDC).

The election was held in two phases. The presidential elections in November 1992 saw Rawlings poll a clear majority of 58%, almost twice as many votes as his closest rival Boahen, who polled 30%. The election was declared substantially free and fair, but this was contested by the NPP and NDC who decided to boycott the constituent elections held on 29 December 1992 in protest. As a result, the NDC took 189 out of a possible 200 seats, with only a 29% poll recorded.

Despite this, the years since 1992 have seen many positive developments on the economic front, as well as an increased level of political freedom with the release of political detainees and the re-emergence of a free press. The government has managed to weather two major storms since 1992, to the extent that it was voted back into power in December 1996. The first of the crises to beset Ghana in recent years was an outbreak of ethnic violence in the northern regions, which originated from a land dispute between the Konkomba and Nunumba of the Bimbilla district in February 1994. Within months, the violence had spread to many parts of the north, leaving as many as 6,000 people dead and a further 100,000 displaced as 200 villages were razed. The second was an attempt to replace the existing sales tax with a new VAT system in February 1995, an unpopular decision which resulted in widespread rioting, the death of five people in Accra, and – eventually – the reinstatement of the familiar sales tax system. The above events notwithstanding, most observers agree that Ghana's days of coup and countercoup are long since gone, and that the combination of political freedom, sustained stability, and continued economic growth means its outlook is as bright as it has been at any time since independence.

ECONOMY AND INFRASTRUCTURE

Ghana is a country of great mineral and natural wealth, for which reason it has been an important centre of trade since prehistoric times. Skipping briefly through subjects covered more fully in the above history section, Ghana is thought to have been the main West African producer of kola nuts (sharp tasting and mildly narcotic, favoured by Muslims who are forbidden from drinking alcohol, and available in any Ghanaian market today) prior to the fifteenth century, at which time it also supplied amounts of gold and salt to Islamic traders in the Sahelian region to its north. From 1471 until the late seventeenth century, the Gold Coast supplied roughly 10% of the world's gold, as the empires of the south entered into a maritime trade with Portuguese and later Dutch traders. From the late seventeenth until the early nineteenth century, this trade in gold and other natural assets was swamped by the nefarious trans-Atlantic slave trade, operated by British and Dutch traders out of the Gold Coast and by several other European powers elsewhere off the west coast of Africa.

The roots of the modern Ghanaian economy can be traced to Britain's attempts to re-establish what they termed 'legitimate trade' after the slave trade was legally abolished in 1807. The main problem facing Britain in this regard was that many traditional trade-related skills such as gold-mining were lost during the era when slaves were the main item in demand by European merchants. In any case, the powerful Ashanti empire of the interior had been built largely on the slave trade, so that it was in both their interest and that of many European merchants to continue operating a clandestine trade in slaves, one that continued out of the Gold Coast at least until Britain's first defeat of Ashanti in 1826.

The first important item of legitimate trade to emerge in the nineteenth century was palm oil, used for cooking and in the manufacture of detergents, and exported from the Gold Coast as of 1820. This was of necessity a small-scale trade harvested from wild palms (the oil palm still cannot be properly cultivated), but plantations were slowly established in many areas, notably in what is now the interior of Eastern Region, and the emergent industry had the important affect of restoring respectability to agriculture after a century in which cultivation had been seen by many Africans as work fit only for slaves. By 1850, palm oil was the principle export from the Gold Coast, and by the 1880s it accounted for almost 75% of export revenue raised by the recently established Gold Coast colony. At the peak of the palm-oil era in 1884, some 20,000 tonnes of pure oil and twice that of palm kernels were exported, mostly to Germany.

Two other relatively important crops that took hold in the nineteenth century were cotton and rubber. The former never became an export crop due to infestations of disease and insects, but the crop was generally adequate to supply local needs, sometimes with a bit to spare for export. Rubber trees, by contrast, had been grown and tapped in the forest zone since the seventeenth century, but it was only in the 1870s that rubber was cultivated on a large scale, when its global importance soared as a result of the invention of the pneumatic tyre. In 1880, the Gold Coast exported a mere 0.05 tonnes of rubber. By 1886 that figure had increased to 692 tonnes, and by the early 1890s rubber was a bigger earner than palm oil, and the Gold Coast had become the world's third largest supplier. In the early 1900s, however, the bottom fell out of the rubber market; prices slid; and the industry in the Gold Coast collapsed, never to recover.

Perhaps the pivotal moment in Ghana's future economic development came in 1879, when Tetteh Quarshie returned home to the Gold Coast from Fernando Po with a few cocoa seedlings which he planted in his garden in Mampong. The climate and soil of the Gold Coast proved ideal for growing cocoa, and the crop was exported from 1891. By the turn of the century, cocoa had replaced rubber as the colony's biggest earner of foreign revenue, and by 1935 the Gold Coast was supplying half the world's cocoa. Cocoa remains to this day Ghana's most important agricultural earner (though it lies second on the production table after neighbouring Côte d'Ivoire), and the failure of the annual crop due to disease has, along with the rise and drop of the internationally determined cocoa price, often had a major influence on the country's politics. This is largely because the cocoa industry still favoured the small-scale farmer – it has been estimated that in 1951 roughly 500,000 people were employed by the cocoa industry or earned their primary income from cocoa production.

Much of Ghana's modern transport infrastructure dates to the colonial era, and there is little doubt that in this regard, if no other, Ghana was reasonably well served by its colonists, particularly by Gordon Guggisberg, the governor from 1919 to 1927. By the end of World War II, the Gold Coast had some 10,000km of roads (about one-third of the present road network) and all its present rail systems had been constructed – the Tarkwa–Sekondi line was completed as early as 1901 and extended to Kumasi in 1903, while the Accra–Kumasi line was finished in 1927. Under Guggisberg, the colonial administration provided a solution to the country's lack of a natural deepwater harbour with the construction of an artificial one at Takoradi in 1928. It was extended in 1956 as the colonial era drew to a close and is still the most important harbour in the country.

Two major engineering projects that were first mooted in the colonial era, but only brought to fruition later, largely at the instigation of Nkrumah, were the development of Tema as a deepwater harbour close to Accra, and the linked construction of a dam on the Volta at Akosombo, the latter not only important to the transport network of the north and east, but also capable of producing enough electricity for the whole country, as well as for export to neighbouring countries.

Just as important to economic development as a healthy transport infrastructure is good education, and here again the colonial administration was unusually forward-looking, with primary school attendance reaching 300,000 by 1951 and secondary school attendance 7,700. By the time of independence, the Gold Coast had 29 teacher training colleges as well as a highly regarded university and a number of trade colleges. The adult literacy rate at this time stood at roughly 25% – nothing to shout about by Western standards, perhaps, but remarkable by comparison with many other African countries at the end of the colonial era.

It is difficult to be so positive about the colonial administration's development of the mining industry – not because the colony's great mineral wealth was left unexploited, but because the industry was structured in such a manner that very little of the significant profit it raised would stay in the colony. Formal gold mining in the Gold Coast started at Tarkwa in 1877 and at Obuasi two years later, and it was also soon discovered that the colony had significant deposits of several other minerals, notably diamonds and manganese. By 1951, the year in which Nkrumah's CPP entered government, annual gold exports exceeded £8 million pounds annually, with manganese and diamonds close behind at around £7 million and £6 million respectively. For the sake of comparison, the value of cocoa exports in this year was a massive £60 million and timber, the second most important agricultural export, stood at £5 million.

At the time of independence in 1957, Ghana had one of the strongest economies in Africa, with foreign revenue reserves ten times greater than the foreign debt. By 1966, the situation had practically reversed, with the foreign debt in the region of US$1 billion. The reasons for Ghana's economic decline in the decades immediately following independence, and particularly between 1966 and 1981, are clearly linked to the political instability of that era, though exacerbated by external factors such as the 60% drop in the cocoa price during the Nkrumah era. More important here and now is that Ghana has undergone more than a decade of substantial economic growth since productivity reached a post-independence nadir in the early 1980s. Many people – not just Ghanaians – regard the country to be the most promising economic prospect in Africa at the moment. Real gross domestic product (GDP) growth since 1984 has typically hovered at around 5%, and an ambitious plan for the next 25 years has set a goal of roughly 8% per annum.

Despite a marked increase in industrialisation in recent times, agriculture remains at the heart of the economy, contributing almost 50% of the GDP and directly or indirectly supporting 80% of the population. Cocoa remains the most important crop in export terms and, although output dropped from over 500,000 tonnes annually in the early 1960s to 158,000 tonnes in 1983, it has recently risen back above the 300,000 tonne mark. Other important crops include cassava, plantains, coco yams, yams, maize, groundnuts, millet, rice, sorghum and sugarcane.

In recent years, mining has become the most important source of foreign revenue: renewed development in the goldfields of the south mean Ghana is now Africa's largest gold exporter after South Africa, with production rising from 17,000kg in 1990 to more than 35,000kg in recent years, while diamond exports have topped 700,000 carats annually since 1991. After gold and cocoa, tourism has recently risen to become the country's third largest earner of foreign revenue, generating an income of US$233 million in 1995 by comparison with US$19 million ten years earlier – an increase of above 100% in one decade!

THE NATURAL WORLD
Geography
Ghana is in essence flat and low-lying. Almost half of the country lies at an altitude of below 150m and nowhere does it top an altitude of 1,000m. The far south of the country is dominated by the low-lying coastal plain which runs between 100km and 150km inland of the Atlantic coastline, except near Accra where the Akwapim Mountains around Aburo rise from the coastal plain only 20km inland. At the heart of the country is the low-lying Volta Basin, Ghana's most important drainage system, stretching from around Tamale in the north to the Volta mouth at Ada. Much of it is now submerged in the 8,500km^2 Lake Volta, the world's largest artificial body of water.

The Volta Basin is flanked by mountains to the east and west. The eastern highlands, part of the Togo-Atakora range that stretches through to Benin, reach altitudes in excess of 900m near the Togolese border. The county's highest peak, Mount Afadjayo, is part of this range. The highlands to the east and west of the Volta Basin are characterised by a high number of waterfalls, most famously the Wli Falls near Hohoe, reputedly the highest waterfall in West Africa.

Climate

The combination of low altitude and proximity to the Equator gives Ghana a typical tropical climate. Daytime temperatures are high throughout the country, approaching or topping 30°C on most days. Temperatures do drop at night, more noticeably in the relatively dry north than the humid south, but visitors from cooler climes will generally consider most parts of Ghana to be hot both day and night. The only really temperate parts of the country are the highlands flanking the Volta Basin, where temperatures can be genuinely cool after dusk.

Owing to its equatorial location, Ghana does not experience the strong seasonal changes to which most Europeans and North Americans are accustomed. Temperatures are reasonably consistent throughout the year, and in many parts of the country the average temperature for the northern hemisphere winter months is actually higher than for the summer months – Accra, for instance, experiences its hottest temperatures from November to January, despite lying in the same hemisphere as Europe. The main seasonal factor to be aware of is rain, which falls almost exclusively during the European summer months of April to September, peaking in May and June. Rainfall figures are highest in the forested southwest, where some areas regularly experience in excess of 2,000mm per annum, and are lowest in the north and the plains immediately around Accra, where it is very unusual for as much as 1,000mm of rain to fall in a calendar year.

A noteworthy phenomenon in this part of the world is the harmattan winds which blow from the northeast during the dry season, bringing dust from the Sahara and reducing visibility to as little as 1km. Generally the winds come in late November or early December and continue until some time in March. The harmattan will have little effect on most tourists, but it is a nightmare for photographers and will cause disappointment to those who've come to admire the scenery in mountainous areas.

Vegetation

Most of southern Ghana for about 250km inland of the Atlantic is naturally covered in rainforest and, while clearing for cultivation and logging activities have left few areas of true rainforest intact outside of designated reserves, southern Ghana remains very lushly vegetated. For most visitors to Ghana, exposure to the rainforest is limited to a day trip to Kakum National Park, noted for its unique and spectacular canopy walkway, but there are countless other opportunities for more adventurous travellers to explore Ghana's forests, ranging from a number of relatively accessible reserves close to Kumasi to a handful of obscure national parks suited to self-sufficient hikers.

The central and northern parts of the country support savannah habitats, gradually becoming drier and more sparsely vegetated as you head further

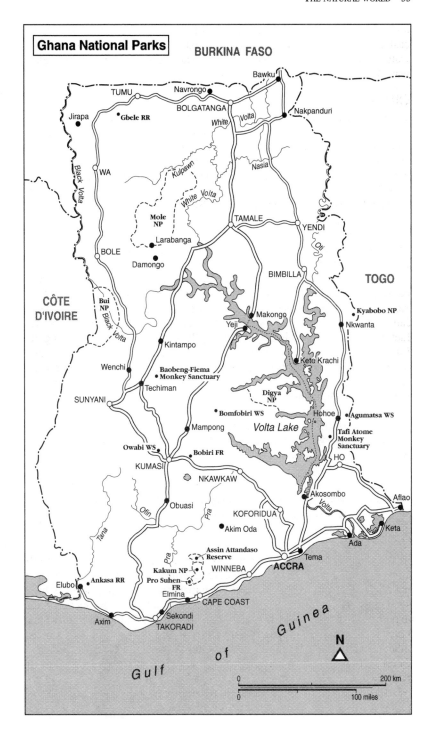

Ghana National Parks

north. In conservation terms, Ghana's most important savannah habitat is Mole National Park, easily visited as an overnight trip from Tamale.

Wildlife

Like other West African countries, Ghana lacks the vast conservation areas and huge herds of wildlife still to be found in most countries in eastern and southern Africa. Several large mammals typically associated with Africa do not occur in West Africa, for instance rhino, zebra, wildebeest and gorilla; while many other large mammal species have been driven to extinction in Ghana in historical times, notably giraffe, cheetah and probably African hunting dog. Within Ghana, the status of several other large mammal species, including lion, is highly vulnerable.

For all that, Ghana still offers some great opportunities for game viewing, with a wide variety of large mammals present and monkeys in particular well represented and easily observed. The following overview of the more interesting mammals to be found in Ghana is designed to help readers who are not carrying a field guide of any sort, but it should also be useful to those carrying a continental guide and seeking more specific information about the distribution and status of various mammal species within Ghana.

It is worth noting that while large mammals understandably draw the attention of most visitors to the game reserves and forests, Ghana does support a tremendous variety of other animals. Several of its forests boast in excess of 400 varieties of butterfly and, while the average visitor is unlikely to see even a fraction of these species, it is quite normal to see ten to twenty visibly different types of butterfly in the course of a walk, many of them quite exquisitely coloured.

Birdwatchers will find Ghana a highly rewarding country and, even if the avian variety doesn't quite match that of East Africa's finest birding countries, there are still plenty of places in Ghana where a reasonably experienced birder could expect to notch up 100 species in a day. For savannah birds, the best spot in the country is undoubtedly Mole National Park, where you can expect to see several varieties of colourful bee-eater, barbet and kingfisher, as well as larger birds such as various storks, herons, eagles, vultures and guinea fowl – enough to arouse the interest even of those with no particular interest in birds. Any forest will offer good birding too, with a greater chance of seeing some genuine rarities, but novices should be warned that the dense vegetation can make birding in the rainforest a frustrating and somewhat tiresome experience by comparison with the same activity in a more open environment. Sadly for birders, little useful literature (aside from a West African field guide) is available regarding Ghana's birds, and although I've included relevent comments based on our experience wherever possible in the guide, a lack of accessible source material means that coverage is less detailed than I would like.

Predators

The **lion**, *Panthera leo*, is Africa's largest predator, and the animal everybody hopes to see on safari. It is a sociable creature, living in prides of five to ten animals and defending a territory of between 20 and 200km². Lions hunt at night, and their favoured prey is large- or medium-sized antelope. Most of the hunting is done by females, but dominant males normally feed first after a kill. When not feeding, lions are remarkably indolent – they spend up to 23 hours of any given day at rest – so the anticipation of a lion sighting is often more exciting than the real thing. Lions naturally occur in any habitat but desert and rainforest, and they once ranged across much of the Old World; these days they are all but restricted to large conservation areas in sub-Saharan Africa (one remnant population exists in India). In Ghana, a small population of lions remains in Mole National Park, though few tourists see them. There may also be lions present in some other relatively unexplored conservation areas.

The powerful **leopard**, *Panthera pardus*, is the most solitary and secretive of Africa's large cats. It hunts using stealth and power, often getting to within 5m of its intended prey before pouncing, and it habitually stores its kill in a tree to keep it from hyenas and lions. Where the two co-exist, the leopard can be distinguished from the superficially similar cheetah by its rosette-like spots, lack of black 'tear marks' and more compact, powerful build (though current information suggests that cheetahs are extinct in Ghana).

Leopard

Leopard

Cheetah

Leopards occur in all habitats, favouring areas with plenty of cover such as riverine woodland and rocky slopes, and there are many records of individuals living for years undetected in close proximity to humans. The leopard is the most common large feline, occurring in many forests, but you'd be extremely fortunate to see one.

Of the smaller cats, the **serval**, *Felis serval*, built rather like a miniature cheetah, with black-on-gold spots giving way to streaking near the head, is seldom seen but widespread and quite common in moist grassland, reed beds and riverine habitats. The **caracal**, *Felis caracal*, closely resembles the European lynx with its uniform tan coat and tufted ears, and it favours relatively arid savannah habitats. The not dissimilar **golden cat**, *Felis aurata*, lives in forested areas, lacks ear tufts and has a spotted underbelly. The markedly smaller **African wild cat**, *Felis sylvestris*, ranges from the Mediterranean to the Cape of Good Hope, and is similar in appearance to the domestic tabby cat.

Caracal

African hunting dog

The **African hunting dog**, *Lycaon pictus*, distinguished by cryptic black, brown and cream

Black-backed jackal

coat, was known to occur in Mole National Park until recent times, but is probably now extinct in Ghana. The **black-backed jackal**, *Canis mesomelas*, and **side-striped jackal**, *Canis adustus*, both occur sparsely in northern Ghana and are listed for Mole National Park. The first species can be identified by its prominent black saddle flecked with a varying amount of white or gold, while the second has an indistinct pale, vertical stripe on each flank and a white-tipped tail.

The **spotted hyena**, *Crocuta crocuta*, probably the most common large predator in Ghana, has a bulky build, sloping back, brown spotted coat, powerful jaws and dog-like expression. Contrary to popular myth, hyenas are not exclusively scavengers: the spotted hyena in particular is an adept hunter capable of killing a large antelope. Nor are they hermaphroditic, an ancient belief that stems from the

Spotted hyena

false scrotum and penis covering the female hyena's vagina. Sociable animals, and fascinating to observe, hyenas live in loosely structured clans of about ten animals, led by females who are stronger and larger than males. The North African **striped hyena**, *Hyaena hyaena*, pale brown with several dark vertical streaks and a blackish mane, may occur in the very far north of Ghana.

A great many small nocturnal predators occur in Ghana. The **African civet**, *Civettictus civetta*, is a bulky, long-haired creature with a rather feline appearance, primarily carnivorous but also partial to fruit, and widespread and common in many habitats but

African civet

very rarely seen. The smaller, more slender **tree** or **(two spotted) palm civet**, *Nandinia binotata*, is an arboreal forest animal with a dark-brown coat marked with black spots. The **small-spotted genet**, *Genetta genetta*, **large-spotted** or **blotched genet**, *Genetta tigrina*, and **panther** or **pardine genet**, *Genetta pardina*, are Ghanaian representatives of a taxonomically confusing genus comprising perhaps ten species, all very slender and rather feline in appearance, with a grey to gold-brown coat marked with black spots and a long ringed tail.

The **ratel** or **honey badger**, *Mellivora capensis*, black with a puppyish face and grey-white back, is an opportunistic feeder best known for its symbiotic relationship with a bird called the honeyguide which leads it to a bee hive, waits for it to tear open the hive, then feeds on the scraps. The **Cape clawless otter**, *Aonyx capensis*, is a brown freshwater mustelid with a white collar, while the smaller **spotted-necked otter**, *Lutra maculicollis*, is darker with light, white spots on its throat.

Six mongoose species occur in Ghana, most of them diurnal, terrestrial and reasonably common – all six have, for instance, been recorded in Mole

National Park. The **marsh mongoose**, *Atilax paludinosus*, is large, normally solitary, with a very scruffy brown coat, often seen in the vicinity of water. The **Egyptian** or **large grey mongoose**, *Herpestes ichneumon*, is also large, and often associated with water, but its grey coat is grizzled in appearance and it is most often seen in pairs or family groups. Restricted to rainforest habitats, where it is often quite common, the **cusimanse**, *Crossarchus obscuras*, is a small, sociable mongoose with a shaggy brown coat, almost always seen in family groups.

The **white-tailed mongoose**, *Ichneumia albicauda*, is a large, solitary brown mongoose, generally found in savannah country, and easily identified by its bushy, white tail. The **slender** or **pygmy mongoose**, *Galerella sanguinea*, is another solitary inhabitant of the savannah, but very much smaller and with a uniform brown coat and blackish tail tip. The **Gambian mongoose**, *Mungos gambianus*, dark brown with the distinctive combination of pale throat and black cheek stripe, is the most sociable mongoose found in savannah country, occurring in groups of up to 30 animals.

Gambian mongoose

Primates

The **common chimpanzee**, *Pan troglodytes*, still occurs in reasonable numbers in the rainforest of southern Ghana. Along with the bonobo, *Pan paniscus*, of the southern Congo, it is more closely related to man than to any other living creature. The chimpanzee lives in large troops based around a core of related males dominated by an alpha male. Females aren't firmly bonded to their core group, so emigration between communities is normal. Primarily frugivorous, chimpanzees eat meat on occasion and, though most kills are opportunistic, stalking of prey is not unusual. The first recorded instance of a chimp using a tool was at Gombe Stream in Tanzania, where modified sticks were used to 'fish' in termite

Chimpanzee

mounds. In West Africa, chimps have been observed cracking open nuts with a stone and anvil. In the USA, captive chimps have successfully been taught Sign Language and have created compound words such as 'rock-berry' to describe a nut. A widespread and common rainforest resident, the chimpanzee is thought to number 200,000 in the wild. In Ghana, there are plans to habituate chimps to humans in Ankasa and Bia National Parks, but until this happens chimpanzees are unlikely to be seen by tourists.

The **anubis** or **olive baboon**, *Papio (cynocaphalus) anubis*, a powerful terrestrial primate, and distinguished from any monkey by its much larger size, inverted 'U'-shaped tail and distinctive dog-like head, is fascinating to watch from a behavioural perspective. It lives in large troops which boast a complex, rigid social structure characterised by matriarchal lineages and plenty of intra-troop movement by males seeking social dominance. Omnivorous and at home in almost any habitat, the baboon is the most widespread primate in Africa. It is quite frequently seen in Ghana, especially in Mole National Park and the Shai Hills.

The **green** or **vervet monkey**, *Cercopithecus aethiops*, is probably the world's most common monkey and certainly the most widespread representative of the *Cercopithecus* guenons, a taxonomically controversial genus associated with African forests. An atypical guenon, in that it inhabits savannah and woodland rather than true forest, the green monkey spends a high proportion of its time on the ground and is more likely to be confused with the much larger and heavier baboon. However, the green monkey's light-grey coat and white forehead band should be diagnostic – as should the male's garish blue

Vervet monkey

genitals. The green monkey is common in most Ghanaian reserves. The terrestrial **patas** or **red monkey**, *Erythrocebus patas*, larger and more spindly than the vervet, has an orange-tinged coat and black forehead stripe. Essentially a monkey of dry savannah, the patas occurs in northern Ghana, and can quite easily be seen alongside the green monkey in Mole National Park.

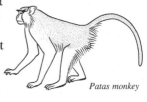

Patas monkey

Probably the easiest to see of Ghana's true forest monkeys, the **mona monkey**, *Cercopithecus mona*, is a pretty and cryptically coloured grey, white and black guenon distinguished by the pale stripe over its eye. It is the common monkey at Baobeng-Fiema and Tafi Atome Monkey Sanctuaries, and occurs in most Ghanaian forests, where it is offered some protection against hunting. There appears to be some taxonomical uncertainty about the relationship between the mona monkey and similar **Campbell's monkey**, *Cercopithecus campbelli*.

Mona monkey

Two other distinctive species of forest guenon occur in Ghana: the **spot-nosed monkey**, *Cercopithecus petaurista*, a small monkey distinguished by its prominent white nose, and the beautiful, white-bearded **Diana monkey**, *Cercopithecus diana*. The spot-nosed monkey is widespread in forests where it hasn't been hunted, while the Diana monkey is restricted to Kakum and a few forests near the Ivorian border. Both are rarely seen in the wild.

The **western** or **Geoffrey's black-and-white colobus**, *Colobus (polykomos) vellerosus*, is a beautiful jet-black monkey with bold, white facial markings and a long, white tail, widespread where it hasn't been hunted to extinction and easily seen at Baobeng-Fiema Monkey Sanctuary. Almost exclusively arboreal, it is capable of leaping distances of up to 30m, a spectacular sight with

Black and white colobus

its white tail streaming behind. The **western red colobus**, *Procolobus (badius) waldroni*, also known as Miss Waldron's bay colobus, is a distinctly red, long-limbed forest monkey restricted to a few forests in southwestern Ghana. The smaller and duller **olive colobus**, *Procolobus verus*, distinguished by two grey patches on its forehead, occurs in several forests in southern Ghana, including Kakum National Park.

The one other forest monkey to occur in Ghana, the **sooty mangabey**, *Cercocebus atys*, is the only West African representative of a genus that's more widely represented in the central African rainforest. It is the only uniform dark-grey monkey to occur in Ghana, but I have no details of where it might be seen.

Also present in Ghana are several species of nocturnal **bushbaby**, *Galago spp*, often quite easy to locate if you know where to find them and have a good spotlight. The **potto**, *Perodicticus potto*, is a sloth-like nocturnal primate of rainforest interiors, also most easily located with the aid of a spotlight.

Antelope

Roan antelope

The **roan antelope**, *Hippotragus equinus*, is the largest plains antelope found in Ghana, with a shoulder height of 120–150cm. It is a handsome horse-like creature, uniform fawn-grey with a pale belly, short decurved horns and a light mane. It occurs in several savannah reserves, and is the common antelope of Gbele Resource Area near Tumu in the north. The roan is quite likely to be seen by visitors spending a few days in Mole National Park.

Defassa waterbuck

The **Defassa waterbuck**, *Kobus (ellipsiprymnus) defassa*, is another very large antelope, easily recognised by its shaggy brown coat, white rump and the male's large, lyre-shaped horns. It is normally seen in small family groups grazing near water, and is almost certain to be seen in the vicinity of the hotel at Mole National Park. The closely related **kob**, *Kobus kob*, is a beautiful, red-gold antelope with a white throat, but otherwise few distinguishing features. It is probably the most common large antelope in Ghana, and family herds are almost certain to be seen by visitors to Mole National Park and Shai Hills.

Kob

Hartebeest

The **western hartebeest**, *Alcelaphus buselaphus*, is a large, ungainly antelope readily identified by the combination of large shoulders, sloping back, red-brown or yellow-brown coat and smallish horns in both sexes. It is resident in several savannah reserves in Ghana, but quite rare everywhere.

Secretive and scarce, the **bongo**, *Tragelaphus euryceros*, is a very large, stocky and clearly striped rainforest species, isolated populations of which occur in several Ghanaian reserves, including Kakum National Park. It is highly unlikely to be seen by a casual visitor. A far more common and widespread resident of forest and thick woodland, though also quite secretive, the **bushbuck**, *Tragelaphus scriptus*, is an attractive, medium-sized antelope. The male is dark brown or chestnut, while the much smaller female is generally a pale reddish brown. The male has relatively small, straight horns. It can be seen in just about any Ghanaian forest or game reserve, and is quite frequently observed in Shai Hills and Mole National Park.

Bushbuck

Less common, the **Bohor reedbuck**, *Redunca redunca*, is a plain, light fawn, medium-sized antelope generally seen in pairs in open country near water. The **Oribi**, (*Ourebia ourebi*), is rather like a miniature reedbuck, uncommon in grassland habitats. Even smaller, the **common** or **grey duiker**, *Sylvicapra grimmia*, is an anomalous member of the duiker family in that it occurs in savannah and woodland rather than true forest. Distinguished by the black tuft of hair between its small horns, it is the only small, grey antelope likely to be seen in non-forested habitats in Ghana.

Reedbuck

Common duiker

The forest duikers are a taxonomically confusing group of 12 to 20 species restricted to the rainforests of Africa. Six species occur in Ghana, all of them widespread (all but the red-flanked, for instance, occur in Kakum National Park), but secretive and rather unlikely to be seen in the wild by tourists. The largest of these is the nocturnal **yellow-backed duiker**, *Cephalophus leucogaster*, a bushbuck-sized antelope with a blackish coat and yellow patch on its back which occurs sparsely in most true rainforests, including Kakum National Park.

Three of Ghana's remaining duiker species are also rather large by the standards of the family, with a shoulder height of up to 55cm. The most distinctive of these, the **black duiker**, *Cephalophus niger*, with a thickish near-black coat and red forehead and throat, is realistically only likely to be seen clearly at Owabi Wildlife Sanctuary outside Kumasi. More widespread, the **bay duiker**, *Cephalophus dorcas*, red-brown with a wide, black dorsal stripe, would be difficult to tell apart at a glance from **Ogilby's duiker**, *Cephalophus ogilbyi*, which is similar but has a narrower dorsal stripe.

The most common forest antelope in Ghana, **Maxwell's duiker**, *Cephalophus maxwelli*, is a small, grey duiker with a distinctive, pale eye stripe, likely to be seen in any forest in southern Ghana. Similar in size to

Maxwell's, but with colouring closer to the bay duiker, the **red-flanked duiker**, *Cephalophus rufilatus*, is best distinguished from members of its genus by habitat and distribution, since it is essentially a species of forest fringe and woodland which differs from *all* other forest duikers in that it occurs only in the northern half of Ghana.

Also occurring in the Ghanaian rainforest, the **royal antelope**, *Neotragus pygmaeus*, is a common, but infrequently observed, brown antelope with a red throat collar, which with a shoulder height of up to 28cm is regarded to be the world's smallest horned ungulate. More closely related to European deer than any antelope, the **water chevrotain**, *Hyemoschus aquaticus*, is an odd, hare-sized nocturnal creature with a brown coat and white stripes and spots, generally associated with wet habitats within rainforests.

Other mammals

The **African elephant**, *Loxodonta africana*, is the world's largest land animal, and both the savannah and smaller forest species occur in Ghana. It is an intelligent, social animal, and often very entertaining to watch. Female elephants live in closely knit clans in which the eldest female plays matriarch over her sisters, daughters and granddaughters. Mother-daughter bonds are strong and may last for up to 50 years. Males generally leave the family group at around 12 years to roam singly or form bachelor herds. Under normal circumstances, elephants range widely in search of food and water, but when concentrated populations are forced to live in conservation areas, their habit of uprooting trees can cause serious environmental damage. Elephants are widespread and common in habitats ranging from desert to rainforest, and despite heavy poaching they are still present in several national parks and reserves. Mole National Park, with a population of between 500 and 800 elephants, is the best place to see them.

Characteristic of Africa's large rivers and lakes, the **hippopotamus**, *Hippopotamus amphibius*, is a large, lumbering animal that spends most of the day submerged, but emerges at night to graze. Strongly territorial, herds of ten or more animals are presided over by a dominant male who will readily defend his patriarchy to the death. Hippos are present in Mole National Park, but not within day-walk distance of Mole Motel, and they are very common in the part of the Volta River protected by Bua National Park. The **West African manatee**, *Trichechus senegalensis*, is an unmistakable large, grey, hairless mammal, related to the marine dugong but entirely restricted to freshwater habitats. Increasingly very rare, manatees are still seen from time to time on Lake Volta and the Volta estuary area near Ada.

African buffalo

The **African buffalo**, *Syncerus caffer*, frequently but erroneously referred to as a water buffalo (an Asian species), is a distinctive ox-like animal which lives in large herds on the savannah and occurs in smaller herds in forested areas. It is common and widespread in sub-Saharan Africa, and historically both the black savannah race and the smaller, redder forest race occur in Ghana, though the latter is now very rare and possibly extinct. The country's largest buffalo population of roughly 1,000 animals is found in Mole, but buffalo also occur in some forest reserves and in Kalapka Resource Reserve near Ho.

The rather endearing **warthog**, *Phacochoreus africanus*, is grey in colour with a thin covering of hairs, wart-like bumps on its face, and rather large upward-curving tusks. Africa's only diurnal swine, the warthog is often seen in family groups, trotting off briskly with its tail raised stiffly (a diagnostic trait) in a determinedly nonchalant air. In Ghana it occurs in most savannah reserves, though is only likely to be seen in Mole National Park, where it is common. The **red river hog**, *Potamoccoerus porcus*, is a larger

Warthog

forest swine, common but primarily nocturnal, and regarded by some authorities to be a race of the East Africa bushpig, from which it is readily distinguished by a decidedly red coat and clear, white stripe along its back. Larger still, the **giant forest hog**, *Hylochoerus meinertzhageni*, a very hairy, dark-brown swine that weighs up to 250kg, is a fairly common but difficult-to-observe nocturnal resident of most rainforests in Ghana.

The **aardvark**, *Orycteropus afer*, is a singularly bizarre insectivore, quite common in dry savannah country, and unmistakeable with its long snout and huge ears, but rarely seen due to its nocturnal habitats. Equally distinctive, **pangolins** are rare nocturnal insectivores with armour-plating and a tendency to roll up in a ball when disturbed. Spiky rather than armoured, several **hedgehog** and **porcupine** species occur in the region, the former generally no larger than a guinea pig, the latter generally 60–100cm long.

One small mammal species that you're quite likely to encounter in the right habitat is the **rock hyrax**, *Procavia capensis*, a rodent-like creature more closely related to elephants and often seen sunning itself in rocky habitats. Probably more numerous in Ghana, but less easily seen, the similar looking **tree hyrax**, *Dendrohyrax dorsalis*, is a nocturnal forest creature which announces its presence

Rock hyrax

with an unforgettable shrieking call.

Of the great many squirrel species present in Ghana, all but one are essentially restricted to forest and woodland. The exception, a widespread inhabitant of the northern savannah, is the **unstriped ground squirrel**, *Xerus inauris*, a terrestrial animal with a white eye ring, silver-black tail, and the characteristic squirrel mannerism of holding food in its forepaws while standing on its hind legs.

Ground squirrel

Chapter Two

Planning and Preparation

WHEN TO GO

In most respects, the best time to visit Ghana is during the northern hemisphere winter. The months of October through to April are not significantly hotter or cooler than other times of the year, but they are a great deal more comfortable since humidity levels are lower. More important, these months form the dry season, which means there are fewer mosquitoes (and correspondingly there's a lower risk of contracting malaria), dirt roads are in better condition, and there is less likelihood of you or your luggage being drenched in an unexpected storm. The dry season is particularly suitable for those with a strong interest in natural history, since game viewing is best when the grass is low and resident bird populations are supplemented by all sorts of Palaearctic migrants.

The main disadvantage of the dry season, particularly from December through to February, is that visibility is seriously impeded by sands blown from the Sahara by the harmattan winds. This won't greatly affect most travellers, but people who plan on doing a lot of hiking will miss the best of the scenery, and serious photographers will find the dull ambient light and grey skies not at all conducive to getting decent pictures.

PAPERWORK

Check well in advance that your **passport** hasn't expired and will not do so for a while, since you may be refused entry on a passport that's due to expire within six months of your intended departure date.

Visitors of practically all nationalities require a **visa** to enter Ghana. This takes up to three days to issue at any Ghanaian Embassy or High Commission, and you will generally have to produce three passport-sized photos and pay a fee of around US$15 for a single-entry visa valid for a stay of up to 30 days. If you plan on spending longer in Ghana, you are likely to be told that you must buy a 90-day multiple-entry visa, at three times the cost of an ordinary visa. This is pure fabrication on the part of some embassies: the purpose of a multiple-entry visa is quite simply that you can enter and exit the country any number of times while it is valid. Upon entering the country with a valid visa, you will be stamped for a maximum of 30 days regardless of what type of visa it is. And if you want to stay on for longer than 30 days, you will have to apply for a visa extension once you are in the country and to pay an additional US$10 for every extra 30 days, regardless of whether you have paid for a single or multiple-entry visa. The good news is that visa extensions can be organised at any time in your trip (we extended ours to three months after a week in the country) and the process seems very straightforward. It's worth knowing that a visa extension in Accra might take two weeks to process, whereas it shouldn't take more than 48 hours at any other regional capital. Obviously, if you expect to leave and re-enter Ghana, then you most definitely do want a multiple-entry visa.

Should there be any possibility you'll want to drive or hire a vehicle while you're in the country, do organise an **international driving licence** (any AA office in a country in which you're licensed to drive will do this for a nominal fee). You may sometimes be asked at borders for an **international health certificate** showing you've had a yellow fever shot.

For security reasons, it's advisable to detail all your important information on one sheet of paper, photocopy it, and distribute a few copies in your luggage, your money-belt, and amongst relatives or friends at home. The sort of things you want to include on this are your travellers' cheque numbers and refund information, travel insurance policy details and 24-hour emergency contact number, passport number, details of relatives or friends to be contacted in an emergency, bank and credit card details, camera and lens serial numbers etc.

Should your passport be lost or stolen, it will generally be easier to get a replacement if you have a photocopy of the important pages.

Something that you no longer need to be concerned about, at least in our experience, is having policemen ask you to produce your passport on a whim.

GETTING THERE
By air

The national carrier Ghana Airways is a reputable airline that flies between Accra and London, Dusseldorf and Rome in Europe, New York in the USA, Harare and Johannesburg in Southern Africa, and eight West African capital cities. Other airlines with scheduled flights to Accra include Air Afrique, Alitalia, British Airways, Egypt Air, Ethiopian Airlines, KLM, Lufthansa and Swissair. Bearing in mind that a Virgin Airways flight from some parts of the USA to London costs as little as US$250, North Americans with more time than money may find it advantageous to fly to London and organise a ticket to Africa from there.

There are dozens upon dozens of travel agents in London offering cheap flights to Africa, and it's worth checking out the ads in magazines like *Time Out* and *TNT* and phoning around before you book anything.

An established London operator well worth contacting is Africa Travel Centre (4 Medway Court, Leigh Street, London WC1H 9OX, tel: 0171 387 1211, fax: 0171 383 7512). Two reputable agents specialising in cheap round-the-world type tickets rather than Africa specifically are Trailfinders (42–48 Earls Court Road, London W8 6EJ, tel: 0171 938 3366, fax: 0171 937 9294) and STA (117 Euston Road, London NW1 2SX, tel: 0171 361 6262, fax: 0171 937 9570). There are STA branches in Bristol, Cambridge, Oxford and Manchester.

Southern Africa Travel (tel: 01483 419133, fax: 01483 860180) features tours to Ghana and can organise tailor-made trips. Guerba Expeditions (tel: 01373 826611, fax: 01373 858351) offers overland trips by truck in and through Ghana.

Unless it's absolutely unavoidable, don't even think about flying to Ghana on a one-way ticket and organising your ticket out once you are there. For starters, you may hit serious problems with airport immigration officials if you don't arrive on a return ticket, and secondly, flights out of Accra are very expensive, so you'll almost certainly end up paying double what you would for a cheap return.

Overland from Europe

There are two overland routes between Europe and Ghana. Both start in Morocco and involve crossing the Sahara, one via Algeria and the other via Mauritania, then continue through Mali and Burkina Faso. The Algeria option has been impassable for some years now, but the situation with either route is highly changeable and you should seek current advice. For readers based in the UK, the best way to gauge the situation would be to get in touch with the many overland truck companies that advertise in magazines such as *TNT* and *Time Out*. And, frankly, unless you've a reliable 4x4, joining an overland truck trip is almost certainly the best way of doing this difficult route, especially if you have thoughts of continuing through the Democratic Republic of the Congo (formerly Zaire) to East Africa.

Travellers visiting Ghana overland from Europe will presumably want to carry a regional or continental guide. If you are taking your own vehicle, then the *Sahara Handbook* by Simon and Jan Glen (Lascelles, 1987) is the essential companion, while *Africa by Road* by Bob Swain and Paula Snyder (Bradt Publications, 1995) is very useful when it comes to general planning, but weak on country-by-country advice. It might also be worth investing in a regional guide to West Africa (see *Further reading,* page 253), or even a more general guide to Africa; but bear in mind that the wider the scope of the guide, the skimpier it is on individual detail.

WHAT TO TAKE

There are two simple rules to bear in mind when you decide what to take with you to Ghana. The first is to bring with you *everything* that you could possibly need and that might not be readily available when you need it. The second is to carry as little as possible. Somewhat contradictory rules, you might think, and you'd be right – so the key is finding the right balance, something that probably depends on personal experience as much as anything. Worth stressing is that most genuine necessities are surprisingly easy to get hold of in Ghana, and that most of the ingenious gadgets you can buy in camping shops are unlikely to amount to much more than deadweight on the road. If it came to it, you could easily travel in Ghana with little more than a change of clothes, a few basic toiletries and a medical kit.

Carrying luggage

Assuming that you'll be using public transport, you'll want to carry your luggage on your back, either in a backpack or in a suitcase that converts into one, since you'll tend to spend a lot of time walking between bus stations and hotels. Which of these you choose depends mainly on your style of travel. If you intend doing a lot of hiking you definitely want a proper backpack. On the other hand, if you'll be doing things where it might be a good idea to shake off the sometimes negative image attached to backpackers, then there would be obvious advantages in being able to convert your backpack into a conventional suitcase.

My current preference is for a robust 35cl day pack. The advantages of keeping luggage as light and compact as possible are manifold. For starters, you can rest it on your lap on bus trips, avoiding complications such as extra charges for luggage, arguments about where your bag should be stored, and the slight but real risk of theft if your luggage ends up on the roof. A compact bag also makes for greater mobility, whether you're hiking or looking for a hotel in town. The sacrifice? Leave behind camping equipment and a sleeping bag. Do this, and it's quite possible to fit everything you truly need into a 35cl day pack, and possibly even a few luxuries – I refuse to travel without binoculars, a bird field guide and at least five novels, and can still normally keep my weight down to around 8kg. Frankly, it puzzles me what the many backpackers who wander around with an enormous pack and absolutely no camping equipment actually carry!

If your luggage won't squeeze into a day pack, a sensible compromise is to carry a large day pack in your rucksack. That way, you can carry a tent and other camping equipment when you need it, but at other times reduce your luggage to fit into a day pack and leave what you're not using in storage.

Travellers carrying a lot of valuable items should look for a pack that can easily be padlocked. A locked bag can, of course, be slashed open, but in Ghana you are still most likely to encounter casual theft of the sort to which a lock would be a real deterrent.

Clothes

Take the minimum, bearing in mind that you can easily and cheaply replace worn items in Ghana. In my opinion, what you need is one or possibly two pairs of trousers and/or skirts, one pair of shorts, three shirts or T-shirts, one light sweater, maybe a light waterproof windbreaker during the rainy season, enough socks and underwear to last five to seven days, one solid pair of shoes or boots for walking, and one pair of sandals, thongs or other light shoes.

When you select your clothes, remember that jeans are heavy to carry, hot to wear, and slow to dry. Far better to bring light cotton trousers and, if you intend spending a while in montane regions, tracksuit bottoms which will provide extra cover on chilly nights. Skirts are best made of a light natural fabric such as cotton. For reasons of protocol, women may prefer to wear a skirt that goes below the knees in the Muslim north – it's by no means necessary, since Ghanaians are relatively relaxed about dress codes, but single women in particular might find that a dress draws much less attention than skimpier attire.

T-shirts are lighter and less bulky than proper shirts, though the top pocket of a shirt (particularly if it buttons up) is a good place to carry spending money in markets and bus stations, since it's easier to keep an eye on than trouser pockets. One sweater or sweatshirt will be adequate, since no parts of Ghana lie at an altitude of 1,000m or above, so night-time temperatures are almost invariably comfortable to sweaty. There is a massive used clothing industry in Ghana, and at most markets you'll find stalls selling jumpers of dubious aesthetic but impeccable functional value for next to nothing – you might consider buying such clothing on the spot and giving it away afterwards.

Socks and underwear must be made from natural fabrics. Bear in mind that re-using sweaty undergarments will encourage fungal infections such as athlete's foot, as well as prickly heat in the groin region. Socks and underpants are light and compact enough that it's worth bringing a week's supply. As for footwear, genuine hiking boots are worth considering only if you're a serious off-road hiker, since they are very heavy whether on your feet or in your pack. A good pair of walking shoes, preferably made of leather and with good ankle support, is a good compromise. It's also useful to carry sandals, thongs or other light shoes.

Camping equipment

The case for bringing camping equipment to Ghana is compelling only if you intend hiking or visiting some of the more obscure reserves, where there is no other accommodation. In most other situations, rooms are cheap and campsites few and far between, so this isn't a country where camping will save huge sums of cash. The main argument against carrying camping equipment is that it will increase the weight and bulk of your luggage by up to 5kg, all of which is deadweight except for when you camp.

If you decide to carry camping equipment, the key is to look for the lightest available gear. It is now possible to buy a lightweight tent weighing little more than 2kg, but make sure that the one you buy is mosquito proof. Other essentials for camping include a sleeping bag and a roll-mat, which will serve as both insulation and padding. You might want to carry a stove for occasions when no firewood is available, as is the case in many montane national parks where the collection of firewood is forbidden, or for cooking in a tropical storm. If you do carry a stove, it's worth knowing that Camping Gaz cylinders are readily available only in southern Ghana (which is where you're most likely to do most of your camping and open-air catering). A box of firelighter blocks will get a fire going in the most unpromising conditions. It would also be advisable to carry a pot, plate, cup and cutlery.

Other useful items

Most backpackers, even those with no intention of camping, carry a **sleeping bag**. A lightweight sleeping bag will be more than adequate in Ghana; better still in this climate would be to carry a sheet sleeping bag, something you can easily make yourself. You might meet travellers who, when they stay in local lodgings, habitually place their own sleeping bag on top of the bedding provided. Nutters, in my opinion, and I'd imagine that a sleeping bag would be less likely to protect against fleas than to be infested by the things.

I wouldn't leave home without **binoculars**, which some might say makes me the nutter. Seriously, though, if you're interested in natural history, it's difficult to imagine anything that will give you such value-for-weight entertainment as a pair of light compact binoculars, which these days needn't be much heavier or bulkier than a pack of cards. Binoculars are essential if you want to get a good look at birds (Africa boasts a remarkably colourful avifauna even if you've no desire to put a name to everything that flaps) or to watch distant mammals in game reserves. For most purposes, 7x21 compact binoculars will be fine, though some might prefer 7x35 traditional binoculars for their larger field of vision. Serious birdwatchers will find a 10x magnification more useful.

Some travellers like to carry their own **padlock**, though in Ghana there are few circumstances where you are likely to need one, unless you have a pack that is lockable. A combination lock might be the best idea, since potential thieves in Ghana are far more likely to have experience of picking locks with keys.

Your **toilet bag** should at the very minimum include soap (secured in a plastic bag or soap holder unless you enjoy a soapy toothbrush!), shampoo, toothbrush and toothpaste. This sort of stuff is easy to replace as you go along, so there's no need to bring family sized packs. Men will probably want a **razor**. Women should carry enough **tampons** and/or **sanitary pads** to see them through, since these items may not always be immediately available. If you wear **contact lenses**, be aware that the various cleansing and storing fluids are not readily available in Ghana and, since many people find the intense sun and dry climate irritates their eyes, you might consider reverting to glasses. Nobody should forget to bring a **towel**, or to keep handy a roll of **loo paper**, which although widely available at shops and kiosks cannot always be relied upon to be present where it's most urgently needed.

Other essentials include a **torch**, a **penknife** and a compact **alarm clock** for those early morning starts. If you're interested in what's happening in the world, you might also think about carrying a **short-wave radio**. Some travellers carry **games** – most commonly a pack of cards, less often chess or draughts or travel Scrabble. A light plastic **orange-squeezing device** gives you fresh orange juice as an alternative to fizzy drinks and water.

You should carry a small **medical kit,** the contents of which are discussed in *Chapter Four*, as are **mosquito nets**.

Photographic equipment

An inexpensive point-and-shoot camera with a 50mm lens should produce reasonably satisfactory photographs of people and scenery, though a 28–70mm zoom lens allows for greater flexibility. You can forget about taking even halfway decent wildlife photographs with anything much less than 200 magnification; a 70–300mm or similar zoom lens would be perfect for anything less than professional purposes. Low-speed 50, 64 or 100 ISO films are ideal in most circumstances, and far less grainy than 400 ISO film.

Don't rely on being able to get anything but 400 ISO print film in Ghana. If you want to use colour print film of other speeds, or any slide or black-and-white print film, then bring as much as you'll need with you.

MONEY
Organising your finances

There are three ways of carrying money: hard currency cash, travellers' cheques, or a credit card. My advice is to bring at least as much as you think you'll need in the combination of cash and travellers' cheques, but if possible to also carry a credit card to draw on in an emergency. I would strongly urge any but the most denominationally diehard of backpackers to bring their cash and travellers' cheques in the form of US dollars, and to learn to think and budget in this currency.

From the point of view of security, it's advisable to bring the bulk of your money in the form of travellers' cheques, which can be refunded if they are lost or stolen. It is best to use a widely recognised type such as American Express and Thomas Cook, and to keep the proof of purchase separate from the cheques, as well as noting which cheques you have used, in order to facilitate a swift refund should you require one. Buy your travellers' cheques in a healthy mix of denominations, since you may sometimes need to change a small sum only, for instance when you're about to cross into another country. On the other hand, you don't want an impossibly thick wad of cheques. For a trip to one country, I'd take five US$20 cheques and the remainder of my money in US$100 cheques. Whatever your bank at home might say, currency regulations and other complications make it practically impossible to break down a large denomination travellers' cheque into smaller ones in most African countries, so don't take denominations larger than US$100.

In addition to travellers' cheques, you should definitely bring a proportion of your money in hard currency cash, say around US$200–300, since you are bound to hit situations where travellers' cheques won't be accepted. Also cash gets a better exchange rate, especially large denomination bills – which isn't much consolation if all your money is stolen, so I'd strongly advise against bringing cash only, but would suggest that you save what cash you do bring for situations where it will buy you a real advantage.

Carry your hard currency and travellers' cheques, as well as your passport and other important documentation, in a money belt – one that can be hidden beneath your clothing rather than the sort of fashionable externally-worn type which in some circumstances will serve as a beacon rather than protection. Your money belt should be made of cotton or another natural fabric, and everything inside the belt should be wrapped in plastic to protect it against sweat.

Credit cards are not widely accepted, though they are of limited use in Accra. You can normally draw up to US$150 daily in local currency against a Visa card at any main branch of Barclays Bank, but I wouldn't rely on this except in Accra. Every time I've travelled in Africa recently I've bumped into at least one person who's strayed a bit too far off the beaten track with only a credit card for support. I would tend to carry a credit card as a fall-back more than anything, and to be conservative in my assumptions about where I'll be able to draw money against it. No matter how long you are travelling, do make sure that you won't need to have money transferred or drafted across to West Africa.

An airport departure tax of US$20 is levied on international flights out of Accra. Before you pay it, check whether it has already been included in the price of your ticket.

Costs and budgeting

Ghana is not an expensive country in which to travel. So far as travel basics go, accommodation for one or two people will probably average out at around US$5 per day for the cheapest room, US$8 per day for a self-contained room, and from US$20 per day for air-conditioned comfort. For food, expect to spend around US$2 per day per head if you eat street food only, and around US$5 if you eat once daily in a restaurant. Depending on how often and how far you travel, public transport shouldn't come to more than US$2 per day per head, while a charter taxi ride in most towns costs at most US$1. The main thing you need to add to the above on a daily basis is liquid. Unless you drink tap water only, which is not always advisable, you'll spend a lot of money just keeping your thirst quenched in Ghana's hot climate – say US$2 per head daily if you stick to mineral water and soft drinks, perhaps US$4 daily if you add on a couple of beers.

Put this together, and you're looking at a rock-bottom budget of US$10/15 daily for one/two people (considerably more for any nights you spend at Mole National Park, unless you camp there). To travel in reasonable comfort, eat and drink what you feel like within reason and take the odd taxi, a budget of around US$20/30 for one/two people would be about right. If you want air-conditioning, two solid meals and the rest, I'd budget on US$40/50 for one/two people.

The above reckoning excludes one-off expenses such as entrance fees to museums or guiding fees in parks, factors that tend to create the occasional expensive day, markedly so for those on a tight budget. In countries such as Tanzania where national park fees and safari costs are very high, I've sometimes found it a useful budgeting device to separate one-off expenses from the more predictable day-to-day costs. As a rule, you'll have relatively few major one-off expenses in Ghana, though tips and guide fees, etc can start to add up in some places. If you are very tight for cash, rather than allocating yourself a budget of, say, US$15 per day, it might work better to aim for a daily budget of US$10 and set aside the rest for one-offs.

Chapter Three

Travelling in Ghana

TOURIST INFORMATION AND SERVICES

There is a regional office of the Ghana Tourist Board in each of the country's ten regional capitals. On the whole, these offices should be worth visiting if you want to check up on new developments in the region, though our experience was that the staff are often surprisingly ignorant about even the most important local attractions – I find it remarkable that the person manning the slick, air-conditioned office in Cape Coast was adamant that no accommodation is to be found near Kakum National Park, or that it took three people in the Kumasi office to give us (incorrect) directions to a wildlife sanctuary barely 20km away. The most pro-active tourist office in Ghana is undoubtedly the one for Volta Region, in the town of Ho – if you plan to explore this eastern part of Ghana then do pop in there.

All in all, however, your best source of current practical information will be travellers who have already been to the places where you are heading. Good places to connect with the travellers' grapevine include the Hotel de California in Accra, the Presbyterian Guesthouse in Kumasi, the motel in Mole National Park, Cape Coast, Busua on the west coast, and (as soon as it becomes better known) the Estuary Beach Camp near Ada on the east coast.

Contact addresses for regional tourist offices are as follows:

Accra Regional Admin Office, Barnes Rd, PO Box 3106, Accra. Tel: (021) 23-1817.
Bolgatanga (Upper East) Information Services Dpt, PO Box 395, Bolgatanga. Tel: (072) 3416.
Cape Coast (Central) Jackson Road, PO Box 847, Cape Coast. Tel: (042) 32062.
Ho (Volta) SIC Building, PO Box 568, Ho. Tel: (0756) 22431.
Koforidua (Eastern) SIC Building, PO Box 771. Tel: (081) 23209/32128.
Kumasi (Ashanti) National Cultural Centre, PO Box 3065, Kumasi. Tel: (051) 26242/22421.
Sunyani (Brong Ahafo) Regional Admin Office, PO Box 802, Sunyani. Tel: (061) 7108.
Tamale (Northern) Regional Admin Office, PO Box 1053, Tamale. Tel: (071) 22212.
Wa (Upper West) Ministry of Trade and Industry, PO Box 289, Wa. Tel: (0756) 22431.

PUBLIC HOLIDAYS

Although several public holidays are recognised in Ghana, the only major impact they will have on tourists is that banks and government offices are closed and the volume of public transport decreases to a level you'd expect on a Sunday. There are five variable-date public holidays: the Christian Good Friday and Easter Monday, the Muslim Eid il Fitr and Eid il Adel, and Farmers' Day (first Friday in December). In addition, the following fixed-date public holidays are recognised:

New Year's Day	January 1
Independence Day	March 6
May Day	May 1
June 4 Anniversary	June 4
Republic Day	July 1
Christmas Day	September 25
Boxing Day	December 25

MONEY

The unit of currency is the cedi, formerly divided into 100 pesewas, but now so heavily devalued that any further subdivision would be meaningless. The value of the cedi has been in steady decline for some years. Since the early 1990s, it has devalued by roughly 100%. Even during the relatively short period of time we spent in Ghana, the most favourable exchange rate for US dollars cash advertised in Accra dropped by roughly 3%. As of early 1998, the rate of exchange against the US dollar stands at between 2,000 and 2,350 cedis, depending on where and how you change your dollars and whether they are in the form of travellers' cheques or cash. It is impossible to predict what the exchange rate will be by the time readers of this guide visit the country.

Foreign exchange

The most widely recognised foreign currency is the US dollar. US dollars in cash can be exchanged for local currency in practically any town or border post, often at a bank or a private bureau de change (forex bureau). In Accra, Kumasi and to a lesser degree the other regional capitals, there's generally a large number of places where you can exchange US dollars cash and the rate may vary by as much as 10%, so it's worth shopping around. In smaller towns your options will probably be limited to one bank or forex bureau, so you'll have to take whatever rate you're offered. In towns where there are no banks, or if you want to exchange money outside the normal banking hours of 08.30 to 14.00, you'll rarely have a problem finding a private individual to exchange your US dollars. There is always a danger of being conned in such a situation, however, particularly when you deal with 'professional' money-changers at borders, so I would advise against changing significantly more money than you need to get to the next town with banking facilities.

The situation is less straightforward with more obscure currencies and with travellers' cheques. With other currencies, even major ones like the British pound or the German Mark, you can forget about exchanging money with private individuals, and should plan ahead to ensure that you don't run out of money in a town without a bank or forex bureau. The same goes for travellers' cheques, with the added complication that practically no forex bureau will accept them, and that even the larger banks outside Accra have to get rates on a daily basis from the capital, a procedure that becomes less reliable the further north you go. If you are carrying mostly travellers' cheques, you should probably rely on being able to exchange money only in the regional capitals. North of Kumasi, you may be held up a day or two waiting for the rates to be faxed up. The simple solution to all this is to carry enough US dollars in the form of cash.

The three main banks with foreign exchange facilities are the Commercial Bank of Ghana, Barclays and the Standard Chartered. In general, they offer a lower rate of exchange for cash than the private forex bureaux. When we were in the country, the best exchange rate for travellers' cheques was invariably at the Standard Chartered Bank, which normally charges no commission.

If you are changing a large sum of money, do check that the bank or forex bureau can give you the bulk of your local currency in 5,000 cedi notes – the next largest denomination bank note is 2,000 cedis, worth less than US$1! It's also worth thinking about how and where you will carry your newly acquired pile of bank notes after a major transaction. You don't want to be walking around the streets of Accra with a few hundred US dollars worth of cedis and nowhere to conceal them.

Small change
The largest bill available in Ghana is 5,000 cedis (worth less than US$2) yet finding small change is an ongoing problem for Ghanaian traders – not to say for travellers. It's not at all unusual to be unable to make a purchase for, say, 100 cedis because nobody can find change for a 500 or 1,000 cedi note! The simple solution to this is to try to keep a reasonable balance of small bills and coins on you at all times. Bear in mind that tro-tro conductors and taxi drivers *always* seem to be able to find change, so never use your last 2,000 cedi bill on a taxi or tro-tro ride. And if you are in a hurry and don't have the right amount when you buy something like a Coke, then pay before you start drinking so the vendor has time to find change.

Prices
With few exceptions (basically a handful of upmarket hotels in Accra), pretty much everything in Ghana can be paid for in the local currency. In many situations, attempting to pay for something in anything but cedis would create complete confusion. Nevertheless, when I wrote this guide in 1998, I chose to quote prices in US dollars, partly to create a more useful impression of costs at the planning stage of a trip, but mostly because the high rate of inflation in Ghana and ongoing devaluation of the cedi threatened to make any price quoted in local currency look meaningless a few years on.

The prices quoted in this book were collected between November 1997 and January 1998 and converted to US dollars at a rough conversion rate of 2,000:1. This means that a hotel room which cost 12,000 cedis in 1997/8 is quoted at US$6. Many hotel and restaurant rates have increased in cedi terms since the guide was written, but in many instances this increase corresponds to the devaluation of the cedi to around 3,500 to US$1 in January 2000. In dollar terms, some hotels may be marginally more expensive than they were in 1997/8, but multiplied by 3,500 the prices quoted in this guide shouldn't be out by more than 10–20%, and they will still give an accurate reflection of the relative cost of hotels in any given town. Do note that prices are approximate, since exchange rates vary widely, depending on where you change your hard currency and whether it is in the form of travellers' cheques or cash, and are generally rounded up or down to the nearest US$0.50.

A government levy of 15% is charged on all accommodation and restaurant meals in Ghana. At the lower end of the price range, hotels and restaurants generally include the levy in any advertised price, hence the frequency with which one comes across a room rate such as 6,900 or 8,050 cedis, seemingly designed to do nothing but waste time in a country where finding small change is a constant precipitator of mini-crises. By contrast, most upmarket hotels and restaurant quote prices exclusive of the levy, so that a room quoted at US$40 will actually cost you US$46. Where I am aware of the latter situation, I've upped accordingly to reflect what the room will actually cost.

GETTING AROUND
Driving
Unusually for a former British colony, Ghana drives on the right side of the road. Ten years ago, the state of Ghana's roads was appalling. In recent times, however, there has been large-scale upgrading of all the main routes, most of which are now surfaced. You could easily drive the entire coastal road from Aflao to Elubo in a saloon car, as could you the main north–south road from Accra to Paga via Kumasi and Tamale. In fact, there are now very few parts of the country which aren't accessible to practically any carefully driven vehicle – as evidenced by the ancient Peugeot taxis that cover the most unlikely of routes throughout Ghana. All the same, it would be prudent to seek local advice repeatedly as you move around the country, particularly if you visit more remote areas during the rainy season.

If you've never before driven in Africa, be aware that the general approach to driving is quite different to that in more developed countries. Ghanaians tend to be complete maniacs on the road, and visitors should be very cautious, particularly if they are also adapting to driving on the right side if the road. In addition to a heart-stopping approach to overtaking, you will have to contend with potholes, pedestrians and domestic animals on the road. And be acutely aware that it's customary not to slow down on a blind curve but to race around it hooting wildly – if you don't hoot back, it will be assumed that no vehicle is coming! Driving at night is inadvisable, not so much for security reasons, but because the general chaos on the road is exacerbated by a lack of street lights and many vehicles without headlights.

Public transport
Rail
What is effectively a triangle of railway lines connects Accra, Kumasi and Takoradi. The most popular rail service in the country is the one between

Kumasi and Takoradi, largely because the equivalent road is in relatively poor condition. Details of this service are in the *Getting there and away* section under Kumasi.

Road

All major roads through Ghana are covered by a variety of public transport, divisible into three broad categories: buses, *tro-tros* and taxis. By comparison with many African countries, getting around Ghana's roads is very straightforward and comfortable, though the standard of driving leaves a great deal to be desired on the safety front.

In small towns and villages, there is generally one place from where all public transport leaves, referred to by Ghanaians as the 'station' or 'lorry station'. In larger towns, there will often be several different stations, each serving a set of destinations in one direction. STC, OSA and City Express buses may well leave from a different station to the one used by private *tro-tros*. This can become very confusing and, while I've tried to indicate the most important stations in most large towns, I'd advise readers to do things the easy way. Cough up a taxi fare (often as little as 50 cents) and ask the driver to take you to the right place. The convention is to ask for the 'station' for the destination you want – in other words, should you be looking for transport to Mampong, then ask to be taken to Mampong Station.

Buses As a rule the safest and most efficient way of travelling is by bus. This is particularly the case when you travel directly between two major centres, for instance from Accra to Kumasi or Accra to Takoradi, since the government State Transport Company (STC) runs regular, reliable direct bus services along most major surfaced routes. STC buses typically cover around 80km/hour with one scheduled 15-minute meal break. Most STC buses will drop off passengers along the way, provided that they are prepared to pay full fare – in other words, the Accra–Kumasi bus will drop you at, say, Nkawkaw, but you must pay the same fare as you would to get to Kumasi. STC buses run to fixed departure times, and it's normally a good idea to have a ticket booked at least 30 minutes in advance.

On practically every major route in the country, even those where there is no STC bus, a cheaper service is provided by the OSA and/or City Express lines. Also run by the government, these lines are just as safe as the STC, but they are generally slower, partly because they stop for passengers more often and partly because the buses are older. OSA and City Express buses generally pick up and drop passengers as required, and fares are charged accordingly.

Bus fares in Ghana are very reasonable. A ticket for the STC bus between Accra and Kumasi, for instance, costs US$3.50 for a 250km ride that takes four to five hours. OSA and City Express buses are slightly cheaper for comparable distances.

Tro-tros If anybody is aware of a more precise definition of a tro-tro than 'pretty much any passenger vehicle that isn't a bus or a taxi', then they are welcome to let me know about it. Tro-tros cover the length and breadth of

Ghana's roads, ranging from comfortable and only slightly crowded minibuses to customised, covered trucks with densely packed seating, a pervasive aura of sweat, no view, and not much more chance of finding an escape route should you be involved in an accident. You will have little choice but to depend on tro-tros when you travel between smaller towns, but I would advise you to use buses wherever possible, not so much because tros-tros are slower or less comfortable than buses (though generally they are both) but because the risk of being involved in a fatal accident is so much greater.

Most tro-tros leave when they are full, and on all main roads you'll rarely wait more than 30 minutes for a vehicle heading in your direction. Be warned that many of the touts whose task it is to fill up tro-tros have a quite neurotic need to physically 'see' bums on seats. It can take all your powers of persuasion to convince them that if they could only use their imagination and pretend you are sitting in your seat, then you could stand outside while you wait for the vehicle to fill up rather than having to practise being uncomfortable in a sweaty, cramped, motionless vehicle for half an hour. And even when you think that you've had an incandescent moment of cross-cultural communication, as the tout appears to light up with recognition of the good sense of your position, he'll be edging up to you two minutes later hissing 'you sit, white man, you sit!'

Only on routes where there is very little transport do you need to think in terms of set departure times, and in such circumstances you should definitely check the situation the day before – it may, for instance, be the case that all the transport leaves before 06.00. It is also worth being aware that many tro-tros don't run on Sundays, particularly in Christian parts of the country, which means you'll generally wait longer for something to leave along main roads and may be delayed for hours or find that nothing is going at all along minor routes. Where possible, I would avoid travelling on a Sunday, though we frequently did and usually got where we wanted to in the end.

Fares on tro-tros are cheaper than on buses. I've not quoted fares in this guide, because they are subject to inflation and generally pretty predictable once you've been in the country for a few days. Typically, you can expect to pay around US$1 per 100km on a good road, and a little more on an inferior road because the journey takes longer. In many places, you have to buy a ticket at the booth of the Private Transport Union (or the GRPTU of TUC to give its full set of initials) for that specific route, and even when you just pay the conductor on the road, fares are fixed and overcharging is not a significant concern.

Some Ghanaians refer to both buses and tro-tros as 'lorries'.

Taxis I've never seen a country with so many taxis as Ghana, and I'd not be surprised to be told that they account for more than 80% of the vehicles on the road. Typically battered old Peugeots, Ghanaian taxis can be split into two systems of operating: dropping and passenger taxis. The dropping system is essentially the one we are familiar with, where you charter a taxi privately, with the major difference being that Ghanaian taxis are not metered, so a price must be agreed in advance. The passenger system is where a taxi plies a specific route at a fixed fare, either picking up passengers along the way or else filling the vehicle at a recognised terminal.

Whichever system you use, taxis in Ghana are quite incredibly inexpensive, and it is well worth making use of them. In most parts of the country a dropping taxi will charge between US$0.50 and US$1 for a ride within a town (the price is a little higher in Accra) and a fare on a passenger taxi within any given town may be as little as 200 cedis (US$0.10) and will rarely be more than 400 cedis (US$0.20).

Passenger taxis are often the main form of transport between two nearby towns, notably in the part of Ashanti northeast of Kumasi. They also often cover short roads between a junction and a nearby town, especially along the coast, where many towns and villages lie a few kilometres south of the main road. Generally these taxis take six passengers, two in the front and four in the back, but on some routes the convention is five or four passengers – don't ask me why! It will often be assumed by taxi drivers that any foreigner prefers a private taxi, so always specify when you want a 'passenger' not a 'dropping' vehicle. In most towns, you can normally assume that any empty taxi that stops for you will be offering you a 'dropping' service to wherever you like at a negotiable fare, whereas a vehicle that already has passengers will be offering you a lift in a specific direction at a fixed fare.

There may often be circumstances where you do want to use a private taxi. In Accra, for instance, it's barely worth figuring out the passenger taxi routes if you're only spending a night or two there. When you arrive in a town with luggage, it is often pleasant to catch a taxi to a hotel. Likewise, you may consider it a waste of time to wait an hour for a passenger taxi to fill up when, for instance, it is covering an 8km road at a cost of 500 cedis per person, and you could charter the whole thing for 3,000 cedis (less than US$1.50)! And note that in such circumstances it would be perfectly acceptable to pay the difference where the taxi is partially full – using the example above, if two passengers each paying 500 cedis were already sitting in the taxi when you arrived, you could offer to pay 2,000 cedis to make up the full fare of 3,000.

It should be understood by travellers that while passenger taxi fares are seen by Ghanaians to be fixed, dropping fares are perceived to be negotiable. You might ask a cab driver how much a passenger fare is and he'll tell you it's 500 cedis, then when you ask how much to charter the same taxi on the same route he'll say 5,000 cedis. It's very difficult to come up with a rule of thumb for determining the right dropping fare – you might ask two different taxi drivers for the same route and one will ask half what the other does – but you'll quickly get a feel for what seems reasonable, and should bear in mind that the dropping fare between two spots should work out at between four and six times the passenger fare.

Boat
The only ferry service in Ghana is the weekly Lake Volta ferry between Akosombo and Yeji, details of which are under *Akosombo* on page 173.

SLEEPING, EATING AND DRINKING
Accommodation

Accra, Kumasi and the major coastal resorts boast a selection of hotels suitable to most tastes and budgets, ranging from international-class skyscrapers to simple local resthouses and church-run establishments. Elsewhere in the country, the majority of hotels are simple and unpretentious places, geared primarily to the local market, and generally very good value for money. For the most budget-conscious travellers, rooms typically start at around US$3–4 in smaller towns and in the north, and US$5–6 in larger towns and along the coast. Even at the bottom end of the price range, you'll rarely have to stay in real dumps of the sort you find in many other parts of Africa – the cheapest hotels generally have fans in the rooms, electricity in towns where there is a supply, and acceptable washing facilities. In most towns US$8–12 will buy you a self-contained (s/c) room with a fan, while for US$15–20 you can expect to find a room with air-conditioning (ac) and possibly television, running hot water and a fridge.

One quirk to watch out for, particularly if you are travelling as a couple, is that a single room in Ghana is sometimes a room with a double bed, while a double room is actually a twin (ie: with two beds). Generally, a couple will first be shown a room with two beds, presumably because it's normally the most expensive option, so if your preference is to share a bed, then ask to look at a single room first. If you're having trouble making your meaning clear, Ghanaians generally talk about big and small beds – you're less likely to be misunderstood if you ask for a room with one big bed as opposed to asking for a double room. Single travellers might also take note that when I went out looking at hotels on my own, my request to see a room at a hotel where no prices were advertised almost invariably resulted in my being shown the most expensive option, often one with two large double beds – quite what the receptionist imagined I would want to do with this prairie-like expanse of soft mattress, I don't know!

It is customary in Ghana for hotels to supply guests with an undersheet only. Many hotels will supply you with a sheet to sleep under upon request, but many won't. Most of the time in Ghana you don't really need a top-sheet to keep you warm, but it can be pleasant to have something to break the direct effect of a fan and to help keep off mosquitoes. And then there are some people who just hate sleeping without some sort of cover. Ariadne says: if you're in that category, bring a sheet or similar with you.

There are relatively few opportunities for camping in Ghana and, accommodation being as cheap as it is, I think that for most people the hassle of carrying a tent and other camping equipment will outweigh the advantages. The major exception is if you expect to spend a lot of time visiting remote wildlife reserves and national parks, many of which are only realistically accessible to people with camping equipment.

Food

We found the food in Ghana to be refreshingly tasty, or perhaps that should more accurately be distinctly spicy, since it is the ubiquitous and liberal use of *piripiri* that distinguishes Ghanaian cuisine from the bland local food served in most parts of eastern and southern Africa.

Among the great many starch-based staples you're likely to encounter in Ghana, the most popular are *fufu, kenkey, banku, tozafi* (TZ), *omo tua* (rice balls), boiled rice, and fried yam or plantain. Particularly popular in the south, *fufu* is made of cassava, plantain or yam, mashed to a pulp then cooked with no water to form a very gooey ball that's normally served submerged in a light soup. Almost identical to each other in taste and texture, and found throughout Ghana, *kenkey* and *banku* are made of fermented maize meal, boiled in a removable wrapping of plantain leaves, and normally eaten with a very spicy tomato relish. Largely restricted to the north, *tozafi* is a millet or maize-based porridge. Fried yam, often sold at markets, is not dissimilar in taste and texture to potato chips, though when bought on the street it often has a lingering, petroleum-like taste, presumably a result of using the same oil for too long. Most travellers find Ghanaian staples to be an acquired taste, and it's probably fair to say that while you wouldn't want to travel in Ghana without trying *fufu* or *kenkey*, you're unlikely to miss them when you return home.

Local food can be eaten in small restaurants known as 'chop bars', where you will generally be served with a plate of *fufu* or *kenkey* or rice along with a portion of meat or vegetable stew. Another typical chop bar dish is *jollof rice* – rice with chicken or meat cooked into it. A more interesting way of eating local food, and dirt cheap, is on the street. Most towns have at least one place where vendors sell a huge variety of dishes from informal stalls, often near the lorry station or the market. One advantage of eating on the street is you can try a bit of this or that, rather than be confronted with one specific dish. In addition to the usual staples, street vendors often sell grilled poultry (chicken, or in the north guinea fowl), spicy beef or goat kebabs, delicious sweet fried plantain with piripiri seasoning, smoked fish, and deep-fried doughnut-like balls.

Fresh fruit and vegetables are widely available, with a degree of regional and seasonal variety. The most characteristic fruits are probably pineapples, coconuts and oranges, the latter skinned in a way that makes it easy to suck the liquid out without getting sticky fingers. Another unexpected pleasure for the sweet of tooth is the locally manufactured chocolate – not a complete surprise when you consider that Ghana is one of the world's major cocoa producers, but unexpectedly good all the same. As for vegetables, tomatoes, onions and yams are available practically everywhere, but most others are mainly restricted to the south and the larger towns of the north.

When it comes to breakfast, you'll pay a small fortune for an egg, bread and tea in your hotel, so head rather for one of the tea stalls that are to be found in most markets and lorry stations. These places serve fresh, tasty tomato and onion omelettes, as well as bread and hot drinks. Note, however, that in Ghana tea seems to be a blanket term covering all hot drinks, so instead of asking for tea or coffee you should ask by brand name for Lipton (tea), Nescafé (coffee) or Milo (a chocolate malt drink). Bread, meanwhile, comes in two forms. The ordinary loaves, squarish but often with a pattern baked in, are known simply as 'bread' and are generally stale and unpleasantly sweet. What you want is tea bread, a crustier loaf that's often not much bigger than a large roll. You'll normally be able to find fresh tea bread somewhere around the market or lorry station, though you may want to resist any offer to have it smothered in margarine, since this is most often rancid.

Finally, most towns of substance have at least one restaurant serving exotic dishes, most often straight Western chicken or steak with chips or rice. Quite why, I don't know, but there's a large number of Chinese restaurants in Ghana, and many of the more Westernised places and superior chop houses serve Chinese-style fried rice and spring rolls. A meal in a proper restaurant generally costs around US$4–6 per head excluding drinks, so it is a lot more expensive than eating on the street or in chop bars. If you are not carrying a lot of cash on you, remember to check the small print of the menu before you order, since many restaurants quote prices exclusive of the 15% government levy and their 10% service charge – so that you actually pay 26.5% more than the stated price.

Drinks

Starting with the familiar, all the usual brand name sodas are widely available in Ghana's fridges, particularly Coca-Cola, Fanta, Sprite and Schweppes soda water and tonic water. Locally bottled minerals cost anything from 600 to 1,000 cedis (less than US$0.50) or you can waste your money on tins of the imported stuff for twice the price. In addition to the international brands, there are a few uniquely Ghanaian minerals available. Now, it's not very nice to take the mickey out of other people's names, but there is such a thing as asking for it. And ask for it, I'm afraid, is exactly what Mr Pee did when he started up a soft-drink factory and decided to name the product after himself – Pee Cola, indeed.

They say that the sound of the African bush is the piercing cry of the fish eagle. Well then, the sound of the Ghanaian bus station is indisputably the banshee wail of *Aaaaiiiiiiiswuhtuh* emitted in best announcement voice by hordes of generally pre-pubescent girls. What they are selling is ice water: sealed plastic bags that contain chilled clear water and cost next to nothing. We drank it without ill effect, which could well have been a triumph of luck over judgement, and more sensible readers will probably prefer to stick to the 1.5-litre bottles of still mineral water that are widely available in Ghana, though rarely chilled and generally quite expensive.

Emphatically worth trying are the surprisingly good, sweetened Refresh fruit juices that come in 250ml packs and sell for around 800 cedis (US$0.40). I never acquired much of a taste for Bruna, a fizzy, locally bottled fruit punch, but we both liked its Togolese equivalent, called Cocktail de Fruits, and widely available in 750ml bottles in the Togolese border area. A cheap, refreshing and highly nutritious drink is fresh coconut juice. You'll often see street vendors selling piles of coconuts, particularly along the coast – just ask them to chop one open and you can slurp down the liquid.

The most widespread alcoholic drink is lager beer, which is brewed locally and generally pretty good. A 750ml bottle costs around US$1, depending on where you drink. Four brands of bottled beer are available: we settled on a preference order of Gulder, ABC, Star and finally Club. In the south, draught beer or Bubra is widely available and can go for as little as US$0.50 per pint. Also widely available (though we never summoned up the courage to try them) are litre boxes of red and white wine, which are presumably Spanish or Portuguese in origin and sell for around US$1 per carton. Local bars in Ghana are also called 'spots', and they can generally be distinguished a mile away by the blue-and-white picket fences that customarily enclose bars.

If you're interested in trying local tipples, several are available, all very cheap and generally rather potent. *Pito* is a type of millet beer, similar to the local beer brewed in villages in many parts of Africa, and most easily located in the *pito* bars that can be found in most towns, especially in the north. Palm wine, easily located on the coast, is called *ntunkum* in its mildest form and *nsa* when it is older and stronger. *Akpeteshie* is a fiery spirit distilled from palm wine. It's frequently offered to visitors when they visit a village chief – the correct protocol is to spill a drop on the ground in honour of the ancestors before you swig it down. Another popular drink is the locally bottled Schnapps, which many chiefs prefer as a libation to money!

INTERACTING WITH GHANAIANS

Ghana has a reputation as the friendliest country in West Africa, a title that is patently absurd but certainly not unjustified. Taken as a whole, Ghanaians do seem to be remarkably affable and friendly both among themselves and in their dealings with tourists, and I find it difficult to think of any other African country where I felt so safe or unhassled. First-time visitors to Africa, or at least those with a white skin, may be surprised at the amount of attention they draw by virtue of their conspicuous foreignness – symptoms of which range from having every passing taxi in Accra blare its horn at you to being greeted by mobs of exuberant children chanting *abruni* as you walk past – but I cannot recall an incident of this type that was underscored by anything approaching malice. Put simply, Ghana is an amazingly welcoming country and, although you'll sometimes encounter people who treat all Westerners like a walking ATM, they are the exception, not the rule. You'd have to be extraordinarily unlucky to experience anything that could be described as seriously threatening or unpleasant.

Etiquette

Ghana, like any country, has its rules of etiquette, and, while allowances will normally be made for tourists, there is some value in ensuring they don't have to be made too frequently!

Perhaps the most important single point of etiquette for visitors to bear in mind is that it is considered highly insulting to use your left hand to pass or receive something or when shaking hands – a common custom in Muslim countries, and practised throughout Ghana. If you eat with your fingers, it is also customary to use the right hand only. Even those of us who are naturally right-handed will occasionally need to remind ourselves of this custom (it may happen, for instance, that you are carrying something in your right hand and so hand money to a shopkeeper with your left) and for those who are left-handed it will require constant effort.

Greeting procedures tend to be more formalised in Ghana than in modern Western societies, especially in small towns and villages, and elderly people in particular should be treated with special respect. If you need to ask somebody directions, or anything else for that matter, it is considered very rude to blunder straight into interrogative mode without first exchanging greetings – even when shopping! At village level, it is polite for strangers to nod to anybody they pass along the way.

It is customary to visit the chief of any village where you intend to stay overnight or to do any local sightseeing. In practice, this is no longer necessary in many villages, and where the custom has been continued in places that regularly receive tourists it tends to feel a bit showy. Only when you travel in really out-of-the-way areas is a visit to the chief likely to feel like a matter of etiquette over commerce, and here you should be especially careful to observe protocol. You will be expected to pay tribute in the form of kola nuts, a bottle of Schnapps, or money (the equivalent of about US$1 is normally fine). In return you may receive a glass of Akpeteshie (local gin), and it would be rude to refuse unless you use the excuse that you don't touch alcohol. Before drinking the gin, pour a few drops on the ground as a tribute to the forefathers. You should always take off your hat or cap in the presence of a chief (or any old person), and should never sit with your legs crossed in his presence.

Guides and tipping

One aspect of travel in Ghana that can become mildly enervating is the constant stream of guides and wannabe guides that tend to attach themselves to travellers. This is not something that's unique to Ghana, I grant you, but it is certainly more prevalent in Ghana than in any other African country I've visited, and it is worth thinking through your attitude to this in advance. There is no doubt in my mind that using guides is in principle a good thing, since it ensures that tourism provides an income to local people, but there is also a line to be drawn; basically that the guide should in some way contribute to your experience.

Starting positively, there are many situations where a guide is an unambiguously worthwhile investment, for instance when visiting game reserves (where it is not permitted to walk without an armed guide) or at many historical sites (where knowledgeable guides are generally provided by request only). In such clear-cut circumstances – basically, where you are allocated a guide by an institution – you *will* normally pay a fee, but since this will not go directly to the guide (who in all probability is poorly paid) it is proper and customary to tip. It's difficult to give an exact guideline for tipping, since this depends on group size and the quality of service, but at current exchange rates a figure of around 1,000 cedis (US$0.50) per group member per hour feels about right. Another way of looking at it would be to tip around half of what you paid as an actual fee, bearing in mind the guide fees in Ghana are generally very reasonable.

The guide situation becomes more ambiguous when it isn't institutionalised. Even here, though, there are some reasonably straightforward scenarios. At places such as Bonwire or Tongo, for instance, visitors are normally approached by a cluster of prospective guides on arrival. There is no reason why you should take one on in such circumstances but, once you've selected somebody who seems a good bet and you've agreed a fee, you'll be left in peace by the other guides, and the one you've chosen will generally be able to add a great deal of insight to what you see. One cautionary note in this sort of situation is that guides will often agree to a fee, but then when you pay them this amount they go on a major sulk because you haven't tipped them. Personally, I don't see any valid reason why an additional tip should be given to a private individual with whom you've already agreed a fee, and nine times out of ten, when people sulk, they are simply chancing it.

The right approach to this sort of situation is to talk through costs at the negotiation stage. Stress to the guide that whatever fee is agreed is final and inclusive of a tip. Check, too, what other fees must be paid – it's not unusual to agree to a guide fee thinking that it covers the full excursion, only to find that the village chief also wants his fee, the caretaker his fee, the guy who thrusts himself unbidden into the middle of your photo his modelling fee, etc. This may feel like nitpicking to our Western mentalities, but Africans are accustomed to negotiation and will not be offended if it is conducted in good humour. The reality is that most of us in most situations are more comfortable when we get a full quote than when there are hidden extras (think of taking your car to a garage!). The overwhelming argument in favour of clarifying things at the outset is that it will decrease the likelihood of bad feeling later.

Now for the difficult bit, difficult because it is so riddled with ambiguity. This might aptly be described as people who are under the illusion (or think that you are under the illusion) that they are a guide. One type is the person who, for instance, greets you at the bus station, asks you where you are going, follows you there, then demands a fee for being your guide. Then there are those who attach themselves to you in a manner that is nothing short of intrusive, butting into your conversation and prattling on about themselves in a way that can only be described as self-absorbed, and then expect you to give them a guide fee or a tip when finally you part ways – penance, presumably, for having been too polite to have told them to bugger off and annoy somebody else in the first place. It's pretty easy to refuse in this sort of situation, but there is a whole hazy area in between, for instance you meet a perfectly likeable guy, get chatting, wander around together for a while, then suddenly find that he is dropping broader and broader hints in the direction of payment for an imagined service. It is easy enough to explain and understand this behaviour, and I don't see any point in reiterating the obvious here. The point is whether tourists should allow guilt or whatever else to make them feel obliged to pay somebody for no other reason than that they have been asked, and the person who asked is poorer than they are. Be generous with genuine beggars. Be generous when tipping genuine guides. By all means, slip a small note to the person who cleans your room, and shrug your shoulders over 100 cedis change. But before you give money to a random individual who in all probability befriended you for the express purpose of financial gain, think – if not about those travellers who will follow in your wake, then certainly about the type of relationship you would like to see develop between the people of Ghana and the tourists who, collectively, are already the country's third biggest source of foreign revenue.

On a less ardent note, it is not customary to tip for service in local bars and chop bars, though you may sometimes want to leave a tip (in fact, given the difficulty of finding change in Ghana, you may practically be forced to do this in some circumstances), in which case 5% would be very acceptable and 10% generous. Most restaurants catering to Western palates automatically add a 5% or 10% service charge to the bill, and this (in theory) goes to the waiter, but it can do no harm to give a cash tip if you feel the service was good.

Bargaining and overcharging

Tourists to Ghana do sometimes need to bargain over prices, particularly in Accra, but generally only in reasonably predictable circumstances, such as when chartering private taxis, organising guides, or buying curios and to a lesser extent other market produce. Prices in hotels, restaurants, shops and public transport are generally fixed, and overcharging in such places is too unusual for it to be worth challenging a price unless it is blatantly ridiculous.

You're bound to be overcharged at some point in Ghana, but it is important to keep this in perspective. Some travellers, after a couple of bad experiences, start to haggle with everyone from hotel owners to old women selling fruit by the side of the road, often accompanying their negotiations with aggressive accusations of dishonesty. Unfortunately, it is sometimes necessary to fall back on aggressive posturing in order to determine a fair price, but such behaviour is also very unfair on those people who are forthright and honest in their dealings with tourists. It's a question of finding the right balance, or better still looking for other ways of dealing with the problem.

The main instance where bargaining is essential is when buying curios. What should be understood, however, is that the fact a curio seller is open to negotiation does not mean that you were initially being overcharged or ripped off. Curio sellers will generally quote a price knowing full well that you are going to bargain it down (they'd probably be startled if you didn't) and it is not necessary to respond aggressively or in an accusatory manner. It is impossible to say by how much you should bargain the initial price down. Some people say that you should offer half the asking price and be prepared to settle at around two-thirds, but my experience is that curio sellers are far more whimsical than such advice allows for. The sensible approach, if you want to get a feel for prices, is to ask the price of similar items at a few different stalls before you actually contemplate buying anything.

In fruit and vegetable markets and stalls, bargaining is often the norm, even between locals, and the most healthy approach to this sort of haggling is to view it as an enjoyable part of the African experience. There will normally be an accepted price band for any particular commodity. To find out what it is, listen to what other people pay and try a few stalls. A ludicrously inflated price will always drop the moment you walk away. When buying fruit and vegetables, a good way to get a feel for the situation is to ask for a bulk discount or a few extra items thrown in. And bear in mind that when somebody is reluctant to bargain, it may be because they asked a fair price in the first place.

Above all, don't lose your sense of proportion. No matter how poor you may feel, it is your choice to travel on a tight budget. Most Ghanaians are much poorer than you will ever be, and they do not have the luxury of choosing to travel. If you find yourself quibbling with an old lady selling a few piles of fruit by the roadside, stand back and look at the bigger picture. There is nothing wrong with occasionally erring on the side of generosity.

Theft

The level of crime against tourists is remarkably low in Ghana, and it is difficult to think of a safer African capital than Accra. In our entire time in the country, we heard one third-hand report of a tourist being robbed. Tellingly, even upmarket hotel managers seem to feel that walking around Accra is safe at any time of day or night, and one said that he doesn't bother locking his car when he parks it in the city centre. While hugely reassuring, this should not be cause for complacency. Firstly, things can change – Malawi was just as safe as Ghana is now when I spent three months there in 1995, yet these days every letter I receive from readers of my Malawi guide stresses that several people they met in the country had been mugged or robbed. And even in a relatively safe African country, tourists are easy game for whatever criminal element exists. As things stand, it would be wholly inappropriate to be anything but relaxed and open in your dealings with Ghanaians; you certainly oughtn't to be ruled by fear. Nevertheless, the risk of being pickpocketed or mugged does exist, and the basic common-sense precautions appropriate to travelling in any African country are worth repeating here:

- Most casual thieves operate in busy markets and bus stations. Keep a close watch on your possessions in such places, and avoid having valuables or large amounts of money loose in your day pack or pocket.

- Keep all your valuables and the bulk of your money in a hidden money belt. Never show this money belt in public. Keep any spare cash you need elsewhere on your person.

- I feel that a button-up pocket on the front of the shirt is the most secure place for money, as it cannot be snatched without the thief coming into your view. It is also advisable to keep a small amount of hard currency (ideally cash) hidden away in your luggage so that, should you lose your money belt, you have something to fall back on.

- Where the choice exists between carrying valuables on your person or leaving them in a locked room I would tend to favour the latter option (only one of the hundreds of thefts I've heard about in Africa happened from a locked hotel room, and that was in Nairobi where just about anything is possible). Obviously you should use your judgement on this and be sure the room is absolutely secure. A factor to be considered is that some travellers' cheque companies will not refund cheques which were stolen from a room.

- Leave any jewellery of financial or sentimental value at home.

Women travellers

It's difficult to imagine a country where women have less to fear on a gender-specific level. We met several women travelling alone in Ghana, and none of them had any serious problems in their interactions with locals. An element of flirtation is about the sum of it, perhaps the odd direct proposition, but nothing that cannot be defused by a firm 'no'. And nothing, for that matter, that you wouldn't expect in any Western country, or – probably with a far greater degree of persistence – from many male travellers.

It would be prudent to pay some attention to how you dress in Ghana, particularly in the more conservative Muslim north. It's not that Ghanaians would be deeply offended by women travellers wearing shorts or other outfits that might be seen to be provocative, but it pays to allow for local sensibilities, and under certain circumstances revealing clothes may be perceived to make a statement that you don't intend.

More mundanely, tampons are not readily available in smaller towns, though you can easily locate them in Accra and Kumasi. If you're travelling in out-of-the-way places, it's advisable to carry enough to see you through to the next time you'll be in a large city, bearing in mind that travelling in the tropics can sometimes cause women to have heavier or more regular periods than they would at home. Sanitary pads are available in most towns of any size.

Bearing in mind that Ariadne and I travelled as a couple, and were thus shielded from hassles facing single travellers (male or female), the thoughts and experiences of women travelling alone in Ghana would be greatly welcomed for the next edition of this guide.

Bribery and bureaucracy

For all that you read about the subject, bribery is not the problem it is often made out to be, and I've heard of no specific incident where a traveller to Ghana was asked for a bribe. Don't worry about it!

As for the tendency to portray African bureaucrats as difficult and inefficient in their dealings with tourists, this says a great deal more about Western prejudices that it does about Ghana. Sure, you come across the odd unhelpful official, but then such is the nature of the beast everywhere in the world. In Ghana, we encountered nothing but friendliness from almost every government official we had dealings with. This, I can assure you, is far more than most African visitors to Europe will experience from officialdom.

A factor in determining the response you receive from African officials will be your own attitude. If you walk into every official encounter with an aggressive, paranoid approach, you are quite likely to kindle the feeling held by many Africans that Europeans are arrogant and offhand in their dealings with other races. Instead, try to be friendly and patient, and accept that the person to whom you are talking probably doesn't speak English. Treat people with respect rather than disdain, and they'll tend to treat you in the same way.

Asking directions

There is no polite way of saying it: most Ghanaians are utterly clueless when it comes to estimating distance or time in any measure more objective than 'far' and 'not far'. Travellers, particularly those needing directions off the beaten track, will have to allow for this.

One regular and reasonably straightforward area of confusion is the difference between miles and kilometres, measurements which many Ghanaians seem to see as interchangeable. It's always better to ask for a distance in miles, the measure still used by most people, even though signposts generally show distances in kilometres. If you're not familiar with one or other system of measurement, you can convert distances using the equation that five miles is roughly equivalent to eight kilometres, while three feet (or a yard) is basically the same as one metre – imprecise equations, I grant you, but more than adequate for practical travel purposes. Another way of verifying distances is to ask both the distance and the time – in reasonably flat conditions, a reasonably fit walker will cover 5km (3 miles) in one hour.

That said, it's difficult to figure out how a bar worker who not only speaks good English, but also has the capacity to make drawing a pint of draught look as exhausting as running a marathon, can say that a hotel 2km distant is three minutes' walk away. Or how people living at Larabanga and Mole, not to say various books, can come up with estimates as divergent as 3km and 10km for the road between Larabanga and Mole Motel. Or how a signpost at Vame reads *Amedzofe 5km* when the two towns cannot be more than 3km apart by road. We hit this sort of problem on a daily basis, and found it difficult to escape the conclusion that a lot of Ghanaians simply say whatever figure first comes into their head – not with the deliberate intent of misleading visitors, but because the measurements that are so important to us mean very little to somebody who has lived in a small town all their life and 'knows' how far one place is from another without ever having had reason to translate that knowledge into hours or kilometres.

It goes without saying that a great deal more interrogation about distances is required when you're researching a travel guide than when you are using one. Still, two points ought to be passed on to readers. The first, particularly if you are hiking, is to ask at least three or four people how far away somewhere is, to use some judgement in interpreting the answers, and to accept that you'll probably never know for sure until you walk there yourself. The second is that I've had to guestimate a great many walking distances in this guide, but they are informed and generally based on first-hand experience and, unlike many of the short distances that are quoted so emphatically by other books, by people you meet, and even on some maps, they will not be wildly out!

Photography
The unwritten law of photography in Africa is that anybody you actually want to photograph will refuse permission, while it is often practically impossible to take a photo of a static subject without having 20 snotty brats leaping uninvited into the frame. Seriously, though, the question of photographing people is a sticky one, most especially in Muslim parts of the country, and the first rule at all times is to ask permission and accept gracefully if it is refused, no matter how much it hurts (and if, like Ariadne,

photography is the main purpose of your trip to Ghana, then it can be really depressing to miss wonderful photograph after wonderful photograph through the potential subject's refusal to co-operate). It is not customary in most parts of Ghana to pay to take a photograph, and I must admit that I'd be sad to see such a custom develop. That said, there are a few instances (the *kente* weavers at Bonwire leap to mind) where you will be expected to pay to photograph a particular subject.

When somebody does agree to let you photograph them, your next question will often be how to go about it without every nearby child leaping into the frame. If you have a point-and-shoot, the answer is to take the picture as quickly as you can. On the other hand, if you have a camera that requires a certain amount of fiddling around, then you may have to compromise by first taking a group photo, and then trying to clear the frame of extraneous kids, bearing in mind that if they then decide to line up behind you, there's a good chance that the photograph will be spoiled by their shadows. Another thing to bear in mind is that people often pose very stiffly when you point a camera at them and relax only when the flash goes off, so it may help to take two shots in quick succession, hoping that the second one will capture a more natural pose. As a rule, you can forget about taking good photos of Africans without fill-in flash, since their skin is very dark by comparison with the bright light.

You should be conscious that until recently there were strict photographic restrictions in Ghana, and that even now you could get in trouble by pointing a camera at any sensitive subject, such as a bridge, dam wall, prison (which includes several of the old coastal forts) or military installation. In general, however, you can photograph what you like, though you may sometimes encounter individuals who will feel a need to interfere in what you're doing. Mostly they're just playing to the crowd, but that doesn't mean you shouldn't recognise when you'd be better off standing down. One way to counter this type of thing is always to ask somebody standing around whether it's OK to 'snap' (as they say locally) whatever subject takes your fancy – once somebody has given you the nod, they will generally back you up should somebody else make a problem, though here again you should be sensitive to not letting anything ugly develop.

One last thought, if you're not particularly keen on photography, why not leave your camera at home and buy a few postcards before you leave? Ultimately, cameras are heavily intrusive, and trying to get good photos of people will often create more frustration than pleasure.

Please give me ...

... are the opening three words of many a one-line interaction with children in Ghana (and elsewhere in Africa). Usually the sentence finishes with a request for one of three things: money, a pen, or an address. In general, I suggest you answer the first two in the negative. Children who ask for money are not necessarily especially needy, more likely just chancing it, and every tourist who accedes to such a request with a pittance is guilty of reinforcing behaviour that has a far greater effect on people's dignity than on their well-being – it is notable that swarms of children asking for money is a phenomenon associated with areas where you find the greatest numbers of tourists, not the worst levels of poverty. And be aware that children who ask tourists for pens are no more worthy than their money-grabbing peers, just a great deal more sophisticated – they know that the average liberal Westerner is more likely to part with a pen than with cash. Finally, there's no need to be rude when fobbing off what are basically light requests; far better to do something that makes the children laugh, like pulling a silly face or something else unexpected.

The address business – a request you can expect at least a dozen times a day – is an odd one. For years I mostly handed out fake addresses when I travelled in Africa, simply because it became too complicated to explain that I'd never get around to writing to the hundreds of people who asked for my address on every trip. Recently, however, it occurred to me that even though I'd also often given out my genuine address, mainly to people with whom I'd actually become friendly, I have only once ever had a response (and this, bizarrely, five years after the event from a person who described a meeting I couldn't recall in a place I'd never visited!). In Ghana, as an experiment, I gave my genuine address to hundreds of people. I've yet to have one response. My only explanation is that we're dealing with the African equivalent of autograph hunting – it is the address itself, not the writing, that is the point of the exercise.

I should probably clarify, just in case anybody thinks I'm being a monster, that the above comments about giving money and pens apply only to children (or occasionally adults) who ask for things purely because you are a Westerner. I see no harm whatsoever in giving money to a genuine beggar (in other words somebody who was begging before you came on the scene) and would actively encourage generosity towards those who obviously have no other means of sustaining themselves – I was struck by the ease with which salaried Ghanaians give to beggars, and would suggest that if they can do it, then so can we.

MEDIA AND COMMUNICATIONS
Newspapers

Several English-language newspapers are printed in Ghana, of which the well established *Daily Graphic* is probably the best. The weekly *Graphic Sport* is of great interest to ardent followers of African football, but coverage of other sports is at best cursory. In Accra you can buy imported newspapers at a highly inflated price – far better to spend a cosy hour catching up on international news in the air-conditioned confines of the British Council in Accra or Kumasi, both of which have a pile of English newspapers from three to four days old.

Telephone

Ghana's telephone system is reasonably efficient. From overseas, it's one of the easiest African countries to get through to first time. The ringing tone is a single short tone followed by a longer pause, and the engaged tone is equal lengths on and off. The international code is +233, and major area codes are as follows:

Accra	021	Ho	091	Takoradi	031
Ada	0968	Hohoe	0935	Tamale	071
Akosombo	0251	Keta	0966	Tema	0221
Axim	0342	Koforidua	081	Wa	0712
Bolgatanga	072	Kumasi	051	Winneba	041
Cape Coast	042	Navrongo	072		
Dunkwa	0372	Sunyani	061		

Post

Post from Ghana is cheap and reasonably reliable, but often very slow. Poste restante letters can be collected in most large towns, and they should be addressed as in the following example:

Philip Briggs
Poste Restante
Accra
Ghana

Electric devices

Electricity is 220V AC at 50 cycles. Stabilisers are required for sensitive devices and adaptors for appliances using 110V. Batteries are useful during power cuts, though such events are increasingly rare.

Radio and television

The Ghana Broadcasting Corporation produces a reasonable television service by African standards, though it's pretty awful by any other. The state-owned radio service, by contrast, is quite exceptional, with some good news and issue coverage and an eclectic mix of music – except on Sundays when it's hijacked by God. You can pick it up on FM 95.7. Travellers with shortwave radios can pick up BBC World Service on 15400 Khz throughout the day and 17830 Khz between 08.30 and 23.30 – programme details are available from the British Council in Accra. Voice of America broadcasts from 03.00 to 22.30, but the frequency changes regularly throughout the day.

Many upmarket hotels pick up the South African television channel M-Net and, as part of the same service, other international satellite channels such as CNN and the BBC.

Internet

The internet is catching on in Ghana in a big way, though it's not as yet very accessible to the man in the street nor to tourists. There is an internet café in Accra, opposite the Niagara Hotel, and more are bound to spring up during the lifespan of this edition.

Chapter Four

Health and Safety

Written in collaboration with Dr Jane Wilson-Howarth and Dr Felicity Nicholson, with thanks to Dr Vaughan Southgate of the Natural History Museum, London, for information on bilharzia transmission.

This is the chapter which always gives me the creeps when I read a travel guide, and I'm quite sure that some readers will question the sanity of travelling to Ghana by the time they finish it. Don't let it get to you – with the right vaccinations and a sensible attitude to malaria prevention the chances of serious mishap are small. It may help put things in perspective to point out that, after malaria, your greatest concern in Ghana should not be the combined exotica of venomous snakes, stampeding elephants, gun-happy soldiers and the Ebola virus, but something altogether more mundane: a road accident.

HEALTH
Preparations
In addition to considering the points made directly below, do read this entire section before you leave, since subjects such as malaria prevention are discussed under a separate heading.

Travel insurance
Don't think about travelling without a comprehensive medical travel insurance policy, one that will fly you home in an emergency. The ISIS policy, available in Britain through STA (tel: 0171 361 6160), is inexpensive and has a good reputation. Pack a good insect repellent, at least one long-sleeved cotton shirt and one pair of long trousers, a hat and sunscreen; these are important insurance measures.

Immunisations
You must have a yellow fever immunisation, and you my be required to show an international immunisation certificate as proof of this upon entering the country. Yellow fever is not valid until ten days after your vaccination and lasts ten years. It is also wise to be up to date on tetanus (ten-yearly), polio (ten-yearly), diphtheria (ten-yearly), hepatitis A and typhoid. Immunisations against meningococcus, tuberculosis and rabies are also worth considering. The majority of travellers are advised to have immunisation against hepatitis A with hepatitis A vaccine (eg: Havrix

Monodose, Avaxim). One dose of vaccine lasts for one year and can be boosted to give protection for up to ten years. The course of two injections costs about £100. The newer typhoid vaccines last for three years, are about 85% effective and should be encouraged unless you are leaving within a few days for a trip of a week or less when the vaccine would not be effective in time. Immunisation against cholera is currently ineffective. Hepatitis B vaccination should be considered for longer trips or for those working in situations where contact with blood is increased. Three injections are ideal, given at 0, 4 and 8 weeks before travel. If you need several immunisations, it's best to go to a travel clinic a month or two before departure.

Travel clinics
United Kingdom
Trailfinders Immunisation Clinic, 194 Kensington High St, London W8 7RG. Tel: 0171 938 3999.

MASTA (Medical Advisory Service for Travellers Abroad), London School of Hygiene and Tropical Medicine, Keppel St, London WC1 7HT. Tel: 0891 224100. This is a premium line number. Readers on the Internet may prefer to check their large website: http://dspace.dial.pipex.com/masta.

British Airways Clinics These are now situated in 35 towns in the UK and three in South Africa (UK tel: 01276 685040 for the nearest). Apart from providing inoculations and malaria prophylaxis, they sell a variety of health-related travel goods.

Berkeley Travel Clinic, 32 Berkeley St, London W1X 5FA. Tel: 0171 629 6233.

Tropical Medicine Bureau This Irish-rin organisation has a useful website specific to tropical destinations: http:/www.tmb.le.

USA
Centers for Disease Control This Atlanta-based organisation is the central source of travel health information in North America, with a touch-tone phone line and fax service. Travelers' Hot Line: (404) 332 4559. Each summer they publish the invaluable *Health Information for International Travel* which is available from the Center for Prevention Services, Division of Quarantine, Atlanta, GA 30333.

IAMAT (International Association for Medical Assistance to Travellers), 736 Center St, Lewiston, NY 14092, USA. Tel: 716 754 4883. *Also at* Gotthardstrasse 17, 6300 Zug, Switzerland. A non-profit organisation which provides health information and lists of English-speaking doctors abroad.

Medical kit
Take a small medical kit. This should contain malaria prophylactics, as well as a cure for malaria and a thermometer (the latter is crucial should you need to diagnose yourself), soluble aspirin or paracetamol (good for gargling when you have a sore throat and for reducing fever and pains), plasters (band-aids), potassium permanganate crystals or another favoured antiseptic, iodine for sterilising water and cleaning wounds, sunblock, and condoms or femidoms. Some travel clinics in Britain will try to persuade you to buy a variety of antibiotics as a precaution. This is not necessary: most antibiotics are widely

available in Ghana, and you should be hesitant about taking them without medical advice. Restaurant meals in Ghana tend to be based around meat and carbohydrate, so you might like to carry vitamin pills.

Further reading
Self-prescribing has its hazards so if you are going anywhere very remote consider taking a health book. For adults there is *Bugs Bites & Bowels,* the Cadogan guide to healthy travel by Dr Jane Wilson-Howarth, and if travelling with children look at *Your Child's Health Abroad: A manual for travelling parents* by Dr Jane Wilson-Howarth and Dr Matthew Ellis, published by Bradt.

Medical facilities
There are private clinics, hospitals and pharmacies in most large towns, and doctors generally speak fluent English. Consultation fees and laboratory tests are remarkably inexpensive when compared to most western countries, so if you do fall sick it would be absurd to let financial considerations dissuade you from seeking medical help. Commonly required medicines such as broad spectrum antibiotics and Flagyl are widely available and cheap throughout the region, as are malaria cures and prophylactics. Fansidar and quinine tablets are best bought in advance – in fact it's advisable to carry all malaria-related tablets with you, and only rely on their availability locally if you need to restock your supplies.

If you are on any medication prior to departure, or you have specific needs relating to a known medical condition (for instance if you are allergic to bee stings or you are prone to attacks of asthma), then you are strongly advised to bring any related drugs and devices with you.

Travellers' diarrhoea
Most travellers to the tropics suffer a bout of travellers' diarrhoea during their trip. The newer you are to tropical travel, the more likely you are to suffer. Travellers' diarrhoea is caused by getting other people's faeces in your mouth, which most often results from cooks not washing their hands after a trip to the toilet, but even if the restaurant cook does not understand basic hygiene, you will be safe if your food has been properly cooked and arrives piping hot. As for what food is safe to eat, any fruit or vegetable that you've washed and peeled yourself should be fine, as should hot cooked food. Raw food and salads are risky, as is cooked food that has gone cold or been kept luke-warm in a hotel buffet. Avoid ice-cream, often not kept adequately frozen due to power cuts. Ice may have been made with unboiled water or deposited by the road on its journey from the ice factory.

It is less common to get sick from drinking contaminated water, but it can happen. To be absolutely safe, you should avoid drinking tap water wherever possible (mineral water is relatively cheap and widely available). Any dodgy water should be brought to the boil, filtered through a good bacteriological filter or purified with iodine. Chlorine tablets (eg: Puritabs) are slightly less effective and taste nastier.

By taking precautions against travellers' diarrhoea you will also avoid typhoid, cholera, hepatitis, dysentery, worms, etc.

Treatment

Dehydration is the reason you feel awful during a bout of diarrhoea, so the most important part of treatment is to imbibe lots of clear fluids. Sachets of oral rehydration salts (eg: Electrolade) give the perfect biochemical mix, but any dilute mixture of sugar and salt in water will do you good. Try a solution of a four-finger scoop of sugar with a three-finger pinch of salt in a glass of water, with a squeeze of lemon or orange juice to improve the taste. If no safe drinking water is available, then Coke or similar with a three-finger pinch of salt added to each glass will do the trick. Drink two large glasses after every bowel action, more if you are thirsty – if you are not eating you need to drink three litres a day *plus* the equivalent of whatever is coming out the other end.

With most diarrhoea attacks, medication will be less effective than simply resting up and forsaking greasy foods and alcohol. If you have bad stomach cramps avoid solids completely for a day or so or stick to dry biscuits, boiled potatoes or rice. The bacterium responsible for diarrhoea and related symptoms normally dies after 36 hours. Avoid taking blockers such as Imodium, Lomotil and codeine phosphate unless you have no access to sanitation, for instance if you have to travel by bus, since they keep the poisons in your system and make you feel bad for longer. It is dangerous to take blockers with dysentery (evidenced by blood, slime or fever with the diarrhoea). Should diarrhoea or related symptoms persist beyond 36 hours, or you are passing blood or slime or have a fever, then consult a doctor or pharmacist. Chances are you have nothing serious, but you may have something treatable, for instance giardia (indicated by severe flatulence, abdominal distension, stomach cramps and sulphurous belching), which is cured by taking a single 2g of tinidazole with another dose one week later if symptoms persist. If this is unavailable then metronidazole 2g daily for three days can be used. Do not drink alcohol with either of these. If you can't get to a doctor, a three-day course of an antibiotic such as ciprofloxacin (500mg twice daily), is effective against dysentery and severe diarrhoea.

Malaria

Malaria kills a million Africans annually, and (after accidents) it poses the single biggest serious threat to the health of travellers to tropical Africa, where it should be assumed to be present at altitudes of below 1,800m, a category that includes *all* of Ghana. The *anopheles* mosquito which transmits the malaria parasite is most abundant near the marshes and still water in which it breeds. As a rule the danger of contracting the disease is greatest during the hotter, wetter months. This mosquito comes out from dusk till dawn and flies low to the ground.

It is unwise to travel in malarious parts of Africa whilst pregnant or with children: the risk of malaria in many parts is considerable and such travellers are likely to succumb rapidly to the disease.

Prophylactic drugs

There is no vaccine against malaria, but various prophylactic drugs offer a level of protection against the disease. Just as important as taking malaria pills is avoiding mosquitoes bites between dusk and dawn - see *Insects*, page 80. Travellers to Africa cannot acquire any effective resistance to malaria, and those who don't make use of prophylactic drugs risk their life. Mefloquine (Lariam) is the most effective prophylactic agent for Ghana, but is not suitable for everyone, so should only be taken on a doctor's recommendation If this drug is suggested, then start two and a half weeks before departure to check it suits you. The usual alternative is chloroquine (Nivaquine or avloclor) two weekly and proguanil (Paludrine) two daily. Doxycycline (100mg daily), is considered by many to be more effective than chloroquine and Paludrine and need only be started one day before arrival in a malarial region. It can only be obtained from a doctor. There is a possibility of allergic skin reactions developing in sunlight in approximately 5% of people. If this happens the drug should be stopped. Women using the oral contraceptive should use additional protection for the first four weeks. All prophylactic agents should be taken after or with the evening meal, washed down with plenty of fluids and continued for four weeks after leaving the last malarial area.

Diagnosis and cures

Even those who take their malaria tablets meticulously and try to avoid being bitten may contract a malaria that is resistant to prophylactic drugs. Untreated malaria is likely to be fatal, unless prompt treatment is obtained.Travellers to remote parts are encouraged to carry a treatment to cure malaria, since a high fever can develop rapidly over hours. Presently quinine and Fansidar is the favoured regime. This should be obtained from a doctor before departure. You should visit a doctor or hospital as soon as you experience malarial symptoms: any combination of a headache, flu-like aches and pains, a rapid rise in temperature, a general sense of disorientation, and possibly nausea and diarrhoea. Carrying a thermometer is always wise. Local doctors regularly deal with malaria, and any laboratory or hospital will be able to give you a quick malaria test.

Another popular cure called Halfan has been recognised as causing some deaths and is no longer a recommended treatment.

Malaria takes at least a week to incubate but can take much longer. Continue prophylaxis for at least four weeks after returning home, and, if you display possible malaria symptoms up to a year later, then get to a doctor and ensure that he/she knows you have been exposed to malaria.

Finally, if you have a fever and the malaria test is negative (which does not completely exclude malaria), you may have typhoid, which should also receive immediate treatment. Where typhoid testing is unavailable, a routine blood test can give a strong indication of this disease.

Bilharzia

Bilharzia or schistosomiasis is a common debilitating disease afflicting perhaps 200 million people worldwide. Those most affected are the rural poor of the tropics who repeatedly acquire more and more of these nasty little worm-lodgers. Infected travellers and expatriates generally suffer fewer problems because symptoms will encourage them to seek prompt treatment and they are also exposed to fewer parasites. But it is still an unpleasant problem, and worth avoiding.

When someone with bilharzia excretes into fresh water, the eggs hatch and swim off to find a pond snail to infest. They develop inside the snail to emerge as torpedo-shaped cercariae, barely visible to the naked eye but able to digest their way through human or animal skin. This is the stage that attacks people as they wade, bathe or shower in infested water.

The snails which harbour bilharzia are a centimetre or more long and live in still or slow-moving fresh water which is well oxygenated and contains edible vegetation (water-weed, reeds). The risk is greatest where local people use the water, bearing in mind that wind can disperse cercariae a few hundred metres from where they entered the water. Wading in slow-moving, reed-fringed water near a village thus carries a very high risk of acquiring bilharzia, while swimming in a rocky pool below a waterfall in a forest carries a negligible one.

Water which has been filtered or stored snail-free for two days is safe, as is water which has been boiled or treated with Cresol or Dettol. Some protection is afforded by applying an oily insect repellent like DEET to your skin before swimming or paddling.

Cercariae live for up to 30 hours after they have been shed by snails, but the older they are, the less vigorous they are and the less capable they are of penetrating skin. Cercariae are shed in the greatest numbers between 11.00 and 15.00. If water to be used for bathing is pumped early in the morning from deep in the lake (cercariae are sun-loving) or from a site far from where people excrete there will be less risk of infestation. Swimming in the afternoon is riskier than in the early morning. Since cercariae take perhaps 10 to 15 minutes to penetrate, a quick shower or a splash across a river followed by thorough rubbing dry with a towel should be safe. Even if you are in risky water longer, towelling off vigorously after bathing will kill any cercariae in the process of penetrating your skin.

Only a proportion of those cercariae which penetrate the skin survive to cause disease. The absence of early symptoms does not necessarily mean there is no infection, but symptoms usually appear two or more weeks after penetration: typically a fever and wheezy cough. A blood test, which should be taken six weeks or more after likely exposure, will determine whether or not parasites are going to cause problems. Treatment is generally effective, but failures occur and re-treatment is often necessary for reasons that aren't fully understood, but which may imply some drug resistance. Since bilharzia can be a nasty illness, avoidance is better than waiting to be cured and it is wise to avoid bathing in high-risk areas.

Other diseases
Sleeping sickness

This is carried by tsetse flies, which look like oversized houseflies and have a painful but (sleeping sickness aside) harmless bite. Tsetse flies commonly occur in low-lying game reserves in Ghana; they bite in daylight and are attracted to blue clothing. Sleeping sickness has a patchy distribution within a small limit of the tsetse fly's range; it is a minor threat to travellers and treatable.

AIDS and venereal disease

HIV and other sexually transmitted diseases are widespread in the region to a degree that is unimaginable in Western countries, and AIDS-related deaths in many African countries have reached epidemic proportions. The risk attached to having unprotected sex with anybody but a regular partner is prohibitively high. Condoms and femidoms offer a good level of protection against HIV and other sexually transmitted diseases. The additional use of spermicide pessaries further reduces the risk of transmission. If you notice any genital ulcers or discharge, seek prompt treatment.

Hospital workers in Africa deal with AIDS victims on a regular basis. Contrary to Western prejudices, health professionals do realise the danger involved in using unsterilised needles, and you are unlikely to be confronted with one in a town hospital or clinic. If you need treatment in a really remote area where supplies are a problem, you might be glad to be carrying a few needles and hypodermic syringes in your medical kit.

Meningitis

This is a particularly nasty disease as it can kill within hours of the first symptoms appearing. The tell-tale symptoms are a combination of a blinding headache, a blotchy rash and a high fever. Immunisation protects against the most serious bacterial form of meningitis and is usually recommended for Ghana. Other forms of meningitis exist but there are no vaccines available for these. Local papers normally report localised outbreaks. If you show symptoms, get to a doctor immediately.

Rabies

Rabies is carried by all mammals – beware the village dogs and small monkeys that are used to being fed in the parks – and is passed on to man through a bite, or a lick of an open wound. You must always assume any animal is rabid (unless personally known to you) and seek medical help as soon as possible. In the interim, scrub the wound with soap and bottled/boiled water then pour on a strong iodine or alcohol solution. This helps stop the rabies virus entering the body and will guard against wound infections, including tetanus. If you intend to have contact with animals and/or are likely to be more than 24 hours away from medical help, then vaccination is advised. Ideally three pre-exposure doses should be taken over four weeks. If you are bitten by any animal, treatment should be given as soon as possible, but it is never too late to seek help as the incubation period for rabies can be very long. Tell the doctors if you have had pre-exposure vaccine. Remember if you contract rabies, mortality is 100% and death from rabies is probably one of the worst ways to go!

Tetanus

Tetanus is caught through deep, dirty wounds, including animal bites, so ensure that such wounds are thoroughly cleaned. Immunisation gives good protection for ten years, provided you do not have an overwhelming number of tetanus bacteria on board. If you haven't had a tetanus shot in ten years, or you are unsure, get a tetanus toxoid injection and a tetanus booster as quickly as possible. Keep immunised and be sensible about first aid.

Insects

Even if you take malaria tablets, do all you can to avoid mosquito bites. The imperative reason for this is the increasing level of resistance to preventative drugs, while of lesser concern are several other mosquito-borne viral fevers which could be present in low- and medium-altitude parts of the region. The *anopheles* mosquito which spreads malaria emerges at dusk, as do most other disease-carrying mosquitoes, so you will greatly reduce your chances of being bitten by wearing long trousers and socks after dark and covering exposed parts of your body with insect repellent, preferably a DEET-based preparation such as Repel 100 or Jungle Jell. Sprays or roll-ons of this sort are not available in Ghana, so bring one with you. The *anopheles* mosquito hunts mostly at ground level, so it is worth putting repellent on your ankles, even if you wear socks. When walking in scrub and forest areas by day, you should also cover and spray yourself, since the *aedes* mosquito which spreads dengue is a day-biter (solid shoes, socks and trousers will in any case protect you against snakes, sharp thorns and harmless but irritating biters like midges).

Like many insects, mosquitoes are drawn to direct light. If you are camping, never put a lamp near the opening of your tent, or you will have a swarm of mosquitoes and other insects waiting to join you when you retire. In hotel rooms, be aware that the longer you leave on your light, the greater the number of insects with which you are likely to share your accommodation.

Once you are in bed, the best form of protection is a net, which is not normally supplied in hotel rooms in Ghana. Mosquito coils, which are widely available and cheap in Ghana, will also reduce (but not eliminate) the biting rate, and (even though strains of mosquito have evolved that are skilled at flying in turbulent air) so will a fan. Far better, though, is to carry your own *permethrin*-impregnated net, which will protect you against everything. Nets and impregnation kits are available from Trailfinders Travel Clinic, MASTA at the London School of Tropical Medicine and Hygiene, and from British Airways Travel Clinics (see page 74).

Minute pestilential **blackflies** spread river blindness in parts of Africa between 19°N and 17°S. You're at risk only near fast-flowing rivers and rapids, where they breed. The flies bite in daylight. Long trousers tucked into socks will help keep them off. Citronella-based repellents don't work against them.

Tumbu flies or **putsi** occur in hot, humid climates, where they often lay eggs on drying laundry. When a person puts on clean clothes or sleeps on a fresh sheet, the eggs hatch and bury themselves under the skin to form a crop of 'boils', each of which hatches a grub after about eight days before the inflammation settles down. In putsi areas, you should dry clothes and sheets in a screened house, or in direct sunshine until they are crisp, or iron them.

Jiggers or **sandfleas** latch on if you walk barefoot in contaminated places, and set up home under the skin of the foot, usually at the side of a toenail where they cause a painful boil-like swelling. They need picking out by a local expert and if the flea bursts during eviction, douse the wound in spirit alcohol or kerosene – or more jiggers will infest you.

There are several unpleasant illnesses which can follow a **tick bite** in Africa, including Lyme disease, but the good news is that even if a tick is carrying disease organisms, it will not inevitably infect you. You are less likely to be infected if you get the tick off promptly and do not damage it. Remove any tick as soon as you notice it on you – it will most likely be firmly attached to somewhere you would rather it was not – grasp the tick as close to your body as possible and pull steadily and firmly away at right angles to your skin. The tick will then come away complete as long as you do not jerk or twist. If possible douse the wound with alcohol (any spirit will do) or iodine. Spreading redness around the bite and/or fever and/or aching joints after a tick bite imply that you have an infection which requires antibiotic treatment, so seek advice.

To balance the warnings, it should be stressed that the overwhelming majority of insects don't bite people and, of those that do, the vast majority are entirely harmless. Mattresses or walls of grotty hotels quite often contain bedbugs and fleas, both of which are essentially harmless.

Skin infections

Any insect bite or small nick gives an opportunity for bacteria to foil the body's defences. It will surprise many travellers how quickly skin infections start in warm, humid climates, and it is essential to clean and cover the slightest wound. Creams are not as effective as a good drying antiseptic such as dilute iodine, potassium permanganate (a few crystals in half a cup of water) or crystal (or gentian) violet. One of these should be available in most towns. If the wound starts to throb, or becomes red and the redness starts to spread or the wound oozes, antibiotics will probably be needed; *flucloxacillin* (250mg four times a day) or *cloxacillin* (500mg four times a day) or, for those allergic to *penicillin, erythromycin* (500mg twice a day) for five days should help. See a doctor if the infection does not start to improve in 48 hours.

Fungal infections also get a hold easily in hot, moist climates, so wear 100% cotton socks and underwear and shower frequently. An itchy (often flaking) rash in the groin or between the toes is likely to be a fungal infection which will need treatment with an antifungal cream such as Canesten (*clotrimazole*) or, if this is not available, try Whitfield's ointment (*compound benzoic acid ointment*) or crystal violet (although this will turn you purple!).

Sun and heat

The equatorial sun is vicious. Although it is impossible to avoid some exposure to the sun, it would be foolish to do so needlessly. Tanning ages your skin and it can cause skin cancer. If you are coming to Africa from a less harsh climate, let your body get used to the sunlight gradually or you will end up with sunburn. Take things too far and heatstroke – a potentially fatal condition – may be the result. Wear sunscreen and build up your exposure gradually, starting with no more than 20 minutes a day. Avoid exposing yourself for more than two hours in any day, and stay out of the sun between 12.00 and 15.00.

Be particularly careful of sunburn when swimming or snorkelling. A shirt will protect your shoulders and a pair of shorts will protect the back of your thighs.

In hot and particularly in humid weather, you may sweat more than normal. To counter the resultant loss of water and salt, you should drink more than usual and eat extra salt if you develop a taste for it (salt tablets are useless). Prickly heat, a fine pimply rash caused by sweat trapped under the skin, is a harmless but very uncomfortable and common problem when you are first exposed to a humid tropical climate such as on the coast. It helps to wear 100% cotton clothing, splash regularly with water (avoiding excessive use of soap), dab the area with talc powder and sleep naked under a fan. If it's really bad, check into an air-conditioned hotel room or head for a higher, cooler place.

SAFETY
Marine dangers
The currents off many parts of the Ghanaian coast are highly dangerous, and swimmers risk being dragged away from shore by riptides, strong undertows and whirlpools, particularly during the rainy season and in windy weather. It is common for those swimmers who underestimate the dangers associated with these currents to drown. Quite simply, you should *never* swim in the sea without first asking local advice, perhaps not at all if you are a weak swimmer, and you are advised against going into water deeper than your waist without some sort of flotation device. If you are ever caught in a riptide or whirlpool, it is generally advisable *not* to immediately fight the current by swimming to shore, but to save your strength by floating on your back or swimming parallel to shore until the tide weakens, and only then to try to get back to land.

The coastal residents of Ghana evidently view beaches in a less aesthetic way than we do. It is customary in most seaside towns and villages for the beach to serve as a communal toilet. While this may not constitute a health threat in most circumstances, dodging between freshly deposited turds does tend to take the edge off a pleasant stroll on the sand, and imagining what the last tide washed away would certainly put me off swimming. Fortunately, most beaches that are regularly visited by tourists are no longer put to the, um, traditional use.

Don't swim or walk barefoot on the beach, or you risk getting coral or urchin spines in your soles or venomous fish spines in your feet. If you tread on a venomous fish, soak the foot in hot (but not scalding) water until some time after the pain subsides; this may be for 20–30 minutes in all. Take your foot out of the water to top up otherwise you may scald it. If the pain returns, re-immerse the foot. Once the venom has been heat-inactivated, get a doctor to check and remove any bits of fish spine in the wound.

Snakebite

Poisonous snakes are widespread but rarely encountered since they generally slither away when they sense the seismic vibrations made by a walking person. You should be most alert to snakes on rocky slopes and cliffs, particularly where you risk putting your hand on a ledge that you can't see. Rocky areas are the favoured habitat of the puff adder, not an especially venomous snake but potentially lethal and unusual in that it won't always move off in response to human foot treads. Wearing good boots when walking in the bush will protect against the 50% of snakebites that occur below the ankle, and long trousers will help deflect bites higher up on the leg, reducing the quantity of venom injected. Snakes rarely attack people unless provoked, most snakes are harmless, and even venomous species will only dispense venom in about half of their bites. To give an example, in South Africa, where venomous snakes are widespread, fewer than ten snakebite fatalities are recorded annually – more people die from being struck by lightning!

In the event of a snakebite, be aware that most first-aid techniques do more harm than good. Cutting into the wound is harmful, tourniquets are dangerous, and suction and electrical inactivation devices do not work. The victim must be taken to a hospital which has antivenom. While being transported, remember that the venom will spread more slowly if the victim stays calm, and if the bitten limb is splinted and kept below the height of the heart. If you have a crepe bandage, bind up as much of the bitten limb as you can, but release the bandage every half hour.

NEVER give aspirin; you may offer paracetamol which is safe.

NEVER cut or suck the wound.

DO NOT apply ice packs.

DO NOT apply potassium permanganate.

If the offending snake can be captured without risk of someone else being bitten, take it to show the doctor, but be aware that a decapitated head can dispense venom in a reflex bite.

Wild animals

The dangers associated with African wild animals have frequently been overstated in the past by the so-called 'Great White Hunters' and others trying to glamorise their chosen way of life. In Ghana specifically, there are few situations in which you would be likely to encounter potentially dangerous large mammals. Furthermore, most wild animals fear us far more than we fear them, and their normal response to human contact is to flee. The likelihood of a tourist to Ghana being attacked by an animal is very low, but it may be worth giving a quick overview of the situation with certain animals.

The need for caution is greatest near water, particularly around dusk and dawn, when **hippos** are likely to be out grazing. Hippos are responsible for more human fatalities than any other large mammal, not because they are aggressive but because they tend to panic when something comes between them and the safety of the water. If you happen to be that something, then you're unlikely to live to tell the tale. Never consciously walk between a hippo and water, and never walk along river banks or though reed beds, especially in overcast weather or at dusk or dawn, unless you are certain that no hippos are present. Watch out, too, for **Nile crocodiles**. Only a very large croc is likely to attack a person, and then only in the water or right on the shore. Near towns and other settlements, you can be fairly sure that any very large crocodile will have been disposed of by its potential prey, so the risk is greatest away from human habitation.

There are only a couple of places in Ghana where a hiker might stumble across an **elephant** or **buffalo**, the most dangerous of Africa's terrestrial herbivores. Elephants almost invariably mock charge and indulge in some hair-raising trumpeting before they attack in earnest. Provided that you back off at the first sign of unease, they are most unlikely to take further notice of you. If you see them before they see you, give them a wide berth and bear in mind they are most likely to attack if surprised at close proximity. If an animal charges you, the safest course of action is to head for the nearest tree and climb it. Black rhinos are also prone to charging without apparent provocation, but they're now very rare except in a few reserves where walking is forbidden.

There are campsites in Africa where **green monkeys** and **baboons** have become a pest. Feeding these animals is highly irresponsible, since it encourages them to scavenge and may eventually lead to them being shot. Monkeys are too small to progress much beyond being a nuisance, but baboons are very dangerous and have often killed children and maimed adults with their vicious teeth. Do not tease or underestimate the strength of a baboon. If primates are hanging around a campsite, and you wander off leaving fruit in your tent, don't expect the tent to be standing when you return.

The dangers associated with large **predators** are often exaggerated. Most predators stay clear of humans and are likely to kill accidentally or in self-defence rather than by design. Lions are an exception, but it is uncommon for a lion to attack a human without cause – in the highly unlikely event that you encounter one on foot, the important thing is not to run, since this is likely to trigger the instinct to give chase. A slight but real danger when sleeping in the bush without a tent is that a passing hyena or lion might investigate a hairy object sticking out of a sleeping bag and decapitate you through predatorial curiosity. In areas where large predators are still present, sleeping in a *sealed* tent practically guarantees your safety – provided that you don't sleep with your head sticking out, or at any point put meat in the tent.

Part Two

THE GUIDE

GHANA AIRWAYS

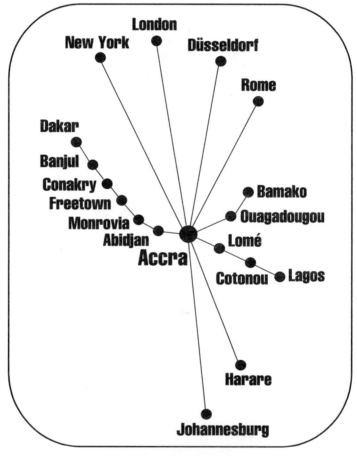

3 Princes Street, London W1
tel: 0171 629 3265; fax: 0171 491 1504
PO Box 7087, Johannesburg
tel: 011 622 4005/4068/4099; fax: 011 615 4625
email: jhbghair@icon.co.za
PO Box 1636, Accra, Ghana
tel: (021) 77 3321; fax: (021) 77 7078

Chapter Five

Accra

It would be tempting to introduce Accra as Ghana's historical capital, or something similarly portentous. This, after all, is a city that started life in the fifteenth century, when the Ga people who still live in the area settled on the west side of Korle Lagoon to found a small village from where they traded with passing Portuguese ships. Later in the same century, near what is now Brazil Lane, the Portuguese built a lodge that was burnt to the ground by locals shortly after it was constructed. No traces of this lodge remain, but modern Accra can still lay claim to three fortified buildings dating from the mid-seventeenth century – Dutch Fort Ussher, British Fort James and Danish Osu Castle. Furthermore, in 1877, when what are now Nairobi, Johannesburg and Addis Ababa were no more than tracts of empty bush, Accra became the capital of the British Gold Coast colony.

Knowing the above, Accra has to be classed a disappointment. The old forts, the city's most obvious drawcards, at least on paper, are closed to the public, their whitewashed stone exteriors patrolled by camera-sensitive military personnel. Osu Castle, the seat of government since colonial times, cannot even be approached closely, since the surrounding streets are barricaded on all sides. And the smaller Ussher and James forts now serve as prisons – approachable, yes, but wholly untouchable. Alone among Accra's historical buildings, the colonial-era lighthouse near Fort James offers an informal welcome to the curious visitor – ask nicely and you may even be allowed to climb the 82-step spiral staircase for a gull's-eye view over old James Town and Ussher Town.

Accra is a modern city, emphatically so, with a population drawing ever closer to the two million mark and an urban landscape of giddy incongruity – scruffy lanes lined with open sewers and colonial-era homesteads lead to untended open spaces, grandiose Independence monuments and arches, dazzling modern skyscrapers and run-down concrete blocks harking from the headiest days of Soviet town planning. The more you try to pin Accra down, the more elusive it seems, and it is in this respect – the way in which the former Danish outpost of Osu, say, still feels like a separate entity to Ussher Town, or Adabraka – that Accra is, if not a historical city, then certainly one whose modern schizophrenia reflects its distant past.

We found Accra to be one of those cities that rewards casual exploration – punctuated in this drenching humidity by frequent stops to sip the juice from a decapitated coconut or gulp down a chilled soft drink. Tourist attractions, it is true, are few and far between, but both James Town and Osu have a certain fading charm, while the frenzied central market area and – even more – Adabraka are vibrantly, brashly modern without ever feeling in any way threatening. Add to this any number of garden bars, inexpensive restaurants and live music venues, and Accra in all its modernity becomes as likeable and absorbing as most African cities.

Not the least of Accra's attractions is its amiability. Hectic it may be, chaotic in places, but as far as visitors need be concerned, there must be few third-world cities of comparable size with such a safe and relaxed mood. I arrived in Accra with defences formed by years of East African travel. Within 24 hours, I realised how wholly inappropriate these defences were. The closest thing to hassle that we encountered in Accra was the relentless horn-blowing of taxi drivers (and can any city be patrolled by such a high proportion of empty taxis?) to whom a white pedestrian evidently spells custom. Yet, remarkably, the selfsame taxi drivers were always happy to point us to a shared taxi if that's what we wanted, rather than try to hustle us into an overpriced charter ride.

In summation, those who have only a short time in Ghana would probably be well advised to spend as little time as is necessary in a city which has little to offer in the way of targeted sightseeing. For those with the time to enjoy Accra – well, enjoy...!

GETTING THERE AND AWAY
By air
You'll fly in at Katoka International Airport, one of the most centrally located international airports that I'm aware of in an African capital, a mere 4km from Sankara Circle and roughly 500m east of Liberation Avenue. Assuming that your passport and visa are in order and you have an onward ticket, the immigration and customs procedures are quick and straightforward. Note, however, that immigration will not stamp more than 30 days in your passport, regardless of what visa you have or how long you intend to stay.

At customs, you may be required to fill in a Currency Declaration Form, stating exactly how much money you are bringing into the country. In theory, you should record on this every foreign exchange transaction and the sums should balance when you depart. In practice, this procedure is no longer taken very seriously, judging by the exasperated attitudes of bank tellers when we asked them to fill it in, and we certainly weren't asked to present it upon departure, nor have we heard of anybody having a problem in this regard.

There *are* money exchange facilities at the airport, though the rate isn't particularly great, so I would change only as much as you need to get you through the first day – for a backpacker, around US$20 should do the trick, unless perhaps you arrive at the weekend or on a public holiday and want enough to see you through to the next banking day. If, like us, you fly in during the wee hours of the morning, then you shouldn't expect foreign exchange facilities to be open, and you'll probably be glad of having a few spare US$1 bills rather than relying on the taxi drivers to provide you with change.

As soon as you leave the terminal building, you'll be mobbed by taxi drivers. As things stand, there would be nothing preventing you from pushing past them all and hopping into a passenger taxi in the direction you want to go, though it's probably fair to say that if any one public transport route in an African capital is likely to attract light fingers, then it's the one from the airport. My inclination after a long flight and loaded down with luggage would be to save your first acquaintance with Accra's bemusing public transport routes for later in the day. A passenger taxi from the airport to anywhere in central Accra really shouldn't cost more than US$2.50, but you'll be asked for a lot more and, again, while you certainly ought to negotiate the fare, this probably isn't the moment to get overtly confrontational.

Should your flight be scheduled to arrive after dark, it might be wise to make an advance booking at a mid- to upper-range hotel, depending on your budget: the Granada, Shangri-La and Golden Tulip are all close to the airport. Be aware that many hotels graded three-star or above have a shuttle service to and from the airport, but you ought to check whether this is the case when you book (or get your travel agent to check it), and should also ascertain until what time it runs.

For internal flights to Kumasi and Tamale, contact **Golden Airways** on Ndabanige Sithole Rd, North Laboni. Tel: 77-7978 or 76-0627; fax: 77-5610.

By road

There are numerous different bus and tro-tro station in Accra, some serving specific lines and others a specific cluster of destinations. The most important stations to travellers are the main STC station on Ring Road, a short distance east of Lamptey Circle, Kaneshie station on Winneba Road about 1km northwest of Lamptey Circle, and Tudu station in the city centre north of Makola Circle.

I would strongly advise travellers heading out of Accra to use an STC bus, assuming that they are going far enough to make it worthwhile (the STC buses charge full fare to their end destination even if you 'drop' along the way). From the main STC station, buses leave hourly to Kumasi, ten times daily to Takoradi, and several times daily to Cape Coast. At least one Kumasi bus daily continues northwards to Tamale, Bolgatanga and Bawku. You should arrive with half an hour to spare to be reasonably certain of getting a ticket, but at worst you could take a City Express bus from the City Express station 100m down the road. Telephone 22-1912 to check current timetables – the people are very helpful on the phone.

All tro-tros and other buses to destinations along the coast and north towards Kumasi leave from Kaneshie station on a fill-up-and-go basis – you'll rarely wait more than 30 minutes for a vehicle to leave for anywhere you want to go to. STC buses and tro-tros to destinations in the east leave from Tudu station. Destinations for STC buses heading in this direction include Aflao (on the Togo border), Ho and Akosombo. For some destinations east, for instance Shai Hills and Prampram, you may have to pick up a tro-tro from Tema station

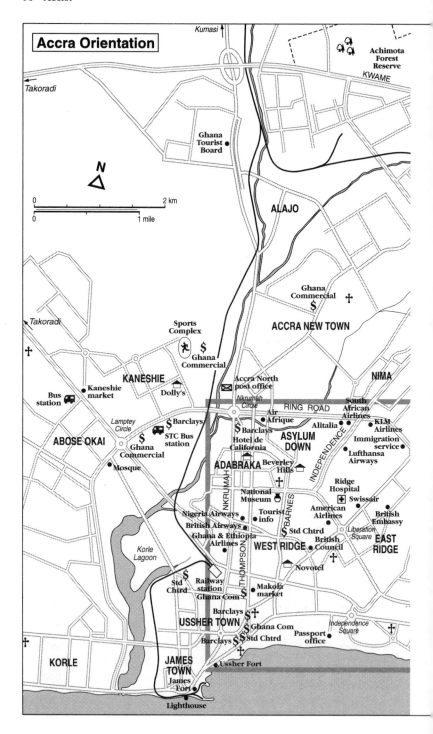

Accra Orientation

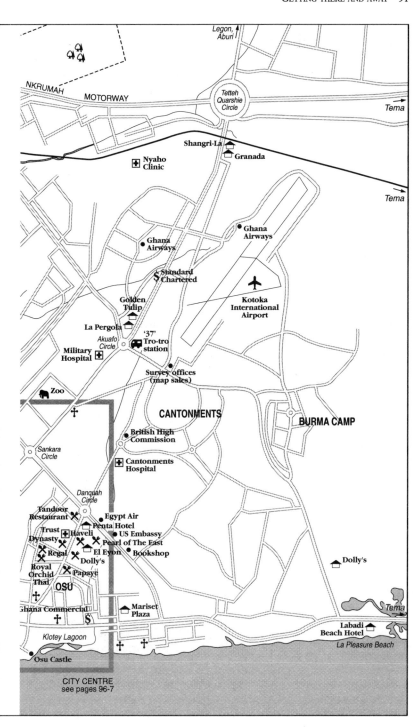

Legon,
Aburi

NKRUMAH

MOTORWAY

Tetteh
Quarshie
Circle

Tema

Tema

Shangri-La

Granada

Nyaho
Clinic

Ghana
Airways

Ghana
Airways

Standard
Chartered

Golden
Tulip

Kotoka
International
Airport

La Pergola

'37'
Tro-tro
station

Akuafo
Circle

Military
Hospital

Survey offices
(map sales)

Zoo

CANTONMENTS

BURMA CAMP

British High
Commission

Sankara
Circle

Cantonments
Hospital

Danquah
Circle

Tandoor
Restaurant

Egypt Air

Penta Hotel

Trust
Dynasty

Haveli

US Embassy

Regal

Pearl of The East

El Eyon

Bookshop

Dolly's

Royal
Orchid
Thai

Dolly's

Papaye

OSU

Ghana Commercial

Mariset
Plaza

Tema

Klotey Lagoon

Labadi
Beach Hotel

La Pleasure Beach

Osu Castle

CITY CENTRE
see pages 96-7

(just south of the Novotel) to Ashaiman and change vehicles there.

Wherever you are going, hail a tax to take you to the right station – the drivers know exactly from where vehicles leave for even the most obscure destinations, and at around US$1–2 per ride it saves immense hassle and asking around. Likewise, when you arrive in Accra, it really is worth the small price of a taxi to get to your hotel swiftly and simply.

ORIENTATION

Central Accra is bounded to the south by the Atlantic Ocean and to the west by Korle Lagoon. In other directions, it is bounded by Ring Road, which starts at the old Winneba Road on the seafront immediately west of Korle Lagoon, before running northeast via Lamptey Circle to Nkrumah Circle, then east from Nkrumah to Sankara Circle, and then southeast from Sankara Circle via Danquah Circle to the junction with Labadi road near the seafront.

Tourists who spend some time in Accra will probably come to regard Nkrumah Circle as the city's most significant landmark. Not only is it the local transport hub of the city, but it marks the intersection between Ring Road and Nkrumah Road, the latter the main north–south thoroughfare through Accra's commercial heart of Adabraka (in the north), Ussher Town and James Town (on the seafront). Running parallel to and east of Nkrumah Avenue, Kojo Thompson and Barnes roads are arguably the city's second and third most important north–south thoroughfares, the former well supplied with budget accommodation, the latter effectively the eastern border of the most built-up part of the city centre, and notable for two important landmarks, the National Museum and Novotel Hotel.

The suburbs that lie within Ring Road can be divided into three broad clusters. In the west are the three central suburbs mentioned above, essentially the commercial city centre. Of these, Adabraka is the main haunt of budget travellers since it is dotted with cheap accommodation, bars and restaurants, while the older suburbs of Ussher Town and James Town are of some historical interest. To the west of this, bounded roughly by Barnes Road to the west and an imaginary north–south line running between Sankara Circle and Independence Square, lies a cluster of more spacious, green suburbs comprising from north to south: Asylum Down, North Ridge, East Ridge, West Ridge and Victoriabourg. The main thoroughfare through this part of Accra is Independence Avenue, which connects Sankara Circle on Ring Road to the seafront at the south end of Barnes Road. The most easterly suburb is Osu (aka Christiansbourg), another old part of town focused towards Osu Castle and bisected by Cantonments Road, an important commercial centre notable for its many restaurants.

Several important trunk roads fan out from Ring Road. The main road to Winneba and the West Coast leaves Ring Road at Lamptey Circle, the main road to Nswawam, Kumasi and the north leaves from Nkrumah Circle, while Liberation Road, which leaves from Sankara Circle, heads past the airport to Tetteh Quarshie Circle and the Kwame Nkrumah Highway for Tema and other destinations east of Accra. At the very southeast of Ring Road, Labadi Road heads to La Beach, Coco Beach and Tema via the coast.

GETTING AROUND

Accra is serviced by a remarkably cheap and efficient system of tro-tros, passenger (shared) taxis and dropping (charter) taxis, though getting to grips with the main routes used by passenger vehicles takes time and a certain degree of trial and error. In my opinion, travellers who are spending only a couple of days in Accra may as well stick to dropping taxis, which can be picked up practically anywhere and at any time. You're unlikely to have to pay more than US$1.50 for a ride within the bounds of Ring Road, though you may sometimes have to negotiate to get a fair price, and prices seem to go up on days when traffic is particularly heavy. Dropping taxis to places outside Ring Road such as La Beach, the STC bus station, Accra Zoo or the airport cost more, but are still very cheap by international standards.

Passenger taxis and tro-tros are absurdly cheap (between 250 and 400 cedis – less than US$0.20) depending on the route, and we heard and experienced nothing to suggest there is any serious need to worry about pickpockets and the like, especially on the taxis. Once you are reasonably well oriented to Accra, the system is quite easy to assimilate. The most important local transport hub is Nkrumah Circle, and you can pretty much assume that you'll find a shared taxi or tro-tro from here to wherever you want, at the worst involving one change of vehicle. Shared taxis to the Novotel Hotel (via Farrar Avenue and Barnes Road) and to Osu leave from the southeast side of the circle, while those to Sankara Circle, '37', the airport, La Beach and Nungua leave from the northeast side behind the Shell garage next to the overpass. Minibuses heading right down Nkrumah Road to Jamestown can generally be picked up by waiting on the west side of Nkrumah Road immediately south of the circle. Tro-tros to destinations slightly further out of town, for instance Legon University and Aburi Botanical Gardens, generally leave from the northwest side of the circle.

An important tro-tro station in the city centre is Tema Station on Independence Avenue below the Novotel Hotel, where you can pick up tro-tros to coastal destinations in the direction of Tema as well as northeast along Independence Avenue to Sankara Circle and along Liberation Avenue past the airport. Outside the Ring Road, a landmark worth knowing is 37 station at Akuafo Circle on the junction of Liberation Avenue and Gifford Road, where you'll pick up shared taxis to most destinations including Nkrumah Circle (via Sankara Circle), Osu (via Cantonments Road and Danquah Circle) and Nungua (via Burma Camp Bypass and La Beach).

WHERE TO STAY

Upmarket: Three to five star; US$100 and above

It isn't difficult to see why the **Labadi Beach Hotel** (tel: 77-2501, fax: 77-2520) is the only hotel in Ghana to be awarded a five-star grading. The most striking feature of the hotel is the rare attention to detail noticeable not only in the architecture and the attractive landscaped gardens (complete with large reed-fringed dam and adult and children's swimming pools), but also in the standard of service. The location, too, is a major boon, adjacent to one of the country's most attractive and lively public beaches, yet only ten minutes by taxi to the city centre. Facilities include tennis courts, sauna and health club, an excellent business centre, a poorly stocked curio and bookshop, three highly regarded restaurants, and 15-channel satellite television in every room. According to a Ghanaian resident of ten years, the hairdressing and beauty salon here is very good and reasonably priced. The rooms are as good as any available in the capital, with the bathrooms in particular less cramped than is often the case in international-class hotels. Rooms cost US$230/270/520 single/double/suite inclusive of an outstanding buffet breakfast.

Out on Liberation Road, towards the airport, the four-star **Golden Tulip Hotel** (tel: 77-5360, fax: 77-5361), part of a Dutch chain, is quite clearly the only hotel in Accra to approach Labadi's standards and is difficult to fault in its own right. Well situated for access to the city centre, its facilities are easily the equal of the Labadi – swimming pool, tennis courts and mini-golf course, good restaurants, an excellent curio and bookshop and a (rather sluggish) business centre. Three things let it down by comparison with the Labadi: the uninspiring grounds, the indifferent location, and the inferior standard of service. Were the Golden Tulip closer in price to the Novotel, then I could comfortably recommend it as Accra's second best hotel. As things stand, I feel that if you're going to pay the sort of room rate asked by either the Golden Tulip or the Labadi, then the Labadi has a great deal more to offer. Rooms cost US$215/250 single/double including a good buffet breakfast.

Part of the well-known French chain, the **Accra Novotel** (tel: 66-7546, fax: 66-7533), on the southern end of Barnes Road, is the other four-star hotel in Accra, and its height makes it something of a landmark in the city centre. Very much a businessman's hotel, the Novotel is the obvious choice if you plan on doing a lot of walking around the city centre and, although the atmosphere is negligible and the rooms are not as plush or spacious as those at Accra's other four- and five-star hotels, facilities are similar and just as good (swimming pool, tennis court, business centre, outstanding restaurant, curio shop, satellite TV in all rooms), and the price is a considerable jump down at US$140/160 single/double including a good buffet breakfast.

A long-standing favourite amongst Accra's tourist-class hotels is the three-star **Hotel Shangri-La** (tel: 77-6993, fax: 77-4873), situated on Liberation Road a short distance past the airport. The major strength of this hotel is its communal areas, which make tasteful use of natural materials and ethnic art and crafts, and are centred around a palm-fringed fountain and large, illuminated swimming pool. Facilities are comparable to those of the hotels listed above, and include a business centre, book and imported newspaper stall, gymnasium, sauna, tennis court, horse-riding and a good restaurant known for its pizzas. Accommodation in s/c chalets with ac, fridge, satellite TV and large private safe costs US$110 single, US$140 small double or US$175 large double.

Mid-range: One to three star; US$100 and under
If eating out plays a big role in your life and you're comfortable staying quite centrally, then look no further than the cluster of decent hotels lying

off Cantonments Road in Osu, also home to Accra's main conglomeration of international restaurants. Perhaps the best of these is the new **El-Elyon Hotel** (tel: 77-4421, fax: 77-6343, email: elelyon@africaonline.com.gh), a small three-star place situated on 18th Lane opposite the Côte d'Ivoire Embassy. Both rooms and facilities here approach those of more expensive hotels, so it seems very reasonably priced at US$70/85 single/double for an attractively furnished s/c room with ac and satellite TV.

Other places in this part of Osu include the **Penta Hotel** (tel: 77-4529, fax: 77-3154), a pleasant two-star hotel where s/c rooms with ac and TV cost US$55/60 single/double; the **Raj Guesthouse** (tel: 77-8760), a bit overpriced at US$60/85 single/double; and the more low-key **Ghalebon Guesthouse**, where you should be able to haggle down the somewhat optimistic initial price of US$45/50 single/double. Finally, at the southern end of Osu, just off Labadi Road, you'll find the three-star **Mariset Plaza** (tel: 77-4434, fax: 77-2085), which has a swimming pool, as well as ac double rooms with satellite TV for US$80/90.

Moving away from Osu nearer to the airport, the two-star **Grenada Hotel** (tel: 77-5343, fax: 77-4880) next to the Shangri-La seems good value at around US$60 for a s/c ac double, making it a good place to head for if you want to be in relatively suburban surroundings. There is a good bar and restaurant attached or you can eat next door at the Shangri-La.

On the north side of Ring Road, between Nkrumah and Sankara circles, the **Hotel Paloma** (tel: 22-8700, fax: 23-1815, email: Paloma@ africaonline.com.gh) is outstandingly good value for money at US$55/60/75 single/double/suite including breakfast. Rooms are all large and comfortably furnished, with satellite TV, ac and hot water, and the suites have kitchenettes. There is a good selection of restaurants in the attached shopping arcade.

On Kojo Thompson Road, well positioned for exploring the nightlife of Adabraka, the **Niagara Hotel** (tel: 23-0118, fax: 23-0119, email: niagara@ighmail.com) seems very good value at US$52/73 single/double with ac and satellite TV. The restaurant looks good too.

Moderate: Ungraded to One Star; US$35 and under
If you want to stay somewhere quite central, you'll find a string of hotels in the moderate price range on Farrar Avenue within easy walking distance of the bars and restaurants of Adabraka. The best of these is probably the **Hotel President** (tel: 22-3343), which has s/c doubles with ac and TV for US$25, as well as a good patio bar and affordable restaurant. Next up, and a bit seedier, the **Avenue Club Hotel** has a lively outdoor bar and rather nice s/c rooms with ac, TV and fridge for US$19/23 double/twin. Further down, on the junction with Samora Machel, the **Beverley Hills Hotel** (tel: 22-4042) also seems good value at US$20/30 s/c double/twin with ac and TV.

On Kojo Thompson Road, a short way south of the intersection with Castle, the **Hotel Avenida** (tel: 22-1354) is as good value as any of the above. Here, a s/c ac double with cold water only costs US$17, while a s/c ac double with carpet, TV and hot running water costs US$23. Nearby, on

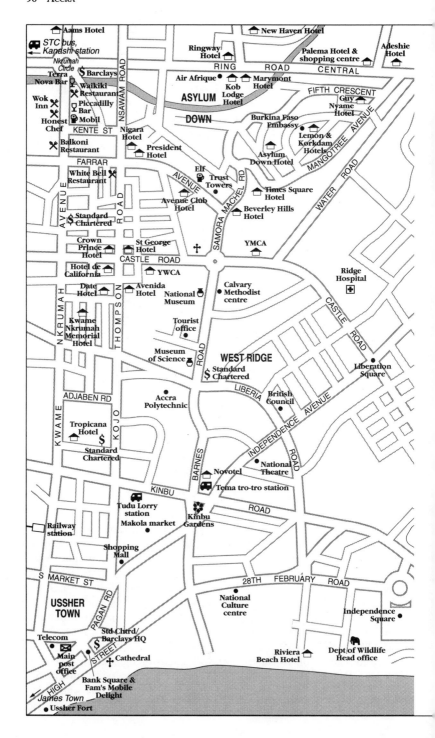

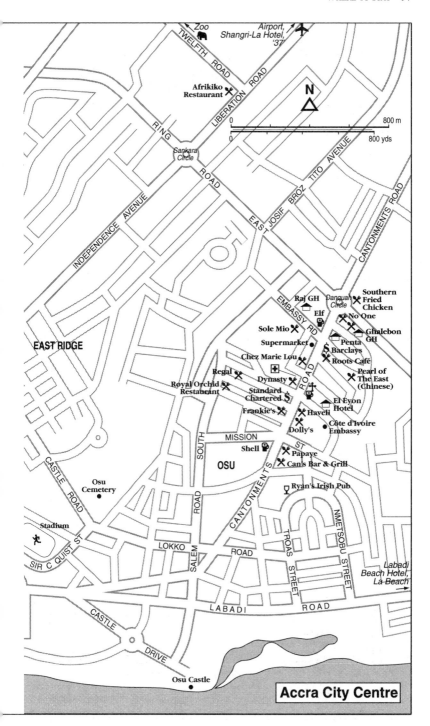

Accra City Centre

Chatfield Road, the **Hotel St George** (tel: 22-4699) has good s/c rooms with ac, fridge, TV and hot water for US$23/27/30 single/double/suite.

Two hotels in this range lie on Ring Road east of Nkrumah Circle. The **Ringway Hotel** has seen better days and seems poor value at US$20/25 for a s/c single/double. The **Adeshie Hotel** (tel 22-1307) by contrast is very plush and reasonably priced at US$34 for a s/c double with ac, TV and phone.

Tucked away in North Ridge right next door to Lemon Lodge, the popular **Korkdam Hotel** (22-3221) has ac s/c rooms for a very reasonable US$14/20/28 single/double/suite.

An odd little place on the beachfront near Independence Square, perfectly positioned to catch the evening breeze, the **Riviera Beach Hotel** is rather run-down but not without a certain appeal, and reasonable value with s/c rooms at US$16/23 single/double with hot water and fan. It also has a quiet, sea-facing bar and serves tasty meals in the US$3–4 range.

Shoestring: Ungraded; US$12 and under

There's no shortage of shoestring accommodation in Accra, especially in Adabraka where a cluster of affordable hotels and hostels lie within 500m of the junction of Castle and Kojo Thompson Roads. A good starting point, right on the junction, the **Hotel de California** (tel: 22-6199) is not quite the lush beach hotel that the name might lead you to expect, notwithstanding the shady palm and mango trees in the grounds, but a creaky old colonial building complete with high ceilings, lazy fans, wooden floors and patio bar. This place is difficult to beat on the combination of price, atmosphere and location, and it's a reliable place to meet other travellers (as well as a clique of 'guides' and other hangers on). Rooms using communal showers cost US$6/7 single/double. The breakfast is good value.

Opposite the Hotel de California, the **Hotel Crown Prince** (tel: 22-5381) doesn't have much atmosphere, but the rooms seem fair value at US$7/8/12 single/double/suite. Similar in standard, and two blocks away on Adama Road, the **Date Hotel** (tel: 22-8200) is OK at US$5/6 for a single/double using communal showers and US$8 s/c double, though be warned that I've had reports of theft from the rooms.

On Castle Road, about 500m east of Kojo Thompson, the **YMCA** is a good place to meet travellers and excellent value at US$2.50 per person. The **YWCA**, barely 100m from the junction with Kojo Thompson, is more basic, and few travellers use it. One of the best budget options in Accra, the **Calvary Methodist Guesthouse**, lies just off Castle Road, on Barnes Road opposite the National Museum. This has s/c rooms with fan for US$6/10 single/double and with ac for US$9/12 single/double. It also serves inexpensive meals.

Back on Kojo Thompson Road, about 500m south of the Hotel de California, the **Kwame Nkrumah Memorial Hotel** can hardly be accused of serving the great man's memory in grand style, offering rather scruffy rooms using communal showers for US$7/9 single/double. Further south, just off Kojo Thompson Road, the **Bellview Hotel** has large and acceptably clean s/c rooms with fan for US$7/12 single/double, as well as rooms with ac, fridge and TV for US$20.

There are a few affordable places within a few hundred metres of Nkrumah Circle. The closest is **Aams Hotel**, which is rather run-down but reasonably priced at US$5 for an ordinary double and US$7 for a s/c double. On Ring Road, the **Marymart Hotel** wouldn't let me look at a room until I paid the asking price of US$9 for a s/c double, from which you're free to draw your own conclusions – one traveller had the same experience and said the rooms were actually very good value. The **Kob Lodge Hotel**, a little further along the same road, seems pleasant enough at US$12 for an ac single.

A more appealing cluster of inexpensive hotels lies in North Ridge, an area with a rather suburban feel despite lying inside Ring Road and being within walking distance of most interesting parts of Accra. The most popular place with backpackers is **Lemon Lodge** (tel: 22-7857), where clean s/c doubles with fan cost US$7.50. Similar in price, the nearby **Asylum Down** and **Mavis Hotels** are also very comfortable and the latter hotel has a good garden bar serving cheap meals. Close by, but just outside Ring Road, the **New Haven Hotel** is quiet, pleasant and good value at US$5/8 for a s/c single/double with fan.

The central **Gasotel Hotel** (formerly the Tropicana) has large, scruffy rooms with double bed, fan but no running water for an uncompetitive US$8.

Recommended by one traveller in late 1999 as the 'best budget place' in Ghana, the **Salvation Army Hostel** at the end of Embassy Road, 200m from Danquah Circle, charges less than US$2 per person for a clean room with a fan and net.

Further out of town, the **Coco Beach Hotel**, 20 minutes' walk from Nungua on the Tema road, charges US$2.50 per person to camp, and has a good bar and restaurant. The **Beachcombers Guesthouse**, also in Nungua, has been recommended as excellent value at US$22 for a s/c chalet in a pretty garden next to the beach. The signposted turn-off to both these places can be reached from Nkrumah Circle by shared taxi.

WHERE TO EAT AND DRINK

Accra is a pretty good city for eating out, with a diverse range of restaurants to suit all budgets. The main cluster of cheaper bars and restaurants is in Adabraka, between Nkrumah Circle and the Hotel de California, while the more upmarket restaurants are clustered on and around Cantonments Road in Osu. Because of this, and bearing in mind that all else being equal most people would prefer to eat within walking distance of their hotel rather than to cross town, I've clumped restaurants and bars by area rather than by cost or type of cuisine.

Adabraka

This is the best part of town for cheap eating and drinking, with a good selection of restaurants serving meals for comfortably less than US$5, as well as a great many bars.

Our favourite place in the area is **The White Bell** on the junction of Farrar Avenue and Kojo Thompson Road. The only open-sided first-floor bar in this part of town, there's usually a good breeze here, not to say cold beer and a reasonably eclectic music selection. Above all, the food is varied, inexpensive, and very good – everything from vegetable curry with rice to a big cheeseburger with chips, and nothing much more than US$3.

Two minutes away, the dining hall at the **Hotel President** looks pretty dismal in atmospheric terms, but the food is good, the price is certainly right at around US$2.50 for a chicken or steak dish, and you can ask to be served in the pleasant garden bar. Another nearby spot for an outdoor drink is the garden bar at the **Club Avenue Hotel**, though food here is restricted to grilled kebabs.

There's a cluster of eating and drinking places along Nkrumah Avenue just south of the Circle. The Chinese food in the **Wok Inn** is not the best in town, but it's certainly very acceptable, and good value at around US$3.50 for a main dish with a huge portion of rice – and the freshly cooked spring rolls really are excellent. The **Honest Chef** next door does various grills for around US$3–4, as does the rather more comfortable **Waikiki Restaurant** opposite.

Approaching the circle, you'll find all manner of street food, including good spicy kebabs, and the **Terra Nova Bar**, a place we liked for its garden ambience and chilled draught. There are several other bars in this part of town, most notoriously the **Kilimanjaro** and **Piccadilly Night Clubs** – the latter (often dubbed Pick-A-Lady for reasons that will be clear to any single guy walking in this part of town at night) has live music on Wednesday and weekend nights.

On the northeast side of Nkrumah Circle, the spotlessly clean, air-conditioned **City Gardens Chinese Restaurant** does a variety of Chinese and other take-away dishes in the US$2–3 range. There are tables at which you can eat, if you want.

The most upmarket place to eat in this part of town is the swanky Chinese restaurant in the **Niagara Hotel**, where most dishes will work out at around US$8–10 with rice or chips. Also relatively upmarket, but quite a bit cheaper, is the garden restaurant in the **Beverley Hills Hotel**.

Osu

Accra's main cluster of mid- to upper-range restaurants lies on and around Cantonments Road in the suburb of Osu south of Danquah Circle. As a rule, you should bank on spending around US$8–10 per head at the better restaurants in this area, though there are a few cheaper places. Please note that the Number One and Roots Restaurants shown on the map had both closed in 1999.

Of the cheaper options, a recommended starting point is **Southern Fried Chicken** on Danquah Circle, on the face of it an inferior Kentucky clone, but of more interest for the good and very affordable pizzas, curries and burgers. Less appetising and more generic fast foods options on

Cantonments Road include **Dolly's** and **Papaye Fast Foods**, the latter specialising in spicy grilled chicken.

Also on Cantonments Road, **Frankie's** has for some time been known for its excellent pastries, cakes and ice-cream, and the recently opened restaurant and coffee shop have been recommended by several readers.

As is so often the case in Ghana, Chinese restaurants dominate the Osu area. One of the best, and more affordable than most, the **Pearl of the East** on 15th Lane also gives you the choice of eating inside or in the open courtyard it shares with the popular **Mapee's Jazz Club** (live music at weekends) and **Kotton Klub** (live music Wednesday and Sunday, plus darts and pool). Also recommended is the **Dynasty Restaurant**, while the **Regal** and **Royal Orchid Restaurants** are reputedly also very good.

There are two good Indian restaurants in this part of town: the **Tandoor Restaurant** alongside the Raj Guesthouse and the **Haveli Restaurant** down an unmarked side road opposite the Dynasty Restaurant. The **Lebanese New Club 400** near Sankara Circle has been recommended. For European cuisine, the **Restaurant Sole Mio** serves Italian dishes and pizzas, while the **Chez Marie Lou** is a Swiss restaurant serving various continental dishes.

For something completely different, **Ryan's Irish Pub**, popular with expats and well signposted from Cantonments Road, sustains an Irish country bar atmosphere remarkably convincingly – you could easily forget you're in Africa after half an hour here. Various grills are served at moderate to high prices, and there's a popular weekend barbecue.

Another drinking hole that's popular with expats and Ghanaians alike is the **Fusion Bar** close to the Elf Garage on Embassy Road. The nearby **Connections Nightclub** has been recommended as one of the best in town; it asks a cover charge of around US$2.

Elsewhere in Accra

For the combination of an affordable tasty meal and after-dinner drinking or dancing, catch a shared taxi to '37' station or a private one along Liberation Avenue to the Elf garage between Akuafo Circle and the Golden Tulip Hotel. Here, right behind the Elf garage, you'll find the excellent little **Restaurant La Pergola**, which serves tasty fish, chicken and meat grills as well as various Ghanaian dishes in the US$3.50–4.50 range. Perhaps 100m back towards the circle, continue to **Mr Rees**, a very lively garden bar and dancing spot which plays a good variety of African, American and reggae music, serves cheap draught beer, and boasts several kebab stalls. One advantage of this place for those with cars is that there's enclosed, guarded parking, while those without cars can stumble from the bar right on to a taxi rank from where they can hail a private taxi or catch a tro-tro direct to Nkrumah Circle.

Further out on Liberation Road, past the airport, the restaurant at the **Shangri-La Hotel** has long had the reputation of serving the best pizza in Accra, as well as a variety of grills in the US$5–7 range. A good time to visit is on Friday evening, when it's happy hour from 18.00 to 20.00. There is live jazz every Saturday night.

Also on Liberation Road, but very close to Sankara Circle, is the **Afrikiko Restaurant**, a shady garden bar and restaurant, with live music every night (no cover charge), chilled draught beer, and a variety of good salads, burgers and fish dishes in the US$3–4 range. On Independence Avenue, almost immediately south of the same circle, the **Canadian High Commission Restaurant**, open for lunch only, is known for its good, inexpensive meals and sandwiches.

On Ring Road, about halfway between Nkrumah and Sankara circles, the Paloma Shopping Centre boats a cluster of restaurants, including the **Paloma Restaurant**, which does the usual grills and pizzas and has live music most nights. In the same centre, **Life Westward of Eden Restaurant** is, so far as I'm aware, the only vegetarian restaurant in the country, with dishes starting at US$4. Nearby, the **Bus Stop Restaurant** serves inexpensive Western dishes and ice-cream.

Few travellers head to the southern half of central Accra by night, but if you're there during the day, **Fam's Mobile Delight**, a van parked permanently in front of the central post office, serves really tasty hamburgers for around US$1.50. One of the few places in Accra where you can eat overlooking the sea is the open-air restaurant of the **Riviera Beach Hotel**, which serves tasty meals in the US$3–4 range.

At La Beach, next to the Labadi Beach Hotel, are quite a number of bars, inexpensive restaurants, and guys selling freshly grilled kebabs and chicken.

LISTINGS
Airlines
Air Afrique On Ring Road East, roughly 300m east of Nkrumah Circle. Tel: 66-4122 or 230014/5. Airport tel: 77-7414.
Air Ivoire Trinity House, Ring Road East. Tel: 22-4666.
Alitalia Ring Road Central. Tel: 22-7873/9813. Fax: 22-0759. Airport tel: 77-2766.
American Airlines Valco Trust House, behind USIS. Tel: 23-1804/5/6.
British Airways Cnr Kojo Thompson & North Liberia Rd. Tel: 66-7800/7900. Airport tel: 77-6172 ext 1335.
Egypt Air Ring Road East (near Danquah Circle). Tel: 77-6585/3537. Airport tel: 77-6171.
Ethiopian Airlines Cocoa House, Kwame Nkrumah Av. Tel: 66-4856/7.
Ghana Airways Agostino Neto Rd. Tel: 77-7401. Reservations 22-8417/1150.
KLM Ring Road Central. Tel: 22-4020/30/50. Airport tel: 77-5729/6509.
Lufthansa Off Water Road, North Ridge. Tel: 22-1086/4030. Airport tel: 77-9052.
Middle East Airlines Airport tel: 77-5492.
Nigeria Airways Danawi Building, Kojo Thompson Rd. Tel: 22-3749/3916.
Swissair Pegasus House, 47 Independence Av. Tel: 22-8150/90. Airport tel: 77-5634/3363.

American Express
The sole agent for American Express is Scantravel, in Enterprise House on High Street, Ussher Town, open from 08.00 to 17.00 Monday to Friday.

Books

An excellent second-hand bookshop called **Books For Less** lies just off Cantonments Road, around the corner from the defunct Roots Café. Second-hand novels can also be bought at a few stalls on the south side of Nkrumah Circle, on Pagan Road near the central post office, and at '37' taxi station near Akuafo Circle. The going rate for second-hand paperbacks, even recent bestsellers, is less than US$1.

Accra is the best place in the country (if not anywhere in the world) to pick up historical and other works about Ghana. If casual browsing and bargaining is the way you prefer to make your purchases, then head to the cluster of bookshops and stalls on and around Pagan Road, where you can often pick up the most unlikely books for next to nothing. The bookshop at Legon University, open on weekdays and Saturday mornings, stocks all sorts of oddities, with probably the best range of historical books I could find, as well as plenty of cheap secondhand novels.

The Omari Book Shop is in the building signposted Omari Computer Systems on East Ring Road close to the US Embassy. It stocks a good selection of travel guides, new and secondhand novels, local fiction, maps and historical books, but it tends to be very expensive compared with elsewhere. Similar is EPS Book Services on Abafun Crescent, which you can reach by using any transport heading between '37' and La Beach. In Osu, a good range of new and secondhand novels and other books can be found at Books For You Enterprises off Cantonments Road behind Papaye Fast Foods.

Curios

A good place for general curio shopping is the market at the National Cultural Centre on the seafront on 28th February Road. Here, you can buy just about anything you want, from genuine *kente* and other local cloths to carvings, masks and statues from all over Ghana and elsewhere in West Africa. It's also a good place to pick up colourful dyed shirts and cheaper trinkets such as imitation *kente* wallets and bead necklaces. The one drawback to doing your curio shopping here is the high level of pushiness and histrionics – this is certainly not the place to go if you want a life-affirming experience.

Unless you're tremendously pressed for time, you may prefer to do your curio shopping in a more haphazard way. Most curios sell primarily to Ghanaians, not to tourists, and for all but the most esoteric requirements (face masks, for instance) you'll find that there are stalls selling interesting items all over the city – around '37' and the Golden Tulip Hotel, on Ring Road next to Danquah Circle, and on La Beach, for instance. Alternatively, the main markets – Makola in the city centre and Kaneshie on Winneba Road – also stock a wide range of textiles and beads, and although the markets are generally more busy than the National Cultural Centre, the stall owners are not as dependent on the tourist dollar, so the atmosphere is less pushy.

Finally, if your budget is up to shipping it home, surely the ultimate in Ghanaian souvenirs must be your very own customised coffin, carved Posuban-style in whatever shape you like (elephant, boat, minibus, whale!) at the celebrated coffin shop in Teshie on the Tema Road.

Embassies and High Commissions
Australia *contact Canadian High Commission*
Belgium Mile 4, Independence Av. Tel: 77-6561. Fax: 77-3927
Benin 19 2nd Close, off Volta St. Tel: 77-4860
Burkina Faso off Sobukwe Rd, Asylum Down. Tel: 22-1928
Canada 46 Independence Av. Tel: 77-3791. Fax: 77-3792
China 6 Agostino Neto Rd. Tel: 77-4527.
Ivory Coast 9 18th Lane, Osu. Tel: 77-4611/2.
Denmark 67 Dr Isert Rd. Tel: 22-6972/9830. Fax: 22-8061.
Finland 7 3rd Rangoon Close. Tel: 77-6307. Fax: 77-4513.
France 12th Road, off Liberation Av. Tel: 22-8571 or 77-4480. Fax: 77-8321.
Germany Valdemosa Lodge, 7th Av ext, North Ridge. Tel: 22-1311/26. Fax: 22-1347.
Guinea 4th Norla St, Labonie. Tel: 77-7921.
Italy Jawharlal Meru Rd. Tel: 77-5621/5536.
Japan 8 Tito Ave. Tel: 77-5616/5719. Fax: 77-5951.
Liberia Odiokwao Rd. Tel: 77-5641/2.
Mali 8 Agostino Neto Rd. Tel: 77-5939/5160.
Netherlands 89 Liberation Rd. Tel: 77-3644. Fax: 77-3655.
Niger E104-3 Independence Av. Tel: 22-4962.
Nigeria Tito Av. Tel: 77-6158/9. Fax: 77-4395.
Norway *Resident in Lagos*
Russia F856/1 Ring Rd East. Tel: 77-5611. Fax: 77-2679.
South Africa Golden Tulip Hotel, suite 507/8 Tel: 77-5360.
Spain Lamptey Av ext. Tel: 77-4004. Fax: 77-6216.
Sweden 11th Lane, Osu. Tel: 77-3145. Fax: 77-3175.
Switzerland 9 Water Rd, North Ridge. Tel: 22-8125/0509. Fax: 22-3583.
Togo Togo House, Cantonments Circle. Tel: 77-7950.
United Kingdom 1 Abdul Nasser Rd. Tel: 22-1665/1715. Fax: 66-4652.
United States of America Ring Rd East. Tel: 77-5347/8/9. Fax: 77-6008.

Foreign exchange
The best banks for changing foreign currency and travellers' cheques are the Barclays and Standard Chartered Banks, both of which have head offices on Bank Road, 100m from the High Street Post Office in Ussher Town. There are also branches of both banks in Adabraka and Osu. You will generally get a better exchange rate for cash (provided that the currency isn't too obscure) at any of the dozens of forex bureaux dotted throughout the city. It's worth looking around for the best rate. Few forex bureaux accept travellers' cheques. In an emergency, there is a forex bureau in most of the upmarket hotels, though rates tend to be very poor.

Credit cards can generally be used to settle bills at the more expensive hotels and restaurants, and to obtain cash advances at certain banks. Barclays Bank is the best place to go with Visa and MasterCard (many branches have autotellers from which money can be drawn directly). The Social Security Bank behind the National Theatre handles Diners Club cards, and Scantravel (see American Express above) handles American Express.

Hospitals
For laboratory tests, visit Medlab in SGS House, 14 Ridge Road, tel: 77-6844. Hospitals and clinics recommended for emergency treatment and

other medical requirements are as follows (note that North Ridge Hospital has a doctor present 24 hours):

Military 37 Hospital, Liberation Rd near Akuafo Circle and '37' Station. Tel: 77-6111/2/3/4.
North Ridge Hospital, Castle Rd near African Liberation Square. Tel: 22-7328.
Nyaho Clinic, Aviation Rd, Airport Residential Area. Tel: 77-5341/5291.
Trust (SSNIT) Hospital, Cantonments Rd 500m south of Danquah Circle. Tel: 77-6787/7137.

Information for visitors

The Regional Tourist Office is quite easy to locate, along an apparently anonymous side road to the west of Barnes Road between the major intersections with Liberia and Castle roads. The people who work here are reasonably friendly, but making friends is about the only purpose that a visit is likely to serve.

A far better source of current information about Accra is the excellent book *No Worries: The Indispensable Insiders' Guide to Accra*, compiled and published by the North American Women's Association and sold at most large bookshops and upmarket hotels for the equivalent of US$12. Geared primarily at people spending a while in Accra rather than the casual visitor, it provides a useful combination of detailed listings and common-sense advice on everything from swimming in the sea to hiring a domestic servant.

Internet

The Cybercafé in the Paloma Centre charges less than US$2 for 30 minutes use, and is open from 07.00 until 23.00 daily except on Sundays when it closes an hour earlier. Other cafés include Yankee Ventures opposite the Paloma Centre, a cybercafé on Kojo Thompson Road opposite the Niagara Hotel, and the communications centre on Castle Road close to the Hotel de California. The British Council is another option, provided you enjoy long queues.

Maps

The KLM/Shell Ghana road map (with Accra on the flip side) is widely available in Accra's bookshops and upmarket hotels. For other requirements, head to the map sales office in the Department of Surveys offices on the junction of Airport and Giffard Road, about 500m from '37' Station. Don't buy the 1:1,000,000 one-sheet map of Ghana, which so far as I can see is identical to the KLM/Shell map, but double the price and lacking Accra on the flip. Far more useful is the set of four 1:500,000 sheets which together cover the whole country and cost around US$2.50 each.

Be aware that all the above maps contain some curious omissions, inclusions, displacements and misspellings (one example is the substantial junction town of Ashaiman, only 20km from Accra, which is not shown on any map that I've seen) suggesting they are rather less current than the legend *8th edition Jan 1994* on the 1:500,000 maps would have you believe.

For hikers and walkers, the map sales office sells more detailed sheets to most parts of the country, though again I would use a certain amount of judgement in deciding how far they are to be trusted.

Newspapers

Various Ghanaian newspapers are readily available throughout Accra. If you look around, you can also pick up the American weeklies *Time* and *Newsweek*, as well as the thoroughly salacious British *International Express*, the attractiveness of which depends on how long you've been out of the UK and your interest in sports – try the newspaper stall on the junction of Cantonments Road one block south of Danquah Circle, or the excellent book and newspaper stall in the Golden Tulip Hotel.

Ghana (like most African countries) must be approached with a certain spirit of sacrifice for those of us whose morning ritual is based around a pot of fresh coffee and equally fresh newspaper. So far as the coffee is concerned, *Nescafé* is generally the only solution, but a cheap fix on the newspaper front is provided by the gloriously air-conditioned reading room in the British Council on Liberia Road, liberally stocked with British newspapers from three days to one month old, and open from 09.00 to 17.00 Monday to Wednesday and 09.00 to 12.00 Thursday to Saturday.

For some unfathomable reason, British newspapers published during the days after the death of Princess Diana are displayed everywhere in Accra, even six months after the event, and presumably still will be for some time to come.

Post

Poste Restante addressed to Accra should be collected between 08.00 and 16.30 from the central post office on High Street, near the seafront in Ussher Town. International mail posted in Accra will arrive at its destination more quickly than mail posted from other towns in the country, but it will still most likely take up to two weeks. Mail posted from the post office in the airport is reputedly a bit quicker. For express and courier services, contact DHL on North Ridge Crescent; tel: 22-7035.

Supermarkets

There are a number of good supermarkets in Accra, selling a variety of imported goods ranging from breakfast cereals to Californian wine, though only those in the city centre are likely to be of great interest to travellers. In Osu, Afridom and Kwatsons are both on Cantonments Road, and the latter, close to Danquah Circle, is regarded as one of the best supermarkets in the city centre, with a good ground-floor bakery. In the city centre proper, the best range of goods is probably at Multistores on High Street. If you are looking for vegetarian products and herbal teas, try Relish Health Foods on the corner of 11th Lane and 6th Street in Osu.

Telephone

International telephone calls can be made from the Telecommunication offices near the Central Post Office on High Street, on Cantonments Road, and on Nkawam Road just north of Nkrumah Circle. A little more expensive, but considerably more time effective, are dozens of business centres offering international telephone and fax facilities in Osu, Adabraka and elsewhere.

PLACES TO VISIT

As mentioned in the introduction to this chapter, Accra is not especially rich in sightseeing. There is, however, a fair amount to busy yourself with in and around the city. A walking tour through the city centre, perhaps making some use of taxis, would be a good way to occupy a morning, followed perhaps by an afternoon visit to the National Museum, taking lunch at the adjacent Edvy Restaurant. Less centrally, La Beach is perhaps the most obvious tourist attraction, certainly for sun-worshippers, though the excellent Du Bois Centre and more mundane Accra Zoo will attract some.

In addition to the places listed below, there are quite a number of places covered along routes in the regional chapters which would make for realistic day trips (or, using public transport, overnight trips) from the capital. On the west coast, I would lump anywhere as far as Apam in this category (though these places would be more suited to overnight than day trips), as well as pretty much anywhere on the east coast as far as Ada (and Tema would be an easy day trip even on public transport). Inland, you could lump Akasombo, Aburi, Shai Hills and arguably Boti Falls and Somanya in the short-trip category.

City centre

Although Accra is well suited for random exploration, the following 'highlights' in and around the city centre are described along a rough route that starts in James Town and follows the main road along the seafront east as far as Independence Square or Osu Castle, before turning back inland past the National Theatre and British Council to the National Museum, a total distance of roughly 6km.

This is a longer distance than you might think in a city that's not only very busy but also really hot and sweaty. One look at the map, however, and you'll see that several shorter variations are possible. You could also make use of a taxi part of the way – a charter along the 2km run from Independence Square to the National Museum shouldn't cost more than US$2. It's also worth mentioning to new arrivals in Ghana that a walk of this length will seriously dehydrate you should you not drink a lot. One of the most refreshing and healthy drinks on offer is coconut juice – keep an eye out for the coconut vendors who hang out all over the city centre, and will cut a fresh coconut for a pittance.

James Town The most atmospheric part of Accra, James Town is a pleasure to walk around, with its colourful small markets, colonial-era shops and houses, and strong sense of community. A highlight is the whitewashed 30m high colonial-era lighthouse – you should be allowed to climb to the top for a small tip. Also worth visiting is the old fishing harbour on the beach below Fort James, the second largest harbour in Ghana until the construction of Tema, which is a riot of colourful traditional pirogues in the early to mid morning after the fishermen come in. Shared taxis from James Town to Nkrumah Circle leave from in front of the lighthouse, and you can also pick up a charter taxi here.

Ussher Town From James Town, follow High Street northeast and you'll soon cross the ill-defined border into Ussher Town, which is centred around the Dutch-built Fort Ussher (to your right walking up High Street about 500m past Fort James) and, more than any other part of Accra, lays claim to being the true city centre. Even before you reach Fort Ussher, look out for Brazil Lane, the seaward end of which is the former site of a long-vanished Portuguese Lodge, built above the cliff in the late fifteenth century. Past Fort Ussher, I would turn left from High Street along Bank Lane, a large square around a parking lot where you'll see not only several old buildings, the main banks, and the central post office, but also Fam's Mobile Foods, which has acquired a deserved reputation along the overland truck routes of Africa for its cheap, tasty burgers. At the end of Bank Lane, turn right into Pagan Road, where the pavement spills over with stalls (this is an excellent place to pick up cheap secondhand novels and cassettes of Ghanaian music) until you reach Makola Square, from where you can join the throngs that mass around **Makola Market**, the largest open-air market in Accra and a good place to buy beads and fabrics. Then turn back down Thorpe Road to High Street.

Nkrumah Mausoleum Set in attractive gardens on the seafront side of High Street between the junction of Thorpe and Barnes roads, the current resting place of Kwame Nkrumah is an altogether colder and more ostentatious affair than its quaintly low-key precursor in Nkrumah's home town of Nkroful on the West Coast. Students of African history in particular shouldn't miss the adjoining museum, which contains photos and other artefacts relating to Ghana's first president.

National Cultural Centre At the intersection with Barnes Road where High Street becomes 28 February Road, you'll see to your left the National Culture Centre (or Arts Centre), somewhat misleadingly named – at least from a tourist's point of view – since by day it amounts to nothing other than Ghana's biggest craft market. Unfortunately, despite being a good place to buy practically any type of curio, the craft market has a rather aggressive atmosphere, not at all conducive to relaxed browsing. If you are heading on from here to Independence Square, you might want to take a right-hand diversion to the Riviera Beach Hotel, for a cold drink, possibly a meal, and as good a view as you'll get of Osu Castle – though you're advised to ask the hotel staff about safety before wandering down to the beach itself.

Independence Square Also known as Black Star Square, this conglomeration of Soviet-inspired monuments to pan-Africanism and Ghanaian independence, constructed under Nkrumah, is a stark anachronism, not least – ironically – because of the absolute lack of African influences apparent in its angular design. The thematic centrepiece of the square is Independence Arch; the adjective that springs to mind is ugly. The parade ground between the square and the sea is a barren concrete eyesore, at least when void of the 30,000 people it is intended to accommodate, though it would take a hard heart to be wholly unmoved by the enclosed Flame of African Liberation, lit by Nkrumah himself in 1961.

Osu Castle Also known as Christiansbourg Castle, this is one of the three main castles on the Ghanaian coast, and it has a more chequered history of occupation than the others. The original castle, much smaller than the modern one, was constructed by Denmark shortly after they bought a piece of land from the chief of Accra in 1661. It was briefly occupied by the Portuguese after the Danish commander was killed in a mutiny in 1679, returned to Denmark four years later, captured by the chief of Akwama in 1693, and sold back to Denmark barely a year later (though the keys of the original castle were never returned to the Danes and remain the hereditary property of the chief of Akwama to this day). After that, the castle remained the Danish coastal headquarters for 150 years, during which time it was greatly expanded, before being sold to Britain along with four other Danish forts in 1850.

The seat of government from 1876 to the present day, Osu Castle etched its name indelibly into the modern African history books on February 28 1948. This was the day when an anti-colonial demonstration outside the castle, initiated by recently returned veterans of World War II, was fired upon by colonial police, who killed 29 demonstrators and injured another 237 – a landmark event not only in the history of Ghana, but in the change in tide that led to almost all of Britain's African colonies being granted independence over the 15 years that followed.

As already mentioned, Osu Castle may not be visited without special permission, and the surrounding roads are cordoned off to prevent close access. The best views of the castle are from the Riviera Beach Hotel and Independence Square. Photography from any angle is absolutely forbidden.

National Theatre Built by China and opened in 1992, this impressive modern building is host to regular plays and dance performances, and it's well worth checking if there'll be anything on while you are in town (tel: 66-3449/3559). In any case, you might want to look in to see the small ethnographic display of traditional instruments and carvings. You might also want to pop into the Theatre Gardens for a meal or cold drink.

National Museum Even if you explore the city centre no further, do pop into the National Museum on Barnes Road, which is open from 09.00 to 18.00 daily except Mondays, and charges an entrance fee of US$1 plus a nominal extra for photography. Most of the displays here are ethnographic in nature, with some excellent examples of traditional crafts ranging from an elaborately carved *oware* board to several *akyeamepoma* (the decorated staffs used by royal spokesmen). There are also reasonable displays on Larabanga mosque and Cape Coast castle. The Edvy Restaurant in the museum grounds does fair meals in leafy surrounds for around US$4 (not open evenings), and it serves cold drinks of all types.

Further afield
Du Bois Centre
Situated at 22 First Circular Road, Cantonments (tel: 77-3127), this is the former home and now burial place of the prominent American pan-Africanist Dr William E Burghardt Du Bois, leader of all the Pan-African congresses between 1919 and 1927, vocal anti-segregationist and later communist, and prolific writer and speaker. Visitors are welcome to the centre, which now serves as a research institute and library for students of pan-Africanism, as well as being a memorial to Du Bois himself. Open on weekdays from 08.00 to 17.00, the Du Bois Centre is most easily reached by taking a shared taxi east from '37' Station along Giffard Road, and hopping off after about 1km, roughly 100m after passing Awak Stadium to your right.

Accra Zoo
Fifteen minutes' walk from Sankara Circle, Accra's small zoo is hardly an exemplar, and many visitors find it depressing, which it is – particularly when you see highly sociable animals such as monkeys locked away in confined isolation. On the other hand, as is often the case in small African zoos, most of the enclosed animals were orphaned or injured or born in captivity. More unusually, most of them do seem to be in good physical condition. The only real alternative to the animals' current situation is death (most would die horribly, of starvation or at the hands of a predator, were they to be released into the wild) and it strikes me as somewhat assumptive to transpose our feelings about captivity on to other creatures (lions, for instance, spend up to 23 hours of the day lazing around even in their natural state). This is a good place to see a fair cross-section of Ghana's large mammals and, who knows, perhaps leaving an extra donation might be a more appropriate response to its downfalls than indignant condemnation.

University of Accra
Situated in attractive grounds 14km from Accra along the Aburi Road, this is the oldest university in Ghana. In addition to a good bookshop and a library rich in colonial documents, the university boasts a mellow botanical garden (behind the Department of Zoology) of special interest to birdwatchers, and – obviously – it is a good place to meet Ghanaian students. To get there, catch a tro-tro from the station located on the northwest side of Nkrumah Circle.

La Beach
This is Accra's best swimming beach, situated in front of the Labadi Beach Hotel, and easily reached by using a shared taxi or tro-tro from Nkrumah Circle or Tema station to Nungua. In addition to the beach itself, which is reasonably safe for swimming depending on the strength of the undertow, there are several shady outdoor bars here, a couple of cheap restaurants, and at least two pool tables, warped ingeniously by the constant exposure to the sun. Thursday night is the best time to come partying here.

Coco Beach

Further out of town, about 20 minutes' walk and signposted from the Tema Road between Nungua and Teshie, this is another good beach, based around a resort that's popular with overland trucks and a good place to head for if you fancy camping near Accra. In addition to the good bar and restaurant, there's live music here most weekends.

Kaneshie Market

This large market lies along the Winneba road about 1km past Lamptey Circle, next to the synonymous tro-tro station. In terms of what you can buy, it differs little from Makola Market in the city centre, but it is generally quieter and less frequented by tourists, so the pressure to buy is minimal.

Kokrobite Beach (AAMAL)

Located about 20km west of Accra and 7km from the Winneba Road, Kokrobite Beach is best known as the site of the Academy of African Music and Arts Ltd (AAMAL), founded by the internationally known Ga percussionist Mustapha Tettey Addy. This is a good place to spend time if you'd like to be instructed in African drumming or music, and it also hosts a popular drumming and dancing show every Saturday and Sunday afternoon. The beach here is also good, though the potentially dangerous undertow means that you should ask before you swim. If you are thinking of staying here, you can camp inexpensively or take a room, the latter very good value at comfortably under US$10 double, while the restaurant serves top-quality seafood. For more information about AAMAL, tel: (021) 66-5987 or (027) 55-4042, or fax: (021) 66-7533.

For cheaper accommodation at Kokrobite, **Big Milly's Backyard** is a good backpackers' set-up, with dormitory beds for US$3 and rooms for US$6/8 single/double. Facilities include a bar and restaurant, book swap service, drum and dance lessons at around US$3 per hour, and live music on Saturday nights.

Be warned that Kokrobite Beach is developing an unenviable reputation as the one place in Ghana where casual theft is a regular problem, so don't take any valuables to the beach.

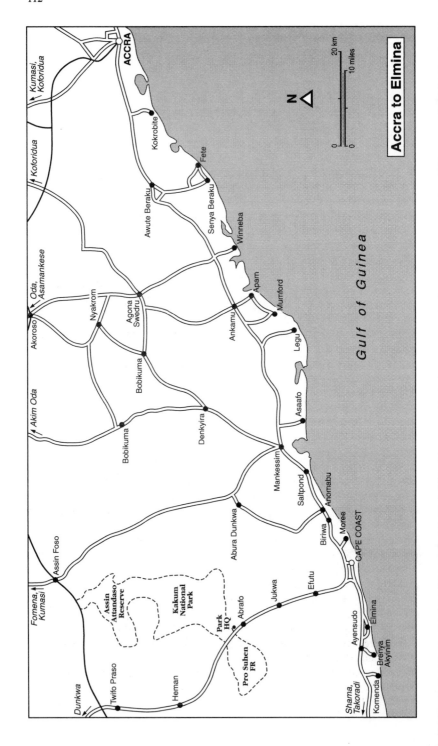

Accra to Elmina

Chapter Six

The Coast West of Accra

It is hardly surprising that Ghana's coast lies at the centre of its tourist industry. But what *is* remarkable – I daresay unique – is that such a magnificent chunk of tropical coastline should support a tourist industry based almost entirely around historical sightseeing. The reason for this is not that the beaches of the west coast fail to live up to every archetype of white-sanded, palm-fringed tropical nirvana – many of them do, even if riptides and currents pose a potentially fatal threat to swimmers in several places. No, it is that Ghana, alone in Africa, bears tangible physical evidence of an episode as barbarous and shameful as any in the recorded history of the continent: the trans-Atlantic slave trade.

For the sake of historical accuracy, I think it important to stress that the west coast of Ghana is scarcely unique in having supported a substantial slave trade before 1850. On the contrary, the large-scale trade in human lives arrived much earlier at several other parts of the West African coast, whereas Ghana remained relatively immune as a result of its importance to the international gold trade. Even in the mid-eighteenth century, by which time the slave trade out of Ghana had peaked, a greater volume of slaves was being exported annually from French Dahomey alone than from the entire coast of what is now Ghana.

What makes Ghana different to any other part of West Africa is simple. Elsewhere along the coast, trade was generally conducted out of makeshift buildings of which nothing is left today. In Ghana, by contrast, the slave trade was run out of a string of solidly built forts and castles, many constructed at the height of the gold-trading era and later adapted to include slave dungeons. The most substantial of these castles and forts are still standing today, the scratched walls of their dank dungeons a graphic reminder of two centuries of cruelty and despair, from the Fort of Good Hope in the east to Fort Apollinia in the west, via the imposing whitewashed castles that dominate the beachfronts of Cape Coast and Elmina.

The west coast of Ghana is neatly divided in two by the towns of Cape Coast and Elmina, which lie 15km apart roughly halfway between Accra and the Côte d'Ivoire. Formerly the Gold Coast headquarters of Britain and Holland respectively, Cape Coast and Elmina today form the main tourist focus in the region, their fully restored castles holding immense historical significance and impact. Both towns, however, warrant further exploration, as in different ways they both retain something of the mood of an older Africa, not merely in terms of historical buildings, but in their tangible sense of community. An added attraction of Elmina is that it boasts what is perhaps the country's most impressive selection of posuban shrines (see box on page 142).

While Cape Coast and Elmina could hardly be described as heaving with tourists, they do have a definite tourist industry, something that cannot be said of many other places along the west coast. True, relatively upmarket beach resorts at places such as Ankobra, Biriwa and Fete attract a steady trickle of well-heeled custom, while Kakum National Park near Cape Coast is probably the country's busiest game reserve, and Busua, and to a lesser extent the Beachway Hotel in Takoradi, sometimes host a busy backpacker scene. But such places are the exception on a coast that's dotted with strange, time-warped backwaters such as Senya Beraku, Apam, Anomabu, Shama, Sekondi, Prince's Town, Axim, Beyin and Mzulezu stilt village.

BETWEEN ACCRA AND CAPE COAST
Although Cape Coast is the first port of call for the majority of travellers exploring the coast west of Accra, a number of interesting possibilities lie on the coast between these two towns. Apam and Anomabu are probably the highlights for those with an interest in history, while Fete and Biriwa both have good beaches with relatively upmarket hotels and Winneba offers a more affordable opportunity to laze around on the beach.

Senya Beraku and Fete
Roughly 40km southwest of Accra as the crow flies, the small and somewhat isolated town of Senya Beraku is an obvious first port of call for unhurried travellers heading west from the capital. The main point of interest here is the eighteenth-century Fort of Good Hope, which boasts a dramatic cliff-top position overlooking a beach covered in colourful fishing boats and reportedly safe for swimming. The town itself is larger than you might expect, unbelievably run-down and populated by perhaps the noisiest children in Ghana but not without some curiosity value, notably a clutch of old churches and – bizarrely – a group of cracking concrete graves that date from the early twentieth century and stand right in the middle of a road (or at least what appears to have been a road before it was eroded to its present topographic state).

Senya Beraku first attracted the interest of Holland in the 1660s when a small trading lodge was built there, to be abandoned shortly afterwards. In 1704, the Dutch returned to the site, and with the permission of the Queen of Agona they started work on what would turn out to be the last fort they were to build in West Africa. Originally a very small, triangular construction designed to facilitate a low-key trade in gold, the Fort of Good Hope – would it be too heavy handed to note the irony? – ended up serving almost exclusively as a slave trading centre. In 1724, the fort was extended to cover more or less its present area, and a large slave dungeon was built into the southwest bastion. The Fort of Good Hope was handed to Britain as part of the 'fort exchange' treaty of 1868, and apparently fell into disuse at some point during the colonial era, since by the time of independence it was a partial ruin. In the 1980s, the fort was restored as a joint historical monument and resthouse.

Senya Beraku doesn't lack atmosphere. On the contrary, the combination of its beautiful coastal setting, grandiose European fort, slave dungeons, crumbling buildings, eroded streets and abject poverty could be seen to encapsulate much of what is disturbing about modern Africa. Senya Beraku is, in a word, depressing, and visitors may want to take a break to visit the nearby town of Fete – or Fetteh – reached from Senya Beraku by a scenic 6km dirt road, and overlooking a beach that's not only one of the prettiest in Ghana, but reportedly also offers some of the country's best surfing.

Getting there and away
Both Senya Beraku and Fete lie roughly 15km south of the main road between Accra and Winneba. Either town is reached via a reasonably good dirt road, leaving the main road about 2km west of Awutu Beraku. This road passes through the small town of Ojobi (notable for its bright pink church) and then about 5km before reaching the coast it forks, with the left fork going directly to Fete and the right fork directly to Senya Beraku. The best place to pick up public transport heading this way is not at the junction itself but at Awutu Beraku, where regular shared taxis leave for both Senya Beraku and Fete. It is advisable to pick up a taxi heading specifically to the town you want to visit.

Unless we were there on a bad day, it seems that no shared taxis run along the 6km road directly connecting Senya Beraku to Fete. If you want to visit one town from the other, your options amount to using shared taxis via Awutu (with the option of getting off at the fork, bearing in mind that most vehicles coming past here will already be full), to hiring a charter taxi (this shouldn't cost more than US$2 one way) or to walking, the latter a reasonably attractive option in one direction, provided that you're not carrying luggage.

Where to stay and eat
Oddly, when you consider the shabbiness and isolation of Senya Beraku itself, the **Fort of Good Hope** easily ranks as the most organised of the various forts now serving as a resthouse. Rooms cost between US$6.50 and US$7.50, and each of them has a double bed, electric light and fan. Other facilities include a communal lounge, clean shared toilet and shower, gift shop, bar with fridge, and restaurant serving chicken or fish with fried rice or chips for around US$3. The staff, too, seem unusually well-tuned to the needs of travellers. Bearing in mind that this fort at one point served as a slave dungeon, the very slickness of this operation (slick, that is, by Ghanaian standards) does teeter on the edge of tastelessness. Then again, you could argue that any economic uplift offered to this town by tourism must outweigh historical sensitivities. Still, it's difficult to imagine that

anybody would want to hold their wedding reception here, though the facility is advertised.

Fete is rapidly emerging as a popular beach resort area, and is now a recommended first stop out of Accra for relatively well-heeled travellers. Set on a beautiful beach 500m from town, the plush German **Till's No 1 Hotel** (tel: 027 55-0480, fax: 027 55-8247, website: www.till.net\TillsNo1) offers outstanding value for money in its price range, with eight standard rooms at US$40/45 single/double and four suites at US$63 (all with hot shower, ac and TV, and suites also have a video machine and fridge). Seafood and German meals are served, in the US$5–10 range, while facilities and activities include beach and indoor games, mini-golf, canoe trips, fishing, windsurfing, drumming and dancing lessons, as well as minibus excursions with a driver. Tills is due for expansion in 2000, and it was joined in 1999 by the similarly priced **Whitesands Beach Club** (tel: 027 55-0707, fax: 027-774064, email: whsands@ighmail.com), a Hopi Indian-style building on the beach east of Fete town.

Winneba

The largest coastal settlement between Accra and Cape Coast, Winneba is the traditional capital of the Afutu, whose King Ghartey IV was the prime initiator behind and president of the Fante Confederation of 1868–73. Winneba was also the site of a reasonably important British fort from 1673 until 1812, when the town was evacuated by its settler community following an Ashanti invasion in which the British commander was tortured to death (for decades after this, passing British ships fired a broadside when they passed the site of the fort). Traces of the old fort can be seen in the Methodist church built on the same site by missionaries in the late nineteenth century. Otherwise, Winneba's compact town centre has the atmosphere of a historical port, all winding alleys, malodorous fishy markets and fading colonial buildings, but no individual buildings of great historical interest, so far as I am aware.

For travellers, Winneba is most attractive for its busy fishing harbour and the beach that lies immediately to its west. You might want to take a look at the old European and Royal cemeteries, which face each other about 300m from the fishing harbour, and hopefully you'll have more luck than us trying to locate the worthwhile posuban shrine that reportedly lies between town and beach. The one time of the year when Winneba changes status from diverting backwater to must-visit is on the first weekend of May, when it hosts the Aboakyer Festival. This 300-year-old festival, probably the most famous in the country, is centred on the 'deer hunt', in which Winneba's two oldest *asafo* companies, dressed in full traditional regalia, compete to be the first to hunt down and capture alive an antelope using only their bare hands. The festival carries on throughout the weekend, climaxing twice: on Saturday when the deer hunt takes place amid much noise and colour until one or other company wins, then at 14.00 on Sunday when the captured animal is sacrificed to the oracles at the Pemkye Otu fetish.

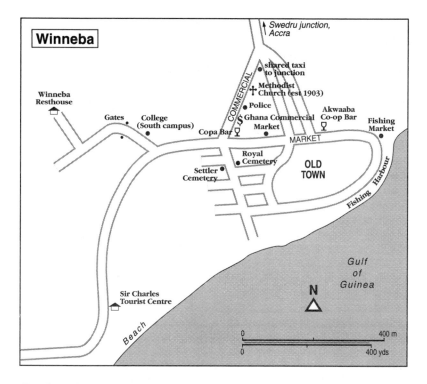

Getting there and away

Winneba lies about 10km south of the main road between Accra and Cape Coast. From whichever direction you are coming, you'll be unlikely to find transport heading directly into Winneba. Instead, take a tro-tro to Winneba junction (also known as Swedru junction) from where regular shared taxis make their way to the old town centre.

Where to stay and eat

There's a pretty good selection of accommodation in and around Winneba; nothing very plush, but most of it at prices which only go to reinforce the feeling that relatively few tourists make it down this way.

Winneba's nominal tourist hotel is the **Sir Charles Tourist Centre** (tel: 0432 22189), a sprawling chalet complex right above the beach about 1km from the town centre. The accommodation, though hardly lavish, is very reasonably priced. A basic room with one double bed costs US$6, a similar room with a fan costs US$7.50 and a sea-facing room costs US$8.50. Larger suites cost US$12, while chalets cost US$14 and bungalows from US$24 to US$45. The restaurant is in a circular hall of absurdly vast proportions; the menu is correspondingly small (fish with rice or yam when we visited!) and prices lie somewhere in between at US$4.50 per plate. The main drawback of the Sir Charles is quite simply that it is ugly: the combination of brutal 1970s architecture and tackily fading pink and blue paint entirely negates any visual pleasure that might otherwise be extracted from this attractive beach.

Altogether less aesthetically confrontational is the **Winneba Resthouse** (or 'Army Resthouse' as it's also known), which lies within the College of Education Southern Campus off the road between the town centre and the Sir Charles. This place has a great view, perched on a hilltop facing a beach to the west, and the large s/c double rooms with fan are really good value at US$5. The only drawback is the distance from the beach – a good ten-minute walk.

There are a couple of hotels along the road between Winneba and the junction, but they are no better than the ones in town and more expensive – in any case, it is difficult to see why any tourist would bother coming to Winneba only to stay in the scruffy suburbs miles from the sea. Worth mentioning, however, is the **Yes Motel**, in a field about 300m and signposted from the Cape Coast side of Winneba junction opposite the tro-tro station. Again, it's difficult to see *why* any traveller would stay here with such good options available near the beach, but if you do then it is indisputably good value – basic room with double bed, fan and bathroom shared with one other room for US$3.50 and large s/c twin with two double beds, fan and sitting room attached for US$7.50. The Yes Motel has a bar but no restaurant – there's plenty of cheap chop available at the junction and Western food at a smart garden restaurant called **Hut de Eric** on the Accra side of the junction.

Apam

Memorable for its picturesque fishing harbour laden with colourful pirogues, Apam would perhaps be my first choice were I in a position to stay in only one place between Accra and Cape Coast. The centrepiece of the town is Fort Leydsaamsheid (Fort Patience), built by the Dutch in 1697, captured by the British in 1782, returned to the Dutch three years later, then finally handed back to Britain in 1868. Now a resthouse, this must be about the smallest extant fort on the Ghanaian coast, and the cramped dimensions of the prison cell suggests that it was never used to store slaves to any serious extent, if at all. The most impressive thing about the fort is its position, on top of a sharp little hill which offers a great view over the town and harbour to one side, and a pretty, secluded beach to the other. Several other buildings in Apam strike me as being of some antiquity, including the turn-of-the-century Methodist Church and the house belonging to Chief Quaye.

Getting there and away

Apam lies about 15km south of the main Accra–Cape Coast road. The junction at Ankamu is easily reached by tro-tro coming in either direction, and regular shared taxis run from the junction to the town.

Where to stay and eat

Fort Patience doubles as a **resthouse**. There are seven small bedrooms, each containing one three-quarter bed, and going for US$2.50. The only facilities are bucket showers. There is no restaurant in the town, but you can buy a

Patas monkey

Above: *Africa's only 'canopy walk' is suspended through the rainforest of Kakum National Park*

Below: *Kintampo Falls*

Above left: *Bay duiker*
Above right: *Mona monkey, considered sacred in some villages*
Centre: *Elephant, Mole National Park*
Below: *Sacred crocodile, Paga*

Above: *The mud-and-stick mosque at Larabanga, said locally to date to 1421*

Below: *Traditional compound, Nakpanduri*

fair selection of food and drinks around the market and tro-tro station. The only other accommodation in the area is the **King Pobee Hotel** at least 1km out of town, just off the road towards the junction and close to the police station – any shared taxi coming from the junction will know where to drop you. Rooms here cost around US$7–10.

Mankessim and Saltpond

The busy junction town of Mankessim may not be much to look at today, but it is widely regarded to be the focal point from which the Fante expanded into much of what is now south-central Ghana. The Fante tradition is that Mankessim was founded by three priests who went by the name of Obunumankuma, Oson and Odapagyan, an event that evidently occurred at least half a century before the Portuguese reached the Ghanaian coast. Mankessim has had its moments in more recent history too: it was here in 1868 that the chiefs of the Akan states of south-central Ghana met to form the Fante Confederation, of which Mankessim served as *ipso facto* capital under the presidency of King Ghartey IV of Winneba until the confederation disbanded in 1873.

The most likely reason you'd want to stop at Mankessim is to see the famous posuban that lies about 300m from the central traffic circle along the same road as the tro-tro station. This must be about the largest shrine of its sort in Ghana, a peculiar three-storey construction adorned with around a dozen life-size human sculptures (see also page 142). You might also want to ask about visiting a sacred shrine called Nananompow – Grave of the Fathers – traditionally thought to be where the three founding fathers of Fante were buried, as well as the seat of the Fante gods. The most interesting days to visit Mankessim are Wednesday and Saturday, when there is a good market.

Saltpond is basically Mankessim's coastal twin, lying about 8km to its southwest. Aside from having a reasonably attractive beach, Saltpond boasts two good posuban shrines, but offers little else that's of interest to travellers.

Getting there and away

Mankessim is an important transport hub, easily reached by tro-tro from Winneba, Cape Coast and points in between. There is little direct transport to Saltpond except from Mankessim, though there is the option of disembarking from a vehicle heading to Cape Coast at Saltpond junction and then walking or hiring a taxi to cover the last 1km or so.

Where to stay

The only accommodation that I'm aware of in Mankessim is the inexpensive **Clare Palace Hotel**. Alternatively, you could stay at the **Palm Beach Hotel** at Saltpond junction, with its view over the town and beach, and good s/c doubles with ac, fan, TV and fridge for US$17. There is no restaurant, but the rooftop bar would be a nice place to sit in the evening. Also near the junction, the **Nkubeom Hotel** has more basic double rooms for around US$10. There are chop houses in both Mankessim and Saltpond, but no proper restaurants.

THE AKAN

The most numerically significant of Ghana's four ethno-linguistic groupings, the Akans of the southern and central part of the country embrace several dozen culturally similar and historically allied peoples, the best known of whom are probably the Ashanti of the Kumasi area and the Fante of the central coast. Most travellers to Ghana will find themselves coming into regular contact with several Akan cultural institutions, not least because the country's two main travel circuits pass almost exclusively through Akan territories, but even those who travel further afield – into the Ewe heartland of Volta Region for instance – will soon recognise the tangible Akan influence over the cultural and political organisation of many of their neighbours.

Every Akan village has its chief, whose position is not as you might expect determined by pure hereditary. Most Akan chiefs are selected by a Council of Elders; although a nominated chief will generally be of aristocratic birth, he will be selected on the basis of his perceived capabilities and may be stripped of his powers if he does not perform satisfactorily or indulges in tyrannical behaviour. Practically throughout Ghana the power of a chief is denoted by his possession of the royal stool, which is typically made of blackened wood (notable exceptions being the famous golden stool of Ashanti and the silver stool of Mampong). So significant is the royal stool that Akan chiefs are referred to as having been enstooled when they ascend to power and destooled should they lose that position. In many Akan territories, a traditional hierarchy of chiefs is maintained – the King of Ashanti, for instance, is considered paramount to the chiefs of such vassal states as Mampong and Jauben, who in turn preside over several small local chieftaincies. It is customary in Akan societies as well as in other parts of Ghana for visitors to a village to pay their respects to the chief, a custom that is still enforced in villages that receive few foreign visitors.

Most Akan societies show remarkably similar political structures, and the chief is far from being the only figure of importance. Every chief is served by a Council of Elders, a body to which he must refer all important matters and which, as already mentioned, has the power to destool him. Another very important figure is the queen mother, a misleading title since she will not necessarily be the mother of a queen, but serves as spiritual mother to the chief. A queen mother will traditionally work closely with the Council of Elders in selecting a new chief, as well as sitting in on all council meetings and presiding over all births and menstruation rites. Other important figures in Akan society include the Akyeame, the chief's official spokesman and carrier of a royal staff, as well as the Adontenhene, the leader of the main military body. Every Akan society is divided into several *asafo*, military companies that play an important role in defence as well as in the arts (see box Posuban shrines page 142), and one of the few Akan institutions to follow purely patrilineal lines of inheritance.

The basic unit of traditional Akan society is the extended family, an institution that is maintained along matrilineal lines, evidently on the basis that one can always be certain of the identity of a child's mother but not of its father. This is changing in modern Ghana, where patrilineal inheritance lines have assumed greater importance than in the past, and (in urban areas particularly) the nuclear family is seen by many to be of greater importance than the extended one. Traditionally, the Akan regard every person to be comprised of three parts: blood, semen and soul. Blood is perceived to be the most significant of these, and is inherited from the mother as a signifier of family. Semen, as you might expect, is the father's contribution, and it determines the personality and other individual

Anomabu

This small seaside town situated about halfway between Mankessim and Cape Coast has been an important trading centre since before Britain settled at Cape Coast, when it served as the coastal trade outlet for the Fante Empire based at Mankessim. Anomabu has a strong history of attributes of the person. The soul is believed to be the part of God that enters each child at birth.

Interestingly, the Akan regard a person's soul to be linked to the day of the week on which he or she was born. For this reason, most Ghanaians' first name is not a given name as such, but a name determined by his or her day of birth. It is in fact the child's second name that is chosen by the parents, eight days after the child is born. It is normally that of a respected family member, selected in the belief that the child will grow to have some of the attributes of the person after whom it has been named. Names associated with the day of birth are as follows:

Day	Male	Female
Sunday	Kwasi	Akosua, Asi
Monday	Kwadwo, Kojo	Adwoa, Ajao
Tuesday	Kwabena, Kobina	Abena, Araba
Wednesday	Kwaku	Akua
Thursday	Yao, Ekow	Yaa
Friday	Kofi	Afua, Afia, Efua
Saturday	Kwame, Kwamena	Ama

The religious ideas of the Akan are too complex to do justice to here. Briefly, all Akan societies believe in one omnipotent God, but they also pay homage to any number of minor local deities (some villages in Ghana have more than 70 local shrines, which may take the form of trees or rocks or any other natural feature) and like most African societies place high emphasis on the veneration of ancestors. Many Akan villages have a totem, often a particular type of animal that may not be killed or eaten by members of that village (one of the best-known totems in Ghana is the sacred monkeys of Baobeng and Fiema). Often the totem has been for selected for reasons bound up in the oral history of that village. At Paga, for instance, it is believed that the founder of the village was saved by a crocodile, while the people of Baobeng believe that the sacred monkeys are the descendants of villagers transformed into monkeys by the magical powers of a king who died before he could return them to human form.

At some point in their travels, visitors are likely to encounter one of the most remarkable aspects of Akan society: its colourful and vibrant funerals. Unusually, Ghanaian societies tend to separate the burial ceremony from the actual funeral – generally by a period of at least three months and sometimes by as long as two years! At the risk of gross oversimplification, a person's burial is generally a quiet and dignified moment, though it is often preceded by wailing and singing, and it is followed by at least nine days of quiet mourning and fasting by close relatives. The funeral itself is traditionally held on a Monday or Thursday several months after the person died, though these days it is most often held on a Saturday for obvious pragmatic reasons. The general tone of the occasion is one of celebration rather than mourning, marked by exuberant drumming and dancing, not to say heavy drinking – on attending a Ghanaian funeral, you can't help but feel that it displays an altogether more convincing belief in some sort of afterlife than its sombre Christian equivalent.

For a good overview of the more complex aspects of Akan culture, I recommend Peter Sarong's book *Ghana in Retrospect* (Ghana Publishing Company, 1974), which is readily available and inexpensive in most Accra bookshops.

independence, despite having been settled intermittently by various European powers. In 1630, the Dutch built a fort at Anomabu, only to abandon it in 1664 due to pressure from Britain. After the British constructed Fort Charles on the beach in 1674, Anomabu became perhaps the biggest slave emporium on the Gold Coast, dealing mainly with the freelance 'ten-percenters'. Britain left Anomabu in 1731, largely as a result of disagreements with the local traders, and destroyed the fort so that it couldn't be captured by a rival power. The French then settled at Anomabu for a period, attracted by the established trade in slaves, but they were expelled by Britain in 1753.

Anomabu today has more to occupy visitors than first impressions might suggest. Away from the somewhat mundane main road, the skyline is dominated by a large, sandstone church and the fort, constructed by the British over the foundations of the older Fort Charles in 1756. One of the most solidly constructed pre-twentieth-century buildings anywhere on the Gold Coast, Anomabu's fort was extended upwards by one storey during the mid-nineteenth-century reign of King William IV, since when it has been known as Fort William. It now serves as a prison, and entrance is forbidden for security reasons (as is photography from most angles), but there is nothing preventing you from walking around the perimeter.

Adjacent to Fort William, there's a substantial ruin which, according to one knowledgeable local, actually predates the fort. About 100m further east, on a beach dotted with coconut palms and (be careful!) fresh turds, there's a sanded-up swimming pool in the rocks, probably dating to the eighteenth century – a good spot from where to take a discreet snap of the fort. Look out to sea and you'll see the rock after which Anomabu is named – seasonally the site of a breeding colony of gulls.

Several of Ghana's most notable posuban shrines lie in Anomabu. There are in all seven shrines in the town, one built by each of the seven asafo companies, and all easy to find. Don't miss the shrine belonging to Company Three, an improbable assemblage of sculpted animals ranging from a cheetah to a whale, adorned with several smaller carvings of animals in grotesque proportions. This shrine is situated about 50m from the main road facing the Ebenezer Hotel behind a contorted strangler *ficus* tree that's one of the most impressive of the town's 70-plus gods. There are also three substantial posuban shrines tucked away in the tight network of alleys lying immediately west of the fort, notably the shrine built by Company Seven, shaped like a European ship and the size of a small house. The oldest shrine, built by Company One, is not as impressive to look at, but it is of special importance as the site where a new village chief must be sworn in – symbolised by the lock and key depicted on the shrine.

You're free to wander around Anomabu and look at the shrines, and you're unlikely to be asked for money unless you take photos. Be warned, however, that the moment you do show a camera you'll not only be expected to pay a separate libation at each shrine (which gets costly!), but are likely to get caught up in all sorts of unpleasantness. (See also *Posuban shrines* box on page 142.)

Alongside the main road next to the Ebenezer Hotel, you may notice a small memorial, erected in 1937 to commemorate Anomabu's most famous son, George Ekem Ferguson (born Ekow Atta in 1864), a trained geographer and natural linguist who was perhaps the single most important pioneer in expanding Britain's knowledge of the Ghanaian interior before his death in battle near Wa at the age of 33.

Getting there and away
Anomabu is bisected by the main coastal road between Mankessim and Cape Coast, and tro-tros heading between these towns will drop you right in front of either hotel. When you are ready to move on, it's easy to find a seat in a passing tro-tro in either direction – just walk outside your hotel to the main road! If you are coming to Anomabu directly from Accra or Takoradi, you may be tempted to use the STC bus which stops at the Ebenezer Hotel for a meal break – bearing in mind that you'll have to pay the full fare even if you disembark here.

Where to stay and eat
The new **Anomabu Beach Resort** lies on an expansive beach nestled in a stand of coconut palms. Large mud-clad and thatched rooms start at US$30 for a double, while standing tents are available at US$12 per double and camping costs US$3 per person. Good meals are served between 07.30 and 21.00.

The friendly and central **Ebenezer Hotel** has large rooms for US$5/7 with carpets, fan, hot water and balcony. The restaurant is where STC buses between Accra and Takoradi stop, and it serves excellent and inexpensive chop. The more upmarket **Adaano Hotel**, on the Accra side of the main road, has doubles with fan for US$7.50 and ac s/c doubles for US$17. The restaurant serves good meals in the US$2–3 range, and ice-cold drinks, best enjoyed on the rooftop balcony.

Biriwa
Regarded as one of Ghana's most attractive beaches, Biriwa was something of a hippy hangout in the 1970s, but these days – except at weekends – it is used more or less exclusively by residents of the Biriwa Beach Hotel (tel: 042 33333, fax: 042 33555/33666, email: bbh@ncs.com.gh, web: www.biriwabeach.com.gh). One of the most appealing upmarket retreats on the Ghanaian coast, positioned on a bluff overlooking the beach, the Biriwa Beach Hotel is less expensive than appearances suggest at US$62/69 single/double (you'd pay in the US$100–200 bracket for this sort of luxury in East Africa) and it has an excellent restaurant with a menu reflecting not only its proximity to the sea, but also its German ownership.

Moree
This large village (or should that be small town?) about 5km northeast of Cape Coast is the site of Fort Nassau. This was the first fort built by the Dutch on the Gold Coast, using bricks brought from Holland, and it served as their headquarters from its construction in 1612 until the capture of Elmina Fort in 1637. Now a substantial ruin, Fort Nassau is clearly visible on a hill above the town, where the standing walls are interspersed with the circular, mud, fish-smoking ovens so characteristic of this part of the coast. More engaging than the ruined fort, however, is the view from the hill: on one side, Moree stretches out in all its corrugated-iron-roofed glory; on the

other side is a beach as beautiful as any in Ghana, dotted with typically colourful fishing boats.

Moree lies only 2km from the main Accra road (though it feels so isolated that could be 200km). At the junction you'll find some of the most dilapidated taxis in Ghana waiting to trundle down to Moree in blissful, pothole-dodging lethargy. Alternatively, direct shared taxis between Moree and Cape Coast take about 15 minutes. There is no formal accommodation in Moree, but you could ask about a room in a private house or try camping on the beach.

CAPE COAST

The first capital of Britain's Gold Coast colony and modern capital of Ghana's Central Region, Cape Coast is steeped in history. Architecturally, it has little in common with the old Swahili towns of Africa's east coast; in atmosphere, however, the streets and alleys of the town centre share with, say, Lamu or Mombasa a comfortable, lived-in feel, and a genuine sense of community – this is one of those towns where the distinction between administrative, business and residential districts is so blurred as to be meaningless. Cape Coast is a fascinating town to explore, its relative antiquity reflected not only in an endlessly surprising range of architectural styles spanning three centuries, but also in the organic shape of the old town, with roads hugging the curves of low hills.

Cape Coast was probably founded in the early fifteenth century. Its English name is a derivation of *Cabo Corso* – Short Cape – the name given to it by the Portuguese captains Joao de Santarem and Pedro de Escobar in 1471. Two contradictory traditions relate to the origin of Cape Coast's vernacular name: Oguaa. One tradition holds that Oguaa is a derivation of the Fante word *Gua* (market) and that Cape Coast was originally founded as a market town. The other explanation is that it derives from that of the village's founder, a hunter from Efutu remembered by the name Egya Oguaa.

While the truth of the local traditions is difficult to verify, we do know that by the time the British captains John Lok and William Towerson reached the Gulf of Guinea, in 1555 and 1556 respectively, Oguaa was a fishing village of roughly 20 small houses enclosed within a reed fence and presided over by a chief who went by the rather intriguing name of Don Juan. Nothing more is heard of Oguaa for two generations, until 1610, when a Portuguese lodge was built at an undetermined site on the outskirts of the village, which by that time probably extended from the beach north to what is now Jackson Street.

The rapidly growing village changed hands several times in the seventeenth century. In 1652, the abandoned Portuguese lodge was occupied by Swedes, then a mere six years later it was captured by the Danes, who signed a treaty with the Efutu paramount chief allowing them to construct a larger, triangular fort at nearby Amanful. The new fort fell briefly into the clutches of the Dutch – the dominant European power in the region at that time, with large forts at nearby Moree and Elmina – before it was taken over by Britain following the Anglo-Dutch War of 1664–45. From that time onwards, Cape Coast was Britain's headquarters on the Gulf of Guinea, and from 1672 onwards the British begin work on expanding and converting the fort to become modern-day Cape Coast Castle.

By the late seventeenth century, Cape Coast had grown from a small fishing village to one of the largest and most important trading ports along the coast. In 1693 the Paramount Chief of Efutu moved his capital from the inland village of Efutu to what is now Victoria Park, on the west side of modern-day Cape Coast Castle. Two years later, a visitor estimated the number of houses in the small town to exceed 500, and it is clear that by this time the modern town centre had more or less assumed its present shape.

Cape Coast's importance derived from its position as the link between the maritime trade routes of the European powers and the terrestrial trade routes through to the Sahel. Throughout the eighteenth century, Cape Coast's economy was dominated by its role at the heart of the trans-Atlantic slave trade – at any given time before 1807, when trading in slaves was abolished by the British parliament, there would have been up to 1,500 captured individuals awaiting shipment in the dungeons of the expanded Cape Coast Castle.

Following the re-establishment of legitimate trade from the Gulf of Guinea in 1821, all British castles along the coast were formally taken over by the British Crown and placed under the governor of Sierra Leone. Cape Coast served as the administrative headquarters of Britain's castles from 1828 until 1874, when it became the first seat of government of Britain's Gold Coast colony. Three years later, this role was assumed by Accra, and although Cape Coast has hardly slid into backwater status since, one still senses that the town centre would be instantly recognisable to a time traveller from the Victorian era.

Getting there and away

Several STC buses run directly between Accra and Cape Coast daily, taking roughly three hours in either direction, the exact timing strongly dependent on how quickly the bus can get through the outskirts of Accra. The STC bus station is opposite the Methodist church.

There are also regular tro-tros from Cape Coast to most main coastal towns from Takoradi to Accra. Tro-tros to Accra and other destinations along the Accra road east of Cape Coast generally leave from the vicinity of the main lorry station on the junction of Sarbeh and Residential roads. Tro-tros to Kakum National Park leave from Kotoka station near Kotokuraba Market. Shared taxis to Elmina and other local destinations leave from Kotokuraba taxi station. Tro-tros to Takoradi and points west along the coast leave from in front of Joyce Lovers Spot at the Elf garage at the junction of Elmina and Jukwa roads.

Where to stay

The most upmarket hotel in Cape Coast is the new and not very imaginatively named **Cape Coast Hotel** (tel: 33632, fax: 33457) on the

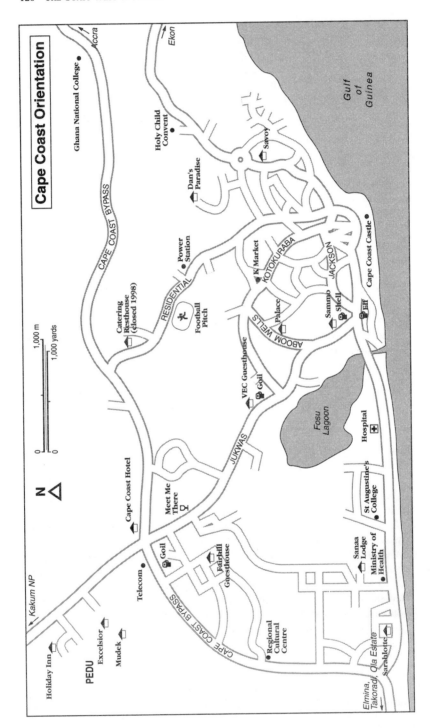

traffic circle at the junction of Jukwa Road and the Cape Coast bypass. It seems a very pleasant place, though lacking atmosphere, and the rooms are good value at US$40 for a s/c double with ac, fridge, TV and hot water. A major disadvantage of staying here is that it's a good 30-minute walk from town, though you can easily pick up a shared or charter taxi to the town centre at the traffic circle.

More homely, but rather out of the way, the **Fairhill Guesthouse** (tel: 33322, fax: 33323) has very good s/c doubles for US$34 with ac, fridge, TV and video (there's a library of videos to watch), fridge and hot water. It is a bit difficult to find, perched on an isolated hill in the marshy area to the west of Fosu Lagoon. With private transport, the guesthouse is about 1.4km and clearly signposted from next to the Goil garage on the Cape Coast bypass about 500m from the traffic circle mentioned above. Without private transport, I'd get a taxi out there, though once you know the way it's only 10 minutes' walk from Jukwa Road where you can pick up shared taxis to the town centre.

The **Sanaa Lodge** (tel: 32391, fax: 32898) is probably the most comfortable of Cape Coast's upper-range establishments, with 30 rooms costing around US$40/50 single/double, all s/c with satellite TV, fridge and ac. Facilities include a large swimming pool and a good restaurant. The lodge is set on a rise above the Ministry of Health, with a view over the beach, about 2km west of the bridge across Fosu Lagoon.

One place you needn't bother yourself about at present is the **Catering Resthouse**. Formerly owned by the government, and presumably now private, this place was closed in early 1998 and I was unable to ascertain when – and indeed whether – it is ever likely to resume business.

About the smartest of the reasonably central places, **Dan's Paradise** (tel: 32942) has good-value s/c, ac rooms with a bed large enough to sleep a rugby team for US$20, or US$25 should you want TV, fridge and radio. The path up to the hotel is steep enough to justify taking a taxi if you have luggage. There's a fair restaurant attached with meals costing around US$5.

Even more central, the long-serving and relatively atmospheric **Savoy Hotel** is adequate without being anything special, and the run-down s/c double rooms are indifferent value for money at US$14 with fan or US$18 with ac. Far more modern, but otherwise much of a muchness, the **Amkred Guesthouse** has adequate s/c doubles with ac for US$18.

Dropping in price, the **Palace Hotel** is a well-established travellers' haunt some 15 minutes' walk from the castle on Aboom Road close to the junction with Aboom Wells Road. Large clean rooms with fan and basin cost US$7/8 single/double, while s/c doubles cost US$10. The communal showers are well kept and appear never to run out of water. There's a good bar downstairs, a reasonable restaurant upstairs, and grilled kebabs on the pavement in the evening.

Similar in standard, and consistently recommended by travellers, the three-storey **Sammo Guesthouse** is conveniently close to a tro-tro station, and less than ten minutes' walk from the castle. Several types of room are available, starting at US$5/6 for a single/double with fan using communal showers to US$13 for a large s/c double. The breezy rooftop bar is one of the best places in Cape Coast for a drink and meal.

Marginally cheaper accommodation is available in the suburb of Pedu, about 5km from the town centre along the road towards Kakum National Park. Quite why anybody would want to spend their time in Ghana's most rewarding town stuck away in the scruffy suburbs, I don't know, but if saving cents is the order of the day, try the **Pedu Holiday Inn, Hotel Mudek** or **Excelsior Guesthouse**, all within 500m of the main road.

A more attractive out-of-town option is the **Sarahlotte Hotel** in Osa Estate, which lies about 4km from Cape Coast centre along the Elmina Road, a mere 50m from the beach and no more than 500m from the intersection with the main Takoradi–Accra road. A small family-run place, this has a variety of rooms ranging from a large double with fan, using clean communal showers, for US$10, to a s/c double with fan, TV and fridge for US$16. Meals can be prepared by request, or you could eat in town – all shared taxis and tro-tros between Cape Coast and Elmina run right past this place.

Where to eat and drink

The beachfront **Castle Restaurant**, once *the* place to eat in Cape Coast, burnt to the ground in May 1998; rumours that it will eventually be rebuilt hadn't translated into reality in late 1999. For the meantime, an attractive place for an evening meal is the Sammo Guesthouse – the food is good and reasonably priced, and although the ground-floor restaurant lacks atmosphere, you can ask to eat at the rooftop bar, which usually catches a breeze and offers a good view over the town.

For breakfast and lunch, several travellers have recommended the **Cape Café** (aka Women's Centre) above the Methodist Book Shop on Commercial Street opposite Barclays Bank. In addition to offering decent, inexpensive meals and selling some lovely local fabrics, this is a non-profit organisation that provides shelter to the homeless etc.

The **Aloumie Krom Garden Bar and Restaurant** is in a closed courtyard, so it can get rather stifling, but otherwise it is a good place for a chilled beer and local meal. It's particularly convenient if you're staying around the corner at the Palace Hotel.

Near London Bridge, **Coconut Delight** does memorable fresh fruit juice as well as good spring rolls and various other snacks and light meals, including breakfast. There are a great many small chop bars in and around the town centre: the snack bars in the court and the Kingsway Department Store are worth a visit.

Finally, you can normally buy fresh coconuts for drinking from a vendor who stands in front of the Mobil garage on Jackson Street, while pineapples and other fruits are sold by vendors along Itsin Street near the castle.

Where to visit
Cape Coast Castle

This World Heritage Site warrants at least two hours' exploration, at least if you want to see it properly. Visitors must pay for a ticket to see the castle at the entrance: the charge is US$2 per person for a self-guided tour (with a useful pamphlet provided), or US$4 per person with a guide. The ticket is good for one visit only, except by special arrangement. Photography is permitted at no extra fee.

It is widely accepted that the modern Cape Coast Castle stands on the site of the Swedish Fort Carolusbourg, built from wood in 1653 and fortified with stone the next year (note that there is little foundation for the claim that the original Portuguese lodge at Cape Coast stood on this site). After Cape Coast was captured by Britain in 1665, the fort was expanded to be comparable in size and strength with the nearby Dutch fort at Elmina, and in the 1680s the slave dungeons were constructed in such a way that they were accessible only from the seaward side of the fort. A second phase of expansion, prompted in part by the notorious leakiness of the roof, took place roughly between 1760 and 1795. By the end of this period, the castle had assumed its modern, loosely pentagonal shape, and practically no traces of the original Swedish fort remained.

It is difficult to know quite how to react to Cape Coast Castle. For all the horrors that have taken place within its dungeons, the first thing that impresses about the building is its architectural scale. And the pervading mood, far from being sinister or evil, is innocuously bureaucratic. The castle has been so sanitised as to be – well, if not quite unreal, then wholly un-African, remote from everything around and outside it. I don't know what to make of the recently whitewashed bastions adorned with neat rows of freshly painted black cannon; or of staff so breezily well-trained that you half expect them to spout 'have a nice day' as they hand you a ticket; or of the gift shop that lies within the castle, or of the lively and aesthetically pleasing Castle Restaurant on the adjacent beach – or of the only 'washroom' that I've ever seen in anglophone Africa. I mean, for goodness sake, if you cannot call a urinal a urinal, then how on earth are you supposed to take in the fact that you are inside a building which for a time stood at the heart of *the* greatest involuntary diaspora in human history?

The museum helps place things in perspective – it houses an absorbing, sobering sequence of displays charting the origin and mechanisms of the slave trade, the scale of the resultant diaspora, and its aftermath in the hands of inspirational black leaders such as Marcus Garvey and Martin Luther King. It is emphatically worth taking a guided tour, to help interpret what you see. But, ultimately, it is the time you spend in the slave dungeons that cuts most closely, their stone walls still marked by the desperate scratching of those imprisoned within them. There are three dungeons in all. The oldest was built before 1790 on the southeastern bastion. The later male dungeon was built below Dalzel's Tower in 1792, while the female dungeon is on the eastern wall, near the exit to sea that bore the grim nickname 'Door of No Return'.

Those buried in the courtyard of the castle include the Reverend Philip Kwakwe (1741–1816), a native of Cape Coast who became the first Anglican priest of African origin. Also buried here is the novelist Letetia Elizabeth London (1802–38) and her husband George Maclean (1801–47),

Cape Coast Town Centre

governor of Cape Coast from 1830 until 1843 and Judicial Assessor of the town from 1843 until his death.

Around the old town

Several of the hills in Cape Coast have been fortified at some point in their history, but only two such outforts now survive. Fort Victoria, to the northeast of the castle, was constructed in 1837 on the site of a ruined fort known as 'Phipp's Tower' and built in 1712. On Dawson's Hill, Fort William is now a lighthouse and has been since 1855, but it was constructed over the older Smith's Tower, built of mud and stone in 1820. Both forts are in good condition and welcome visitors.

Otherwise the centre of Cape Coast may lack individual landmarks, but it is certainly well endowed with Victorian-era buildings, especially along Commercial and Jackson streets and Beulah Lane – and there is even a bust of Queen Victoria standing in her namesake park to prove it! Many of these old buildings are solidly constructed brick homes with an enclosed upper-floor balcony. The area around Dawson's Hill is one of the best preserved parts of the old town, with Coronation Street in particular boasting several two- and three-storey buildings architecturally characteristic of Cape Coast in the mid- to late nineteenth century. Particularly notable is the now derelict building near the junction with Commercial Street, built as a hotel in the 1880s and later a convent.

Possibly the oldest unfortified building in Cape Coast, albeit now rather run-down and imposed upon, is the three-storey former Government House opposite the Methodist Church off Jackson Street, also known as 'Hope Smith House' and now the STC office. It is known that this building was leased to the government by one Caroline Jackson in 1850, but it is unclear how much older it actually is – it seems reasonable to assume it was built before or during the period 1817–22 (when John Hope-Smith was governor), and it may conceivably have been built in the late eighteenth century.

Near to this, on Royal Lane, the former Convent of St Mary is perhaps the best-preserved building of its kind in Cape Coast. Originally built by an Ashanti prince in around 1850, this building was bought by a community of nuns in 1891 and served as a convent until 1975, since when it has been only intermittently occupied. I only read about this after we were in Cape Coast, but based on descriptions it could well be the building that now houses the tourist office.

There are a few posuban shrines in Cape Coast, but none is very impressive. At the centre of the traffic circle on the junction of Ashanti and Commercial roads, there is a small posuban-like sculpture of a crab. Although recently placed there, this statue has a great significance as the crab is one of the important symbols of Cape Coast – one tradition has it that the village was first founded because of the good crab meat available, and that it was originally called Kotokuraba (crab village), still the name of the town's main market and the nearby tro-tro station.

Near the above junction, London Bridge is a rather odd and unimposing little bridge dating to the late nineteenth century and appropriately garnished with painted Union Jacks and the like – it's worth crossing if only to have a fruit juice at Coconut Delight.

Further information
The regional tourist office is probably the best source of up-to-date information about Cape Coast and other places in Central Region, though the not unfamiliar prevailing attitude seems to be that all the answers must be in the handful of pamphlets and maps they stock. It's not that you'll meet with an unhelpful response – on the contrary, the person who looked after me couldn't have been more obliging – it's just that it doesn't appear to have occurred to anybody involved that tourists visit a tourist information office to get information.

On a more positive note, two excellent and inexpensive books giving the historical background to Cape Coast are available at the Castle curio shop. These are the *Cape Coast and Elmina Handbook*, edited by Kwame Arhin of Legon University (Institute of African Studies, 1995) and *Cape Coast in History* by James Erskine Graham Jr (Anglican Printing Press, 1994). Here you can also buy the useful *Central Region Tourist Map* with large maps of both Cape Coast and Elmina on the reverse.

KAKUM NATIONAL PARK
Less than an hour from Cape Coast by private vehicle or tro-tro, Kakum National Park – along with the contiguous Assin Attandaso Game Production Area and Pra Suhien Forest Reserve – protects a patch of rainforest that not only ranks among the most extensive remaining pristine habitat of its sort in Ghana, but is also the most accessible to the casual visitor to the country. Covering a total area of 607km^2, the protected area is classified as moist, semi-deciduous forest, and like any true rainforest, it is characterised by high rainfall figures (especially between May and December) and a humidity level averaging around 90%. Although vital purely in conservation terms, forests such as this often form important watersheds – the rivers that rise in Kakum, for instance, provide water to more than 130 towns and villages, Cape Coast among them.

The Kakum complex of reserves protects at least 40 large mammal species, including giant forest hog, six types of duiker, bushbuck, bongo, forest elephant, various flying squirrels, leopard, spot-nosed monkey, Diana monkey, mona monkey and black-and-white and olive colobus. None of these mammals is likely to be seen by day visitors, but it is possible to arrange overnight camping trips to Antikwaa Camp, where elephants in particular are encountered with some frequency. Kakum is an excellent place to see forest birds, with roughly 275 species recorded, though to see even a tiny proportion of these you would need to spend a couple of days in the area and do some early-morning guided walks. A full checklist of large mammals, birds and reptiles, together with detailed notes and line drawings of the more common and interesting species, is included in the outstanding 124-page *Field Guide to the Kakum National Park*, written by Roell, Helsens and Nicolet, and available at the park headquarters for around US$3.

HANS COTTAGE BOTEL

This very attractive and original set-up, situated at Efutu about 8km from Cape Coast centre along the road to Kakum National Park, is not only an excellent place to spend a night or two, but well worth visiting as a day trip from Cape Coast, and would make a convenient brunch stop en route back to Cape Coast after a morning walk at Kakum. The centrepiece of the 'botel' is a double-storey wood and thatch restaurant built on a stilted platform over a small lake and connected to the shore by several wooden walkways.

The main attraction here is the dozen or so crocodiles resident in the lake, easily lured to the surface by throwing bread in the water to attract the fish on which they feed. The lake also supports a plethora of colourful lizards and a varied avifauna. Aurally, things are dominated by the ceaseless chattering and swizzling that emanates from various weaver colonies around the lake (we identified village, golden and Viellot's black weaver), but several types of kingfisher appear to be resident, and herons and egrets are well represented – patient photographers with adequate lenses could find it very rewarding.

The rooms form a separate unit about 100m from the platform, centred around a residents' swimming pool. Different types of room are available to suit different budgets: a smart s/c double with ac, fan, TV and hot water costs US$30, whereas a 'backpacker' double with fan and use of hot communal showers costs US$10. Camping is permitted at a negotiable rate, with access to the ac conference room when it's available. The restaurant is a great place to sit, and it serves a good variety of reasonably priced meals – mostly in the US$4–5 range – as well as chilled drinks of every variety.

The Botel lies to the left of the main Kakum road at Efutu. Coming from Cape Coast, you can't really miss it if you have private transport or are sitting in the left side of a tro-tro. To find a tro-tro from Cape Coast heading in this direction, go to Kotoka station.

The diversity of Kakum's flora is such that there are parts of the forest where the number of plant species per hectare comfortably exceeds 200! This vegetation is divided into five broad layers. The sparsely vegetated floor of the forest interior is dominated by herbaceous plants, above which a layer of shrubs reaches up to about 4m. The upper three layers together form the canopy: the lowest layer consists of spreading trees reaching a height of around 18m, above which lies the main closed canopy of larger trees, typically around 40m high, and then finally there are the emergent trees, many of them very old, reaching a height of up to 65–70m.

The main tourist attraction at Kakum is the much-publicised canopy walk. Constructed in 1995, this 350m long, 40m high wood-and-rope walkway is suspended between seven trees and broken up by a number of viewing platforms. Unique in Africa so far as I'm aware, the canopy walk offers a rare opportunity to actually look into the forest canopy, a breathtaking experience in itself (though emphatically *not* for those with a poor head for heights), and one that will immediately excite birdwatchers. Be warned, however, that the canopy walk can get quite busy, especially at weekends, when the whole exercise starts to feel a bit frogmarched, something that's reflected in the price of US$10 for the first hour (including the 15–20-minute walk in either direction from the park

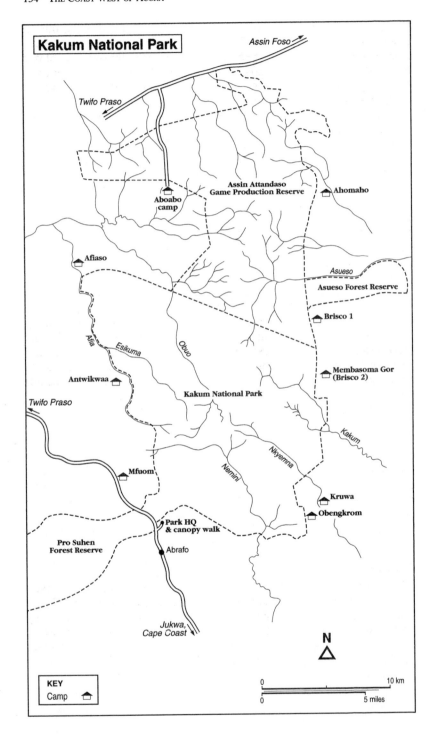

Kakum National Park

Assin Foso

Twifo Praso

Assin Attandaso
Game Production Reserve

Ahomaho

Aboabo
camp

Afiaso

Asueso

Asueso Forest Reserve

Brisco 1

Afia

Esikuma

Obuo

Membasoma Gor
(Brisco 2)

Antwikwaa

Kakum National Park

Twifo Praso

Kakum

Mfuom

Nkyemna

Nemini

Kruwa

Obengkrom

Park HQ
& canopy walk

Pro Suhen
Forest Reserve

Abrafo

Jukwa,
Cape Coast

N

KEY

Camp

0   10 km

0   5 miles

headquarters) plus another US$1 for every extra hour. Bearing this in mind, you'll get the most from the experience by being at the headquarters as soon as possible after the opening time of 08.00. Better still, should you be spending the night in Abrafo, you can arrange the previous afternoon to be met by a guide before 08.00, when everything is quiet and the forest is at its most atmospheric. Before heading out on the walk, spend a few minutes looking around the informative natural history displays in the information centre.

We felt that the canopy walk dominated thinking around the park headquarters to an extent that became mildly irritating. This richly diverse forest has so much more to offer visitors than this one (perhaps slightly over-hyped) novelty, and those with the time and an interest in natural history are encouraged to think about doing a more general walk. This costs US$2.50 per person for the first hour plus US$1 per extra hour, and you can arrange on the previous afternoon to be met before 08.00 the next day – the early morning is the best time to see birds and monkeys (though not butterflies, of which 400 species have been recorded in the area, since they tend to peak in activity in the mid- to late morning).

A recent introduction at Kakum are guided night walks, which offer the chance to see nocturnal animals by spotlight. With suitable equipment, an overnight camping trip deeper into the park would be an even more alluring option. A trip of this sort must be arranged privately with an individual guide (around US$10 per person per day seems a fair fee), though a letter I received in late 1999 suggests this may no longer be permitted due to understaffing. If you are able to set up an overnight trip, goals might include elephant tracking, birdwatching, the Kuntan trail (for medicinal and other plants) and the Masomagor Bamboo Orchestra.

Getting there and away

The Kakum National Park headquarters is clearly signposted along the Jukwa Road roughly 33km from Cape Coast. You can easily get there either by chartering a taxi or by using a tro-tro heading to Jukwa from Kotoka station in Cape Coast. If you intend sleeping over at the nearby tourist resthouse, then you're advised to get out of the tro-tro at Abrafo, leave your luggage at the resthouse, and walk the last 1km to the park headquarters.

Where to stay

The **Tourist Resthouse** in Abrafo, about 1km south of the park headquarters, is a pleasant enough place, though can hardly be called a bargain at US$7.50 for a basic double without running water or fan. In any case, staying there is the only realistic option for those who want to do an early walk in the forest. Reasonable meals and a limited range of semi-chilled drinks are served at the covered tables in the garden.

So far as I could ascertain, camping is not permitted at the headquarters or elsewhere in Kakum, unless it's as part of a guided overnight trip into the park.

It would be possible to use **Hans Cottage Botel** (see box on page 132) as a base from which to explore Kakum, but I find it difficult to see any real advantage in doing this rather than simply heading up as a day trip directly from Cape Coast.

There is a restaurant at the **park headquarters**, but if our experience is representative then cold beer and disgusting coffee are about all that's on offer – neither of which is wholly enticing at 08.00.

ELMINA

Situated on the thin strip of land that separates the shallow Benya Lagoon from the Atlantic, Elmina is a fascinating small town, at least the equal of nearby Cape Coast in terms of historical sightseeing, though often overlooked by tourists in favour of its larger neighbour. The town started life as a fishing and salt producing village roughly 700 years ago and, despite having served as first the Portuguese and later the Dutch headquarters in West Africa, an overgrown fishing village is basically what Elmina remains today, the rich harvest of the surrounding ocean supplemented by the production of salt from the brackish lagoon. Back in its economic heyday, however, Elmina lay at the heart of the West African gold trade.

Known as Edina in prehistoric times and by the Portuguese as *Aldea das Duas Partes* ('Village of Two Parts' – a reference to the lagoon), Elmina has probably gone by its modern name only since the Dutch took over in 1637. Nevertheless, the name Elmina is almost certainly derived from a Portuguese term which referred to this whole stretch of coast – *Da Costa de el Mina de Ouro* (The Coast of Gold Mines) – though some sources suggest, without any apparent foundation, that Elmina is derived from the Arabic phrase *el mina* (the harbour).

Traditional accounts suggest that Elmina has been settled at least since AD1300, when it was chosen as the capital of Kwaa Amankwaa, the founder of the Edina state, originally a matrilineal chieftaincy though its monarch was selected on patrilineal lines after 1680. The site was probably chosen because of the Benya lagoon, an excellent venue for salt production. An important trade route developed in prehistoric times between the salt mines of Elmina and the goldfields of the Bono Empire (around what are today Tarkwa and Obuasi), and it was due to this that the Portuguese were able to buy gold with such ease when they first landed at Elmina in 1471.

Our best idea of Edina's wealth and political set-up prior to the arrival of the Portuguese comes from a contemporary account of a meeting held in 1482 between the Portuguese captain Diogo de Azambuja and King Caramansa (probably a mistranscription of the common Edina royal name Kwamina Ansah). The narrator writes that Caramansa 'was seated on a high chair dressed in a jacket of brocade, with a golden collar of precious stones ... his legs and arms covered with golden bracelets and rings ... and in his plaited beard golden bars' and that 'his chiefs were all dressed in silk [and] wore rings and golden jewels on their heads and beards'. The same account goes on to describe the king as a man 'of good understanding, both by nature and by his dealing with the crews of the trading ships' and that 'he possessed a clear judgement ... as one who not only desired to understand what was proposed to him, who not only listened to the translation of the interpreter, but watched each gesture made by Diogo de Azambuja; and while this continued, both he and his men were completely silent; no-one as much as spat, so perfectly disciplined were they'.

In 1482, with the permission of Caramansa, the Portuguese began work on the earliest incarnation of the Castle of St George, a rather humble building by comparison with the modern castle. Within five years, several Portuguese traders had settled around the fort, and Elmina had been elevated to city status by the King of Portugal. Elmina remained the Portuguese centre of operations for more than 150 years, though their grip on the fortress gradually waned towards the end of this period. In August 1637, St Jago Hill was taken by the Dutch and the castle was bombarded by cannons, forcing a Portuguese surrender that effectively ended their period of influence in West Africa.

From 1637 until 1872 (when Holland sold all her Gold Coast forts to Britain), Elmina was in many respects the Dutch equivalent to Cape Coast. The castle of St George was substantially expanded shortly after the Dutch took possession of it, and it was further renovated and expanded throughout their centuries of occupation. In 1665–66, a second fort was established on St Jago Hill, ensuring that no other rival power could take Elmina with the same ease the Dutch had. A French trader, describing Elmina in the seventeenth century, wrote that it was 'very long, containing about twelve hundred houses, all built with rock stones [and] divided into several streets and alleys'. Old maps show that the small town centre had assumed much of its modern shape by the late eighteenth century, perhaps earlier. It would appear that the town has seen surprisingly little development since it was abandoned by the Dutch, partly because the British were already well ensconced at nearby Cape Coast, but more significantly perhaps because its very location between ocean and lagoon precluded the sort of expansion that has taken place in Cape Coast since the late nineteenth century.

Much of Elmina's fascination today lies in the way the former Portuguese and Dutch capital has returned to its fishing village roots. There is something decidedly odd about watching the colourful pirogues sail in and out of the lagoon, much as they might in any other small Ghanaian port, except that it is happening right in front of what is the oldest European building in West Africa. And this is the sort of paradox that one repeatedly encounters in a town which has a mood so inherently African juxtaposed against an urban landscape moulded almost entirely by exotic influences. Elmina's apparent contradictions are epitomised by the large posuban shrines that lie to the east of St Jago Hill, monuments unique to this part of Ghana, yet which – on the basis of appearance alone – could as easily have come from practically anywhere in the world.

Getting there and away

Elmina lies about 2km off the main Takoradi–Accra road, and it's connected to Cape Coast by a regular stream of tro-tros and shared taxis. In

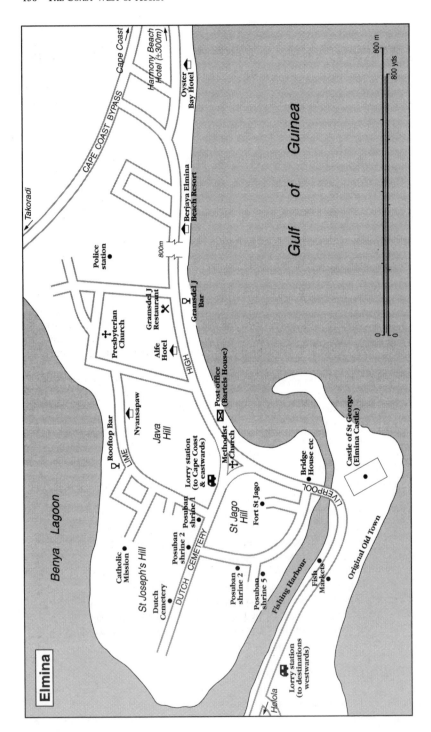

Elmina

most circumstances, your best bet in heading to Elmina is to catch public transport to Cape Coast, then use a local vehicle to Elmina – there are regular STC buses to Cape Coast, as well as tro-tros from Takoradi. The same is true when you leave Elmina – you can pick up a shared taxi to Cape Coast from Chapel Square, and find transport on from there (bearing in mind if you are heading to Takoradi that you'll pass Takoradi station on your way into Cape Coast).

Where to stay

Most travellers on a budget stay at the **Nyansapow Hotel** for the quite simple reason that it offers the only decent and affordable accommodation in the town centre. Fortunately, it's a pleasant enough place, a double-storey building centred around a large, open courtyard, offering smart, clean, s/c doubles with fan and running water for US$7.50. There is a bar on the ground floor, but no restaurant.

The only alternative we could find in the town centre was the **Alfe Hotel**, which seemed a real dump, but is indisputably cheaper at US$5 for a scruffy double using communal bucket showers.

Another relatively cheap place is the **Holola Guesthouse** in the suburb of Bantoma, about 1.5km from Elmina Castle along the Pershie road. The rooms are of a similar standard to the Nyansapow, but more expensive at US$10 s/c double, and the inconvenience of its location, not to say the quantity of mosquitoes that breed in the neighbouring salt flats, make it something of a last resort.

Three upmarket hotels are clustered within 500m of the intersection of Elmina High Street and the Accra–Takoradi road, 2km from the town centre. Coming from Elmina, the first of these is the **Berjaya Elmina Beach Resort** (PO Box 100, Elmina, tel: 042 33742/3, fax: 33714), part of the international Best Western chain and easily the plushest hotel on the coast west of Accra. It has air-conditioning throughout, good business facilities, and satellite TV in every room – not to say an aura of breezy transatlantic efficiency that comes as a mildly comic shock if you've been travelling in Ghana for a while. Rooms cost US$100/140 single/double B&B during the week and US$95/115 over weekends.

The other two hotels in this cluster offer similar facilities in a style that's more Ghanaian and at half the price. The **Oyster Bay Hotel** (PO Box 442 Elmina, tel: 042 33605/6) is attractively situated on a rocky stretch of coast, and although you can't swim in the ocean, there is a saline swimming pool in the rocks below the dining area. Large s/c rooms with ac, TV, fridge and fan cost US$50 double. The **Harmony Beach Hotel** (tel: 33678/9, fax: 33681) is more bland and barely utilises its beachfront position, but the clean rooms are fair value at US$46 for a s/c double with ac, satellite TV, fridge and telephone.

In the same price range, the **Coconut Grove Beach Resort** (PO Box 175 Elmina, tel: 042 33637, fax: 042 33647) is situated on a lovely stretch of beach 5km west of the town centre. The accommodation in detached cottages has been recommended by several readers of earlier prints of this guide, as have the meals at the open beachfront restaurant.

While talk of converting **Saint Jago Fort** into a resthouse has been going around for years, the signs are that it will open in this capacity during the course of the year 2000.

Where to eat

The best place to eat in the town centre is the **Gramsdel J Spot**, which spans High Street on the Elmina side of town. The rather stuffy indoor restaurant is on the town side of the road, but you can ask to have your food served at the breezy wooden platform bar perched on the opposite side of the road above the beach. The menu here isn't all that extensive, but the spicy fish and chicken stew is very tasty and reasonably priced at around US$2.50 per plate, and the beers are reliably chilled.

There is a pleasant rooftop bar on Lime Street, about 100m west of the Nyansapow Hotel, overlooking the salt ponds in Benya Lagoon.

Aside from the above places, your options amount to heading for one of the chop stalls around the market, or wandering out of town to one of the upmarket hotels – if you go for the latter option, the **Oyster Bay Hotel** has the most attractive location and it does really good food in the US$6–8 range.

What to do

The obvious place to start a walking tour of Elmina is **St George's Castle**, perched on a rocky promontory between lagoon and ocean. Freshly whitewashed as of 1995, the castle is now maintained as a historical monument and museum, and there is an entrance fee of US$2.50 per person, plus an additional fee of US$2.50 if you would like a guided tour – well worth doing. The castle is if anything more architecturally impressive than its Cape Coast counterpart, much of it four storeys high, and it offers excellent views across to the beach and over the town. Founded in 1482, St George's Castle is the oldest extant colonial building in sub-Saharan Africa, though it has been so extensively rebuilt and extended over the centuries that even its mid-seventeenth-century shape is radically different to its modern one (I think you could convincingly argue that the 'oldest building' tag hangs more meaningfully on the small Church of Senhora Baluarte on Mozambique Island, barely altered in architectural terms since it was constructed in 1522).

The original St George, a small rectangular fortress, was sufficiently substantial to withstand three Dutch naval bombardments, before it was captured as a result of the bombardment from the top of St Jago Hill. The modern fort must cover about ten times the surface area of the original; the only recognisable relic of pre-Dutch times is the former Portuguese chapel, converted by the Dutch to an auction hall for slaves, now a museum with displays that concentrate on local history rather than the slave trade.

You may want to linger awhile at the pretty **fishing harbour** and fish market directly in front of the castle. Dozens of colourful pirogues can be seen here, making their way in and out of the sheltered Benya Lagoon every morning beneath the small bridge over its mouth. Immediately east of the castle and the harbour, between lagoon and ocean, lay the **original old**

town, depicted in several paintings and lithographs before it burnt to the ground in 1873 as a result of a British naval bombardment.

To get from the castle and fishing harbour to what, I suppose, has to be termed the modern **old town**, you must follow Liverpool Street north over the bridge across the lagoon mouth. During Elmina's prime in the early nineteenth century, this area is where the wealthiest citizens lived, many of them mulattos or prosperous Dutch merchants who married Elmina women and settled in the town. Immediately after you cross the bridge, you'll see a cluster of these houses running up the right side of Liverpool Street, large double-storey buildings now trimmed of many of their more ornamental touches. Built in the 1840s, this cluster of buildings consists of Bridge House (partially destroyed during heavy rains in 1981), Quayson House, the twin Viala Houses and Simons House (now a complete ruin).

From here, a left turn into the road that runs alongside the north bank of the lagoon will, after no more than 20m, bring you to the steep and easily found path to the top of **St Jago Hill**. A wonderful panoramic view over the fishing harbour and the town centre is to be had from the top of this hill. It also provides an excellent vantage point over St George's Castle, something that was exploited by the Dutch in 1637 when they dragged four cannons to its peak and bombarded the castle, forcing a Portuguese surrender. **Fort St Jago** was built on top of the hill in 1665–66, so that the Dutch could be certain that they wouldn't lose possession of the castle in a manner similar to the one they had used to gain it. The resultant relatively modest fortified garrison post was named Fort Coenraadsburg by its Dutch constructors, but for reasons that are unclear it is generally known today by the older Portuguese name for the hill. Though several extensions were made after 1666, the essential shape of the fort is little changed since that time.

When you walk back down to the base of St Jago Hill, turn right, following the road that runs alongside the harbour away from Liverpool Street before curving inland. Here, over the space of perhaps 200m, is Elmina's main concentration of **posuban shrines** (see also page 142). The first two, on the left side of the road a few metres after it curves inland, belong to Asafo Companies Five and Two. The shrine built by Asafo Company Two is a double-storey affair with several life-size figures carved on the ground floor and – strikingly – a ship with three naval officers on the upper one. Number Two Shrine consists of four life-size carvings of people surrounding an older man in a bright blue robe and flanked by two aeroplanes. Most impressive, however, is the shrine built by Asafo Company Four at the junction with Dutch Cemetery Street: a variation on the story of Adam and Eve.

Turn left into Dutch Cemetery Street if you want to nose around the old **Dutch Cemetery**, inaugurated in 1802 and moved to its present site at the base of St Joseph's Hill four years later. Well maintained, the graveyard boasts several marble tombstones as well as a large, neo-classical cenotaph dating to 1806. Turn back along Dutch Cemetery Street, passing the shrines built by Asafo Companies Two and One, and you can take a left turn into Lime Street. Here, the rather run-down, but once grand **Dolphin House**, distinguished by its multi-arched façade, was built in the late nineteenth

POSUBAN SHRINES

Unique to Ghana's central coastal region, *posubans* are the eye-catching and often elaborately decorated concrete shrines that dot the urban landscape of many Fante settlements, reaching something of a garish zenith in such ancient trading centres as Elmina, Anomabu and Mankessim. These shrines are the work of *asafo* companies, the patrilineal military units that are a feature of most Akan societies. *Asafo* companies are traditionally responsible for the defence of their town, but these days they are perhaps more significant for their ceremonial function and for their activity and influence in the arts and local politics. Most towns in the region boast at least five rival companies, and some boast up to 12. Each company is identified by number, name and location, with Number One Company generally being the longest established unit in any given town, as well as the most important and influential in terms of links to the chieftaincy. In Anomabu, for instance, a new chief is always sworn in at the *posuban* built by Number One Company, adorned with a symbolic padlock and key.

Many posubans originated as storage houses, used to hold not only arms but also the company regalia, and they are often decorated in a manner that is both richly symbolic and – to the outsider – decidedly cryptic. The extent of this decoration varies enormously from town to town. You could easily walk right past most of Cape Coast's posubans without noticing them, since at best they are decorated by one small mural. In Elmina and Mankessim, by contrast, the most important shrines are multi-storey affairs decorated with up to ten life-size human forms, and complex enough in their symbolism to keep you guessing for several hours.

Perhaps the most surprising thing about the posubans of the Ghanaian coast is how little they owe to any other African artistic tradition – unique to the area these posubans may be, and ancient too by all accounts, but were you to show a picture of a typical shrine to most Europeans, they'd be hard pushed to guess in what continent it had been photographed. One renowned shrine in Anomabu just about conjures up Africa by depicting lions and leopards (sitting somewhat incongruously alongside a whale and several surreal antelope-like creatures), which cannot be said for the best-known posuban in that town, several metres long and built in the shape of a European warship. Other famous shrines in the region are dotted with European sailors (clad in blue and white) and overgrown clocks, while one startling shrine in Elmina depicts the story of Adam and Eve. It's the sort of thing that's bound to annoy arty ethno-purists, though personally I find it fascinating to see this strange melding of exotic and indigenous influences in a town such as Elmina, a place where Africa and Europe have, after all, been rubbing shoulders for more than five centuries.

Despite vigorous questioning of local elders, I was unable to establish when, why and how these elaborate posubans were constructed. Most of the shrines I saw look as if they took their present form in the post-independence era. It is my understanding (and I'm open to correction on this) that the actual sites of the shrines often *are* centuries old, but that the shrines themselves are resculpted every few decades to reflect changes in fashion and recent additions to the long list of symbols and proverbs boasted by each *asafo*.

Details of important individual shrines are given under the town where they are found. For most short-stay visitors, the obvious place to go posuban viewing is Elmina, though the selection found in Anomabu is arguably more varied and interesting, while the main shrine in Mankessim (traditionally regarded as the first capital of Fante) is probably the largest and most elaborate in the country. Most of the shrines lie on main roads, so viewing them is free, but a donation of around US$1 per shrine will be expected if you want to take photographs.

century by the merchant Fred Dolphin at the foot of the road running to the top of St Joseph's Hill. Walk up this hill to see a clutch of impressive mission buildings, including a large **Catholic church** dating from the 1880s, and a view over the salt ponds in Benya Lagoon.

When you walk back to Dutch Cemetery Street, turn left and follow it to Chapel Square, at the intersection of Liverpool and High streets and marked by an attractive Methodist church. A left turn into High Street will bring you to what is perhaps the best-maintained building of its vintage in Elmina, the stone **post office**. This was built some time between 1825 and 1850 as the domestic dwelling and trading quarters of the merchant C H Bartels (son of Governor Bartels), and it later served as a hospital during the colonial era.

BETWEEN ELMINA AND TAKORADI
The stretch of coast between Elmina and Takoradi has three obvious highlights: the excellent beach resorts at Brenu Akyinim and at Ampenyi, and the off-the-beaten-track town of Shama with its historic fort.

Brenu Akyinim
The small village of Brenu Akyinim, 15km west of Elmina, is known for its attractive and reasonably safe swimming beach. A substantial chunk of beach about 300m east of the village has been fenced off to form the Brenu Beach Resort, and the entrance fee of US$0.50 ensures that villagers do their ablutions elsewhere. Swimming is not advisable unless you check current conditions with the locals, but Brenu is a great place to lounge in palm-fringed, white-sanded perfection, and facilities are suited to those on a budget. Brenu is an easy day trip from Elmina.

Akyinim is pronounced 'Achinim' and, rather confusingly, it is also the name of a suburb in Elmina.

Getting there and away
There is no direct transport between Elmina and Brenu Akyinim, but you shouldn't have difficulty finding a tro-tro as far as Ayensudo junction, from where a couple of shared taxis ply the roughly 5km road to Brenu. These taxis fill up rather slowly, but since the full fare for six passengers works out at around US$1 you could always treat yourself!

Where to stay and eat
The **Brenu Beach Resort** has an excellent restaurant serving mostly seafood dishes in the US$4–6 range, as well as minerals and alcoholic drinks. The only accommodation in Brenu Akyinim is the **Celiamen's Hotel** behind the tro-tro station, where basic but adequate rooms cost US$6/7. There is a bar attached, and the friendly owner can arrange a meal courtesy of the lady who runs the beach resort restaurant.

Ampenyi
The beach at Ko-Sa, 1km from Ampenyi, is arguably the finest on the entire coast of Ghana, boasting a natural rock pool where swimming is both safe

and pleasurable. Situated right on the beach, the **Ko-Sa Guesthouse** offers accommodation in attractive local-style grass huts using clean communal showers and toilets for around US$8 per person, and simple meals are served to advance order. Ampenyi lies about 20km west of Elmina and can be reached via a 5km turn-off signposted from Ajensudo junction on the main Takoradi road.

Komenda

The mouth of the Komenda River was a focal point of Anglo-Dutch rivalry in the 17th and 18th centuries, as testified by two ruined forts on the opposite banks. Fort Vreedenburg was built by the Dutch in 1682, and Fort English by the British five years later. Little remains of these forts, so Komenda is probably worth visiting only if you have private transport – the 5km turn-off is signposted from the main Cape Coast–Takoradi road.

Shama

This small, out-of-the-way town makes for a diverting overnight excursion en route between Cape Coast and Takoradi. Shama is the site of Ghana's third-oldest fortified building, the Fortress of Saint Sebastian, built and named by the Portuguese in 1523. In 1640, the all-but derelict fort was captured by the Dutch, who completely rebuilt it following a brief British occupation in 1664. The ground plan today is almost identical to the Portuguese original, but an extra storey was added by the Dutch. Later in the fort's career, strong buttresses were constructed to prevent the soft foundation rock from being washed away – hence the high semi-circle of steps leading to the main entrance.

Shama's fort is well maintained and looms imposingly above the central market. Entrance costs roughly US$1 inclusive of a guided tour. So far as we could see, the only other building of any great vintage in Shama is the Methodist Church built opposite the fort in 1893. Also of interest is the fish market on the mouth of the Pra River, a short walk to the east of the town centre. During the gold trading era, Shama was renowned for the seaworthy canoes that were crafted on an island a short distance upstream of the Pra mouth, and even today it is possible to organise a canoe ride up the river from near the market.

Getting there and away

Any tro-tro heading between Cape Coast and Takoradi can stop at Shama junction. A steady flow of shared taxis ply the 4km road to Shama.

Where to stay and eat

At the multi-storey **Hotel Applause**, a s/c double with fan and hot shower costs a reasonable US$7.50. There's a great rooftop bar and restaurant, and the staff seem friendly.

SEKONDI-TAKORADI

The twin city of Sekondi-Takoradi is probably the third largest in Ghana, with a total population approaching 300,000. Takoradi is the larger and more modern and industrialised of the two, which lie 10km apart on the coast roughly halfway between Accra and the Côte d'Ivoire border. It is passed through by many travellers since it has good road and rail links, as well as an adequate beach and a large number of hotels and restaurants.

Formerly an obscure fishing village, Takoradi was earmarked for development as a harbour in 1920, and officially opened as such in 1928, since when it has grown to become the most important port in the country. The compact city centre, emanating from the circular central market, has a busy, modern feel without approaching the chaotic atmosphere of, say, Kumasi. Below the city centre is an attractive suburban area that runs along the beach to the west of the golf course. Takoradi boasts no eminent tourist attractions, but together with Sekondi it makes for a pleasant place to spend a night or two.

Sekondi, in direct contrast to its upstart twin, is visibly steeped in history. A solid Dutch fort was built there in 1690 over the foundations of a lodge built 50 years earlier, and the town has served as the administrative capital of Western Region and an important naval base from the very earliest colonial times right up to modern day. Very few travellers make the 20- minute tro-tro ride from Takoradi to Sekondi, but those who do will be amply rewarded. The Dutch Fort Orange is still in use as a lighthouse, and the family who live there seem happy to let visitors wander around the fortifications, which offer a great view over the town. The harbour, with its backdrop of green hills, is bustling with colourful fishing boats. Above the harbour, the quarter still referred to locally as the 'European Town' is a compact jumble of crumbling turn-of-the-century buildings, with an atmosphere as rich as it is depressing.

Getting there and away
Ten STC buses run directly between Accra and Takoradi every day, taking roughly four hours in either direction. The first bus out of Accra leaves at 05.00, after which there is one bus hourly until 11.00, and a couple in the afternoon before the last one leaves at 17.00. The first bus out of Takoradi leaves at around 03.00, then a cluster between 08.00 and 09.30, while the last bus leaves at 16.30. You generally want to arrive at the STC station 30 minutes before the bus leaves to be sure of getting a ticket.

There are direct tro-tros between Takoradi and practically every town of substance on the coast west of Accra. Tro-tros to Elubo, Beyin, Half Assini, Dunkwa and other points west of Takoradi leave from the lorry station on the opposite side of Axim Road to the STC station. Tro-tros to Cape Coast and other points east of Takoradi leave from the station at the corner of Cape Coast and Ashanti roads. Tro-tros to Sekondi leave from a back road off Kintampo Road.

For details of the twice daily train service to Kumasi, see *Getting there and away* under Kumasi on page 199.

Where to stay
If you're literally just crashing the night in Takoradi, you have the choice of half a dozen centrally located budget hotels, all of which charge very similar rates. Top of the list is the well-maintained **Amenla Hotel**, which has large,

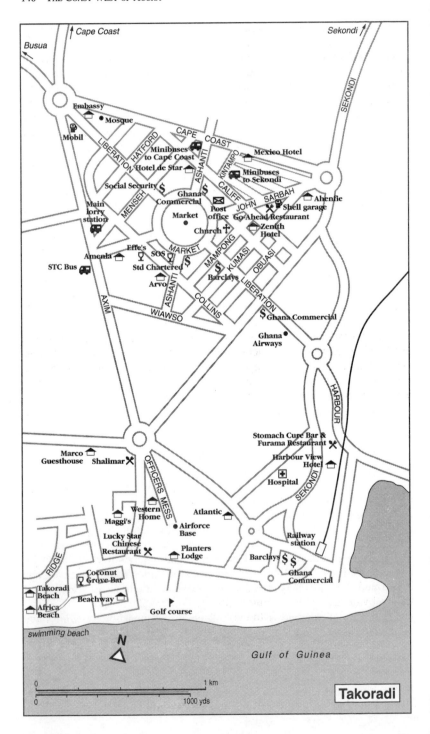

Takoradi

clean rooms with fans and running water. Rooms using communal showers cost US$4/5 single/double, while s/c doubles cost US$7.50. Around the corner, the **Hotel Arvo** is a bit more run-down, but it has identically priced rooms and is definitely the second choice in this bracket. Next best is probably the **Zenith Hotel**, notable more for its colonial architecture and idiosyncratically decorated courtyard than for the large, but rather run-down rooms costing US$4/5 single/double. Still, it's a clear notch above the identically priced **Mexico Hotel** and **Hotel de Star**, and for that matter the less central and slightly more expensive **Embassy Hotel**.

For smarter accommodation in the city centre, the **Melody Hotel**, which opened in late 1999 opposite the STC station, has been warmly recommended and costs around US$25 for a s/c double. Similar in price, the **Ahenfie Hotel** has s/c doubles, a good restaurant, a garden bar, and a disco where – take note – 'all shirts must be tucked into trousers except jumper'! Another relatively central option, offering s/c rooms at around US$15/25, is the **Harbour View Hotel** – and there's a good outdoor bar and restaurant overlooking the harbour in the same complex.

More suitable for those spending a couple of nights in Takoradi is the cluster of accommodation on the beachfront, a 20-minute walk or US$1 taxi ride from the city centre. For budget travellers, the **Beachway Hotel** is without doubt the most attractive hotel in Takoradi, if not along this entire stretch of coast, a creaky, four-storey colonial building with large balconies overlooking leafy grounds facing the beach and the golf course. Rooms using communal showers range in price from US$4.50 for a single to US$7/8 for a small/large double. There is a pleasant garden bar and restaurant serving food by advance arrangement only.

In the same area, there are two medium-priced hotels set back a few hundred metres from the sea. The **Western Home Hotel** on Officers Mess Road seems particularly good value, with ac, s/c chalets for US$14/20 single/double. The **Guesthouse Maggi**, set in a quiet, suburban garden, has double rooms with ac, TV, fridge and hot shower for US$30.

The other hotels in this part of town are more upmarket. Top of the list, in my estimation, is the **Africa Beach Hotel** (tel/fax: 031 23466), which has pleasant grounds centred around a swimming pool and right above the swimming beach. Double chalets with ac, satellite TV, fridge and hot water cost US$60. By contrast, it's difficult to see why any tourist would choose to stay at the nearby **Takoradi Beach Hotel**, an unattractive, multi-storey monolith with no direct access to the beach and rooms that are relatively overpriced at US$70/80 single/double. Much nicer, though separated from the sea by the golf course, **Planters Lodge** (tel: 031 23331, fax: 031 23330) has plenty of ambience, and attractive chalet accommodation for US$82 s/c, ac double. The neighbouring multi-storey **Atlantic Hotel** was closed for renovation at the time of writing and due to re-open as a Holiday Inn.

Where to eat
If you are staying in the city centre, one of the best places to eat is the **SOS Restaurant**, which has an air-conditioned, ground-floor bar as well as a

first-floor restaurant spilling on to a balcony overlooking the market circle. The menu includes roast chicken, spaghetti and various local dishes, all for around US$2 per plate. Other affordable eateries include the **Go-Ahead Restaurant** next to the Shell garage, and **Effe's Home Cooking Spot** near the Alvo Hotel. There is a considerably more upmarket restaurant, complete with air-conditioning, in the **Ahenfie Hotel**.

A bit further from the centre, a nice place to spend the evening is the **Stomach Cure Garden** next to the Harbour View Hotel, an open-air bar with chilled beers and a great view over the harbour by night. There's a guy who grills kebabs and such outside the bar, or you can eat excellent Chinese food for around US$5–6 per head, excluding drinks, at the air-conditioned **Furama Restaurant** next door. Quite a lot of travellers will want to take a picture from the Stomach Cure Bar, and there's no reason why you can't do this except that the 'security manager' is a macho idiot. Just take your snaps, and if he attempts the Rambo approach to customer relations, then do point out that you can take exactly the same photo from right outside the bar – and you can take your custom elsewhere while you're about it. It worked for us!

There's a couple of decent places near the beach and golf course. The **Lucky Star Chinese Restaurant**, popular with backpackers staying at the Beachway Hotel, is similar in standard and price to the Furama. The **Shalimar Restaurant** has a limited selection of Western and Indian dishes in the US$4–5 range.

THE COAST WEST OF TAKORADI

Less touristy than the coast to the east of Takoradi, the far western coast of Ghana offers several worthwhile excursions. For many, Busua will probably be the highlight of this stretch of coast, with a thriving travellers' scene and idyllic beach, and easy foot access to the historical small town and British fort at Dixcove. A more adventurous trip, however, would be to Beyin, site of another British fort and the only place from where you can visit the unique stilt village of Mzulezu.

Busua and Dixcove

Only 20km east of Takoradi, Busua Beach is widely regarded to be among the best and safest in Ghana, for which reason the small fishing village that lies on it has played host to a steady influx of backpackers since the 1960s. Recent years have seen Busua attract a marginally more upmarket crowd than in its hippy heyday, particularly following the refurbishment of the long-serving Busua Beach Resort, but it is also true that the village has never before been blessed with so many affordable lodgings and restaurants, most of which are run by locals rather than out-of-town businessmen. The beach remains magnificent, the village and fishing harbour in particular are very colourful, and the friendly backpacker-oriented atmosphere makes it tempting to label Busua as West Africa's answer to the legendary Twiga Lodge in Kenya and Cape Maclear in Malawi.

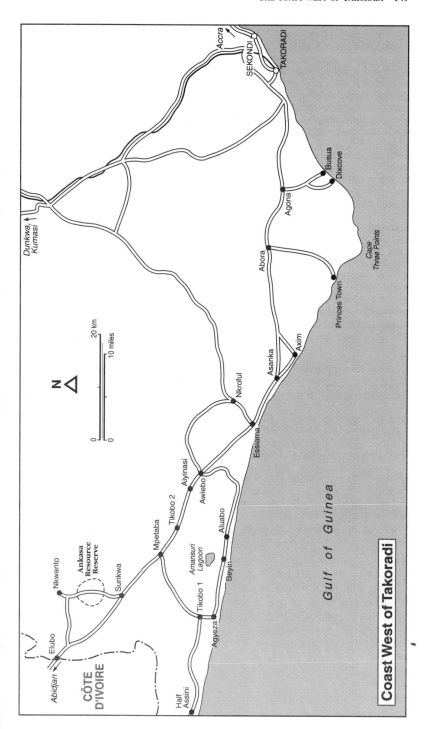

Coast West of Takoradi

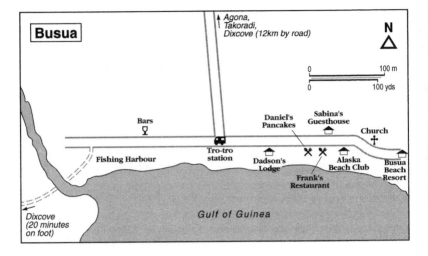

Only 20 minutes' walk from Busua, Dixcove is more a small town than a village, a compact settlement of run-down alleys which carry a definite sense of – well, if not history exactly, then certainly historical continuity. Like many other Ghanaian ports, Dixcove has long been the site of a European fort, and it was probably settled by local fishermen for centuries before that. In 1692, Dixcove (or Dick's Cove as it was then known) was chosen by the British as the site of a fort, construction of which was completed in around 1696. For the best part of two centuries, Dixcove Fort was the only British property in the Dutch-controlled part of what is now the Ghanaian coast. The fort was captured by the Dutch in 1868 and renamed *Fort Metalen Kruiz*, only to be returned to Britain in 1872 along with all other Dutch forts on the Gold Coast – oddly, however, the Dutch name stuck and it is known as Fort Metal Cross today. The fort is the obvious focal point for visits to Dixcove, and it may even be possible to spend the night there for a fee.

Getting there and away

Dixcove and Busua lie no more than 2km apart and roughly 20km east of Takoradi as the crow flies. To reach either town, follow the main Elubo road east of Takoradi to the junction town of Agona, then take the left turn signposted for Busua Beach Resort. This road diverges about 5km out of Agona, with the left fork reaching Busua after another 5km and the right fork reaching Dixcove after a similar distance. So far as I'm aware, no tro-tros connect Takoradi directly to Dixcove and Busua, but there are regular tro-tros from Takoradi to Agona, from where tro-tros run every hour or so to both Dixcove and Busua.

There is no direct road between Busua and Dixcove. If you want to travel between the two, you have three options: to catch a tro-tro back to Agona and change vehicles there, to charter a private taxi between the two, or to walk. The two towns are connected by a 15–20-minute footpath, which leaves Dixcove from alongside the fort and Busua from the opposite side of the estuary next to the fishing harbour. Do be aware that you'll have to wade through the estuary at Busua, which is safe enough at low tide when the water is thigh height, but dangerous at high tide, according to some locals. I'd be reluctant to walk this route carrying luggage at any time, not only because of the risk of drenching it in the estuary, but also because of a few second-hand reports of robberies in 1999.

Where to stay and eat

All of the accommodation and restaurants in Busua lie along a roughly 500m stretch of road running between the main circle (where tro-tros stop) and the Busua Beach Resort. The first place you'll pass, to your right coming from the tro-tro park, is the double-storey **Dadson's Lodge**, which has rooms without fans for US$5/10 single/double using clean communal showers. There's a nice atmosphere in the ground floor bar, but no food.

Further towards the beach hotel, **Sabina's Guesthouse** is a friendly, family-run place with basic, clean rooms for US$5/7.50. Another recommendation in this range is **Mary's Place**. Opposite Sabina's, **Daniel the Pancake Man** ('world-famous' pancakes) and **Frank's Restaurant** (lobster and other fresh seafood) vie for the palates of travellers, with the latter being popular in the evening. Next to Frank's, the **Alaska Beach Club** has simple rondavels for US$12/double and allows camping at US$2.50 per person. In previous prints of this guide I recommended the Alaska for its idyllic beachfront position, but I've since received complaints about the noise at night, theft from rooms, and rude management.

The **Busua Beach Resort** (tel: 031 21210/21857), which re-opened in all its newly renovated glory in late 1996, has a justifiable reputation as one of Ghana's top beach hotels. It is also, by international standards, remarkably good value, with plush s/c, ac rooms for US$45/60 single/double and suites for US$90. Positioned right on the beach, the hotel has attractively landscaped grounds and a good restaurant, also open to travellers who are staying at one of the cheaper places in the village.

The only formal accommodation in Dixcove is the **Quiet Storm Hotel**, the conspicuous, blue and pink building on a slope to your right as you enter the town. It's nothing very special, and lacks the vibe of the Busua hotels (which for some might be an attraction), but is affordable enough at US$7.50/10 for a single/double room with a fan and use of clean bucket showers.

Prince's Town

The isolated village of Prince's Town (or Prince's Terre), with its attractive unspoilt beach near the mouth of the Nyan River, is visited by few travellers as a result of its distance from the main Takoradi–Elubo road. The main attraction here, aside from the beach, is Fort Gross Friedrichsburg, a near ruin at the time of independence, but since fully restored. The fort has an unusual history in that it was built by the

Brandenberg Africa Company, a latecomer to the European struggle for dominance of the Ghanaian coast, formed in 1682 as a representative of Prince Friedrich of Brandenberg. After landing at the village then known as Pokesu in 1683, the Brandenbergers were ceded the promontory on which the fort now stands in exchange for offering the village protection against the Dutch and other slave raiders.

By the 1690s, Fort Gross Friedrichsburg had become the most important smuggling centre on the coast, simply because the officials received so few ships from Brandenberg that they were forced to trade with other nations to make a profit. In 1716, the Brandenbergers abandoned the fort to John Conny, an Ahanta chief who had already acquired the nickname 'King of Prince's Terre' for his role at the centre of a trade network so powerful that it caused a temporary decline in the fortunes of nearby Dutch ports such as Dixcove and Axim. In 1724, following a decade of military clashes, the Dutch captured the deteriorating fort from Conny and renamed it Fort Hollandia. It remained in Dutch hands for almost 150 years, before being handed to Britain as part of the treaty signed in 1872.

Getting there and away
Prince's Town is 18km from Abora junction on the main Takoradi–Elubo road and is signposted. Any vehicle heading between Agona and Axim can drop you at the junction, where you'll probably be in for a long wait – there's not a lot of transport, but you should get through eventually, except perhaps after heavy rain when the road has tended to become impassable in the past.

Where to stay and eat
There is no formal accommodation in Prince's Town, but there are a few spare beds in the fort, and the caretaker has been allowing travellers to stay here for a small fee for some years now. Facilities are limited to a bucket shower. A limited selection of food is available in the village.

Axim
The largest town on the coast west of Takoradi, Axim (pronounced more like *Azsim*) is also the site of Ghana's second-oldest fort. The triangular Fort São Antonio dates to the Portuguese era, and although its exact year of construction is not on record, most authorities reckon it to be around 1515. Positioned on an outcrop, with excellent natural protection in the form of a few small rocky islands and a reef, the fort was captured by Holland in 1642 and remained in their control until it was handed to Britain in 1872.

Axim was once one of the most important trading posts on the Gold Coast, but aside from the fort, which now serves as an administrative centre and generally welcomes visitors who want to take a look around, you would hardly know it today. Axim struck me as perhaps the most characterless port in Ghana, chronically run-down and rather unwelcoming, and any thoughts of exploration are likely to be dampened by the inexplicably high price of hotels, at least by Ghanaian standards.

Getting there and away
Regular tro-tros connect Axim to Takoradi in the east and Esiama to the west.

Where to stay and eat
The **Frankfaus Hotel**, roughly 100m uphill from the tro-tro station and main traffic circle, appears to have serious delusions of grandeur which you're unlikely to want to help finance. A small non-s/c room costs US$9/12 while a s/c double with bucket shower costs US$15 – you'd get the same standard of room for half the price or less in most Ghanaian towns. The management argues that the nearby Ankobra Beach Resort charges a lot more – somewhat beside the point as the Ankobra Beach Resort is several quantum leaps nicer.

The only other place to stay in Axim is the **Hotel Monte Carlo**, about ten minutes' walk and signposted from the tro-tro station. Here, a rather grubby double with fan sets you back around US$9 – again, grossly inflated by Ghanaian standards, especially as the communal toilets reek and the ambience is zero.

About 500m south of the Elubo road, clearly signposted no more than 5km from Axim, the **Ankobra Beach Resort** lies on a perfect, palm-lined beach close to the mouth of the Ankobra River. In addition to having an attractive layout, the resort places a strong emphasis on cultural and historical excursions, for instance to the various slave forts and the stilt village at Beyin. Self-contained rooms are good value at US$25 for a double with standing fan, US$35 for a double with roof fan, or US$55 for a family bungalow with ac. The restaurant looks good too.

Nkroful
This small town 4km north of the main Takoradi–Elubo road is noted as the birthplace of Kwame Nkrumah, Ghana's first president, and the site of the small mausoleum where the former president was buried after his death in 1972. Frankly, this Nkrumah Mausoleum is a rather underwhelming sight by comparison with the vast Nkrumah Mausoleum in Accra (which in any case is where Nkrumah is now buried). It is easy enough to find, however, lying within the bright pink information centre – children, lots and lots of them, will show you how to get there, not to say drape themselves over the memorial, shove their way in front of the camera, etc.

If you want to visit the mausoleum, ask any vehicle travelling along the main road to drop you at Essiama, from where regular and inexpensive shared taxis go directly to Nkroful. There is no accommodation in Nkroful, but you could stay at the Motel de Miegyina in Esiama – lying behind the Goil garage on the Axim side of the main junction, this place sees little custom and could hardly be cheaper at US$3/double.

Beyin
The seaside village of Beyin is the site of Fort Apollinia, the last fort to be built by Britain on the Gold Coast, constructed in 1770 with the permission

of the Nzima chief, Amenihyia. Fort Apollinia was built in a different manner from any other fort in the country, with a substantially stronger seaward bastion that not only served a defensive purpose, but also contained the cells used to store slaves. Beyin's fort was built to endure, using rock quarried from a site 10km away, and it has retained its original shape, despite having been abandoned for long periods of time before it was converted to a resthouse in the 1970s.

Arguably one of Ghana's travel highlights, and certainly a more singular experience than Fort Apollinia, is **Mzulezu Stilt Village** on the freshwater Lake Amansuri about 5km from Beyin. Supporting a population of roughly 500 people, Mzulezu is one solid construction raised above the water, consisting of a central wood and reed walkway with perhaps two dozen individual houses on either side of it. Quite why the people of Mzulezu decided to build their village above the water is an open question – especially as they are not primarily fishermen but agriculturalists, whose fertile fields lie about 1km north of the lake. The villagers welcome tourists, except on Thursdays which are sacred, and they charge a nominal entrance fee which allows you to wander around freely and take as many photos as you like (you'll be asked to send them copies of the best results).

Mzulezu can only be reached by dugout canoe, and the 5km, one-hour ride there is as rewarding as the village itself, following the Amansuri River through areas of marsh and open pools fringed by palm thickets and jungle until it opens out on to the dark, reflective waters of the lake. It's a lovely trip, especially in the early morning cool, and you should see plenty of birds. Pygmy geese and lily-trotters abound on the lily-covered pools, purple and squacco herons are often flushed from the reeds, and a variety of colourful bee-eaters, rollers and kingfishers perch silently on low branches, while hornbills and plantain-eaters draw attention to themselves with their cackling and chuckling – keen birdwatchers and photographers could happily spend an additional morning on the water without visiting the village.

Getting there and away

Beyin lies along a dirt road that follows the coast south of the main Takoradi–Elubo road. Coming from the direction of Takoradi, the junction for Beyin is at Awiebo, something that you don't really need to know if you are using public transport, since Takoradi and Beyin are connected by direct minibuses taking two to three hours in either direction. Heading towards Elubo, there are a few direct vehicles daily, but if nothing is going, you could catch a vehicle bound for Half Assini as far as the village known as 'Tikobo One' and there pick up a shared taxi to Elubo.

A canoe to Mzulezu can be organised through the caretaker at Fort Apollinia – the boat takes about one hour each way and the cost of the return trip appears to be fixed at US$3.50 per person (plus the village entrance fee of US$1 per person).

Where to stay and eat
The two twin bedrooms in **Fort Apollinia** cost US$2.50 per person; facilities include a communal bathroom with an ample supply of well water and a kitchen with a gas stove. Nearby, a local guesthouse opened in 1999 to handle the overspill from Fort Apollinia. There's a bar next to the fort with a paraffin fridge, and local food such as fried yam and *kenkey* is available at stalls along the main road.

INLAND TO THE CÔTE D'IVOIRE BORDER
Few travellers head this way unless they are going to Côte d'Ivoire, and those who do generally rush through in a day. The only reason why you'd be likely to want to linger in this area is to spend time exploring the little-visited Ankasa Resource Reserve, potentially a major attraction for hikers and birders alike.

Ankasa Protected Area
Comprising the contiguous Nini-Suhien National Park and Ankasa Resource Reserve, this little visited but highly accessible 523km² chunk of evergreen rainforest is bounded on the south by the Ankasa River and on the north by the Nini River. Ankasa is regarded as having the greatest biodiversity of any reserve in Ghana. Up to 300 plant species have been counted in one hectare, while a list of 43 large mammal species includes forest elephant, bongo, giant forest hog, chimpanzee and several types of monkey and duiker. Of the 350 birds recorded, the rare and elusive white-fronted guinea fowl is of particular note. Ankasa is currently being developed for tourism: visitors can walk freely along the public road through the reserve, or arrange a guided walk deeper into the forest with a ranger. Large terrestrial mammals are unlikely to be encountered by casual visitors, but the birding is excellent, butterflies are everywhere, and there is a good chance of coming across a few monkeys (mona, spot-nosed and black-and-white colobus are most common, though the localised Diana monkey and white-crested mangabey are also present).

Getting there and away
Ankasa gate and campsite lie some 5km north of the main Takoradi–Elubo road, along a signposted turn-off 22km east of Elubo, and can be reached in any vehicle except after heavy rain. The best day to get to the reserve using public transport is Monday (local market day), when you can catch a tro-tro from Aiyinasi or Elubo to Sowodadem and then another tro-tro from Sowodadem directly to the Ankasa gate. On other days, your options are either to charter a taxi to the gate from Elubo or Aiyinasi (this shouldn't cost more than US$8 one-way) or else to ask a tro-tro heading along the main road to drop you at the junction and hitch or walk the last 5km. If you go for the latter option, it's a pleasant walk on gentle slopes, and you can break the walk at a small bar in Amgakosuaza.

Do note that when you arrange transport to Ankasa, you should make it clear that you want to visit the reserve and not the synonymous town.

Where to stay and eat

Currently there is only one campsite in the reserve. Situated at the Ankasa gate, this consists of two shelters sleeping 12 people, simple ablution facilities, and a covered cooking area. The park supplies kerosene lamps, mosquito nets, camp beds and firewood; even if you don't have a tent it is permitted to sleep under a net suspended from a beam. Camping costs US$5 per person, and a small extra charge is made for using the nets and camp beds. Visitors should bring all food and drink. Rain water is available from tanks, but should be boiled before drinking.

Future plans for Ankasa include the construction of two further campsites over the course of 2000, followed by a more upmarket private camp in 2001. Mountain-biking and canoeing are also on the cards for 2001. For details of progress, contact the Protected Areas Development Plan (PADP) at 031 25322 or padp@africaonline.com.gh.

Elubo

Everything about Elubo screams 'border town', from the exceptionally chaotic market spilling over on to the main street, to the hissing money changers and mandatory clowns who try to overcharge you for everything on the basis that you've probably just crossed into Ghana from Côte d'Ivoire. As a result, Elubo is the sort of place you'll probably want to pass through as quickly as possible. Redeeming features include the street food – the beef kebabs on sale here are as tender, tasty and generous as any we had in Ghana – and (especially if you *have* come from the more expensive Côte d'Ivoire) a couple of very reasonably priced hotels

Getting there and away

Regular tro-tros connect Elubo to Axim and Takoradi, as well as to Abidjan in Côte d'Ivoire. If you are travelling from Elubo to a point before Axim, you may have to change vehicles in Aiyinasi.

Where to stay and eat

The **Hotel Cocoville**, surprisingly large and upmarket in this remote neck of the jungle, is situated about 200m from the lorry station overlooking the Tano River, with a view of the remnant forest patches on the Ivoirian bank and (less picturesquely) a steady stream of locals coming to soap themselves down. The rooms here are indisputably good value at US$10 for a s/c double with fan or US$17 for a s/c double with ac and TV, and the hotel has the only electricity in town. You can eat pretty well in the restaurant or at the waterfront garden bar – meals are a little expensive by Ghanaian standards at around US$5, but portions are generous.

Of the cheaper places, the **Hotel Falun** opposite the lorry station is clearly the best option. Clean rooms with double bed cost US$3 and there are regularly refilled tubs of water outside the communal bucket showers – note, however, that the fans and light fittings are purely ornamental, since there's no electricity.

Bia Protected Area

This 305km^2 reserve on the Ivorian border protects an important area of virgin rainforest and is currently being extensively developed for tourism. In addition to trees reaching a height of 60m, the reserve harbours more than 100 mammal species, notably forest elephant, bongo, red river hog and ten types of primate including chimpanzee. The ever-expanding bird list now stands in excess of 200, while 370 types of butterfly have been recorded. The main entrance to Bia is at the village of New Debiso, most easily reached from the direction of Kumasi, with the last 94km being on a bumpy dirt road. Using public transport, my understanding is that you would first have to bus to Eduikrom, from where tro-tros run to the park boundary, but this has not been confirmed. At present, there is a basic guesthouse close to the entrance gate, with two bedrooms, en-suite bathrooms and kitchen, at a cost of around US$3.50 per person. Camping is permitted next to the guesthouse, and two camps similar to the one at Ankasa will be constructed over the course of 2000. Several trails have been cut through the forest, and more are planned for 2000, along with a number of hides and observation platforms. For more details about Bia, contact the PADP (see facing page).

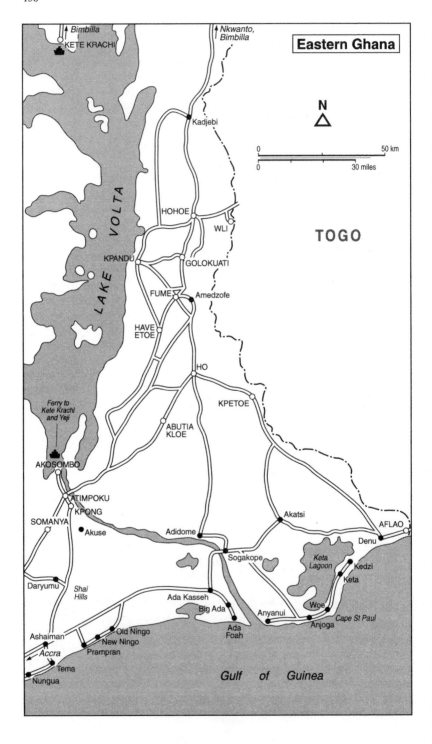

Chapter Seven

Eastern Ghana

The east of Ghana is probably the part of the country that currently attracts the lowest volume of tourists, a situation that's difficult to explain when you consider its great natural beauty, not to say the wealth of low-key, low-cost travel possibilities offered to those with the initiative to take them up. For keen hikers and ramblers, the lush and relatively cool highlands around Ho and Hohoe, boasting not only the country's highest peaks but also a plethora of accessible waterfalls and an excellent little monkey sanctuary at the village of Tafi Atome, will undoubtedly be a highlight of a visit to Ghana. And the east coast, too, is rich in isolated, out-of-the-way gems, most notably the small ports of Ada and Keta.

Travel conditions in Eastern Ghana generally conform to those experienced in other parts of the country, a little cheaper perhaps, but no more arduous. Nevertheless, this region will appeal greatly to those travellers for whom travel means *travel* in the chest-thumping, epic journey sense, rather than, say, soaking up the tropical beach atmosphere at Ada. Two exceptional ferry rides run through this part of Ghana: the daily trip from Ada north to Akuse along the Volta River, and the legendary overnight run from Akosombo to Yeji via Lake Volta. And there is also the bumpy overland trip from Hohoe through to the northern capital of Tamale, the closest thing in Ghana to those interminable bone-crunching trips for which many other African countries are renowned. In short, if the term 'off the beaten track' sets your ears pricking, then this is probably the part of Ghana for you.

THE COAST FROM TEMA TO ADA
Tema
Ghana's fourth largest city and second largest port (after Takoradi), Tema's population has grown almost tenfold from 35,000 in the early 1960s to more than 250,000 now, mainly as a result of its proximity to Akosombo Dam. Tema is often overlooked by tourists as a result of being situated only 25km east of the capital, and, frankly, this is much as it should be, since Tema really is the dullest of cities, redeemed only by the busy central market area, a lively fishing port and – for nature lovers – an alluringly bird-rich lagoon just as you enter the town along the coastal road from Accra.

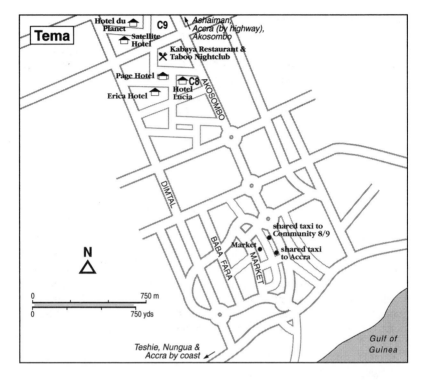

Getting there and away

Regular tro-tros to Tema leave Accra from Tema station in the city centre, taking about 45 minutes each way. Travellers staying in the Adabraka area of Accra may find it easier to catch a shared taxi from Nkrumah Circle to Nungua and pick up transport to Tema from there.

Where to stay and eat

It is difficult to imagine why any traveller would want to stay in Tema, since it's so easy to visit as a day trip from the capital, and – contrary, perhaps, to expectations – accommodation is no cheaper. But if you insist, there *is* plenty of accommodation in Tema, much of it conveniently clustered over a walking distance of about 500m, and all within 50m of a shared taxi route – from central Tema, look for a taxi marked for Community 7, 8 and 9 on the opposite side of the road to the tro-tro station for Accra.

The cheapest rooms are at the **Erica** or **Jakotron Hotel** (though both names are signposted, it appears to be one place) in Community 8; rather scruffy little s/c doubles with fan costing US$8. The nearby **Page Hotel** is far more upmarket, with a restaurant and good snack bar, and ac, s/c double rooms with tv for US$17. Similar in standard, and facing each other as the shared taxis enter Community 9, are the **Hotel du Planet** and **Satellite Hotel**, both of which have s/c doubles with fan for around US$10 and similar rooms with ac for around US$15. Back in Community 8, the **Hotel**

Lucia seems a lot smarter and charges practically identical rates of US$10 for a double room with fan and US$15 for a double with ac.

In the middle of the cluster of hotels, basically in one complex, you'll find the **Kabaya Restaurant** and **Golden Ivy Chinese Restaurant**, as well as the pleasant rooftop **Taboo Nightclub and Bar**.

Prampram and Ningo

The small towns of Prampram, New Ningo and Old Ningo lie within 10km of each other on the stretch of coast between Accra and the mouth of the Volta. Separated by a long, sandy beach as attractive as any in the country, Prampram and Old Ningo are two of the oldest European settlements in this part of Ghana. Prampram was the site of a small British trading post and fort built in 1742, while Ningo was the site of a Danish fort from 1735 until it was handed to Britain in 1850. Neither fort, however, has survived to the modern day: some traces of Prampram's Fort Vernon remain in the walls of a more modern, but also derelict resthouse near the fishing harbour, and even less remains to be seen of Fort Fredensborg in Old Ningo. The main attraction of the area is the beach, particularly the stretch around New Ningo, generally regarded as safe for swimming and dotted with holiday homes – New Ningo even boasts a rather posh-looking polo club. The estuary on the west flank of Old Ningo is also very pretty, its natural beauty enhanced by the colourful fishing boats moored on the beach.

Getting there and away

All three small towns lie about 6km to the south of the main Accra–Aflao road, along a road which on paper forms a roughly 20km-long southward loop. In practice, no vehicles can complete this loop at the time of writing, since the bridge over the estuary on the west flank of Old Ningo is being reconstructed and is open to foot passengers only. Prampram is the main transport hub in the area, but there is no direct tro-tro transport between it and Accra – you will almost certainly have to change vehicles at Ashaiman, a busy junction town to the north of Tema. If you are coming to Prampram from the direction of Ada, ask to be dropped at Dwahenya (also known as Prampram junction) and wait for a lift to Prampram there.

Regular shared taxis connect Prampram to New Ningo and Old Ningo (or more accurately at the time of writing, to the edge of the bridge across the lagoon, from where it's a five-minute walk to Old Ningo).

Where to stay and eat

Visitors to Prampram have two hotels from which to choose. At one end of the scale is the **Prampram Sealane Hotel**, about 500m and signposted from the lorry station. This place is definitely aiming for the Accra weekend crowd with its green neat grounds, reasonable bar and restaurant, and comfortable s/c twin rooms with tv and fan for US$12. At the opposite end of the scale is **Sam's Place**, tucked away in the alleys behind the lorry station, and offering grotty rooms at a rather steep US$5. If the latter place is more in your price range, then rather head on to New Ningo where the

Hotel de Vas, on the eastern side of town just before the Polo Club, seems much better value, with basic but adequate rooms for US$2.50.

The ambience-deficient **Golden Beach Resort** in Prampram, five minutes' walk from the Sealane Hotel, serves chilled drinks on a rather desolate beach dominated by the massive hulk of an abandoned cargo ship. Similar but nicer is the **Comme Çi Resort** on the western side of New Ningo. The only place to eat Western food is the Sealane Hotel in Prampram.

Ada

The port of Ada lies on the mouth of the Volta River, which was readily navigable for several hundred kilometres inland before the construction of the Akosombo Dam in the 1960s. Ada has thus played an important role in Ghanaian history as a combined river and ocean port, but – rather surprisingly – only one rather small fort is ever known to have been built there, Fort Kongensten, constructed by the Danes in 1783 and long ago vanished. Ada probably peaked in importance in the nineteenth century, when it was visited by Henry Stanley, who sailed there from London in a Thames pleasure launch several months after his renowned 'discovery' of Livingstone in Tanzania. It was Stanley, in the company of Captain Glover, who took the first steamer across the perilous Ada Bar and up the Volta. Sadly, Ada is today something of a backwater, with little to show for its illustrious past. It is of interest to travellers mostly for the isolated, backpacker-friendly Estuary Beach Camp, but it also serves as the most obvious base from where to explore the lushly vegetated lower regions of the River Volta, whether by chartered canoe or via the public ferry to Akuse.

Getting there and away

Ada consists of three discrete settlements. Ada Kasseh lies on the main Accra–Aflao road, at the junction of the road to Big Ada and Ada Foah, which lie 15km and 20km respectively to its south. From the point of view of travellers, Ada Foah is the most important settlement, since it lies closest to the river mouth as well as to most of the accommodation in the area. If you can't find direct transport to Ada Foah from elsewhere on the coast, you'll have no difficulty getting a tro-tro to drop you at Ada Kasseh, from where regular tro-tros run up and down to Ada Foah.

Few people would miss the opportunity to arrive at or leave Ada Foah by river ferry (unless, as was the case when we were in the area, the ferries are docked as a result of a diesel shortage). Two boats run up and down the river between Ada and Akuse (15km and a short tro-tro ride south of Kpong), leaving in opposite directions on alternate days. The newer *MS Oko* starts the upriver journey from Ada at 07.00 on Monday, Wednesday and Friday, arriving at Akuse at about 18.00. The same boat leaves from Akuse at 07.00 on Tuesday, Thursday and Saturday, arriving at Ada at about 16.30. The older *MS Sogakope* leaves from Ada at 07.00 on Tuesday, Thursday and Saturday, and from Akuse at 07.00 on Wednesday, Friday and Monday. The fare in either direction is US$1 per person. Simple meals are available on board, but not drinks. Both boats stop at Sogakope on the main Accra–Aflao road. Should you need to stop over in Akuse, the **Volta River Authority Clubhouse** has clean s/c doubles for around US$17 as well as an inexpensive restaurant and bar, and a swimming pool and tennis courts. More basic, cheaper accommodation can be found at the **Africana Stop Over Inn**.

A final possibility is to take a motorised canoe across the Volta to Anyanui for Keta; see *Getting there and away* under Keta on page 166.

Where to stay and eat

The once popular **Estuary Beach Camp** on the mouth of the Volta River was destroyed by a flood in 1998, since when a number of similar set-ups have opened in the Ada area. The most recent addition is the **Cocoloko Beach Camp**, established in late 1999 by the former owner of the Estuary Beach Club about 400m from the beach and half an hour's walk west of the town centre, which offers accommodation in reed huts at around US$3.50 per person. Other possibilities are the **Harmony Beach Club** and **Sea View Cottages**, both of which offer simple accommodation in reeds huts at around US$5 for two people. Meals are definitely available by request at Harmony Beach, but no mention is made of whether meals are offered at the other two places. Of several 'spots' that line the road between Ada Foah and Harmony Beach, the **Brightest Spot** has been recommended for simple local meals. The best place to make further enquiries about current accommodation options is the clearly signposted 'Tourist Centre' on the main road about 100m downhill from the petrol station where all the tro-tros stop.

The only accommodation actually within the bounds of Ada Foah is the **Ada Hotel**, which seems grossly overpriced at US$18 for a scruffy s/c double with fan. About 1km out of town, the three-star **Paradise Beach Hotel** (tel: 0968 275/6/7) is rather more upmarket, and reasonably priced at around US$45 ac, s/c double with TV and hot water.

If for some reason you should get stuck at the junction town of Ada Kasseh, the **Gardens Hotel** is a surprisingly smart-looking place. Another option is the **No Problems Guesthouse** along the main road between Big Ada and Ada Foah.

SOGAKOPE AND AKATSI

On the east bank of the River Volta, some 25km upriver of Ada, the small town of **Sogakope** forms something of a transport hub. Not only is Sogakope adjacent to the most southerly bridge across the Volta, making it the sole funnel for road traffic crossing directly between Greater Accra and Volta Regions, but it is also the main port stopped at by ferries between Ada and Akuse. The Vume area, on the opposite side of the river to Sogakope, is rightfully renowned for its painted ceramic pots, which are displayed for sale on the side of the road.

Aside from changing over vehicles, the only reason you'd be likely to stop off in Sogakope is to visit Villa Cisneros (tel/fax: 0968 311), an unexpectedly large and upmarket complex on the east bank of the river about 1km downstream from the bridge. Facilities include everything from river trips to tennis court, swimming pool and satellite television, and rooms are relatively affordable starting at US$16 for a single with fan and going up to US$30 for a room with double bed, ac, tv and fridge.

The relatively downmarket alternative to Villa Cisneros is the Volta View Hotel, misleadingly named since it's a good ten minutes' walk from the river. It also seems quite steeply priced for what you get. A non-s/c double with fan costs US$9, a s/c double with fan US$17, and you can't help but feel that a lick of paint might be in order before the next price increase. On the plus side, should you have to swap vehicles, the garden bar at the Volta View serves ice-cold draught beer and spicy kebabs a mere 20m from the tro-tro station.

Another important junction town on the Accra–Aflao road is **Akatsi**. We found that we had to change vehicles here when we travelled between Ho and Keta and again when we travelled between Aflao and Sogakope. Of minor interest, should you get stuck here, is an old hunters' collection that serves as an informal natural history museum. Accommodation can be found at the **Black Cat Hotel**, where a double room costs around US$5.

KETA AND THE FAR EAST COAST
Probably the least-visited part of southern Ghana, the roughly 100km stretch of coast between the Volta River and the Togolese border is also one of the most rewarding, and highly recommended to travellers with the inclination to spend a few days away from any established travel circuit. A dramatic feature of this region is the Keta Lagoon, the largest in the country, 40km long and 8km wide. This generally very shallow body of fresh or brackish water is separated from the sea for much of its length by a strip of sand less than 1km wide, causing some concern that many of the settlements on this stretch of coast will eventually be swallowed by the sea. Among other things, Keta Lagoon is a genuine birdwatchers' paradise, and several of its islands are important bird-breeding sites.

The main town along this stretch of coast is Keta, the site of Fort Pridzeinstein, built by Danes in 1784 and now a substantial ruin. In general, Keta seems quite incredibly run-down – a result, presumably, of the water erosion that threatens to engulf the town. The large number of crumbling buildings gives Keta a somewhat bleak mood, one that reminded me of parts of the Tanzanian coast in the 1980s, though based on our experience the advanced urban decay is compensated for by the genuine friendliness you tend to encounter only in places where tourists remain something of a novelty. Further in Keta's favour is its beach, very pretty, relatively turd-free and normally safe for swimming (though you should ask local advice first). And finally, there are the birds, which should hold some interest even for those not normally given to twitching – right in the town centre I saw the largest concentrations of pied kingfisher and avocet that I've ever encountered.

While Keta remains the obvious tourist focus in this region, the opportunities for exploration are excellent, and aided by the presence of a guesthouse or hotel in at least four different settlements. Definitely worth

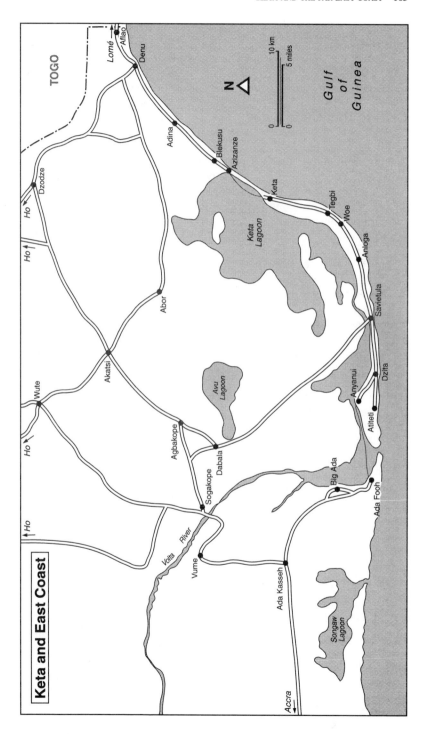

Keta and East Coast

checking out is the lighthouse at Cape St Paul near Woe, reportedly the oldest lighthouse in the country. Also of interest are the extensive shallot farms on the edge of the lagoon, especially around Anloga. Finally, the lagoon itself could reward further exploration by boat – you'll have no difficulty finding somebody to take you out on the water at Keta or elsewhere.

Getting there and away

A good tar road connects Keta to the main Accra–Aflao road at Dabala. You'll have no problem finding transport to Keta from this direction. Coming from Accra, the best place to find a direct tro-tro to Keta is at Ashaiman. Coming from Ho, you'll probably have to catch one tro-tro to Akatsi, then another to Keta. Coming from Ada, you may also have to do the trip in stages, changing vehicles at Kasseh and Sogakope.

A far more interesting way of approaching Keta from the west, however, would be to take a motorised canoe across the Volta River between Ada Foah and Anyanui, from where the occasional tro-tro covers the 10km or so stretch of road to Savietula junction on the main Keta road. Before doing this, it would be wise to check whether any canoes are likely to be leaving the next day, since they generally only go on market days, which are Tuesday, Wednesday, Friday and Saturday. Even on these days, there may be only one boat in either direction. The best source of current advice is the tourist centre in Ada.

Heading east from Keta, most maps show a solid surfaced road following the coast directly to Aflao. In reality, the 5–10km stretch of this road connecting Keta to Azizanze has been engulfed by the narrow bar of shifting sand that separates sea from lagoon (note that Azizanze is not shown on many maps, but it lies about 1km before Blekusu). Local people thus use a taxi-boat to get from Keta to Azizanze, where they pick up a tro-tro to Aflao. These boats leave Keta from in front of the central market 100m from the lorry station, carry around 30 people each, cost next to nothing, and take 30–60 minutes depending on whether they are motorised or not. The boats have to follow a strict course, since the lagoon is so shallow (we saw what appeared to be a man walking on water right in the centre of the lagoon). The best day to travel is market day in Keta, every four days, when you'll rarely wait more than about 30 minutes for something to leave. On other days, transport is less frequent, but you should still get across with ease.

Azizanze has a beautiful position on the lagoon's edge. There are a few stalls selling bread, eggs, etc and you can see where the tar road has literally vanished into the sand. There should normally be a row of tro-tros and shared taxis waiting to go direct to Aflao (certainly this is the case on market days).

The road towards Aflao, once again surfaced and in good condition, passes through a few small villages, palm-lined havens fringed by both lagoon and ocean, and notable for several large, modern burial shrines reminiscent in style of the *posuban* shrines of the Elmina area (see page 142).

Where to stay and eat

The only formal accommodation in Keta is the **Keta Beach Hotel** (tel: 0906 288), a smart, well-run and friendly establishment that's quite popular with Accra residents at weekends, but very quiet during the week. Rooms here start at US$7.50/10 for a non-s/c single/double with a fan and using clean communal showers, and they go up to US$25 for a s/c, ac double with tv, fridge and water heater. Good meals are served in the restaurant and pleasantly wooded garden bar, and cold beers are available. Coming by road from the west, ask the tro-tro driver to drop you at the hotel, clearly signposted and very close to the main road some 2km before you reach the centre of Keta.

If the above sounds too expensive, then there are a couple of cheaper guesthouses on the side of the road coming from the west, well before you arrive at Keta. These are the **Superfine Guesthouse** in Anloga, about 15km before Keta, and the **Abutia Guesthouse** in Woe about 10km before Keta. We didn't stop at these places, but it's difficult to imagine that either would charge much more than US$5 for a room.

Another option, right opposite Keta Beach Hotel, is the **Ghana Highway Authority Resthouse** – the caretaker may allow tourists to stay there for around US$5 per room, assuming that it's not already occupied by GHA staff.

The only accommodation along the stretch of road between Keta and Aflao is at Adiafana-Denu, where the one-star **Hotel Vilcabamba** (tel: 0962 354) lies close to the OSA station about 2km before you reach the main junction. Double rooms here start at around US$10.

AFLAO

This typically chaotic border town, the third largest urban settlement in Volta Region, must be a somewhat disconcerting introduction to Ghana for those coming from Togo. It's one of those places where money changers yell at you from all directions, and you can expect a few blatant attempts at overcharging, especially when you are walking away from the border. For those travelling entirely within Ghana, Aflao lies off any major trunk route, and the only situation in which you'd be likely to pass through the town is if you'd followed the coastal road from Keta and wanted to pick up transport back towards Accra or Ho. Aflao is not without redeeming features, however, most obviously a variety of street food that's second to none in Ghana – wherever you go you'll see women carrying baskets full of crusty baguettes, betraying your proximity to a francophone country.

Getting there and away

Aflao has a lorry station as crowded as any in Ghana, with all manner of tro-tros heading direct to Accra and most points in between. There are also regular STC and OSA buses to Accra. The most interesting route in or out of Aflao, however, is the coastal one to or from Keta described opposite.

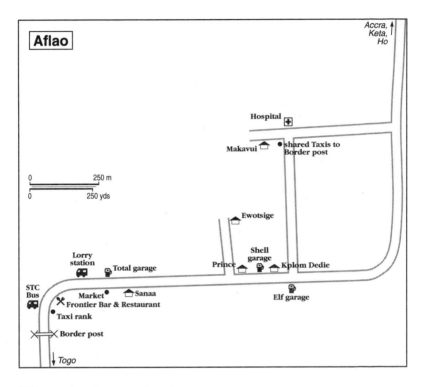

Where to stay and eat

Should you need to stay the night in Aflao, there's no shortage of accommodation. The **Sanaa Hotel**, the closest place to the lorry station, has adequate rooms for US$4.50/5.50. I'll leave it to you to decide whether you transgress the somewhat cryptic ruling that the 'rate applies to one man one flesh only Gen 2:24'.

Clustered about 100m apart and roughly 500m back along the road away from the border post, the **Kplom Dedie**, **Prince** and **Ewotsige Hotels** all have rooms with double beds for between US$3.50 and US$4.50, with the Kplom Dedie definitely the first choice.

The most upmarket place in town is the **Makavu Hotel**, about 1km from the border, which has s/c rooms with fans for US$8/10 and with ac for US$15. The Makavu has the only restaurant proper in Aflao, as well as an attractive beer garden. Shared taxis run between the border post and a taxi rank in front of the hospital that lies about 50m from this hotel.

THE ROAD TO AKOSOMBO

If you simply want to get to the town of Akosombo (see page 171), a great many tro-tros head there directly from Accra. For those with time to spare, however, there are two worthwhile and little-visited spots within easy striking distance of the Akosombo road. These are Shai Hills Resource Reserve and Somanya, currently being developed for low-key ecotourism with the assistance of Peace Corps volunteers. Both of these places would make for easy day trips for motorised Accra residents.

Note that travellers exploring this eastern part of Ghana may well end up changing vehicles at **Ashaiman**, a busy little town at the junction of the main Accra–Aflao highway and the roads south to Tema and north towards Akosombo. Regular tro-tros connect Ashaiman with most of the main lorry stations in Accra. There are a few hotels in Ashaiman should you need to spend the night.

Shai Hills Resource Reserve
Shai Hills is the closest wildlife sanctuary to Accra, and one of the most accessible in the country, since it is bordered by the main Akosombo road. It protects an area of coastal savannah, broken by rocky hills which supports patches of dry evergreen forest rich in endemic plant species. The area now protected by the reserve was home to the Shai people for several centuries until 1892, when they were ejected by the British. There are still a great many traces of Shai occupation in the reserve, including pottery dating to about AD1600. Several active Shai shrines lie within the reserve, but the most important are closed to casual visitors.

Originally demarcated as a forest reserve, Shai Hills was listed as a game reserve in 1962 and, uniquely in Ghana, it has since been fenced off to protect the remaining wildlife. Motorised visitors will be able to explore the reserve from 20km of fairly good roads but, until such time as horseback trails are introduced, other visitors must explore on foot with an armed guide. The most common large mammal in the reserve is the baboon, which most visitors will see, followed by kob antelope and the shy bushbuck. There are plans to reintroduce other antelope species, such as roan and hartebeest. About 90 bird species have been recorded, an improbably low total which suggests that many further species await discovery. There are more than ten dams in the reserve, as well as several caves, of which the most interesting is the bat cave about 4km east of Sayu Camp.

Entrance costs US$2 per person. Guided walks cost US$1 per hour.

Getting there and away
The main entrance gate lies on the main Akosombo road opposite Doryumu junction, easily identified by the prominently signposted Midway Spot bar. A second entrance gate, more difficult to pick up, lies about 10km further towards Akosombo, at Sayu Camp. On public transport, the best way to get to the main entrance gate is to first take a tro-tro from Accra to Ashaiman, from where any tro-tro heading to Doryumu will drop you outside the reserve.

Where to stay and eat
Camping is permitted at the main entrance gate, though we were asked US$20 per person, not particularly tempting even if it is inclusive of entrance and guide fees. You can also camp at **Sayu Camp** in the north of the park, but you must first report to the headquarters at the main entrance gate.

An affordable alternative is to head to Doryumu about 1km from the entrance gate. Here you'll find the **Shai Hills Hotel**, an unsignposted white building on the left side of the Mamre Road about 100m from the lorry station. Basic s/c rooms with running water and electricity cost US$4, good value even if the hotel is – in the words of the management – 'not properly functioning', by which they mean it no longer has a bar or restaurant. There are a couple of bars around the lorry station in Doryumu.

Mount Krobo and Somanya

Mount Krobo is the spiritual home of the Krobo people, who settled there for the natural protection it offered against Ashanti slave raids and whose famous defeat of an Ashanti raid in 1764 led directly to the incumbent Ashanti king being destooled. The Krobo were less fortunate when they resisted a British attempt to impose poll taxes in 1892; they were forced off the mountain, which has remained virtually uninhabited ever since.

The Mount Krobo Community Reserve has recently been developed for tourism with the assistance of a Peace Corps volunteer. A reception centre with summer huts, a shower and flush toilet was constructed at the base of the mountain in 1999, and a number of guided walks are offered, ranging from one to five hours in duration and costing US$1–3 per person. Among the mountain's natural attractions are the rare charcoal tree *Talbotia genetii*, wild baboons, birds, caves and views across to Lake Volta. Of archaeological interest are the ruins of abandoned Krobo villages, still used to enact sacrificial rites, as well as the former chief's palace and the ceremonial 'Dipo Stone'.

Only 8km from Krobo, the small town of Somanya has also been the site of recent tourist development. Activities that can be arranged here include a 40km hike to Boti Falls (see page 195), a visit to the bead factory in Odumasi or the Wednesday and Saturday bead market at Agomanya, and visits to cocoa farms, herbalists, traditional drummers and various fetish shrines.

Getting there and away

To reach Krobo from Accra or Tema in a private vehicle, follow the Akosombo Road as far as the junction to the mountain (about 2km before Akuse Junction) then turn right to reach the reception centre. On public transport, the best option is to catch a bus to Somanya from Tudu Station in Accra or at the Community Two tro-tro station in Tema, then hire a private taxi in Somanya to cover the last 8km to Krobo. Alternatively, any transport heading between Accra and Akasombo should be able to drop you at the mountain junction, from where you can walk to reception.

Where to stay and eat

No accommodation exists on Mount Krobo, though self-sufficient campers are welcome to pitch a tent at the reception area. Alternatively, the **Traycourt Leisure Centre**, only 3km from the mountain, has s/c doubles for around US$17, as well as decent food and a garden bar. In Somanya, the **Palm Hotel** offers s/c doubles at around US$8 and doubles using communal facilities at US$5, while several travellers have recommended staying in the home of Michael Dey, who can normally be located at the Ministry of Agriculture or at an agricultural store next to the Presbyterian bookshop near the main tro-tro station. There is also accommodation in Akuse, about 5km from Mount Krobo (see page 163).

AKOSOMBO AND SURROUNDS
The township of Akosombo was purpose-built in 1961 to house the workers involved in the creation of Ghana's largest dam, a clay and rock construction measuring 370m across and 124m from top to bottom, inaugurated by President Nkrumah in 1966. The body of water dammed by Akosombo, known as Lake Volta, is the most expansive artificial lake in the world, with a surface area of roughly 850,000ha, a length of 400km, and a shoreline measuring almost 5,000km.

Aside from affording an excellent view over the dam, Akosombo is important to travellers as the southern terminus of the weekly Lake Volta ferry to the northern ports of Kete Krachi and Yeji (see page 173). In addition to this local passenger ferry service, the more tourist-oriented *MV Dodi Princess* does a joyride to the Dodi Islands every Sunday, leaving at 10.30 and getting back at around 16.00; tickets cost US$6 and can be booked through the Volta Lake Transport Authority, tel: 0251 686.

For the purpose of orientation, it's worth noting that Akosombo township lies some 8km off the main road between Accra and Ho. The junction to Akosombo is at Atimpoku, a small but impressively chaotic urban sprawl straddling the Accra–Ho road on the west bank of the river. Atimpoku's skyline is dominated by a massive suspension bridge, one of only two places where cars are able to cross the Lower Volta. Travellers on a budget are generally better catered for in Atimpoku than in Akosombo, and Aylo's Bay, 500m from the junction, offers perhaps the best access to the river in this area.

Getting there and away
By road
The main regional transport centre is Kpong, situated on the west bank of the Volta some 10km south of Atimpoku and 10km north of the river ferry terminal at Akuse. Kpong is bisected by the main Accra–Ho road, and it is connected by regular tro-tros to Ashaiman (for Accra), Ho and Akuse. Regular tro-tros run up and down from Kpong to Akosombo via Atimpoku and New Senchie, and you'll rarely wait more than five minutes for a seat between any of these places. STC, OSA and other buses travelling between Accra and Ho will generally drop passengers on request at Atimpoku, provided that they don't mind paying the full fare. If you're heading to Ho from Atimpoku, most vehicles passing in the right direction will be full when they come past, which means it's generally quicker in the long run to take a tro-tro to Kpong and board a Ho-bound vehicle there.

Regular shared taxis run around the sprawling hills of Akosombo. From the lorry station, ask for a taxi to 'Mess' for the Volta Hotel, and one to 'Marine' for the ferry jetty and ticket office.

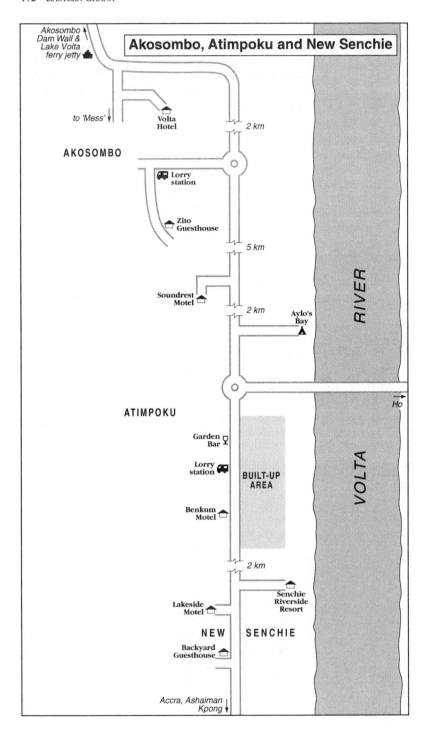

Akosombo
Dam Wall &
Lake Volta
ferry jetty

Akosombo, Atimpoku and New Senchie

to 'Mess'

Volta
Hotel

2 km

AKOSOMBO

Lorry
station

Zito
Guesthouse

5 km

Soundrest
Motel

2 km

Aylo's
Bay

RIVER

Ho

ATIMPOKU

Garden
Bar

Lorry
station

BUILT-UP
AREA

Benkum
Motel

VOLTA

2 km

Lakeside
Motel

Senchie
Riverside
Resort

NEW　SENCHIE

Backyard
Guesthouse

Accra, Ashaiman
Kpong

By ferry

The weekly ferry service across Lake Volta leaves from Akosombo every Monday at 16.00. It arrives at Kete Krachi at 05.00 on Tuesday morning and at Yeji on Tuesday evening. It then starts the return trip out of Yeji at around 04.00 on Wednesday morning, stops at Kete Krachi on Wednesday evening and arrives back in Akosombo on Thursday morning. In both directions, the ferry stops at Kpandu, halfway between Akosombo and Kete Krachi, when the water level is sufficiently high, which is generally only in the rainy season.

Three types of ticket are available for the ferry. First-class tickets for an ac, two-bed cabin cost US$15 per person for the full trip. Only two such cabins are available, however, so it's advisable to book well in advance (tel: 0251 686). Otherwise, a second-class ticket, which can normally be bought early on the day of departure, gives you your own bed in a communal dormitory and costs US$7 per person for the full trip. Third-class deck tickets cost US$5.50 per person for the full trip. Tickets to Kete Krachi are about 20% cheaper than full-fare tickets to Yeji.

The cheap daily ferry service between Ada and Akuse would allow you to travel by boat from the Volta mouth all the way to Yeji, using road transport for a mere 30km between Akuse and the Akosombo dam wall. See *Getting there and away* under Ada on page 162.

Where to stay and eat

The closest hotel to the dam, the **Volta Hotel** (tel: 0251 731, fax: 021 66-3791, email: voltahtl@africaonline.com.gh) is part of the upmarket international Accor chain. It is also one of Ghana's few truly upmarket hotels outside Accra, with a great location on a hill overlooking the dam wall, as well as a large swimming pool and a good restaurant. S/c rooms with ac and tv cost US$90/100. The hotel lies more than 1km from Akosombo township; passenger taxis from the lorry station to 'Mess' pass by the bottom of its steep drive.

In Akosombo township, about 200m and signposted from the lorry station, the **Zito Guesthouse** has comfortable s/c rooms with fan for US$10 or with ac for US$16. It also has a pleasant, small garden and serves meals on request.

Along the road connecting Akosombo to Atimpoku, about 5km from the former and 2km from the latter, the **Soundrest Motel** has an attractively rustic setting, with restaurant and bar facilities. The rooms seem good value at US$6/7 single/double with fan, US$12 s/c double with fan, or US$17 s/c, ac double.

On the same road, less than 500m from Atimpoku and the Volta Bridge, **Aylo's Bay Leisure Spot** has a wonderfully atmospheric riverside location. There is not, as yet, any accommodation here, but you can pitch a tent for US$1.50 per person, and there are toilet and washing facilities. Aylo's is definitely the best place to eat in the area, serving large, tasty plates of fish or chicken with chips or rice for around US$2. Swimming is said to be safe in this stretch of the river (the water is remarkably clear) and a canoe trip from Aylo's to the bridge costs US$2.50 for up to three people. With advance notice, it's possible for groups to organise drumming, dancing and cooking workshops here, sleeping at the nearby Soundrest Motel. Contact PO Box 37, Akosombo, for details.

In the heart of Atimpoku, only 50m from the lorry station, the **Benkum Motel** is the obvious first choice for tentless backpackers. It looks like a dump from the outside, but the rooms are actually very nice and the people seem friendly. Clean rooms with a fan cost US$5 using communal showers and US$7.50 for s/c. There's no restaurant, but the staff will cook breakfast on request, and there's plenty of street food around if you don't want to wander up to Aylo's for a meal – oyster kebabs and packets of smoked shrimp are local specialities. A pleasant place to drink nearby is the garden bar opposite Adomi Spot, about 100m along the road towards Akosombo.

About 2km south of Atimpoku, at New Senchie, the **Lakeside Motel** (tel: 0251 310) has a variety of rooms all with one double bed; prices range from US$10 for a room with fan using communal showers to US$17 for a s/c room with ac. The restaurant has a varied menu and you can eat in the shady, sloping gardens. About 500m from the motel, you can also eat or drink at the clearly signposted **Senchie Riverside Resort**, which as the name suggests overlooks the river. Somewhere you probably don't want to bother with is the nearby **Backyard Guesthouse**, which seems very overpriced at around US$30 for a s/c, ac double.

So far as I'm aware, there is no accommodation in Kpong and only one hotel in Akuse, the inexpensive **Africana Stop Over Inn**.

HO AND SURROUNDS
The former administrative centre of German Togoland and modern capital of Volta Region, Ho is the largest, busiest town in this part of the country, with excellent facilities for backpackers and good transport connections. Aside from a couple of old colonial buildings (notably the old church and school, and the Ewe Presbyterian Mission at Wegbe, founded in the 1850s), about the only tourist attraction within the town is the Ho Museum next to the hospital, where an investment of US$1 will gain you entrance to an oddly eclectic and occasionally fascinating collection of photographs and artefacts, including displays on the mud-and-stick mosques of the northwest and Ashanti fetish shrines in the Kumasi area. Otherwise, Ho is of limited interest, though it remains a pleasant, inexpensive and well-organised place to take a day or two's break between exploring the many beauty spots that lie within a couple of hours' radius by tro-tro.

Getting there and away
Ho is an important transport hub, well connected to most parts of Ghana east of Accra and Lake Volta. Regular tro-tros leave from the lorry station to destinations such as Kpandu, Hohoe, Kpetoe and Accra. Travelling between Ho and eastern ports such as Keta or Aflao, you'll probably have to change vehicles at Akatsi. Travelling to Ho from the Akosombo area, the best place to pick up a vehicle is Kpong.

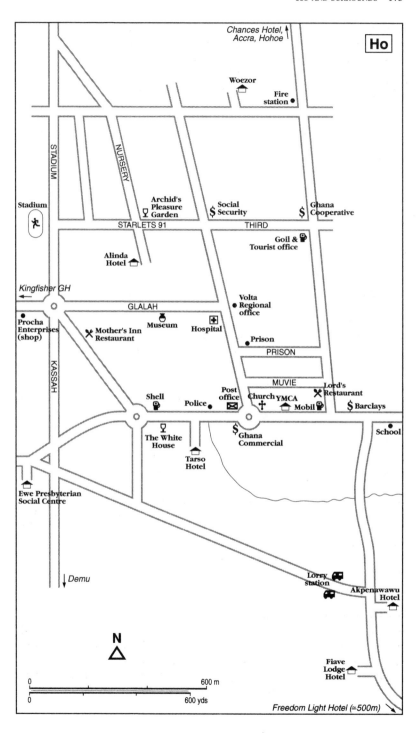

Where to stay

The selection of good affordable accommodation in Ho has to be about the best in the country. One of the best options, and quite handily situated if you're just using Ho as an overnight stop, is the **Freedom Light Hotel** (tel: 091 8158), which lies about 500m from the lorry station along the Kpalime road. Prices here start at US$7 for a room with one double bed and fan using communal bathrooms to US$10 for a similar s/c room, or US$20 for a s/c room with two double beds, ac, fan, fridge and tv. A pleasant feature of this hotel is the garden, which is dotted with traditional statues and boasts a couple of thatched 'summer houses'. The restaurant serves a good variety of Western dishes in the US$3–5 range.

On the main road between the lorry station and the Freedom Light Hotel, **Fiave Lodge** is a clean, unpretentious place with a family-run feel. The large, clean rooms all have fans, and they cost between US$4 and US$6, depending on whether they're self-contained and have one or two double beds. Also very close to the lorry station, the **Akpenamawu Hotel** looks rather sordid from the outside, but the rooms are perfectly acceptable and good value at US$3.50 for an ordinary double with fan to US$5 for a s/c double with fan and running water.

There's a couple of decent places along the main road through the town centre. The very central **YMCA** has basic but clean and pleasant doubles for a very reasonable US$3.50. So far as I could establish, the rooms here are available not only to men but also to couples and single women – but any further queries around the subject of what gender combinations could occupy the rooms and I rather suspect the bemused receptionist would have had me locked up! Not far away, the double-storey **Tarso Hotel** is the oldest hotel in town and looks it, though the atmosphere is very amiable and the spacious s/c rooms are very good value at US$6 (downstairs) or US$7 (upstairs).

Scattered elsewhere around town, the **Kingfisher Guesthouse** is again good value at US$6 for a s/c double. The same can't be said for the **Alinda Hotel**, once popular with travellers, but now absurdly overpriced at US$6/7 for a scruffy single/double using communal showers and US$12.50 for a s/c double. Much nicer and altogether better value, the **Ewe Presbyterian Social Centre** (tel: 091 670) offers a variety of clean accommodation: a dormitory bed costs US$2.50, a single using communal bathroom costs US$5.50, a s/c double with fan costs US$8 and an apartment US$14.

Aside from the Freedom Light, there are only two relatively upmarket options in Ho. The **Woezor Hotel** (tel: 091 8339), formerly a government Catering Resthouse and still a little frayed at the seams, charges US$17 for a s/c, ac double or US$20/25 for a single/double chalet. Far better value, the brand-new **Chances Hotel**, about 3km out of town along the Accra road, has large s/c, ac double chalets for US$26 and the best restaurant in Ho. By the time you read this, it will hopefully also have a swimming pool.

Where to eat

All things considered, the restaurant at the **Freedom Light Hotel** is probably the best place to eat, not only for the food – a good selection of inexpensive, tasty dishes including a tangy vegetable stew – but also for the ambience of the gardens. On the other side of town, the **Woezor Hotel** offers similar dishes at similar prices, but the atmosphere is a little dingy, except perhaps when there's live music. The food at **Chances Hotel** is excellent and not too expensive at around US$5 for a main course, but the location isn't very convenient at night, unless you arrange for a taxi to collect you.

In the town centre, good places to eat include the **Mother's Inn Restaurant**, which does chicken with chips or fried rice for around US$2–3 per plate, and offers the option of eating in or out of doors. Similar in standard, the **Lord's Restaurant** has indoor seating only, and the room you eat in is very hot and sweaty. For a chilled draught, perhaps the nicest spot in town is the **White House Bar**, though the less central **Archid's Pleasure Garden** has a more rustic character.

Street food, as usual, is to be found everywhere, and particularly around the lorry station and market area. A local speciality is cat meat, traditionally popular with the Ewe, but now an unusual and highly prized dish – so no fears about inadvertently chomping on a spicy tiger kebab.

Listings

Books A shop called Procha Enterprises (see map) stocks a small range of cheap secondhand paperbacks. Try also the street stalls between the hospital and the Regional Administrative Office.

Ghana Tourist Board Situated in the SIC Building near the Goil garage, the Volta Region tourist office is perhaps the most enthusiastic in the country, and well worth visiting for the latest information on developing tourist attractions throughout the area, especially those with Peace Corps involvement.

Kalapka Resource Reserve

Situated no more than 10km south of Ho, this 325km^2 reserve, gazetted in 1975, has yet to see much in the way of tourist development. It protects an area of gently sloping land, dominated by dry savannah, but with a few patches of forest, and bisected by the Kalapka River, a seasonal stream lined by borassus palms. Large mammal populations are rather low, though kob antelope, baboon and green monkey are still quite common and likely to be seen by most visitors. Less conspicuous species that are still present in the reserve include buffalo, bushbuck, waterbuck, Maxwell's duiker, patas monkey and a variety of nocturnal creatures such as bushpig and genet. The area has a reputation for good birding, though few details are available.

Although few tourists visit Kalapka, it is perfectly accessible to those who don't mind a bit of walking. At present, the best place to enter the reserve is at the village of Abutia Kloe, a short tro-tro ride south from Ho, where you can pay the nominal entrance fee and arrange an armed guide at the Department of Wildlife office. There's no accommodation at Abutia Kloe, and it would be easy enough to visit the reserve as a day trip out of Ho, but you should also be allowed to camp if you have a tent and fancy an early start in order to catch the animals and birds when they're most active.

It may well be that the next year or two sees more structured visits to Kalapka emanating from the village of Adaklu Helepke, where a Peace Corps volunteer was installed in November 1997 to look at possible tourist development. The main aim of this project is to open up hiking, caving and rock-climbing possibilities on the Adaklu Mountain, the dramatic inselberg that's visible from Ho on a clear day. But since Adaklu Helepke lies close to the eastern boundary of the resource reserve, it would be logical for these places to be developed in tandem. For current information, contact the Ghana Tourist Board office in Ho, which is involved in the project.

If you are in this area, it may be worth asking about the traditionally constructed former German governor's residence that lies on a mango-tree-covered hillside near the village of Abutia Agove, also the site of a famous spring which used to draw people from far and wide during periods of drought.

Kpetoe and Afegame

These small towns near the Togolese border about 30km east of Ho are renowned throughout Ghana for their *kente* cloth weavers. Although *kente* weaving is these days largely associated with the Ashanti, the people of Kpetoe claim that the style originated with them and was later adopted further afield after their best weavers were captured during the Ashanti wars. Two types of cloth are made in Kpetoe: the light and popular Ashanti *kente* and the more durable Ewe *agbamevo*. Curio buyers should note that this area is known for high-quality rather than high-volume production: it is not the place to come to buy cheap cloth, but good cloth. (See also *Kente* box on page 212.)

Kpetoe, the larger of the two weaving centres, lies on the main road connecting Ho to Aflao and Akutsi, so getting there is straightforward. Basic but affordable accommodation can be found here at the **Friends Club Hotel**.

BETWEEN HO AND HOHOE
Amadzofe

Formerly a German mission, Amadzofe is the principal town of the Avatime Mountains and the site of a well-known teacher training college. The town lies at an altitude of more than 600m, and is reached via a spectacular 3km ascent from Vame. Facing Amedzofe, Mount Gemi is one of the highest mountains in the country, and easily picked out by the large cross that was erected in its grassy peak in the 1930s by German missionaries – there is a bizarre local legend that the cross doubled as a communication device in World War II!

Blessed with a relatively temperate climate, substantial stands of rainforest, a great many bird and butterfly species, and three inexpensive government resthouses, the Amedzofe area offers some excellent opportunities for unstructured hiking and rambling – you could easily spend a few days working your way on foot from Amedzofe to Tafi Atome (see below) via Biakpa.

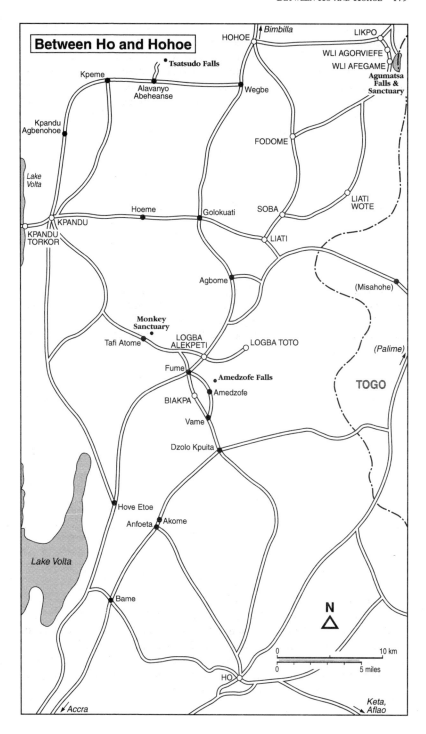

Between Ho and Hohoe

Since this guide was first printed, tourism in Amedzofe has been formalised under the auspices of the Amedzofe Planning and Tourism Council. Visitors must report to the tourism office to pay a tax of US$2 per person and arrange guided walks at a small fee. A good target for a short walk is Amedzofe Falls, 45 minutes from town following a dirt road and then a treacherously muddy footpath through lush forest to come out at the three knee-deep pools separating the upper and lower falls. More ambitiously, ask about visiting the valley at the base of the lower fall, said to harbour a population of black-and-white colobus monkeys. Another worthwhile goal is the peak of Mount Gemi, 30 minutes' walk from town, which offers tremendous views.

Getting there and away

Amedzofe lies about 35km from Ho, and it is reached by a rough dirt road through Akome and Vane. The most dramatic stretch of this road is the roughly 3km ascent from Vame to Amedzofe. Three vehicles plod back and forth between Ho and Amedzofe throughout the day, with one leaving in either direction every hour or so, on average. Note, however, that the vehicles all start out from Amedzofe before 06.30, and the first one generally only gets back at around 10.00, so there's normally a transport lull between these hours. The trip takes slightly longer than an hour in each direction.

Heading northwards from Amedzofe towards Hohoe may look straightforward enough on a map, but the reality is complicated by the absence of public transport between Amedzofe and the junction town of Fume on the main Ho–Hohoe road. The simplest way around this is to walk, with the option of using the road directly connecting Amedzofe to Fume, or else taking a Ho-bound vehicle as far as Vame and using the road that connects Vame and Fume. In terms of distance, there's not much to choose between these routes – both of them are around 6–8km – but the Vame–Fume road is a lot flatter and it allows for an overnight stop at the wonderful government resthouse about 1km past Biakpa.

If you're heading to Hohoe and don't fancy walking, your options are either to catch a tro-tro back to Ho and change vehicles there, or to catch a Ho-bound vehicle as far as Akume, where you should be able to pick up some transport to Bame, 8km away on the main Ho–Hohoe road.

Where to stay and eat

The **Amedzofe Government Resthouse** consists of six large double rooms. All have electricity and a private bathroom (there's an outside tap which has running water) and each pair shares a communal sitting room and balcony with views over the forest to Mount Gema and on a clear day to Lake Volta. Rooms cost US$5 per person. They can be booked in advance at Room 24 in Ho Regional Headquarters, though there's little need to book as things stand. Very little food is available in Amedzofe, so either bring some with you or make sure you're at the market well before sunset when the stalls will have run out of *kenkey* and the like. There are also a couple of bars next to the market; if you're luckier than us, then the one with the fridge and the one with the beer will be one and the same when you visit. Note that the guesthouse isn't actually in town, but on top of the same hill as the large and conspicuous television transmission tower; to get there, hop off the tro-tro at the junction just as you enter Amedzofe and follow the road signposted for the Ghana Broadcasting Corporation to your right and uphill for about 500m.

If you don't mind a bit of walking, the blissfully isolated **Biakpa Government Resthouse** lies about halfway along the 6–8km road connecting Vame and Fume, 1km past the village of Biapka in the direction of Fume. Set on a grassy hill, ringed by forest, and facing Mount Gemi, this is a gorgeous, little-known spot that will appeal greatly to keen walkers and birdwatchers. Accommodation consists of two double rooms, each with a private dining and sitting room, and the charge is only US$2.50 per person. There's water for washing, and the friendly caretaker, a stalwart of more than two decades' service, can organise any food you like from the village (well, within reason), and he'll cook it too – but if you're going to take advantage of his services, then do leave him a decent tip. As things stand, this resthouse goes weeks without a visitor, but it might still be worth booking a room through the District Headquarters in Ho (a different entity to the Regional Headquarters).

According to the caretaker at Biakpa, **Vane Government Resthouse** is on the junction up towards Amedzofe. There are four double rooms, each charging US$2.50 per head, and they can also be booked through the District Headquarters in Ho. In Vane, you'll see several signposts for the **Sikakrom Holiday Resort**, which to the best of my knowledge has never been a functioning entity (the story is that the guy who built the resort abandoned it immediately after it was finished).

In Akome, about halfway along the road between Ho and Amedzofe, the **Gemini Guesthouse** looks to be a clean and inexpensive little place.

Tafi Atome Monkey Sanctuary

Centred around the eponymous village, Tafi Atome Monkey Sanctuary was created in 1993 to protect the sacred monkeys that live in the surrounding forest. The story is that the ancestors of the modern villagers migrated to the area from Brong-Ahafo 200 years ago, and brought with them fetishes for monkeys and tortoises. For many years this taboo protected the monkeys, who were thought to act as spokesmen for the slower tortoises, but numbers had dwindled badly by the late 1980s, largely as a result of the erosion of traditional beliefs by Christianity. In 1996, there were estimated to be 60 monkeys in the area, living in three troops, and anecdotal evidence suggests that numbers have since increased.

Under Peace Corps guidance, Tafi Atome is actively trying to encourage tourism, and in fact seems to be developing into the very model of a multi-faceted community-based ecotourism project. Naturally enough, the monkeys form the centrepiece of tourist activities, and a guided tour of the sanctuary costs US$2 per person. The monkeys are seen by most visitors, bearing in mind that they are generally most active before 09.00 and after 15.00. Several other activities are available to visitors spending a night or two at Tafi Atome. These include a guided walk through the village, and a session of storytelling, drumming and dancing in the evening – the latter particularly enjoyable judging by the visitors' book. The guides can also organise for you to hire a bicycle to explore further afield. Worthwhile objectives include Tafi Abuife, a *kente* weaving village some 7km away; Logba Tota, 12km away via Logba Alekpeti and famous for its waterfall; or even Amadzofe, some 10–12km distant.

Tafi Atome's importance in conservation terms is that it harbours the only Ghanaian population of the nominate race of mona monkey *Cercopithecus mona mona*, distinguished from the Lowe's mona (*C. m. loweii*) of Baobeng-Fiema by its two white hip discs. Given the confusion that surrounds the classification of the *cercopithecus* monkeys, it is possible that, as some authorities maintain, these two types of monkey should be treated as discrete species. At Tafi, you'll be told that their monkeys are the only 'true monas' in Ghana, which could come across as hype, but is perfectly true – though all it means is that *C. m. mona* was formally described before *C. m. loweii*, so that the latter is regarded as a race of the former.

More generally, we were struck by the lack of hustle that characterises the village. Tafi Atome would be a great place to spend a couple of inexpensive and interesting days – and all funds raised from tourism go towards developing the monkey sanctuary or to the development of community projects such as building a much-needed clinic and drilling boreholes.

Getting there and away
Tafi Atome lies about 5km along a good dirt road that leaves the main Ho–Hohoe road at Logba Alekpeti. There is plenty of transport to the village on Logba's market day, which is on a five-day cycle. On other days, the only transport is a tro-tro that leaves Tafi Atome for Ho between 06.00 and 08.00 and returns in the late afternoon – it's best to pick it up at Logba Alekpeti, through where it passes at about 17.00. Alternatively, you can walk out from Logba Alekpeti, an easy hour's trip along a flat road through lush scenery.

Where to stay and eat
Accommodation is in two basic rooms, each of which has a double bed and mosquito net (the latter something you don't see too often in Ghana). A room costs US$3 for one person and US$4 for a couple. Alternatively, a full accommodation package, including simple meals prepared by a trained chef and guided tours through the sanctuary and village, costs US$7.50 per head. A couple of shops in the village sell warm Cokes and beers.

Kpandu
This small town near the Lake Volta shore is of interest to travellers mostly as the one place on the eastern shore where you can board or disembark from the Lake Volta ferry, at least during the rainy season when the water level is sufficiently high. The town centre, set about 4km back from the lake, is notable for several turn-of-the-century German

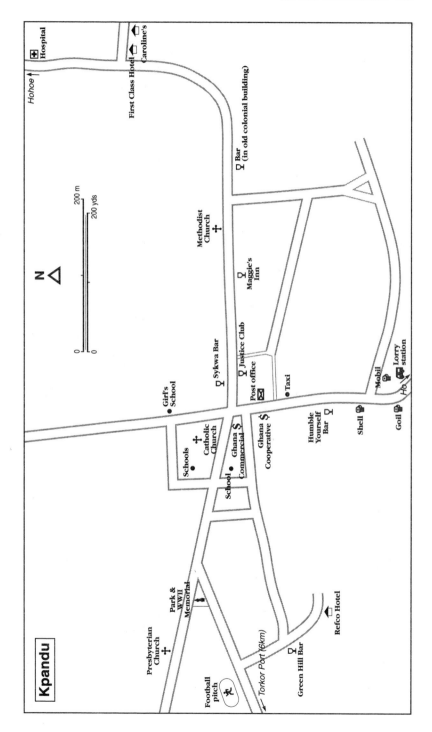

buildings, part of a mission founded there in 1904. The lake port of Kpandu Torkor, connected to the town centre by a steady stream of shared taxis, hosts a busy market selling not only fish, but all manner of cloths, garments and other foodstuffs.

If tourists are an infrequent sight in Kpandu District, the same cannot be said of the Virgin Mary, who evidently makes regular appearances in the area! Two grottos have been established at places where she has been seen. The Catholic grotto, reportedly one of the largest in Africa and open to all, is situated on top of a hill at Kpando Agbenohoe, about 8km north of town. The other, under control of the Ghana Blue Urs (whoever they might be), is at a place called Aziavi, and again open to all.

Note that the 'K' in Kpandu (and in all other place names in this part of the country that begin with 'Kp') is silent – locals pronounce 'Kp' as a slightly more explosive 'P'.

Getting there and away
Kpandu is connected to Ho and Hohoe by regular tro-tros. For details of the Lake Volta ferry, which stops at Kpandu, see *Getting there and away* under Akosombo on page 171.

Where to stay and eat
Situated just off the Hohoe road perhaps 500m from the town centre, the **Caroline Guesthouse** is a quiet place with simple, clean rooms with fan for US$3.50 double and US$4 twin. The neighbouring **First Class Guesthouse** is similar in standard but poor value by comparison, since rooms cost from US$5 to US$7.50. The rooms here are also very noisy when there's music playing in the bar, which, if our stay is representative, seems to be all the time.

On the other side of town, the **Refco Hotel**, the most upmarket in Kpandu, is set in pretty, flowering grounds near the top of a slope. It also seems good value: non-s/c rooms cost US$4/5/6 single/double/twin, while s/c rooms cost US$6/7 double/twin.

Street food is plentiful along the main road between the Ghana Commercial Bank and the lorry station, and there are a couple of indifferent looking chop bars dotted around town. For a sit-down meal, accompanied by cheap, chilled draught beer, try the **Justice Club**, where we had a very good plate of freshly cooked chicken and chips for US$2.50, served with a winning sense of ceremony.

HOHOE AND SURROUNDS
Hohoe is the second most populous town in Volta Region, and much like the regional capital it is a decidedly amiable place, busy without being in any way intimidating and offering good amenities to budget travellers. Hohoe makes a useful base from where to explore several local beauty spots (the waterfalls at Agumatsa, Tsatsodo and Liate Wote are all feasible day trips) but it has no inherent qualities that might conceivably invite superlatives.

Getting there and away

Hohoe is connected by regular tro-tros to Ho, Kpandu, Wli and most other towns in the region. Travellers coming to Hohoe from Amadzofe should note that there is no direct transport: you will either have to take a tro-tro back to Ho and pick up a Hohoe-bound vehicle there, or else walk the 5–6km from Vane or Amadzofe to Fume on the main Ho–Hohoe road.

Where to stay

Right in the town centre, opposite the prominent Bank of Ghana building, the **Grand Hotel** has a few shabby but very acceptable doubles with fan for US$5 and communal showers with running water. It's a good place to stay if you want to be close to the action: the atmospheric courtyard bar serves cheap draught beer and sensibly priced meals, and there are several more bars within a block if you hit a dull night. Fortunately, the noise from the bar doesn't penetrate through to the rooms to a significant degree.

The **Africa Unity Hotel** is the only other option right in the town centre. It is also the cheapest lodge in Hohoe, with basic rooms for US$2.50/4. It's often full, but close enough to the Grand Hotel that you could check it out first.

Of the less central places, the **Pacific Guesthouse** is deservedly popular with travellers, and less than ten minutes' walk from the tro-tro station via a dirt road through the fields. A room with a double bed and fan costs US$6.50 non-s/c or US$9 s/c. Chalets with ac cost US$20. Facilities include running water, a bar and a cosy tv lounge. Breakfast is served but other meals are by special request only. The newer **Geduld Hotel**, not far from the Pacific, is similar in both price and standard.

On the other side of town, the **Matvin Hotel** was once Hohoe's most upmarket hotel, and it has the grounds to prove it, complete with large garden bar overlooking a small stream. The rooms here are surprisingly inexpensive. A non-s/c room with double bed and fan costs US$5, while a s/c room with two double beds costs US$10. The food is reasonable.

Even further out of town, at least 1km along the Wli road, the **Machill Hotel** is a decent little place where spotless s/c doubles with fan and running water cost US$7. The absence of food and distance from town will put off most backpackers, but it is a good choice if you have a vehicle.

The relatively new **Taste Lodge** now ranks as the most upmarket address in Hohoe, and very good value it is too, charging US$20 for a pleasantly furnished s/c double with hot water, ac, fan, tv, radio and fridge.

Where to eat

The restaurant at the **Taste Lodge** has the most varied menu in town, and most dishes cost less than US$3. It would be the definite first choice if you could eat outdoors, but as things stand the dining room is just too sweaty to be a very appealing place to spend an evening. Far better to head to the **Grand Hotel** or **Matvin Hotel**, both of which serve a fair variety of dishes for around US$3 and offer the choice of eating inside or out. For cheaper local dishes, the **Eagle Canteen** and **Inatrip Chop Bar** are recommended.

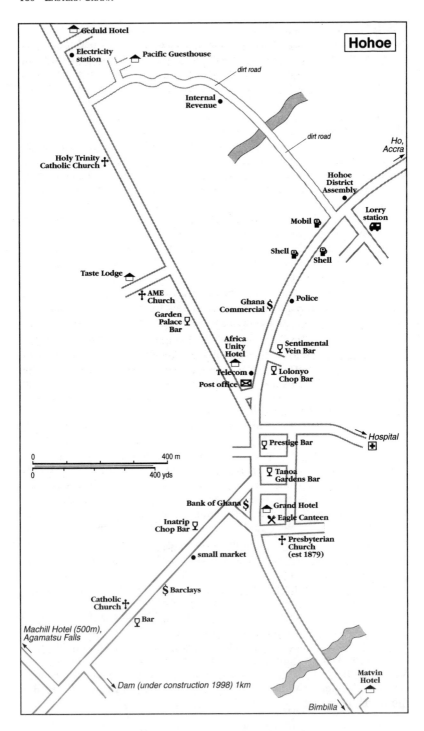

Hohoe

Geduld Hotel
Electricity station
Pacific Guesthouse
dirt road
Internal Revenue
dirt road
Ho, Accra
Holy Trinity Catholic Church
Hohoe District Assembly
Lorry station
Mobil
Shell
Shell
Taste Lodge
AME Church
Ghana Commercial
Police
Garden Palace Bar
Africa Unity Hotel
Sentimental Vein Bar
Telecom
Lolonyo Chop Bar
Post office
0   400 m
0   400 yds
Prestige Bar
Hospital
Tanoa Gardens Bar
Bank of Ghana
Grand Hotel
Eagle Canteen
Inatrip Chop Bar
Presbyterian Church (est 1879)
small market
Barclays
Catholic Church
Bar
Machill Hotel (500m), Agamatsu Falls
Dam (under construction 1998) 1km
Matvin Hotel
Bimbilla

There are quite a number of good bars in the town centre. In addition to the Grand Hotel, the **Tanoa Gardens Bar** and **Golden Palace Bar** both have cheap chilled draught, and the latter might just serve the spiciest kebabs in Ghana. The **Prestige Bar** was very quiet when we visited, but it should liven up when it hosts live music – check the posters around town for the next date.

Agumatsa (Wli) Falls

The Agumatsa or Wli ('*vlee*') Falls, situated on the edge of the 3km² Agumatsa Wildlife Sanctuary near the village of Wli Agorviefe on the Togolese border, is perhaps the most popular tourist attraction in eastern Ghana. Despite being billed as the 'largest waterfall in West Africa', it is not especially voluminous, so I would tend to assume that it is the *highest* waterfall in the region. Odd, then, that nobody seems to agree on how high it actually is. A few metres discrepancy I could understand, but it's difficult to know what to make of local estimates that range from 20m via 60m and 1,800ft to 2km, especially when the only figure I can find in print is 400m (surely a reference to the altitude?). Short of leaping from the top myself with a tape measure attached to my waist, I can only guess, but I would imagine that it is in the region of 50–60m high. It is certainly the tallest single drop of water that we saw in Ghana.

As much of an attraction as the waterfall itself is the footpath from Wli village to its base. The flat, easy path leads through thick, semi-deciduous forest for 45 minutes to an hour, fording the Agumatsa River a total of nine times – there are footbridges at all but the first crossing, which is also the most shallow. The sanctuary is thought to harbour some 220 bird and 400 butterfly species. The birding was disappointing when we visited, but the butterflies were dazzling, perhaps because we were walking during mid-morning. You're unlikely to see large mammals on the waterfall trail, though a small number of monkeys reportedly live deeper in the reserve. As you approach the waterfall, you'll hear the roar of plunging water vie with the high-pitched chirping of thousands upon thousands of straw-coloured fruit bats nesting on the adjacent cliffs – this must be an awesome sight towards dusk when the bats go out to forage. There's a large, rather shallow pool below the falls where you can take a refreshing dip, though the water is chillier than you might expect.

Getting to the waterfall couldn't be simpler. Regular tro-tros run along the 25km road between Hohoe and Wli. You're unlikely to wait more than 30 minutes for a vehicle and the trip out takes less than one hour. Once in Wli, the Department of Wildlife office, no more than 100m from where tro-tros stop, is where you pay the entrance fee of US$1 per person (proceeds are divided between the Wildlife Department and the community) and organise a mandatory guide (free of charge, but a tip would be in order).

Two very basic rooms are available in Wli, or you can camp at the base of the waterfall. If you spend the night, you could ask about the fetish shrine in Wli Afegame, or visit the caves which lie a tough hour's walk from Lipke Todium on the road to Hohoe – give the chief at Lipke a bottle of Schnapps and he'll arrange a guide.

Tsatsudo Falls

This seasonal waterfall on the Tsatsudo River, near the village of Alavanyo Abeheanse, is very accessible to travellers. It is not as spectacular as the Wli Falls, but is just as pretty, consisting of five separate falls, each separated from the one above and/or below by a rocky ledge. The pool at the base of the waterfall is deep enough to swim in properly, but do take care not to bump into one of the many large, submerged boulders. We climbed up a steep rock-face to the ledge separating the bottom fall from the one above, where you could also swim in a pool below a pretty overhang. The route we used to get up (and so far as we could tell the only way up) is not recommended unless you're reasonably agile and sure-footed, since there are a couple of spots where a slight slip would almost certainly lead to a broken limb or worse. So far as animal life goes, frogs seem to be particularly abundant and vociferous here, and the riverine vegetation and cliffs harbour quite a number of birds – we saw what appeared without binoculars to be a pair of auger buzzards and an African goshawk.

Alavanyo Abeheanse lies no more than 20km from Hohoe along a dirt road that branches from the main Ho road at Gibi Wegbe, about 7km from Hohoe. Regular tro-tros connect Hohoe to Abeahense, which is the first of several villages making up Alavanyo. Before you head out to the waterfall, you must visit the chief and pay a fee of US$2 per head, which allows you to visit the falls as many times and for as long as you like. The waterfall lies about 1km from the village; if you have a vehicle, you can drive to within 50m of it. A guide isn't necessary to find the waterfall, but might be a good idea if you want to explore the higher pools. Overnight camping is permitted at no extra charge, assuming that you've paid your entrance fee. Note that there is no public transport along the road connecting Alavanyo directly to Kpandu.

Liate Wote

This pretty village near the Togolese border on the foothills of Mount Afedzeto is yet another part of eastern Ghana that's being developed for tourism in association with a Peace Corps volunteer. The main attraction in the area is probably the Tagbo Waterfall. With a refreshing plunge pool at its base, and surrounded by semi-deciduous forest in an area that boasts one of the country's highest butterfly diversities, this is likely to be protected as a community reserve in the near future. Also of interest is the seasonal Tizor Falls. The peak of Mount Afedzeto, at 968m Ghana's highest, can be reached on foot from Liate Wote in roughly one hour – the views from the top are glorious.

The main obstacle to visiting Liate Wote at present is the low volume of public transport. It's easy enough to get transport from Hohoe to the junction at Golokuati, 20km south along the Ho road, and from there to pick up a vehicle on to Liate Agbonyra. There is, however, no public transport along the final 8km stretch of road between Liate Agbonyra and Liate Wote, so you'll either have to walk or charter a vehicle for around US$5–6 one way.

The only direct transport along the 14km backroad between Hohoe and Liate Wote is a lorry that leaves Liate Wote once daily between 07.00 and 08.00 and Hohoe daily in the late afternoon or evening. There is also a vehicle direct to Accra that leaves Liate Wote every Tuesday and Thursday morning at 05.00, presumably doing the return trip the next day.

There is no formal accommodation in Liate Wote, though a resthouse should be constructed within the lifespan of this edition. Warm drinks and snacks are available at Stella's Bar, and chilled drinks may soon be on the menu if there is truth in the rumour that electricity will arrive before the end of 1998.

FROM HOHOE TO TAMALE VIA BIMBILLA

The rough but scenic backcountry route between Hohoe and Tamale runs to the east and north of Lake Volta via the small towns of Nkwanta and Bimbilla. The trip breaks down into three legs, each of which normally takes one day to tackle. Roads are rough throughout: dusty in the dry season, muddy during the rains, and bumpy at all times. There is little point in attempting any leg on a Sunday, since there is even less transport than normal.

The 150km leg from Hohoe to Nkwanta is covered by at least one bus or tro-tro daily. These leave in the mid-morning in either direction, and take up to five hours depending on the current state of the road, which is surfaced for some distance out of Hohoe but deteriorates rapidly after that. The second leg is a 120km trip to Bimbilla which might entail changing vehicles at Kpaso and/or Damanko, and should take five hours excluding whatever time is lost waiting for vehicles. The final 220km leg between Bimbilla and Tamale is covered by two buses daily in either direction; these leave in the early morning and early afternoon, and take around five hours with a stop at Salaga. For travellers tackling this route in a southerly direction, a daily bus reportedly runs between Bimbilla and Accra, leaving Bimbilla at around 08.00 and taking only six hours to get to Hohoe (via Nkwanta). I've not heard of anybody catching this bus in a northerly direction – perhaps it's normally full when it passes through Hohoe, or possibly it only runs seasonally depending on the state of the road.

Nkwanta is a small but lush town, noted for the colourful yam festival that takes place in November. The **Kilimanjaro Hotel** has been recommended as clean and pleasant: a s/c double with a running shower and fan costs around US$5, though cheaper rooms are available, and the restaurant serves decent meals. Close to Nkwanta, the recently gazetted **Kyabobo Range National Park** borders Togo's Fazao Malfacassa National Park and protects habitats ranging from savannah to montane rainforest. Large mammals such as lion, leopard, buffalo, elephant and various antelopes and monkeys are present. Facilities are limited, but camping and guided hikes can be arranged at the Wildlife Department in Nkwanta. Also of interest, **Shairi** lies at an altitude of 600m on the slopes of **Mount Dzebobo**, the country's second highest peak, only 15km from Nkwanta. Shairi has a cool, misty climate unusual for Ghana, and is known for a nearby waterfall and picturesque terraced houses.

Bimbilla has rather less going for it, but there's no way of avoiding an overnight stay. The basic but friendly **Teacher's Hostel** is situated next to the Goil garage some 20 minutes' walk from the tro-tro station, and charges around US$2 for a double room using bucket showers. Reasonable meals are served at the restaurant at the Goil station.

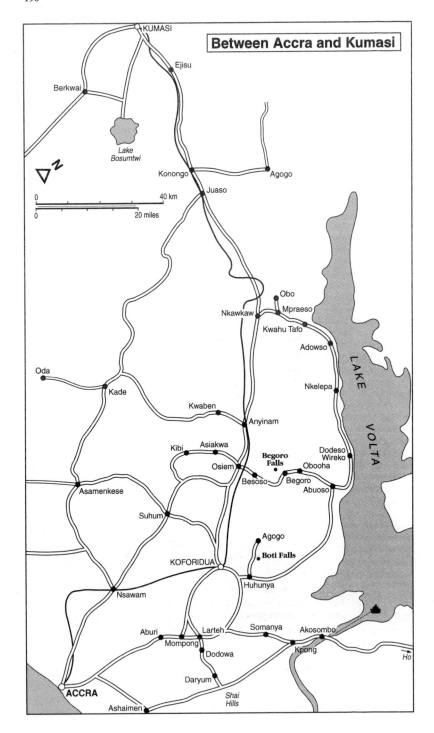

Between Accra and Kumasi

Chapter Eight

Kumasi and Central Ghana

This chapter covers the Ghanaian interior west of Lake
Volta, north of Accra, and south of Tamale and Mole
National Park. Culturally and geographically, this is a
rather incohesive area, but it makes considerable sense in
travel terms, since the chapter follows (with only a few
diversions) the route most likely to be taken by those
travellers heading north from Accra, whether they travel
only as far as Kumasi or continue further north towards
Tamale and/or Mole National Park.

At the core of the area described in this chapter lies
Kumasi, Ghana's second largest city and most important
route focus after Accra. Historically, Kumasi is of great significance as the
capital of Ashanti (also known as Asante – see box on page 206), the most
important empire assembled in the Ghanaian interior in historic times.
Tourism to Kumasi inevitably focuses around the Ashanti cultural legacy (a
legacy I felt to be less tangible in the regional capital than in several
outlying small towns), but it is worth noting upfront that the city also lies
at the centre of one of Ghana's most compact conglomerations of natural
attractions, most notably Lake Bosumtwi, but also a number of obscure
forest reserves.

There is arguably far more to be seen within a 50km radius of Kumasi
than there is along the roads that connect it to Accra or Tamale. The Kwahu
Plateau to the east of the main Accra–Kumasi road is not without its
attractions, particularly for hikers, but Boti Falls aside, it is hardly
comparable with the excellent walking country in the eastern highlands
covered in the previous chapter. The pickings are even poorer along the
Kumasi–Tamale road, the most notable exception being the excellent
monkey sanctuary at Baobeng-Fiema, well worth visiting as a round trip
from Kumasi even if you have no intention of proceeding further north
(true, the turn-off to Mole National Park lies on the Kumasi–Tamale road,
but the realities of public transport mean that this park is more
appropriately seen as part of the northern travel circuit than an excursion en
route to Tamale).

BETWEEN ACCRA AND KUMASI
This is another of the many trips in Ghana that could be done as easily in a
few hours as over a week – Kumasi lies a mere four hours from Accra by

direct STC bus, but there are a number of interesting sites along the way. Of the places listed below, obvious highlights are the Aburi Botanical Garden and Boti Falls, the former a perfectly feasible day trip from Accra.

Aburi Botanical Garden
Established by Britain in 1890, the botanical garden at Aburi lies in the Akwapim Hills, a popular weekend retreat with Accra residents as much for the relatively bracing montane climate as for the lushly scenic setting. The garden would also make an excellent first stop for travellers heading north from Accra, offering the opportunity to acclimatise and unwind for a couple of days in peaceful surroundings only 30km from the capital. It is planted with a mixture of indigenous and exotic trees, notably an immense 150-year-old *kapok* on the main lawn, and is riddled with footpaths from where visitors can see a large variety of labelled trees as well as many birds. In clear weather, the views back to Accra can be amazing.

A short tro-tro ride north of Aburi, the small town of Mampong (not be confused with its namesake in Ashanti Region) has an important place in Ghana's economic history as the site of the country's first cocoa farm, founded by Tetteh Quarshie. Born in what is now Accra in 1842, Tetteh Quarshie was an illiterate, but well-travelled, Ghanaian who lived on Fernando Po from 1870 to 1876 and brought back with him cocoa seeds which would first bear fruit at Mampong in 1879, revolutionising the national economy. The Gold Coast first exported cocoa in 1891, by 1911 it had become the world's largest cocoa producer, and it remains the world's second largest producer to this day. While cocoa was Ghana's leading earner of foreign revenue for decades, it has recently been overtaken by gold. Visitors to Tetteh Quarshie's farm and homestead can see Ghana's first cocoa plant, still in good health, and they will be shown how cocoa is planted and picked.

Getting there and away
Regular tro-tros to Aburi leave Accra from Tema station. There are also regular tro-tros from Aburi to Mampong and Mamre, the latter being where you'll find transport to Koforidua.

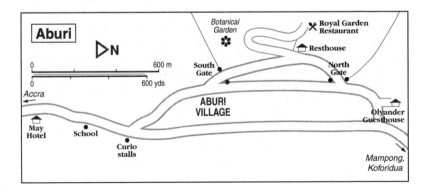

Where to stay and eat

The nicest place to stay is the **Aburi Gardens Resthouse**, a former sanatorium overlooking the main lawns about 200m inside the northern entrance gate. Bedrooms in the main building have three beds each and cost US$7.50, while s/c chalets cost from US$10 to US$17 (depending on whether they have fridge and TV), and ac executive chalets cost US$35. If possible, ring through an advance booking on 0876 22022, especially over weekends and public holidays. The patio bar here serves simple meals for around US$2–3 as well as chilled beers, soft drinks and spicy barbecued kebabs. More substantial, varied and expensive meals are available at the **Royal Garden Restaurant** about 100m away.

If the resthouse in the gardens is full, the **Olyander Guesthouse** about 300m outside the northern entrance has a variety of s/c rooms starting at around US$10. Similarly priced accommodation, as well as meals, are available at the **May Restaurant and Lodge** on the south side of Aburi village, about 1km from the southern entrance gate.

Koforidua

The capital of Eastern Region, Koforidua was founded in the 1870s by the New Juaben people, who were forced to migrate from Juaben in Ashanti after they staged an unsuccessful (and British-inspired) revolt against the authority of the Ashanti King in Kumasi. Today, Koforidua is a substantial and busy town, with a good market and pleasant atmosphere, but it offers little of specific interest to tourists.

Getting there and away

Koforidua is an important transport hub, with good bus and tro-tro connections to most nearby towns, including Accra, Nkawkaw, Begoro and Kumasi.

Where to stay and eat

The most affordable accommodation within walking distance of the town centre is the **Kes Hotel**, where adequate, though slightly overpriced, double rooms using clean communal showers cost US$9. Around the corner, the **Partners May Hotel** (where strangers, presumably, may not!) is a pleasant one-star place with s/c chalet-like accommodation for US$15/20 single/double with fan and hot water, or US$23 double with ac.

There's a cluster of cheapish, decent hotels lying within 100m of the junction of Old Estate and Pentecost roads, about 2km northwest of the town centre. I particularly liked the feel of the **Eastland Hotel**, a quiet, friendly place which has clean, compact s/c rooms with running water and fan for US$6.50. It has no restaurant, but there is a bar and local restaurant right opposite. Similar in standard, the **White Rose Lodge** has s/c rooms with fan for US$5.50/7.50 single/double and ac doubles for US$14. A bit smarter, the **Starland Hotel** has s/c rooms with a double bed for US$9 with fan or US$13 with ac. It also has the best restaurant in the area. To get to any of these three hotels, catch a shared taxi from the town centre to 'Old Estate', or charter a dropping taxi for less than US$1.

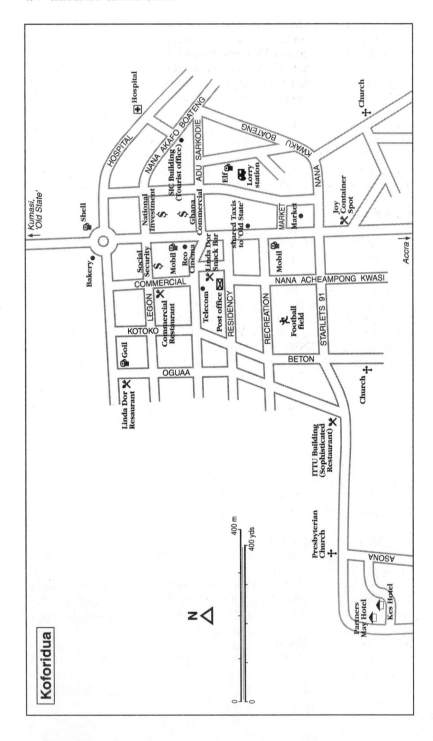

Koforidua

The most upmarket hotel in the region is the two-star **St James Hotel** (tel: 081 23165), 3km out of town along the Densuegya road. A s/c double room here with hot water, ac and TV costs around US$35.

The best place to eat in Koforidua is the **Linda Dor Restaurant** on Oguaa Road. This has a varied menu ranging from steaks and burgers to spaghetti and Chinese dishes, and nothing costs more than US$3. The portions are big and you can eat in or out of doors. There's a second, more central Linda Dor Restaurant next to the Telecom building, with a similar menu, but you can't eat outdoors. Other places you could try are the **Sophisticat Restaurant** on the first floor of the ITTU Building, and the **Commercial Restaurant** on Legon Road. There's also the usual scattering of bars and drinking 'spots' around the market, including the classically named **Joy Container Spot**!

Boti Falls

This 30m-high perennial waterfall, one of the most attractive in Ghana, lies on the Pawnpawn River in the Boti Forest Reserve to the northeast of Koforidua. It is impressive at any time of year, but the flow decreases during the dry season when the waterfall splits into two separate streams. The pool at the base, reached by a sequence of 250 concrete steps, is safe for swimming, provided that you keep clear of the waterfall itself, especially in the rainy season. The scene is made by the surrounding forest, which boasts many enormous trees, including flamboyants with their striking red flowers. An entrance fee of US$0.50 is charged.

The rainforest around the waterfall once harboured chimpanzees and various monkey species. These have reportedly been hunted out, but the forest is still very impressive and supports many different birds and butterflies. It's no problem to arrange a guided walk along the forest paths for a negotiable fee, or to explore the forest fringing the Agogo road on your own. Further afield, you can arrange guided walks to the anonymous caves that lie about an hour from the waterfall, as well as to the so-called 'Umbrella Stone' and a palm tree that reputedly has three trunks.

The Boti Waterfall is a sacred site, and the setting for a celebration every year on 1 July. Many thousands of Ghanaians visit the waterfall on this day, but foreign visitors are welcome to participate.

Getting there and away

Boti Falls lies 21km and 30 minutes' drive from Koforidua. To get there, follow the surfaced road northeast to Huhunya via Kurakan, then take the signposted fork to the left, a 7km dirt road that can be driven in any vehicle. If you're using public transport, a tro-tro from Koforidua to Agogo, a small village shown on no maps, will drop you at the entrance to the falls.

Where to stay and eat

A basic chalet overlooking the waterfall can be rented for around US$3, and camping is permitted at US$1.50 per tent. The friendly caretaker will bring water for washing and arrange for somebody to do your cooking. He keeps two fridges loaded up with ice-cold mineral water, soft drinks and beer, as well as a supply of biscuits and tinned sardines. You can buy other basic foodstuffs at a village 1km up the road, or arrange for the caretaker (who has a car) to run into Agogo to buy you meat or chicken.

Begoro

This small town lies at an altitude of around 500m on the Kwahu Plateau, the name given to the large area of elevated hilly country that lies between the main Koforidua–Kumasi road and Lake Volta. Rather off the beaten track today, Begoro was chosen as the site of a pioneering Presbyterian Mission in 1875 (look for the arch near the Presbyterian church reading *Presbyterian Boarding School 1885*), a decision influenced by its pleasant and relatively disease-free mid-altitude climate. Also worth a look is the Fanteakwa's Palace along the road between the tro-tro station and the Sweet Memories Hotel, easily distinguished by its colonial architecture and the large murals of musicians on the outer wall.

Of greater interest than the town itself, however, is the possibility of using it as a base from where to explore the surrounding countryside, which is great walking country notable for its varied birds and butterflies as well as many streams and waterfalls. An obvious target for day visitors would be the Begoro Falls, which lie less than 20 minutes' walk from town. The Begoro Falls drop about 15m from a large overhang – not much more than a trickle when we visited in the dry season (though even then we were able to wade knee-deep into the muddy pool below the fall for a refreshing natural shower), but reportedly very impressive after the start of the rains.

Getting there and away

Begoro lies roughly 20km east of Osiem on the main road between Koforidua and Nkawkaw. Regular shared taxis run between Begoro and Osiem, as well as directly from Begoro to Koforidua.

To get to Begoro Falls, follow the road leading uphill and to the left as you enter the tro-tro station. After about 100m, where a storm drain crosses the road, turn right and uphill towards the Presbyterian church, then after another 50m, just before the church, turn left and follow this road for a few metres until you reach a football field. Immediately before you reach it, turn right into the footpath that runs parallel to it before leaving town to descend into a valley. After about ten minutes walking downhill, you'll reach the river just below the waterfall.

We didn't use the back route from Begoro to Mpraeso which crosses the Kwahu Plateau through Obooha then descends to Abuoso and follows Lake Volta northwest via Dedeso Wireko and Adowso, but it promises to be a scenic off-the-beaten-track trip for those with the time, patience and curiosity. Tro-tros connected Begoro to Obooha in early 1998, and (we were told) Obooka to Dedeso Wireko via Abuoso. On the other side of the loop, there was definitely transport between Adowso and Mpraeso, but we couldn't ascertain whether anything covered the 20km between Dedeso Wireko and Adowso. Two letters from readers, both dated early 1999, offer conflicting update information. The first states that, according to the police in Mpraeso, travelling from there to Adowso was impassable due to a 'cut in the road'. The other mentions regular tro-tros from Nkwakaw via Mpraeso and Adowso to Abuoso, where a vehicle ferry makes a 'river crossing at Lake Volta' daily at 14.00. I'm not aware of any formal accommodation along this road. If you head this way, do write and tell me how it went.

Where to stay and eat
The only accommodation is the aptly named **Sweet Memories Hotel**, which has cosy, clean, s/c rooms with fan for US$3.50, as well as friendly staff, and a very effective drinks fridge. For food, you'll find plenty of stalls selling kebabs, bush meat, fried yam and other goodies around the lorry station, all overlooked by the **Dorcas Restaurant**, which does chicken with rice or fufu for US$1.50 per plate.

Anyinam
It's difficult to imagine why any traveller would want to sleep over at this moderately sized town situated near the junction where the main roads from Koforidua and Accra to Kumasi converge. Should you be that unimaginable traveller, however, you'll be pleased to hear that there are at least two hotels to choose from. The inexpensive Mensco Hotel, painted bright blue, is to the left as you enter town from the Accra or Koforidua side, but there is also a newer, rather plush and apparently anonymous hotel right in the town centre, with rooftop bar and restaurant attached, as well as a supermarket.

Nkawkaw
This substantial, readily accessible, but rather scruffy town lies 104km from Kumasi on the main Accra road. Nkawkaw is of interest to travellers primarily as a springboard for visits to Mpraeso and Obo on the northern part of the Kwahu Plateau, but it does boast some memorable features, not least a main street that must rank close to being the most hectic and pedestrian-unfriendly in Ghana. Also noteworthy are the forested mountains rising to the northeast, and the preponderence of fading colonial-era buildings complete with red corrugated-iron roofs and balconies.

Getting there and away
There is plenty of transport to Nkawkaw from all directions. STC buses from Accra to Kumasi will drop you at Nkawkaw, assuming that you don't mind paying full fare to Kumasi.

Where to stay and eat
There's a good choice of budget accommodation in Nkawkaw. A particularly pleasant option is **Bertram's Hotel**, which lies about 500m from the main road, signposted just off the road to Mpraeso. A spacious room with double bed costs US$4, and facilities include clean communal bucket showers and a bar with a fridge. Another good bet, the **Top Way Hotel**, is also on the Mpraeso road, but closer to town, and has rooms with fans for US$2.50/5 single/double.

Plenty of street food is available along the main road through the town centre, but a more attractive option would be to walk out of town about 500m in the direction of Kumasi to the Goil garage. Just behind the garage is a reasonable restaurant with indoor and outdoor seating, serving local fare at around US$2 per plate as well as chilled beers. More fun, perhaps, is to nibble your way around the kiosks and shops that circle the STC parking lot just before the garage – everything from imported biscuits to Californian white wine, as well as the usual grilled chicken and kebabs and chilled sodas and beers, are on offer.

Mpraeso

A district administrative centre, Mpraeso is Nkawkaw's high-altitude twin, perched on top of the sandstone cliffs that lie immediately to the east of Nkawkaw and reached by a road as scenic as any in Ghana, a dramatic series of switchbacks up a jungle-clad slope. Like Begoro to the south, Mpraeso is of less interest in itself than it is for the attractive walking country of the Kwahu Plateau on which it lies.

A more appealing base from where to explore this area, however, is **Obo**, a quiet, small town ringed by forested hills and host to a decidedly odd mixture of dirty old colonial mansions and spanking new, brightly painted holiday homes complete with satellite aerials. It's an unusual town, one that might well appeal to photographers, and the surrounding hills offer some good walking and birding – any child will act as a guide should you want one.

Getting there and away

Regular passenger taxis run along the 10km road between Nkawkaw and Mpraeso. There are also regular passenger taxis between Mpraeso and Obo.

Where to stay and eat

There are three hotels in Mpraeso, all of them dumps. The **Osafa Kantanka Motel**, an unsignposted building next to the Goil garage 100m downhill from the tro-tro station, is the best bet, if only because it is a dump that prices itself accordingly. On paper, the s/c doubles with fan and running water probably sound good value at US$4, but then you haven't seen them. Next up is the **Riverside Hotel**, a bright pink, three-storey dump that might more accurately be called the Trickleside Hotel. Situated on the edge of town about 500m from the tro-tro station (ask anybody for directions), this place seems exceedingly optimistic in asking US$8 for a non-s/c double with no fan. Finally, there is the **Afoarima Hotel**, a dump with eyes that light up when a paleskin comes a-knocking – the rooms are absurdly overpriced at US$8.

Better to stay in Obo, where the **Obo Central Hotel**, basic but emphatically *not* a dump, is a friendly, family-run place with simple rooms for US$2.50. The bar serves chilled drinks, and although there is no formal restaurant, the management will prepare a meal given advance warning.

KUMASI

Ghana's second city, with a population of around one million, Kumasi is not only the modern capital of Ashanti Region, but has for three centuries served as royal capital of the Ashanti state. Tradition has it that the city was founded by the first Asentehene, Nana Osei Tutu, who relocated there from his former capital at Kwaman in 1695. Kumasi rapidly acquired the status of largest and most important city in the Ghanaian interior, and was the inland terminus of most of the major eighteenth-century slave-trading routes to the coast.

In the late nineteenth century, Kumasi became the focus of hostilities between aspirant British colonists and the Ashanti. The city was burnt to the ground by Sir Garnet Wolseley in 1873, resulting in the Anglo-Ashanti Peace Treaty of March 1874 and a period of prolonged infighting within the Ashanti state. Following the Yaa Asantewaa War of 1900–01, Kumasi (or Kumase as it was then spelt) was annexed to the British Gold Coast colony on 1 January 1902.

Contrary to expectations conjured up by the epithet 'Ancient Ashanti Capital', your first impression upon arriving in Kumasi, particularly if you disembark near Kejetia Circle, is less likely to be rustic traditionalism than daunting Third World urbanity. Kumasi is one of the most hectic cities I've visited in Africa, far busier than Accra, and the mood is emphatically modern: the surging throngs of humanity and constant traffic jams that emanate in every direction from the market and lorry station feel positively overwhelming if you arrive from the relatively provincial, traditionalist north of Ghana.

Still, Kumasi ranks in most people's books as one of Ghana's 'must-sees', and what it lacks in terms of old buildings – 'historical Kumasi' amounts to little more than the late nineteenth-century fort and the colonial-era buildings clustered in the city centre – it makes up for with a trio of fascinating small museums (see *Things to do* on page 204) and as the base for any number of day or overnight trips to the craft villages and small reserves that dot the lush surrounding countryside.

Getting there and away

The most reliable transport between Accra and Kumasi are the STC buses which leave in either direction every hour on the hour. In theory, seats must be pre-booked but, provided you're at the STC station 15–30 minutes ahead of departure time, you should get a seat on the next bus. The route used by the buses is via Nsawam, Suhum, Kibi and Nkawkaw, with a scheduled stop at Asiakwa's SOS Village, which has clean toilets and serves a range of inexpensive meals and snacks, as well as cold drinks. You can ask to disembark from the bus before Kumasi, but will have to pay the full US$3.50 fare. Depending on the traffic in Accra, the journey takes 4–5 hours.

The best, and most popular, means of transport between the west coast and Kumasi is the rail service from Takoradi, stopping at Tarkwa, Dunkwa and Obuasi. Two trains cover this route daily in either direction, an express service that leaves at 06.10 and arrives at about 14.00 and an overnight sleeper that leaves at 20.30 and arrives at around 07.00 the next day. Tickets may be bought only on the day of departure, starting at 05.30. Tickets for the

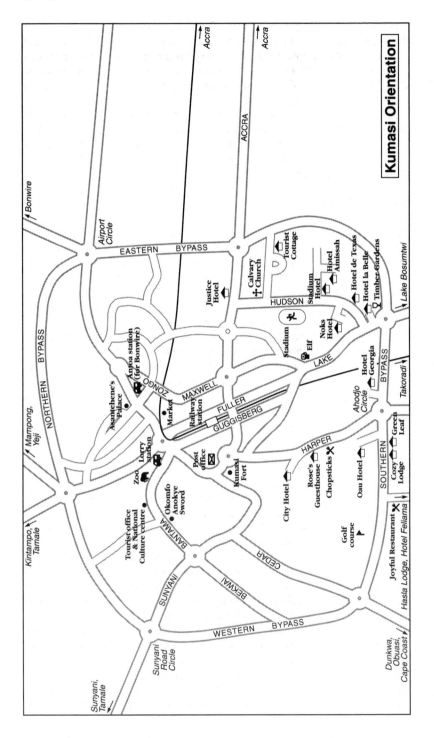

Kumasi Orientation

express train cost roughly US$2.50/3.50 first/second class, while tickets for the sleeper cost US$4 first class (two-berth compartment) or US$3 second class (four-berth compartment). In our experience, the train is both punctual and reasonably comfortable, but it's worth paying the slight extra to go first class. No meals are available on the train, and the selection of food on sale at stations is limited, though the dining car does sell drinks and biscuits.

Regular tro-tros leave Kumasi in practically every direction. Tro-tros for destinations to the north and west generally leave from Kejetia station, below the synonymous traffic circle, while those heading south and east – for instance to Accra, Lake Bosumtwi and Cape Coast – leave from Asafo station on Fuller Road.

Where to stay

Probably the single most important traveller crossroads in the Ghanaian interior, the **Presbyterian Guesthouse** (or just 'The Presby' once you feel sufficiently familiar) is a ramshackle, double-storey, colonial building with attractive, wide, wooden balconies overlooking leafy grounds. The high-ceilinged rooms with fan aren't especially good value at US$3–6, but the atmosphere and popularity of the place go a long way to compensating for this – except perhaps when you're forced to do your socialising in the morning queue outside the only communal bucket shower. The Presby is nothing if not conveniently located, practically in the city centre and perhaps 100m from the STC bus station using a footpath that skirts a football pitch.

There are two budget hotels in the city centre. First is the **Hotel Montana**, tucked down an alley off Odum Road, where large, slightly scruffy rooms with a fan seem good value at US$3.50, especially as the communal shower has running water. Closer to the central market and main lorry station, the **Narum Inn Annexe** has acceptable rooms spanning the US$4.50–6 range. Also very central, but a great deal more expensive, the **Hotel de Kingsway** seems rather poor value at US$25 for a fairly ordinary double with ac, and US$35 for a s/c double.

Dozens of other hotels are dotted around suburban Kumasi. Of interest to budget travellers, and very convenient because it's right on the Accra road, the **Justice Hotel** (tel: 22525) has ordinary non-s/c rooms with fan for US$7–8, s/c rooms with fan for US$9–11 and ac s/c rooms for US$14–17.

Several mid-range hotels are clustered on or near Hudson Road, which runs from opposite the Justice Hotel south past the stadium and is covered by innumerable shared taxis. Running from north to south, the **Tourist Cottage Hotel** (tel: 5219) is a pleasant, well-run, small hotel where s/c rooms with fan cost US$10–12 and ac rooms cost US$17. The **Stadium Hotel** (tel: 23647) has s/c rooms with a fan for US$17 and s/c rooms with ac and TV for US$30. The **Hotel de Texas** has s/c rooms with fan for US$10–15 and ac doubles for US$20. The **Hotel La Belle** (tel: 27934) seems particularly good value at US$15 for a s/c ac double.

Moving up in standard, and also just off Hudson Road, the two-star **Noks Hotel** (tel: 24438, fax: 24162) is regarded as one of the city's best hotels, with pleasant grounds, a good restaurant, and ac, s/c doubles with TV and

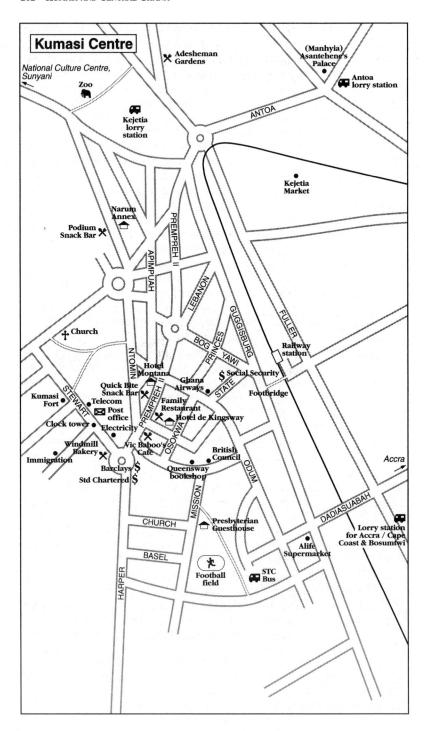

hot water for US$45. Comparable in price and standard, the two-star **Roses Guesthouse** (tel: 24072, fax: 23500) on Harper Road seems exceptional value for money: s/c doubles with hot water, fan, ac, fridge and satellite TV for US$37. The nearby **City Hotel**, a rather soulless, high-rise affair, also seems pretty good value with s/c doubles for US$13 (with fan) or US$26 ac.

The three-star **Hotel Georgia** (tel: 23915, fax: 24299) on Ahodjo Roundabout has shabby s/c rooms with ac and satellite TV for US$77/88. A better bet at US$60/double is the newer three-star **Royal Basin Hotel** (tel: 60144, fax: 60168) off the Accra Road.

Where to eat

An excellent place to eat in the city centre is **Vic Baboo's Café**, diagonally opposite the Hotel de Kingsway, which serves a varied selection of meals ranging from burgers and pizzas to vegetarian curry and tandoori chicken for around US$2–4 per main course. The restaurant is air-conditioned, and it serves chilled soft drinks and beer. The **Family Restaurant** next to the Hotel de Kingsway does reasonable Western and Lebanese meals, but the service is slow and the lack of ventilation makes it an uncomfortable place to wait around. The **Old Timer's Bar** below is, by contrast, one of the most pleasant drinking holes in the city centre.

In the same part of town, the air-conditioned **Quick Bite Restaurant** on Prempreh II Road serves dishes such as chicken and chips or spaghetti bolognaise for around US$2.50. The **Windmill Bakery** on Prempreh II Circle has its aficionados, but the menu is somewhat more varied than the actual selection of dishes, and yet another plate of regulation chicken and rice is unlikely to hold much appeal if you've been in Ghana for a while – then again, perhaps we were there on a bad day.

Near Kejetia Circle, the **Kentish Restaurant** at the National Cultural Centre serves a selection of uncomplicated Western and Ghanaian dishes at reasonable prices indoors or in the fairly attractive garden. It's a good place to eat should you be planning on seeing one of the musical concerts or plays that are put on occasionally at the cultural centre. On the other side of Kejetia Circle, practically facing the chaotic lorry station, **Adesheman Gardens** is a surprisingly tranquil place to down a few draught beers, often with live musical accompaniment later in the evening. There's a good, but rather expensive, Chinese restaurant in the gardens, and plenty of roast kebabs and other chop available in the vicinity.

The more upmarket restaurants are generally found away from the city centre. Most of the more expensive hotels do food: there are good Chinese restaurants in the **Hotel Georgia** and the **City Hotel**, but the long-standing **Chopsticks Restaurant** near the Roses Guest House is considered to be the best in town. For Indian food, try the excellent **Moti Mahal Restaurant** in the OAU Hotel. At most of these places you'll be looking at close to US$10 for a full meal.

For cheap Ghanaian dishes in the Hudson Road area, try the restaurant at the **Hotel de Texas**. Nearby, on the junction of Lake and Southern Bypass roads, **Timber Gardens** is a busy outdoor spot serving cold draught beer, spicy grilled kebabs and chicken, as well as more ordinary chop.

Information for visitors

Books and newspapers A limited selection of secondhand novels can be bought for around US$1 at the stalls on Prempreh II Road close to Vic Baboo's Café, and at the Queensway Bookshop near the British Council. The British Council itself has a stack of recent British newspapers in the air-conditioned reading room.

Foreign exchange Several forex bureaux can be found dotted around the city centre. Most accept cash only, for which they offer a better rate than the banks. The Standard Chartered Bank and Barclays Bank are situated opposite each other off Prempreh II Circle. Both exchange travellers' cheques without charging commission. At the time of writing, the Standard Chartered had the better exchange rate but will not change more than US$200 per person in travellers' cheques on any given day.

Immigration The visa extension service here is far quicker than in Accra: two or three days as compared with two weeks, and you may even be able to get it done overnight if you can persuade the immigration officers that it's urgent.

Supermarkets Quite a number of reasonable supermarkets are to be found in the vicinity of Prempreh II Road. By far the most varied selection of groceries in Kumasi is available at the excellent A-Life Supermarket (between the STC and railway stations), which also serves ice-cream cones and other snacks on the veranda café.

Tourist office The Ghana Tourist Board office in the National Cultural Centre can be a reasonable source of local information, depending on to whom you end up speaking. Our first visit was genuinely productive, and most of the information we were given proved to be more or less accurate. On our second visit, a month later, we were misinformed on several relatively straightforward points, and the staff seemed interested only in persuading us to charter a taxi to visit Bonwire and other cultural villages.

Things to do

To get some feel for Ashanti history, visit the **Prempreh II Jubilee Museum** in the National Cultural Centre on Bantama Road, about five minutes out of town from Ketejia Circle. The museum is named after the popular Asantehene, Nana Osei Agyeman Prempreh II, who ascended the Golden Stool in May 1931 and reigned until his death almost 40 years later in 1970. Most of the artefacts in the museum relate to the reign of Prempreh II, a largely peaceful period during which the Ashanti empire, shattered in several respects by the British colonists, re-established much of its former cultural cohesion. Several black-and-white photos are on display, most strikingly a vibrant portrait of the young Asantehene taken at his coronation. There are also a number of royal stools in the museum, notably the fake Golden Stool that was handed to Lord Baden-Powell in an attempt to fool the British authorities in 1900, and a photo of the real Golden Stool, which last appeared in public at the enstoolment of the present Asantehene in 1970. Perhaps the most historically significant artefact in the museum is the royal cask which dates back 300 years to the rule of Nana Osei Tutu; contents unknown, since tradition holds that opening it would bring about the fall of Ashanti. The entrance fee of around US$1 covers an informative guided tour. Photography is forbidden.

About 300m further out of town along Bantama Road, fenced in behind Block C of the Okomfo Anokye Hospital, the **Okomfo Anokye Sword** is traditionally held to have been stuck in the same position in the ground for 300 years, marking the spot where the Golden Stool initially descended from the sky. In common with the cask mentioned above, the sword is an important symbol of Ashanti unity – legend has it that the state would collapse should the sword ever be pulled out of the ground.

Walking back towards town, just before you reach Kejetia Circle and lorry station, the **Kumasi Zoo** consists of a few depressingly cramped cages harbouring various primates (many are in solitary confinement, a fate as cruel to a chimp or a monkey as to a person) as well as a rather more aesthetically pleasing duiker-breeding scheme. Altogether more phenomenal than the inmates of the zoo are the thousands of fruit bats that rest of their own volition in the trees above – a quite incredible sight (not to say sound – they chatter away like demented mice) and worth the nominal entrance fee if you've never before seen a large bat colony. While you're in this part of town, pay a visit to the vast, sprawling **Kejetia Market**, reputedly the largest in West Africa, with some 10,000 traders operating in an area of 12 hectares, and now restored to its gloriously hectic former self after it was partially destroyed by fire in 1995.

On Antoa Road, about 1km from the National Museum, **Manhyia Palace** was built in 1926 following the return from exile of Prempreh II's predecessor and uncle, Asantehene Nana Prempreh I. Surprisingly low-key, the palace remains in use today, though the present Asantehene lives in a more modern building on the same property, and it was temporarily closed in late 1997. Assuming that it's reopened by the time you get there, the entrance fee of US$1 will allow you to wander freely through the old palace (photography costs more) and it may be possible to make an appointment to meet the Asantehene with a couple of days' notice. The best time to visit the palace is between 10.30 and 13.00 on Adae festival days, about every three weeks, when the Asentehene receives homage from his subjects.

Back in the centre, near Prempreh II Circle, is the **Kumasi Fort**, presumably the oldest building in the city. The foundation and some of the walls date to 1820, when Asentehene Osei Tutu Kwamina decided to build a replica of the fort at Cape Coast, but the fort as a whole was completed in 1897 by the British using granite blocks transported to Kumasi from the coast. The fortress was surrounded in March 1900, during the so-called 'Ashanti Rebellion', and 29 Britons were trapped within its walls for several weeks before they were able to escape. The Queen Mother of Ejisu, Ohemaa Yaa Asantewaa, the prime initiator of the Ashanti Rebellion, was imprisoned here for a week before being exiled to Cape Coast and later the Seychelles, where she died.

THE ASHANTI KINGDOM

The Ashanti (also spelt 'Asante') are one of the few African peoples whose name is instantly familiar to many Westerners. Undoubtedly, this situation is in part a result of the unique role played by Ashanti in the pre-colonial and modern history of Ghana. No less, however, should it be recognised that the Ashanti owe their notoriety to the fact that, like, for instance, the Zulu or the Maasai, they were one of the few sub-Saharan African peoples to provide effective (if ultimately ineffectual) resistance against Britain's late-nineteenth-century drive for colonialism.

The Ashanti Kingdom only started to take a recognisable modern shape under King Osei Tutu of the Oyoko clan in the dying years of the seventeenth century. What little is known about Ashanti history prior to this is fogged by myth. This is partly as a result of the ban, placed by Osei Tutu on his subject states, on passing down their own foundation legends to subsequent generations. Some oral traditions claim that the Ashanti people emerged from a hole in the ground near Lake Bosomtwi, others that they descended from the sky, yet others that they migrated to the area from Mesopotamia or Israel (the last based somewhat tenuously on a few similarities in Jewish and Ashanti tradition, notably the observance of a Saturday Sabbath and the reserved use of the word 'Amen' for dialogue with God).

More probable than any of the above scenarios is that the ancestral Ashanti, like other Akan peoples, migrated into modern Ghana from its ancient namesake in what is now Mali some time before the thirteenth century AD. It is likely that they had settled in their modern homeland north of the confluence of the Pra and Oda Rivers by the early seventeenth century. The Oyoko clan, generally seen as the true founders of the Ashanti Kingdom, lived in the vicinity of Lake Bosomtwi, an area they called Amanse (*'Beginning of Nations'*), where they built a capital called Asantemanso (from which the name *Asante* or *Ashanti* derives).

For much of the seventeenth century, the proto-Ashanti consisted of several loosely linked chieftaincies scattered through an area radiating some 30–50km around modern-day Kumasi. All the evidence suggests that the people of this region enjoyed an immensely high standard of living, as a result of the fertility of the soil and their strategic position at the conjunction of the main trade routes to the north and south. In these days, the area was noted particularly for its production of mildly narcotic kola nuts, exported via Salaga to the Muslim states of the Sahel and North Africa. The one thing that these chieftaincies lacked, however, was true political autonomy, since they were all essentially vassal states of the mighty Denkyira Empire, which retained control of the all-important gold trade to the coast throughout the seventeenth century.

The trend towards military unification in Ashanti is thought to have emerged under Oti Akentem, who ascended to the stool of Asantemanso in around 1650. It continued under his successor Obiri Yeboa, who moved his capital to the more central location of Kwamaan before being killed in battle in 1697. Obiri Yeboa's successor to the stool of Kwamaan was Osei Tutu, who with the help of the respected priest Okomfo Anokye would become the first true Asantehene (*King of Ashanti*), and who is still widely regarded as having been the greatest of Ashanti leaders.

In response to the death of his predecessor, Osei Tutu called upon the states of Juaben, Nsuta, Mampong, Bekwai and Kokofu to form a formal confederation with Kwaaman. Legend has it that when the chiefs of the six states assembled to discuss this union, the priest Okomfo Anokye summoned a golden stool from the sky to land in the lap of Osei Tutu, signifying that he should assume the role of paramount king of the new confederation. It is also claimed that the priest planted three palm (*kum*) trees in various parts of the union, and the first one to start growing was nominated

A highly informative guided tour of the fort, which now doubles as an **Armed Forces' Museum**, costs US$1 and is well worth the expenditure. The tour starts unpromisingly with a collection of weapons and the spoils from various campaigns in which the Gold Coast Regiment has been as the site of the Ashanti capital, Kumasi (which means 'under the *kum* tree'). When the Denkyirahene (King of Denkyira) heard about the newly formed Ashanti confederation, he responded by increasing tax demands, and dictating that the union should be dissolved, that each of its chiefs should chop off a finger to send him, and that the Asantehene should hand over the golden stool. The chiefs of Ashanti decided to go to war with Denkyira, though Okomfo Anokye warned that the chief who led Ashanti to victory would not live for more than seven days after the battle, and he advised that Osei Tutu should remain in Kumasi. The Mamponhene (king of Mampong) volunteered to serve as general provided that his stool was made second to that of the Asantehene (the silver stool of Mampong is to this day regarded to be second in importance only to the golden stool of Kumasi). In 1701, the Denkyirahene was captured and beheaded at Feyiase, and his kingdom became the first subject by conquest of the Asantehene.

Using revolutionary military tactics, and fuelled by its growing importance in the emergent slave trade, Ashanti grew from strength to strength in the eighteenth century. Osei Tutu was killed by snipers while crossing the Pra river and, after a brief period of internal instability, his successor Opuku Ware (1720–50) pursued a policy of military expansion that resulted in most of the Akan states of southern Ghana being subject to Ashanti by 1740. In 1744, Accra was briefly captured by the Ashanti army, and later in the same decade much of what is now northern Ghana fell under Ashanti rule. By the time of Osei Bonsu (Asantehene from 1801 to 1824), the kingdom covered an area larger than that of modern Ghana, spilling over into parts of what are now Côte d'Ivoire, Togo and Burkina Faso.

The nineteenth-century decline of Ashanti is linked to the parallel decline in the trans-Atlantic slave trade, which lay at the heart of the kingdom's economy. It was more or less sealed in 1896 when Britain occupied Kumasi and deported the Asantehene and several other important dignitaries to the Seychelles. In 1900, led by the aged queen mother Yaa Asantewaa, the Ashanti made one last brave but ill-fated attempt to remove Britain from Kumasi Fort, with the net result that even more of its traditional leaders were deported and Ashanti was formally annexed to Britain's Gold Coast colony. However, while this may have resulted in the core states of the Ashanti confederation losing their autonomy, they have never lost their identity – Britain was practically forced to restore the Asantehene to his stool in 1924, and the king of Ashanti is regarded as being the second most important political figure in Ghana to this day.

It is one thing to sum up the history of the Ashanti, another altogether trying to come to grips with their cultural institutions, rather like asking a foreigner to sum up the British obsession with regionalism and class in a paragraph or two. Every Ashanti is a member of one of seven matrilineal 'families' as well as of his or her clan, and of a patrilineal spiritual group known as an *nton*. Like many African cultures, great emphasis is placed on communality and the subservience of the individual to the nation (as an example, until recent times all land was communal, the nominal property of the Asantehene), yet paradoxically the highest of all Ashanti goals is personal power (one classic Ashanti proverb translates thus: 'If power is up for sale, then sell your mother to obtain it – once you have the power there are several ways of getting her back!'). If you are interested in finding out more, I advise you to seek out a couple of the following books, all written by Ghanaians and available for next to nothing in bookshops in Accra: *Ashantis of Ghana* by J W Tufuo and C E Donkor, *An Outline of Asante History* by Osei Kwadwo, or *Ancient Ashanti Chieftaincy* by Ernest Obeng.

involved (I was surprised to see how heavily the Gold Coast Regiment had featured in booting the Italians out of Ethiopia during World War II). More interesting, in my opinion, are the many portraits of Ashanti notables (notably Yaa Asantewaa), the first African soldiers to be promoted to

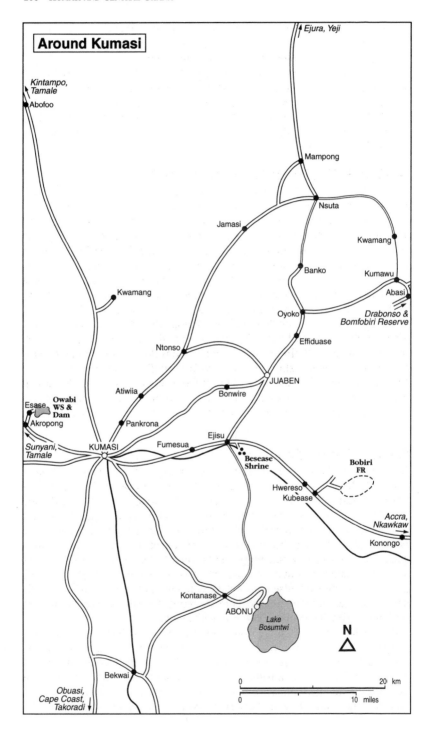

Around Kumasi

various ranks during colonial rule, and two of the World War II veterans who were killed when an anti-colonial protest outside Osu Fort in Accra was fired upon by colonial police. The tour gradually takes on several unexpected dimensions: a potted history of twentieth-century conflict, as seen through the collected memorabilia of an obscure African regiment, and, more tellingly, a cruel exposure of the minutiae of colonial arrogance which, for instance, forbade all African soldiers, even those poor souls who were shipped across the Atlantic to the muddy fields of Flanders in 1914–18, to wear shoes.

SHORT EXCURSIONS FROM KUMASI

A great many possibilities for unstructured travel lie in the lush countryside within a 50km radius of Kumasi, an area that is generally regarded to be the core region of Ashanti since it is occupied by the various states that combined forces under the golden stool in the late seventeenth century. Attractions in this area range from Lake Bosumtwi (the country's largest natural body of water) to several pedestrian-friendly forest reserves, a number of craft villages, and a few small towns that might as easily be used as a base for exploration as Kumasi itself. Many of these places would make ideal destinations for a day trip out of Kumasi, or you could travel around the region sleeping wherever you end up on any given night. It would, I think, be restrictive to describe these places in the form of a prescribed circuit, so I've chosen to follow them in roughly anti-clockwise sequence, starting with Owabi Wildlife Sanctuary and Lake Bosumtwi. With the exception of Owabi and Bosumtwi, you could travel between any two places listed below without returning to Kumasi, making use of the small tro-tros and shared taxis that connect just about any two villages in the area.

Owabi Wildlife Sanctuary

One of Ghana's smallest conservations areas, covering a mere 13km^2, Owabi Wildlife Sanctuary was gazetted in 1971 to protect the chunk of pristine forest surrounding Owabi Reservoir, for many years Kumasi's sole source of drinking water. Crossed by several footpaths, the sanctuary harbours a great many varieties of butterfly, as well as 145 bird species – the raucous pied (or allied) hornbill is the most conspicuous of the forest birds, while the pygmy goose and purple heron can be seen on the reservoir. A fair number of large mammals are present: casual visitors stand a reasonable chance of glimpsing black-and-white colobus and mona monkey in the trees, but are unlikely to see more secretive terrestrial species such as bushpig, bushbuck or black and Maxwell's duiker.

Owabi lies roughly 16km from Kumasi and only 3km from the main Sunyani road. The turn-off to the sanctuary is at Akropong, which can be reached by a regular tro-tro service from Kejetia station. Most tro-tros going from Kumasi to Akropong continue along the Owabi turn-off as far as Esase, from where it's a ten-minute walk to the entrance to the reserve – you may even be lucky and get a lift with a waterworks vehicle. At the entrance gate, you'll have to pay the entrance and guide fees (visitors may not enter the forest without a guide), which shouldn't work out at more than US$2 per person.

There's no formal accommodation at Owabi, but for a small fee you can pitch a tent on the lawn between the entrance gate and the dam wall. The bar at the entrance sells chilled beers and soft drinks, and you shouldn't have a problem finding food in Akropong – it's a fairly large town with a couple of chop bars. Without a tent, it's easy enough to visit Owabi as a day trip from Kumasi. Otherwise, the closest accommodation is at Abuakwa, about 5km from Akropong along the Kumasi road.

Lake Bosumtwi

Situated some 30km south of Kumasi in a vast crater, Lake Bosumtwi is, at 28km^2, the most expansive natural body of fresh water in Ghana. It is also the deepest, reaching a maximum depth of 80–100m, and rising, which has resulted in the submersion of several lakeshore villages within living memory. Debate about the origin of the crater in which Bosumtwi lies was settled by a recent geological study which confirmed it isn't volcanic but the result of a meteorite impact. The lake is a beautiful spot, encircled by raggedly mountainous, thickly vegetated crater walls that reach an altitude of greater than 600m, and with ample opportunities for walking, birding, fishing and canoeing.

As you might expect, Lake Bosumtwi is held sacred by Ashanti traditionalists, though the finer details of its exalted status are rather elusive. Some claim that Bosumtwi is where a deity called Twi resides, others that it is visited by the souls of the departed on their passage to eternity. It is also the sacred water body of the Bosumtwi (one of five divisions in the patrilineal Nton system which the Ashanti and other Akan peoples believe passes a father's attributes to his children), on account of it being as round as the sun, the model for members of the Bosumtwi Nton. There is a taboo on the use of traditional pirogues on the lake; local fishermen get around by lying on customised tree trunks and using their hands as paddles.

The normal base for visits to the lake is Abono, a picturesque village on the northern shore. Direct tro-tros from Kumasi to Abono take no more than one hour, though you may have to wait a while for something to leave. The alternative is to take a tro-tro to Kuntansi, where you can pick up a shared taxi to Abono. Either way, all vehicles heading in this direction leave Kumasi from Asafo station, and the total fare to Bosumtwi should be less than US$1.

There is a hotel in Abono, apparently anonymous and clearly intended to be something more grandiose than the unfinished-looking concrete eyesore it was when it closed for renovations in 1999. This hotel boasts a great lakeshore location above a swimming beach (reputedly there's no bilharzia), though rooms will presumably cost more than the US$5 we paid in 1998 when eventually it does re-open. A second, smarter hotel was reportedly also under construction a short distance west of Abono in mid-1999. For the meantime, the only certain accommodation in the area is a fully furnished, self-catering government resthouse at the top of the crater on the road to

Abono; an air-conditioned room here costs around US$20 and can be booked at the local government office in Kuntunase. In Abono village, a couple of shops have a fridge and sell beer (unfortunately they don't necessarily keep any beer in the fridge!).

Ejisu

This busy little junction town, 20km from Kumasi at the intersection of the Accra and Effiduase roads, could easily be used as a base for exploring the Kumasi area. In addition, it currently offers the closest budget accommodation to the Bobori Forest in the form of the excellent little Ejisu Hotel. Only 50m away and signposted from the main road, this hotel has large, clean s/c rooms with fan and running water for US$5, making it one of the best deals in the region. A constant stream of minibuses runs through Ejisu in all directions, street eats are available in abundance, and there are numerous small 'spots' blessed with fridges.

Within easy walking distance of Ejisu, signposted roughly 1.5km further along the Accra road, **Besease Traditional Shrine** is probably the most accessible remaining Ashanti *abasomfie* (the name given to a fetish temple dedicated to a local deity or Abasom). The Besease shrine is regarded as the most important abasomfie in Ejisu, itself one of the major Ashanti states, and it is still where the elders of Ejisu gather for important meetings. The shrine has existed in some form for at least 300 years, though the current building is relatively recent – according to the curator of the Armed Forces' Museum in Kumasi, it was built and lived in by Ohemaa Yaa Asantewaa, the queen mother who led the resistance to British occupation in 1900. The caretaker priestess who lives next door to the shrine, called to the task by ancestral spirits more than 30 years ago, seems happy to let tourists look around. When I visited, one local suggested that an advance visit to the National Cultural Centre might have been in order, but my feeling that a small cash donation or bottle of Schnapps for the priestess would be altogether more appropriate than a ream of official documentation has since been confirmed by a reader who recommended an 'exuberant' local guide named Augustus.

One footnote: a few weeks after I visited the Besease shrine, I read that Dwenease Shrine near Ejisu is the only abasomfie left with a fully intact interior, and that it boasts the original of the crocodile decoration duplicated on the outer wall of the Prempreh Jubilee Museum in Kumasi. My strong suspicion is that Dwenease and Besease are one and the same shrine – Besease certainly had a complete interior, though I don't recall seeing a crocodile fresco. If you do head out this way, then let me know...

Bobiri Forest Reserve

This substantial pocket of near pristine forest, situated some 30km from Kumasi within walking distance of the main Accra road, has been used as a research site by the Forestry Research Institute of Ghana for some 50 years. The forest supports a rich fauna, most prolifically butterflies and birds (nearly 400 butterfly species have been recorded), but also mona, white-nosed, green, and black-and-white colobus monkeys. Bobiri has been earmarked for future

KENTE AND ADINKRA CLOTH

Of all the crafts practised in West Africa, few are more readily identifiable with a particular country than **kente cloth** with Ghana. Strongly associated with the Ashanti, modern *kente* is characterised by intricately woven and richly colourful geometric designs, generally dominated by bold shades of yellow, green, blue, orange and red. However, in its earliest form, before the introduction of exotic fabrics and dyes through trade with the Europeans castles of the coast, kente cloth was somewhat less kaleidoscopic, since white and navy blue were the only available dyes.

According to Ashanti tradition, kente design originated at Bonwire, the small village close to Kumasi which still serves as the main centre of kente production in south-central Ghana. This claim is disputed by the Ewe people of Volta Region, the country's other important centre of kente production, who maintain that they were the first kente weavers and that their techniques were adopted in Ashanti at a later date. While the Ewe claim has a certain ring of truth, the reality is that most people now associate kente cloth with Ashanti, where the most complex and beautiful designs, not to say the skills of the finest weavers, are to this day reserved for the use of royalty.

These days, much of the kente cloth you see on sale in Ghana is mass produced, and considered by experts to have little intrinsic merit. At Bonwire, however, it is still possible to see traditional weavers (a role reserved for men only) working at their looms, and to buy top-quality cloth, though it will be a lot more expensive than the stuff you see in, say, Accra. Visitors to Volta Region may also like to visit ancient centres of the kente craft, such as Kpetoe, a small town on the main Ho–Aflao road, and the more obscure village of Afegame. The best example of kente weaving that you are likely to see in Ghana today is the century-old piece of cloth on display in the National Museum, formerly the property of one of the kings of Ashanti.

Adinkra cloth is popular in many Akan societies, but most strongly associated with the Ashanti. Like kente cloth, *adinkra* is generally worn by men in the form of a toga, but its use is reserved for funerals and other relatively sombre occasions (the word *adinkra* means 'farewell') rather than for celebrations, and adinkra symbolism takes the form of monochrome graphics as opposed to the colourful geometric abstractions of kente. Most contemporary adinkra cloth is made using a plain white calico textile which is then decorated with various ancient designs using calabash stamps and a dye obtained by boiling the bark of the badie tree, *Bridelia micranta*.

More than 60 different adinkra symbols are in use, each of them signifying a specific tradition or proverb. The most popular of these is the rather Chinese-looking *Gye Nyame*, symbolising the omnipotence of God, and is easily recognised since it is depicted on the 100 cedi banknote. Another popular symbol is *sankofa*, heart-shaped with two whirls inside, which has taken on a particular resonance in the post-independence era since it signifies the value of building on one's cultural roots. The *kuntinkantan* design of five interlocking circles depicts the value of pride in ones state or society over pride in oneself, while the *pempansie* (like two opposing figures of '3' linked by a concave bar) symbolises a chain and stresses the importance of each member of a society as part of the whole. While these and other traditional designs remain at the core of most adinkra designs, many modern craftsmen are prepared to experiment with variations reflecting the changing nature of Ghanaian society.

The origin of the adinkra dyeing technique is uncertain. It is thought to have been adopted by the Ashanti in around 1818, during the reign of King Osei Bonsu, but oral traditions differ as to whether the craft originated in the neighbouring territory of Denkyira or in the Jaman kingdom in what is now Côte d'Ivoire, both of which were vassal states of Ashanti during its early nineteenth-century peak. Today, the main centre of adinkra production is the village of Ntonso on the main Kumasi–Mampong road, where it is easy to arrange an informal guide to show you around.

tourist development (a Peace Corps volunteer was installed in late 1997 for this purpose), and even as things stand it makes an excellent day trip from Kumasi or, better for an early start, Ejisu.

To reach the forest from Kumasi or Ejisu, ask any Konongo-bound minibus to drop you at Kubease, about 1km past Hwereso and perhaps 8km past Ejisu along the Accra road. The turn-off to the forest is clearly signposted, and it's a lovely 3km walk out. The first part of the road passes through lush, marshy vegetation, dotted with palms, and absolutely heaving with birds in the early morning (serious twitchers could spend a happy two hours along this stretch sorting out the myriad weavers, waxbills and bulbuls). The only place where you could go wrong here is at the fork 1km out of Kubease, where you ought to head to the right. About 500m past this fork, a signpost and abrupt change in vegetation and drop in temperature signal your entry to the forest proper, after which it's a straightforward 10–15-minute walk to the resthouse.

It would be possible to stay in the resthouse, a comfortable looking building with a generator and running water, though the current asking price of US$30 per person (or US$10 if you're 'forestry-affiliated') is unlikely to find too many takers. At present camping isn't permitted, though it does seem likely that any realistic tourism assessment would recognise the value of dropping the resthouse rates and permitting campers – the set-up is ideal. If you're interested, the best bet would be to telephone or stop by at the Forestry Research Institute in Fumesua (tel: 0572 392), right on the side of the road between Kumasi and Ejisu, so easy to visit on the way out. As things stand, you'd have to stop here anyway to pick up the keys to the resthouse.

Bonwire

A 30-minute ride from Kumasi (tro-tros leave from Manhyia station near the palace of the same name), Bonwire is known throughout Ashanti and elsewhere in Ghana as the home of the country's most skilful *kente* weavers (*kente* being the luxuriant cloth characterised by complex, colourful geometric patterns that's worn by the Ashanti on festive occasions). According to local tradition, Bonwire was founded by exiles from Denkyira who settled close to Kumasi shortly after 1701, the year in which Denkyira was conquered by King Osei Tutu. They soon developed the art of weaving *kente* using cotton they grew themselves and colourful dyes extracted from plants in the nearby forest. Bonwire first received royal patronage in King Osei Tutu's time, and for centuries after this its most skilful weavers were forbidden from selling cloth to anybody without the express permission of the Ashanti king. This version of events is accepted throughout Ashanti, but disputed by the Ewe of Volta Region who claim that they invented kente cloth and the Ashanti copied them.

Whatever the truth, Bonwire is a good place to buy some of the best kente cloth woven in Ghana. Even if you're not buying (and be warned that the kente cloth here is no cheaper than it is elsewhere), Bonwire makes for a good day out from Kumasi. The village has a pleasantly relaxed atmosphere, some good examples of traditional Ashanti buildings, and it's no problem to watch the weavers at work. Many of the weavers work indoors or in an enclosed courtyard, so it's easier to find your way around with a guide, who will also be able to provide you with some insight into the various types of cloth and the symbolism of their patterns. Several guides are bound to approach you on arrival; they won't ask a fee but will expect a fair tip.

Effiduase
Some 40km from Kumasi along a good, surfaced road through Ejisu, Effiduase is the sort of friendly, relaxed town where nobody pays visitors a great deal of attention, and as such it makes for a pleasant retreat into busy small-town Ashanti, away from the main roads and major tourist circuits. Effiduase is also conveniently situated for exploring the Kumasi area, with good tro-tro links in every direction, and it could be a useful base in which to settle for a few days.

A couple of exceptional little hotels lie on the outskirts of Effiduase. Firstly, about 500m from the lorry station, and signposted from the road towards Effisco Secondary School, the Zanamat Hotel is a clean, friendly place with a bar and restaurant, running water, and rooms starting at US$3.50–5 non s/c with fan, or US$6 for a s/c double and US$9 for a s/c twin. Another 500m along the same road, opposite the school, the Lizpo Hotel is not quite as homely, but the rooms are even better value at US$5 for a large s/c double with fan.

The winding, 20km dirt road connecting Effiduase to Nsuta passes through some of the most attractive scenery in the region: hilly jungle broken up by sandstone cliffs and a couple of remote small towns notable for their traditional Ashanti and colonial architecture. Reasonably regular passenger taxis ply along this track, and keen hikers and birders could do worse than ask to be dropped at the forest-fringed village of Adutwam (a small, rustic settlement lying at the base of a cliff about halfway between Effiduase and Nsuta) to explore the road on foot from there.

Bomfobiri Wildlife Sanctuary
Gazetted in 1975, the 53km^2 Bomfobiri Wildlife Sanctuary is centred around the seasonal waterfall on the Boumfoum River after which it is named. The sanctuary harbours a variety of forest mammals, including mona monkey, baboon, bushbuck, black duiker and all three West African crocodile species. A great many birds can be seen along the 2.5km path between the entrance and the waterfall, though it will require some luck to see the reserve's speciality, the bare-headed rock fowl. This is a strange-looking and highly localised bird, loosely related to the crow family, but placed in a monospecific genus unique to the rainforest belt of West Africa.

The entrance to Bomfobiri lies around 10–15km from the town of Kumawu along the Drabonso road. Kumawu itself is easy to reach on public transport, only 30 minutes from Effiduase along a good, surfaced road. Without private transport, getting from Kumawu to the entrance could be problematic. More

Above: *Kpandu market, Lake Volta*

Below left: *Girl selling oranges, Larabanga*

Below right: *Woman in Mzulezu*

Canoeing near Mzulezu stilt village

Above: *Bar in Tongo outside Bolgatanga*

Below: *A colourful and cryptically decorated bar in Sekondi*

Sekondi fishing harbour

accurately, you can get to the entrance with ease using one of the tro-tros to Drabonso that leave Kumawu every afternoon between 15.00 and 16.00. The difficulty is finding transport back, since vehicles returning to Kumawu from Drabonso are generally full when they come past the entrance. Short of walking back, the only viable option at present is to charter a taxi, which will cost around US$15–20 for a round day trip, and double that if you want to be taken out on one day and picked up a day or two later.

Before heading out to the sanctuary, you are obliged to visit the Department of Wildlife office in Kumawu, clearly signposted as you enter town from the direction of Effiduase. This is where you'll pay your entrance fee (US$2 per person) and collect a guide (US$1 per hour for a day trip, negotiable for an overnight trip). It is also the best place to seek current advice about accommodation and camping, and to organise a taxi charter to the sanctuary.

There is no formal accommodation in the area at present, either in the sanctuary or in Kumawu. Rumour has it that a new hotel is under construction in Kumawu, but I have no idea when it is likely to open. In the meantime, travellers with a tent are free to camp within the sanctuary, and they may also pitch a tent outside the Department of Wildlife office in Kumawu the night before they leave for Bomfobiri.

Mampong

The seat of Ashanti's second most important chieftaincy, the silver stool of the Mamponhene, Mampong is also one of the largest towns in the region, with a population well in excess of 20,000. It is a rather attractive place, notable for the steep ascent by which it is reached coming from Kumasi, but otherwise unremarkable, except perhaps for the great many fading colonial-era buildings in the compact town centre.

There are two hotels in Mampong. The Midway Hotel, about 500m from the tro-tro station along the Kumasi road, has very ordinary rooms for US$5, using communal bucket showers. The relatively upmarket Video City Hotel, closer to the tro-tro station, is a conspicuous, bright-blue building attached to a cinema, with a courtyard centred around an empty pond and dotted with traditional statues. Non-s/c doubles without a fan cost a rather steep US$7.50, while nicer s/c doubles with running water and fan go for a more realistic US$10. The Simple Stores Restaurant on the main road between the tro-tro station and the Midway Hotel serves local meals and ice-cold drinks indoors or in a courtyard bar.

The Mframaboum Caves can be reached from Mampong by catching a shared taxi to Kwamang (possibly changing vehicles at Nsuta) where the chief can organise a guide. The caves lie two hours from Kwamang on foot, with the last stretch being rather tough – with luck you'll be offered lunch and liquid at a cocoa farm near the caves. There is nowhere to stay in Kwamang, though vague plans to build a resthouse may be abetted by an increase in tourism. Note that Kwamang lies within sight of Kuwamu, but the gorge that separates the towns is passable only on foot, a 5–10km hike depending on who you believe.

Ntonso

Straddling the main Kumasi–Mampong road, only 5km from Bonwire, Ntonso is the major centre of *adinkra* cloth design and manufacture in Ashanti. This is the dyed, red-and-black cloth that you often see older Ghanaians wearing draped around them as a toga, especially on Saturdays, since it is the customary attire for funerals. It is not the cloth itself – either plain *kente* or imported cotton – that is made in Ntonso, but the dye stamps: it is possible to buy stamped cloth here, but also to buy the actual stamps. As is the case in Bonwire, the mood in Ntonso is welcoming and the pressure to buy is minimal. There are no organised guides as there are in Bonwire, but it is easy to find an articulate person to show you around and explain the complex symbolism that lies behind the various *adinkra* designs.

Ahwiaa and Pankrona

On the outskirts of Kumasi, these two craft villages are known respectively for their wood carvings and pottery. In both cases, however, you've little chance of seeing the craftsmen at work, and the level of aggro means that they're really only worth visiting if you plan to buy – in which case you can get just as good quality stuff at lower prices in Kumasi itself.

THE TAMALE ROAD

Most travellers heading northwards from Kumasi travel along the main north–south highway to Tamale, passing through Techiman and Kintampo (note that contrary to the impression created by many maps, the direct stretch of road between Kumasi and Techiman is in poor condition, so most drivers prefer to use the slightly longer but better road via Sunyani). This 400km trip takes about six hours by STC bus, the best way to go if you're doing it in one stretch. Alternatively, it can be broken up using a mixture of shared taxis and tro-tros. The most alluring diversion would be to visit the excellent and readily accessible Baobeng-Fiema Monkey Sanctuary near Nkoranza, though more adventurous travellers might be tempted to head out to the little-visited Bui National Park on the River Volta northwest of Wenchi.

Sunyani

Capital of Brong-Ahafo Region since 1909, Sunyani lies at the heart of one of Ghana's main areas of cocoa and kola nut production. The name Sunyani derives from the Akan phrase '*ason ndwae*', a reference to a time when the elephants that lived in the surrounding forest provided hunters with a rich source of income in the form of ivory. These days, there's not a great deal of virgin forest left in the region, and the elephants have long since been hunted out, but the substantial forest patch about 1km out of town along the same road as the Providence Bar might be worth investigating for birds, butterflies and possibly monkeys. Otherwise, Sunyani battles it out with Koforidua as the least compelling of Ghana's regional capitals, and there is little of interest to travellers in the immediate vicinity.

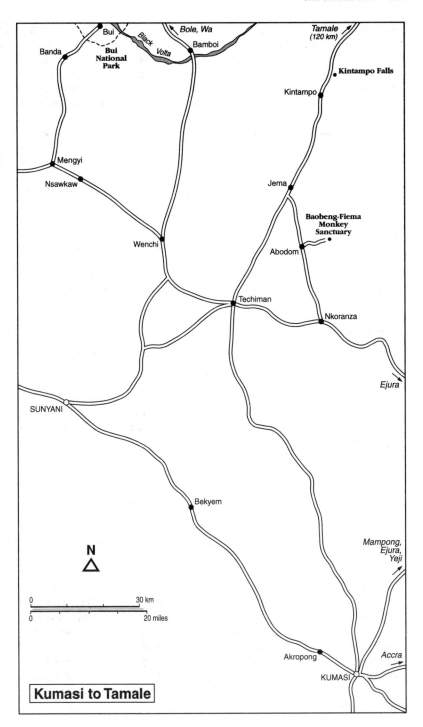

Kumasi to Tamale

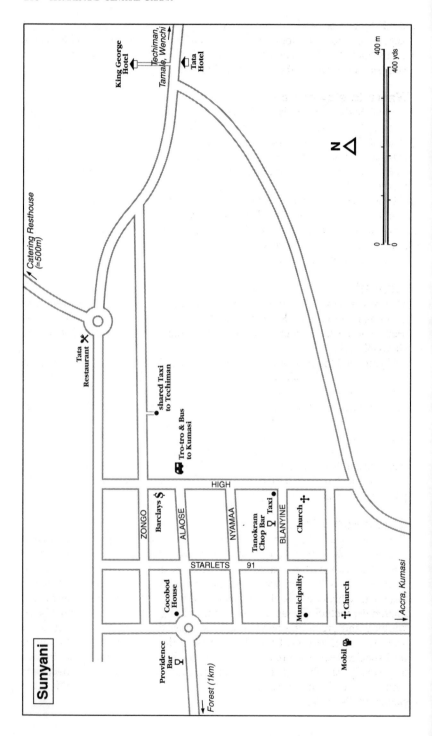

Getting there and away

Regular tro-tros run along the 130km road between Kumasi and Sunyani, taking about two hours either way. There is also plenty of transport between Sunyani and Wenchi, Techiman and Tamale.

Where to stay and eat

A good budget choice is the **Tata Hotel**, which lies about 1km from the town centre (a taxi there will cost less than US$1) and has large, spotless rooms with fans for US$3.50. Unsignposted, on a roundabout a similar distance from the town centre, the more upmarket **Catering Resthouse** has s/c chalets for around US$20 and the food is rated by expatriates as the best in town.

Under the same management as the synonymous hotel, but some five minutes' walk away, the **Tata Restaurant** serves a variety of tasty, inexpensive local and Western dishes. It also wins the award for the ultimate African misspelling of the word 'spaghetti', in case you're wondering just what 'supergaity' might taste like!

Wenchi

This reasonably large town, linked by regular tro-tros to Sunyani and Techiman on the main Kumasi–Tamale road, is something of a local route focus, but mostly of interest to travellers as the springboard for visits to Bui National Park.

If you need to spend a night in Wenchi, the **Baah Hotel**, 100m from the bus station along the Wa road, has pleasant rooms with a double bed and fan for US$3 non-s/c or US$6 s/c, and the owner seems to keep himself up-to-date with the practicalities surrounding visits to Bui. The only other place we could find is the **Kaaf Hotel**, 200m along the Busia road, which has more basic rooms in the US$2–4 range.

There are no restaurants, but dozens of chop stalls serve inexpensive meals in the lorry station. The breezy **Rooftop Bar**, about 500m from the main traffic circle, serves cheap, ice-cold draught beer and on occasion presents live music.

Bui National Park

The little-visited Bui National Park near the Côte d'Ivoire border protects an area of 1,821km^2 on either side of the Black Volta River, including the large Bui Gorge, long mooted as the site of a possible hydro-electric scheme. Bui is best known for its population of roughly 200 hippos, the largest in Ghana, but it also protects small numbers of several terrestrial mammals, including roan antelope, hartebeest, waterbuck, kob, bushbuck, warthog and green and patas monkeys, most of which are unlikely to be seen by casual visitors. Crocodiles occur in the river, and several hundred bird species have been recorded. Tourist facilities at Bui are basic, but it's a perfectly feasible goal for backpackers, and inexpensive overnight camping and hiking trips can easily be organised through the flexible rangers at Bui Camp.

Getting there and away

The park headquarters at Bui Camp lie 8km from the village of Banda and 2km from the village of Bui on the Black Volta. The best route to the camp is from Wenchi. One large tro-tro daily does the 85km run from Wenchi to Bui village via Bui Camp, leaving Bui at 05.30, arriving in Wenchi about three hours later, and starting the return trip any time after that. The tro-tro is normally only half-full when it passes Bui Camp, so you'll have no problem finding a seat when you leave. If for some reason you can't find direct transport to or from Bui, there are at least thee tro-tros daily in either direction between Wenchi and Banda, from where it's a reasonably flat 8km walk to Bui Camp. What you shouldn't do is take a vehicle from Wenchi that's going only as far as Nsoko or Mengyi, since you may well get stuck and neither village has any accommodation.

The only alternative to the Wenchi route is the signposted side-road that leaves the main road to Bole and Wa from near Banda Nkwanta, the site of a well-known mosque (see page 243). Motorists should be warned, however, that the signpost at the junction, blithely proclaiming Bui Camp to be 50km away, omits to mention that the unbridged and unfordable Volta River lies about 2km before the camp! For those using public transport, this road is a more realistic possibility, but only on Mondays when a few tro-tros leave Banda Nkwanta for the riverbank opposite Bui in the early morning and start the return trip in mid-morning. Passengers can cross the river in a local canoe.

Bui Camp actually lies some 4km outside the national park boundary, so you'll need to arrange to walk there with a guide. Day walks into the park work out at around US$0.75 per hour guide fee, while overnight camping trips cost around US$2.50 per day, plus there is a US$1 entrance fee. The alternative to entering the park on foot would be to organise a canoe trip out of Bui village.

Where to stay and eat

One of the wooden chalets at Bui Camp is reserved for visitors. The facilities amount to little more than one bed with a foam mattress and no bedding, and a bath where you can take a bucket shower. There is no charge for using the chalet, but a donation will be expected. Camping is also permitted. You should be able to organise local food with the caretaker, and may even be able to buy a few sodas or beers, but it would be prudent to bring some provisions with you, especially if you have thoughts of an overnight foray deep into the park.

At present, the only possibility for those who enter the park overnight is to camp in their own tent. In the near future, however, it is likely that a few tree houses will be constructed next to some established hippo viewing sites.

There is no accommodation in the villages of Banda, Bui or Banda Nkwanta.

Baobeng-Fiema Monkey Sanctuary

This small sanctuary was created in 1974 to protect the monkey population of the 4km^2, dry, semi-deciduous forest centred around the villages of

Baobeng and Fiema, which lie 1km apart in Nkoranza District. Two monkey species occur here in significant numbers, the mona monkey and black-and-white colobus, but there are also unsubstantiated reports of sightings of green, patas, spot-nosed and Diana monkeys in recent years. The mona monkey population is thought to stand at around 350 individuals, living in troops of 15–20 animals, several of which now have a territory in the forest fringe and adjacent woodland. The black-and-white colobus monkeys, with a population of 165 animals divided into 13 troops, are rarely seen outside true forest.

The reason why significant monkey populations have survived here but not in most other parts of Ghana is that the inhabitants of both villages regard them as sacred. This tradition has been undermined somewhat in recent years by the rising influence of Christianity, for which reason it is now illegal to hunt monkeys within a 5km radius of either village. Oral tradition dates the monkey taboo to 1831, when the villages were founded, and a special festival is held to this day for the monkeys every November. So serious is the taboo that whenever a monkey dies it is given a formal burial and funeral service by the villagers.

As for how the taboo arose, one story is that Baobeng was founded by a Brong warrior who saw two mona and two black-and-white colobus monkeys guarding a piece of white calico, consulted his patron god, Daworoh, and was told that the monkeys would bring him good fortune. Another story is that Daworah married Abodwo, the patron saint of Ashanti-founded Fiema, and that the monkeys are their offspring. Yet another tradition is that a former chief who had the ability to turn people into monkeys and back at will, something that was useful in battle, died before he was able to transform some 'monkeys' back into human form. According to this version of events, the colobus monkeys are men and the monas are women, and the two interbreed freely!

The main centre for monkey viewing is Baobeng village, ten minutes' walk from the resthouse, where an entrance fee of US$2.50 (most of which goes towards community projects) must be paid to the game scouts. The mona monkeys that scavenge from the village are particularly tame and they spend a great deal of time on the ground; it is highly rewarding to be able to watch these normally shy forest monkeys interact at such close quarters. The colobus monkeys are shyer and they stick to the trees, but you should easily get a clear view of them, and it's wonderful to see them leap between trees with their feathery white tails in tow. Although the village is the best place to see monkeys at close range, you can also do a guided walk along some of the 10km of footpaths that emanate from it; an opportunity to see some of the many birds and butterflies in the forest, as well as a giant mahogany tree thought to be more than 150 years old.

Getting there and away

The monkey sanctuary lies about 6km along a clearly signposted turn-off running eastwards from the dirt Nkoranza–Jema road. The springboard for visits is Techiman, a substantial and ancient town on the main

Kumasi–Tamale road about 60km northeast of Sunyani. You'll have absolutely no problem finding a tro-tro or shared taxi to Techiman from Kumasi, Sunyani, Kintampo or Tamale. From Techiman, take a shared taxi to Nkoranza about 25km to the east. From Nkoranza, you shouldn't have to wait too long for a shared taxi heading directly northwards to Fiema, another roughly 25km trip. Ask to be dropped at the resthouse, on the left side of the road about 1km before you enter Fiema. With luck, you can get from Techiman to Fiema in about one hour, and even on a slow day you should be there in two hours.

Travellers leaving Fiema for points further north should note that, while shared taxis do run along the road connecting Nkoranza to Jema, they are normally full when they pass the Fiema junction. In other words, rather than trying to head directly between Fiema and Jema, you might be better heading back to Techiman and picking up a northbound vehicle there.

Where to stay and eat
Established as part of a community project, the **resthouse** charges US$4 for a large, clean room with a double bed or US$2 per person to camp. There is no electricity or running water, but a borehole provides a good supply of water for bucket showers and paraffin lamps are available. At the time of writing, meals can be provided by private arrangement with the caretaker, but this situation is likely to be formalised in the medium term. Beers and soft drinks can be bought in Baobeng village, albeit at rather inflated prices.

Should you get stuck in Techiman, the **Agweya Hotel** has a pleasant garden, decent meals, and rooms in the US$6–15 range. There is at least one hotel in Nkoranza.

Kintampo
This moderately sized town lies on the main north–south road, almost precisely halfway between Kumasi and Tamale. It is best known for its waterfall, which is reportedly seasonal, but impressive even when we visited in the dry season. The Kintampo Falls must measure about 25m high, with a wading or swimming pool at the base, easily reached by a series of concrete steps, and a large cave a short distance upstream. The fringing riparian forest is dominated by mahogany trees up to 40m high and looks promising for birding. Also near Kintampo, Fuller Falls is notable for the stream below the waterfall, which disappears underground for some 40m before re-emerging.

Getting there and away
There is plenty of direct transport between Kintampo and Tamale, Kumasi, Techiman, Wenchi and Nkoranza. The Kintampo Falls lie 6km from town, a short walk from the Tamale road, and are signposted at the 191km marker. Fuller Falls lie a similar distance from town along a more obscure side road. In either case, the best way to get to the waterfall is to charter a taxi from Kintampo's lorry station – we were quoted about US$4 for either return trip.

THE OLD TAMALE ROAD 223

Where to stay and eat

There's nothing wrong with the **Midway Hotel** opposite the lorry station, which has large, clean rooms with fan and use of communal bucket showers for US$3. About 200m back towards Techiman, the **Wood Green Hotel** has clean, s/c rooms with fan and fridge, but no running water, for US$5.50 and smaller, scruffier s/c rooms for US$8. For food, there are plenty of chop stalls and bars serving chilled drinks dotted between the lorry station and Shell garage.

THE OLD TAMALE ROAD

Once the main trunk route north from Kumasi, the road through Mampong to Ejura and Yeji is now something of a byway, poorly maintained, of limited interest, and likely to be visited only by those travellers who plan on hopping on or off the Lake Volta ferry at Yeji.

The main attraction in this part of the country is **Digya National Park**, the second largest sanctuary in Ghana, protecting a 3,478km² knuckle of rolling hills, large, granite inselbergs and varied vegetation jutting into the west shore of Lake Volta. Digya protects one of the most varied faunas of any Ghanaian reserve, including elephant, leopard, possibly lion, warthog, buffalo, bushbuck, waterbuck, reedbuck, kob, roan antelope, six types of duiker and eight primate species. It is rumoured that this part of the lake supports a small population of manatees, large aquatic mammals similar in appearance and closely related to the dugong of the Indian Ocean. The Department of Wildlife office at Ejura must be visited by all prospective visitors to the park, but the park itself is accessible only to self-sufficient campers with a private 4x4. The only accommodation that I'm aware of in Ejura is the Liberty Avenue Hotel, a basic place with rooms for around US$2.50.

Yeji is essentially a port town, and not a particularly attractive one at that. The Lake Volta ferry from Akosombo pulls in here every Tuesday evening, assuming that it's running to schedule, and departs again at around 04.00 the next morning. There's no shortage of accommodation in Yeji: the Alliance Hotel has rooms for around US$2.50, or you could try the Volta or Ebenezer hotels. Heading north from Yeji, a twice-daily ferry to **Makongo** is supplemented by small motorised boats that take around 45 minutes. Regular transport runs along the 160km road between Makongo and Tamale, though you may change vehicles at Salaga. There is nowhere to stay in Makongo, so don't cross from Yeji in the afternoon unless you can be sure of reaching **Salaga** 40km along the Tamale road. The Salaga Community Centre has a few large air-conditioned s/c doubles for US$7.50; it lies 500m from the lorry park close to a football pitch.

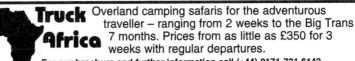

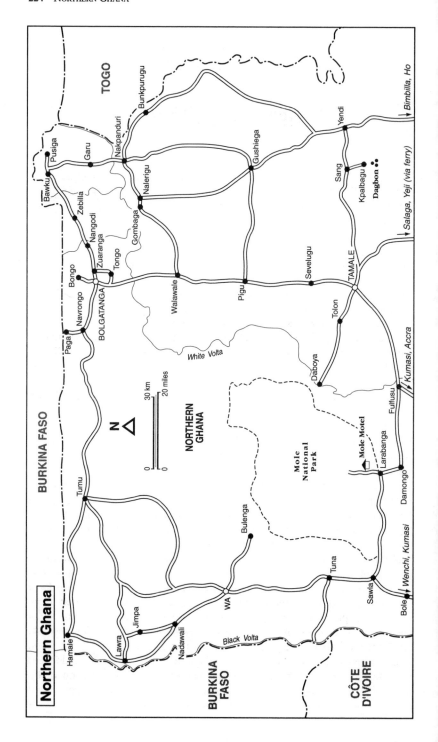

Chapter Nine

Northern Ghana

The vast and relatively thinly populated savannah country
that lies to the north of Lake Volta and the Black Volta River
was annexed to the Gold Coast colony in 1902. Formerly
known as the Northern Territory, it is now divided into three
administrative regions. The Northern Region is the largest
of these, covering an area of 70,384km^2 (more than one
quarter of the country's surface area), and its regional
capital Tamale boasts a population of roughly 250,000,
which puts it in competition with Tema and Takoradi as
the country's third most populous city. Much smaller than
Northern Region and – somewhat paradoxically – lying to its
north are the Upper East and Upper West Regions, the respective capitals of
which, Bolgatanga and Wa, each support a population of between 45,000 and
60,000.

The north of Ghana can in many respects be viewed as a historically and
culturally discrete entity from the southern and central regions. Unlike the
various Akan groups who live to the south of the Black Volta, the
predominantly Mole-Dagbani groupings of the north generally follow
patrilineal lines of inheritance and they share a common oral tradition that
suggests they arrived in modern-day Ghana in the twelfth or thirteenth
centuries following a militarised migration from the Lake Chad region.
Historically, the Mole-Dagbani have had far stronger trade and cultural links
with the Islamic world than with the Christian Europeans who settled along
the Gold Coast, as witnessed by the large number of mosques throughout the
region, including several centuries-old west Sudanese-style whitewashed
mud-and-stick mosques in the northwest.

Not as dense with tourist attractions as the coast, northern Ghana has a
relatively untrammelled, parochial atmosphere that seems far removed from
the cosmopolitan bustle of Accra or Kumasi. And, in Mole National Park,
the region does boast the country's best and most easily visited game
reserve, a patch of open, tsetse-fly-infested savannah where close
encounters with elephants are an everyday occurrence on what must be
about the most affordable guided foot safaris on the African continent. Close
to the entrance to Mole, at the small village of Larabanga, is the oldest and
most famous mosque in the country. Another important attraction of the
region is the traditional architecture which reaches its peak at Paga on the
Burkina Faso border, where large, flat-roofed, mud constructions have

grown organically over decades, even centuries, to house as many as a dozen related families. Similar homesteads are to be found around Nakpanduri, on the famed Gambaga escarpment, an area that's also notable for having some of the best scenery and birding in the country, as well as a magnificently positioned and highly affordable government resthouse.

The city of Tamale, itself of marginal interest to tourists, boasts the best facilities in the north, and it's the obvious gateway to the region if only because it's connected to both Accra and Kumasi by daily STC buses and a plethora of tro-tros. Tamale can also be reached by using the weekly ferry service from Akosombo to Yeji on Lake Volta. A second main access road to the north, connecting Kumasi to Wa via Wenchi and Bole, is in worse condition than the main Tamale road, but it's traversed by regular buses and allows you to see several beautiful, old mosques. For convenience sake as much as anything, this chapter describes the north in an anticlockwise loop out of Tamale, with Mole National Park, approachable from several directions, tagged on at the end.

TAMALE

The main route focus in northern Ghana, not to say the largest urban conglomeration, Tamale is hot, flat and quite incredibly dusty: first impressions arriving in the harsh light of day are less than flattering, unless perhaps you're a homesick construction worker, though the sunset, filtered through a misty suspension of fine red dust, can fleetingly make it look like one of the most beautiful construction sites in the world!

Despite being nominated as the capital of Northern Territory less than ten years after the region was annexed to the Gold Coast, Tamale has a rather provincial atmosphere, and it holds little of interest to travellers – the most remarkable aspect of the city is the infestation of whimsically weaving bicycles that makes walking, particularly in the vicinity of the central market, seem positively hazardous. Demented cyclists aside, Tamale's other shortcomings are largely compensated for by a friendly, hassle-free atmosphere, and good, inexpensive amenities ranging from several hotels and restaurants to one of the best and cheapest secondhand bookshops in Ghana, Grasrut Ventures Annex near the mosque.

As for sightseeing, the central market itself is worthwhile, and you'll certainly want to pause to watch the Gonja cloth weavers at work. As a taster for architectural styles found to the north, you could wander past the engagingly low-key palace of the Gulpke Na, clearly signposted on Hospital Road near Barclay's Bank, and consisting of several small, thatched buildings connected by 2m-high walls – be warned, however, that neither photography nor poking around the palace compound appear to be encouraged. Near to the palace is the Centre for National Culture, mentioned prominently in every piece of travel literature about Tamale that I've come across; I have no idea why. Finally, and most unexpectedly on the outskirts of this dry city, is a substantial teak forest and dam about 1.5km from the centre along Education Ridge Road, a good place for a walk and highly promising for birds.

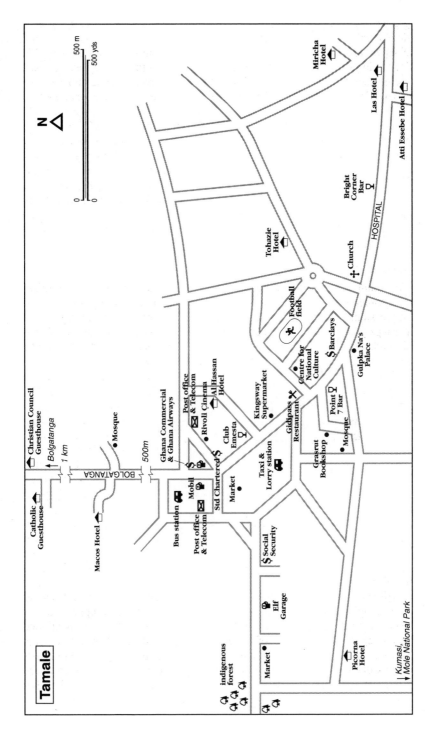

Getting there and away

Tamale is the main transport hub in northern Ghana. Note that since the map on page 227 was drawn up, the Lorry Park and OSA bus station have relocated to an area behind the Elf Garage, close to the Picorna Hotel. STC buses still leave from the bus station behind the post office.

Regular STC buses connect Accra, Kumasi and Tamale, and at least one continues to Bolgatanga and Bawku daily. The weekly air-conditioned luxury express bus between Accra and Tamale costs US$15, leaving Accra at 05.00 on Thursdays and Tamale at 09.00 on Fridays, stopping at Kumasi for 15 minutes. Many tro-tros run between Tamale and main towns along the Bolgatanga–Kumasi road.

For Mole National Park, a daily OSA bus leaves Tamale at 14.00 to overnight at the Mole Motel before heading back to Tamale at 05.30 the following morning. Without booking a few hours in advance, you'll probably have to stand most of the way. Alternatively, catch a bus connecting Tamale to either Bole or Wa as far as Larabanga (see *Getting there and away* under *Mole National Park* for further details).

Travellers coming to Tamale via Lake Volta ferry are advised to disembark at Yeji rather than Kete Krachi, since the City Express bus from Kete Krachi to Tamale can takes in excess of 15 hours. For details of transport between Yeji and Tamale, see page 223. For crossing between Hohoe and Tamale via Bimbilla, see page 189.

Where to stay

The **Macos Hotel**, clearly signposted about 2km from the town centre on the Bolgatanga road, has the cheapest rooms in Tamale. Aadequate doubles with a fan cost US$4.50, with the use of clean communal showers. Similar in standard, a little more expensive, and considerably more central, the **Al Hassan Hotel** has long been a favourite with backpackers and it remains good value at US$4.50/5.50 single/double using communal showers or US$7 for a s/c double.

Two good church guesthouses are situated no more than 200m apart on the Bolgatanga road, about 1km past the Macos Hotel. The **Catholic Guesthouse** is outstanding value, offering clean, comfortable, s/c rooms with fan for US$6/8 single/double. The rambling green grounds are an added attraction, along with cheap breakfasts and – a little unexpectedly – a great outdoor bar! The **Christian Council Guesthouse** charges roughly the same price, and it's clean enough, but it seems a poor deal by comparison.

There are three more expensive hotels clustered about 1km out of town off Hospital Road. The **Atti Essebe Hotel** is no better than the cheaper places, for which reason it seems overpriced at US$11 for an unremarkable double with a fan. Far better is the **Miricha Hotel** (tel: 22735), which has pleasant grounds and comfortable, ac, s/c doubles with hot running water for US$18. The more upmarket and highly regarded **Las Hotel** (tel: 22158) has s/c rooms with a fan for US$17/20 single/double and ac rooms for US$23.

fan and US$17 with ac – very good value assuming that the water's running by the time you get there. The restaurant has an inexpensive breakfast menu.

Finally, the most upmarket option in Tamale in the **Picorna Hotel** (tel: 22070), which seems good value at US$20/30 for an ac, s/c single/double with hot water. The grounds and restaurant are fairly attractive.

Where to eat
The **Gillipass Restaurant**, on the roof of a three-storey building, is the breeziest place to eat in the city centre, and arguably also the best, with a good selection of Western and Chinese dishes costing around US$5 per plate. Even if you don't eat here, it's a great place to sip on a chilled beer while you watch the sun set over the city, or stargaze. Directly opposite Gillipass, there's cheaper beer and less breeze at the popular **Point Seven Bar**, where you have the choice of sitting indoors or on the semi-enclosed pavement.

The **Crest Restaurant** in the Al Hassan Hotel is under the same management as Gillipass and serves similar food at about half the price, but the dining room is unbearably hot, even if you switch the fan on, so try to persuade the waiter to let you put your table in the courtyard. Also very reasonably priced, **Sparkles Restaurant** next to the National Cultural Centre is similarly marred by the lack of breeze, though you can at least sit outdoors.

The **Sweet Gardens Chinese Restaurant** on the first-floor balcony of the Las Hotel is popular with expatriates and the food is very good, though you should expect to pay around US$7 per head for a main course with rice.

For Western and Ghanaian dishes in the US$3–5 range, try the restaurants in the **Tohazie** or **Picorna hotels**.

NAKPANDURI AND THE GAMBAGA ESCARPMENT
The Gambaga escarpment, which lies to the east of the main Tamale–Bolgatanga road, is the most significant physical feature in northeastern Ghana, measuring more than 60km from east to west and rising several hundred metres above the surrounding plains. Named after the town of Gambaga, capital of the ancient Mamprusi kingdom, the escarpment is of great interest to birdwatchers and hikers, with the excellent government resthouse at Nakpanduri forming the most obvious base for exploration, as well as boasting some fantastic traditional architecture in the form of sprawling *kraals* – extended family homesteads in which each nuclear family unit has its own hut and courtyard area enclosed within one walled compound.

Mamprusi is widely regarded to be the oldest of the Mole-Dagbani states; the Dagomba chief, or Nayiri, is still sometimes called upon to settle internal disputes in neighbouring Mossi and Dagomba. It is also probable that Mamprusi is the oldest extant political unit in Ghana. All Mole-Dagbani traditions agree that it was founded before AD1200 by the descendants of a light-skinned chief remembered by the name Toha-jie ('The Red Warrior'), who led his people from somewhere further east to Pusiga on what is now

EXPLORING DAGOMBA

Tamale lies at the heart of Dagomba, an ancient Mole-Dagbani state founded by an offshoot of the even older Mamprusi. I can find no evidence to suggest that Tamale itself is of any great historical significance: on the contrary, even today Tamale doesn't serve as the seat of the paramount chieftaincy of Dagomba. According to oral tradition, the first Dagomba capital was Dagbon, founded in the mid-fifteenth century, and over the ensuing decades the base from where the militaristic chief, Nyagse, expanded his empire to incorporate a great many smaller kingdoms, most strategically the salt-producing village of Daboya on the White Volta. Now an obscure and somewhat remote village, Dagbon in its heyday must have been one of the most architecturally impressive settlements in West Africa: when archaeologists discovered the ruined city in 1962, they unearthed traces of a five-storey building and a rock-hewn subterranean reservoir.

Dagomba's influence appears to have declined with the rise of the Gonja kingdom in the early seventeenth century: in roughly 1620, Gonja expansionists forced the Dagomba chief, Dariziogo, to relocate his capital to Yendi, some 30km northeast of Dagbon. From around 1750 to 1874, Dagomba was a vassal state of Ashanti, and from 1902 until after World War I the state was split between the British Gold Coast and German Togoland, with Yendi falling into the latter territory. Despite this, not to say the economic ascendency of Tamale since it was made colonial capital of the Northern Territory in 1907, Yendi remains the modern seat of the Ya-Na (the paramount chief of Dagomba) almost four centuries after it was founded.

Although it's perhaps a rather esoteric pursuit, several of Dagomba's more historic towns can be reached on public transport. There are several tro-tros daily from Yendo to Tamale, a 100km trip that takes about three hours in either direction. Yendi is best visited on Monday or Friday mornings, when the Ya-Na holds an open court in the company of his two dozen shaven wives. The old salt-production centre at Daboyo, now better known for its Gonja cloth weavers, lies on the northwest bank of the White Volta, some 60km and two hours by tro-tro from Tamale. Also of great historical interest is the former slave market town of Salaga on the Yeji road, though I understand that few visible relics of its past remain. As for Dagbon, it lies about 100km from Tamale, 25km along a side road heading south from Sang on the Yendi road – I've no idea how much transport runs along this side road, but if you can find transport as far as Kpalbagu, Dagbon shouldn't be more than an hour's walk from there.

Be aware that none of these towns has any formal accommodation so, if you don't want to visit them as a day trip out of Tamale, you'll have to take a tent or rely on making private arrangements.

the Ghana–Burkina Faso border. Toha-jie's grandson, Naa Gbewa, is thought to have been the first true Mamprusi chief, settling first at a place called Mamprugu (from which the name Mamprusi derives), then at Gambaga, where he forged a union with the indigenous people by assuming political control, but allowing religious power to remain in the hands of traditional *Tengdana* priests.

The section that follows describes in an anticlockwise direction a loop through the Gambaga region, departing from the main Tamale–Bolgatanga road at Walewale, then running through Gambaga and Nalerigu to Nakpanduri, from where you could either turn back directly towards Walewale or else continue north via Garu, Bawku and Zebila to Bolgatanga.

Situated at the junction to Nakpanduri, **Walewale** lies some 40km south of Bolgatanga and 120km north of Tamale, and although at least one (seriously dilapidated) bus runs daily in either direction between Nakpanduri and each of Tamale and Bolgatanga, you can also do the trip in short hops. Coming from Tamale, it's probably worth paying the extra to catch a tro-tro heading directly to Bolgatanga and then asking to be dropped at Walewale. Coming from Bolgatanga, look for a tro-tro that terminates in Walewale itself. At the junction, you'll find a couple of bars selling chilled drinks. Directly opposite, there's an intriguing, if not particularly attractive, mosque of indeterminate age (one source claims it is very old, but when I suggested this to locals they nodded sagely and said it was built at least 20 years ago – who knows?) and notable mostly for its Moorish tower. Should the need arise, there's also a small private guesthouse in Walewale, a short distance back from the junction towards Bolgatanga.

You're unlikely to wait too long at the junction for a lift of some sort, at least as far as **Gambaga**, 45km along the dirt road leading east from Walewale. It is difficult to determine the historical relationship between Gambaga and Nalerigu 8km to the east: most sources refer to Gambaga as the ancient capital of Mamprusi, and it was certainly the colonial capital of the Northern Territory until 1907 (it remains district capital to this day), but Nalerigu appears to be the older settlement and it houses the palace of the Mamprusi Nayiri. Gambaga itself isn't much of a place today, and assuming that your vehicle is continuing to Nalerigu you may as well stay on board.

Of passing interest in **Nalerigu** are the attractive dam and pretty, sandstone church as you enter town from the Gambaga side. More ambitiously, ask a local guide to show you traces of the so-called 'Nigeria Walls' that surround the town, the remains of sixteenth-century fortifications that relate to the Sahelian slave trade. You'll probably also need a guide to locate the government resthouse, where for less than US$1 you'll be offered a bare room with no mattress, no lock, and not much of a ceiling to form a barrier between you and the several hundred bats that roost in the roof. Ask instead to be shown the government *guesthouse*, which is a little more expensive but reasonably habitable, consisting of three mud-walled rooms around a central courtyard, at least one of which might lock, definitely has a foam mattress, and seems entirely bat-free (the caretaker adamantly refused to let us look in another room after poking his own head round the door, so goodness knows what evil lurks inside). Be warned, too, that you should look at the accommodation only if you're reasonably serious about staying over, or you might well find yourself victim to a conspiracy of misinformation aimed to keep you in town overnight – it's a long story...! If you do have to wait around a while, check out the small garden bar next to the bus station (cool but not chilled drinks). Right next to that, a chop stall sells deliciously spicy guinea fowl stew.

The main draw in the region is **Nakpanduri**, perched on the edge of the highest point on the Gambaga escarpment, roughly 25km east of Nalerigu and connected to it by reasonably regular transport. There's little in the way of prescribed sightseeing in the area, but the combination of an excellent guesthouse, attractive surroundings and a relatively cool climate makes it a pleasant place to settle in for a few days. The town itself is a quite striking collection of sprawling, traditionally built compounds interspersed with massive baobab trees, while the area around the guesthouse affords great views to the northern plains, and is excellent for birdwatching. A good day walk would be to follow the Bawku road through a forest reserve to the base of the escarpment, where a bridge crosses a forest-fringed tributary of the Volta River. There's also supposedly a seasonal waterfall nearby, worth asking directions to if you are there in the rainy season.

As for practicalities, the first thing you'll want to do upon arrival in Nakpanduri is make certain of a room at the government resthouse, where a comfortable double room with a fan (but no electricity within a 25km radius!) costs US$2, and there is plenty of water for bucket showers. To get to the resthouse from the main circle (which is where most tro-tros and buses stop), walk along the Bawku road for about ten minutes until you pass the Agricultural Rehabilitation Centre for the Blind to your right and see a three-way fork to your left opposite a signpost reading 'Caution: Slow Down'. The guesthouse is about 200m down the central fork. For food, either ask the caretaker about using the kitchen or head back to the main circle where there are several chop stalls. Spicy guinea fowl stew is the local speciality, sold from mid-afternoon until late evening, and stale bread is sold at all times, but on the basis of our experience *kenkey* (or whatever other hot starchy accompaniment is available) evidently sells out well before nightfall.

Heading on from Nakpanduri, your options more or less amount to beating a retreat back to Walewale or striking on northwards to **Bawku**, a large and busy market town that can be rather absorbing on market days (every third day), but is less than memorable the rest of the time, unless perhaps you want to buy a sample of the attractive *fugu* shirts that are characteristic of the far northeast. Before you go clothes' shopping, however, you'll need to find transport from Nakpanduri through to Bawku, apparently a more hit-and-miss affair than local advice ('you get lorry any time') might have you believe – we waited about seven hours for a lift on market day. As compensation, once you finally get going the 60km road offers some magnificent views. Accommodation in Bawku appears to be limited to the seedy but reasonably central Paradise Guest House, and the Hollywood Hotel, 3km out of town just off the Bolgatanga road, which has unexpectedly smart rooms with a fan for US$5, bucket showers, and a fridge loaded with ice-cold drinks. The best place to eat in the town centre is the Him Restaurant, next to the Mobil garage, while those staying at the Hollywood Hotel will find tasty grilled guinea fowl served outside the open-air bar on the junction 200m away. The only sightseeing in the area that I'm aware of is the ancient shrine to Naa Gbewa, the founder of the Mamprusi state, at nearby Pusiga.

Heading west from Bawku isn't a problem: not only do tro-tros to Bolgatanga leave from in front of the Mobil garage every half hour or so, but there's also a daily STC bus to Kumasi and Accra, leaving at 13.00, which you can use to hop as far as Bolgatanga or Tamale, assuming seats are available. You could also do the trip to Bolgatanga in hops, with the main attraction being the geometrically painted family compounds around

Zebilla and **Amkwalaga**, better examples of which can be seen by 'dropping' from a tro-tro at an appropriate spot along the road than by actually getting off in one of these small towns.

BOLGATANGA

The burgeoning capital of Ghana's Upper East Region may be smaller than Tamale, but it is no less hectic. Bolgatanga, you can't help but feel, is about to do the urban equivalent of bursting at the seams, and it comes as no surprise to discover that the population of this amorphous, bustling city has grown from fewer than 20,000 in 1970 to about 50,000 in 1998. Like many towns in the north, Bolga (as you'll soon come to call it) lacks specific tourist attractions, but definitely worth an hour or two is the small, but interesting, ethnographic museum behind the Catholic Social Centre. You might also want to pop in at the nearby regional library and Ghana Tourist Board office, the latter your best source of current local tourist information. Bolga's most interesting feature, however, is the busy market, which peaks in activity every three days and is best known elsewhere in Ghana for the fine and often very affordable leatherwork, basketry, colourful straw hats and striped cloth shirts produced by the Frafra people for a predominantly local market. Hat salesmen, heads layered high with samples of their wares, are a familiar sight around town.

Getting there and away

Bolga is an important regional transport hub and you'll have little difficulty finding transport in any direction. The greatest volume of transport runs to and from Tamale and points further south. The Tamale road is serviced by regular tro-tros, plus at least one OSA and City Express bus daily. An STC bus to Kumasi leaves Bolgatanga at 16.30 every Monday, Wednesday and Friday. In the opposite direction, the STC bus leaves Kumasi at 18.00 on Tuesday, Thursday and Saturday.

There are two main lorry stations in Bolga. Tro-tros to destinations further north, such as Navrongo, Paga and Bongo, leave from the old station in the town centre. Tro-tros to destinations in the south and east, such as Bawku and Tongo, leave from the new station behind the Shell and Goil garages on Zaurangu road. City Express buses also leave from the new station, while the OSA station is near the fire station and the STC station is out of town on the Tamale road.

Note that the only transport to Wa is run by City Express (see *Getting there and away* under Wa on page 240).

Where to stay

When it comes to finding a decent, inexpensive room in Bolgatanga, you're spoilt for choice. My nomination for best deal in town has to be the **Sand Garden Hotel**, 15 minutes' walk from the town centre and ten minutes from the new lorry park off the Bawku road near the fire station. Clean, comfortable rooms with a fan cost US$3/4 single/double, using spotless communal bucket showers and toilets, while s/c doubles cost US$6 and ac

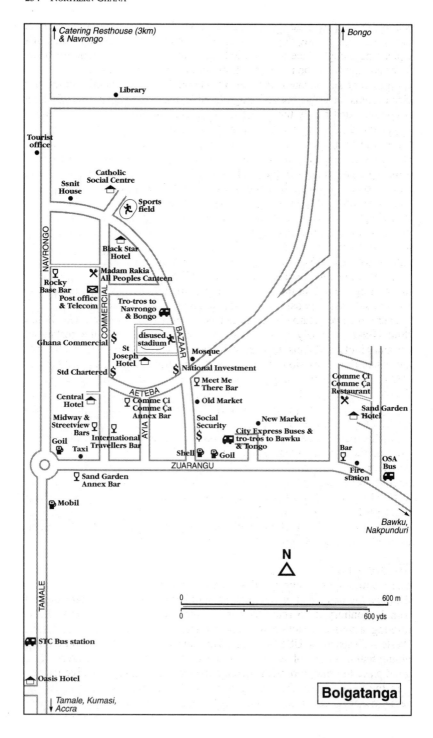

rooms US$9. The large and indisputably sandy garden may be lacking on the aesthetic front but, depending on what's blaring from the tape deck, it's a pleasant enough place for a chilled beer – and the sound system, for once, is far enough from the rooms to allow for an undisturbed night.

More centrally located, the **Sacred Heart Catholic Social Centre** has clean rooms for US$3.50/5.50 single/double, the slight shabbiness of which is compensated for by the excellent communal showers and toilets. Cheap meals and drinks are available from the canteen. There are dorms, too, but these aren't especially cheap and are intended for self-contained groups of at least three people rather than for travellers arriving alone. Also very affordable and central is the **St Joseph Hotel**, next to the old lorry park, where you can get a slightly run-down s/c double with fan for US$5.

Another possibility in this price bracket is the **Oasis Hotel**, a very clean, friendly place which, unfortunately, leaves you stranded in suburbia with few obvious eating options, and is probably only worth thinking about should you arrive in Bolgatanga by STC bus. Large rooms with a fan cost US$3.50/4.50 and s/c rooms US$5.50. The easiest way to get there is to follow the Tamale road out of town for about 200m past the STC bus station, then turn right into the road signposted for the State Housing Company, then left after about 50m into the side road opposite The Point Bar, then right after about 100m.

There are two relatively upmarket hotels in the city centre. The **Black Star Hotel** is widely accepted as the top spot in town; the restaurant certainly looks and feels the part with blasting air-conditioning, swish decor and chattering television. The rooms, by contrast, seem very ordinary at US$11 for a double using communal showers and US$17 for a s/c, ac double. They might also get noisy at weekends. Nearby, and better value in my opinion, the appropriately named **Central Hotel** has large s/c, ac rooms for US$8/10 single/double.

Finally, there's the **Catering Rest House**, a grand folly situated 3km out of town off the Navrongo road. A massive, partially unfinished concrete eyesore with comic modernist pretensions, the Catering Rest House is redeemed from utter absurdity only by the pleasant s/c, ac chalets, which are excellent value at US$17. The bar and restaurant also seem OK, and it may even host the occasional disco, but ultimately the atmosphere is just too depressing – it's difficult to see why anybody without private transport would want to be isolated in such unattractive surroundings so far from the town centre.

Where to eat

The **Comme Çi Comme Ça Restaurant**, on the outskirts of town close to the Sand Garden Hotel, is not quite as indifferent as the name might suggest – on the contrary, it's perhaps the best restaurant of its sort in northern Ghana, offering a varied selection of tasty, attractively presented and substantial Western dishes in the US$3–4 range. You can eat either in the air-conditioned dining hall or in one of several fan-cooled, thatched, outdoor shelters. It's a good place to drink, too, with friendly service and a highly effective fridge.

In the town centre, the restaurant in the **Black Star Hotel** is under the same management as the Comme Çi Comme Ça, and the menu and prices are practically identical. For cheap grilled beef kebabs and whole guinea fowl, try the courtyard bar at the St Joseph Hotel. The usual range of street food is available around the market and lorry parks.

Excursions from Bolgatanga

About 15km north of Bolgatanga, the small town of **Bongo**, a district administrative centre since 1988, lies at the heart of a memorable landscape of massive boulders, magnificent baobab trees and attractive kraals covered in childish stencil-like painted figures. The main attraction here, the aptly named Bongo Rock, emits a convincingly resonant vibrating boom when struck, while the general landscape offers much to photographers. Regular tro-tros to Bongo leave Bolgatanga from the central lorry station, taking about 30 minutes. Bongo Rock lies 20–30 minutes' walk from Bongo; to get there follow the main road back from the tro-tro station past the Catholic church, until after about 300m you see a footpath to your left leading to the taller and more distant of two hills. There's no accommodation in Bongo, but there is a bar serving coolish soft drinks and beers about 100m from the tro-tro station in the opposite direction to the Catholic church.

A similar distance south of Bolgatanga, **Tongo** lies at the base of a horseshoe-shaped chain of low mountains, famous not only for their balancing rock formations and the views offered across the border to Burkino Faso, but also for the whistling sound made by the harmattan wind as it passes through cracks in the rocks from December to February. The mountains above Tonga support the ethnically distinct Talensi people, who live in several small, scattered villages, most notably Tengzugu, where an important oracle and fetish shrine is located in a nearby cave. A popular site of pilgrimage for many Ashanti, who believe the oracle to have mystical curative and visionary powers, Tengzugu Cave lies roughly an hour's walk from Tongo along a rather steep road suitable for 4x4 vehicles only. The cave is visited with increasing frequency by adventurous travellers: initial arrangements must be made through the chief in Tongo, who'll expect the usual gift or payment, and you'll also have to visit the chief in Tengzugu to go through a similar ritual before actually visiting the shrine (only 200m from his palace). When you arrive in Tongo, expect to be approached by a few guides offering to set up the trip: make sure that you pick one you like, because you'll be stuck with him after he's taken you to see the chief. Tro-tros to Tongo leave Bolgatanga from the new station and they take about 30 minutes. There is no formal accommodation in Tongo, but this seems likely to change in the near future, and at present you should have no problem finding a hut in which to sleep, or pitching a tent with the permission of the chief. In addition to visiting the shrine, it's possible to arrange longer hiking trips into the mountains. It may be of interest to some readers that relatively formal excursions to Tongo are in the process of being developed by an Accra-based company called Fredina Tours (tel: 021 77-2494 or 77-5554).

Also of interest is the sacred bat-tree at **Baare**, 3km from Tongo, though whether it's worth the hassle of visiting yet another chief is debatable, especially as the bats aren't always there and the numbers pale by comparison with the bat colonies you can see in parts of Accra and Kumasi.

Note, too, that **Paga** (see page 239) would make a perfectly feasible day trip from Bolgatanga.

NAVRONGO

This quiet, rustic town, situated close to the main border crossing into Burkina Faso, is notable for its many traditional homesteads, which are typical of northern Ghana, though angular where those in Gambaga curve, and often painted in monochrome geometric patterns. Should you arrive in Navrongo from Tamale or Bolgatanga, your first impression is likely to be how neat, orderly and shady it feels by comparison; this, despite the large number of uncompleted concrete buildings dotting the small town centre, skeletal relics of an absurdly over-ambitious development plan initiated by the short-lived Acheampong government of 1972–75.

Historically, Navrongo's claim to fame is as the home of Catholicism in northern Ghana. The Catholic Mission on the outskirts of town was founded in 1906 by pioneering 'White Fathers' under the French Canadian missionary Oscar Morin, who travelled to this then little-known part of West Africa overland via what is now Burkino Faso. Definitely worth a visit is the Cathedral of Our Lady of the Seven Sorrows: consecrated by Father Morin in 1919, this large, traditionally constructed building is notable above all for the simple, but beautiful frescos that were painted on the pillars by local women using kerite oil and soil-based pigments. Also in the mission grounds is a remarkable grotto, reportedly a replica of the one at Lourdes, protected by a high stone wall constructed in a manner reminiscent of the Zimbabwe ruins in the country of the same name.

Getting there and away

Regular tro-tros connect Navrongo to Bolgatanga, and there are shared taxis running back and forth throughout the day to Paga. To get to nearby Lake Tono, the turn-off to which lies 3km along the Wa road, you'll probably have to charter a taxi for around US$3.

If you're heading towards Wa, the City Express buses from Bolgatanga do pass through Navrongo, but seats are generally full by that time, which means standing at least as far as Tumu, three hours away. Far better to go to Bolgatanga and pick up the bus at the terminus.

Where to stay and eat

The most central accommodation is at the **Hotel Mayaga**, a likeable little place clearly signposted about 500m from the lorry station along the Wa road. A spacious s/c room with fan and running water costs US$4/5 single/double, while an ac double costs US$10. The restaurant is better than you'd expect and not too expensive, and the outdoor bar serves chilled beer and cold drinks. There are several bars and chop houses in Navrongo; we had a wonderful plate of spicy guinea fowl and lettuce for little more than US$1 at the **Crossroads Bar**.

Less centrally, another option is the **Catholic Church Social Centre Guesthouse**, which faces the cathedral about 10–15 minutes' walk from the lorry station. There's nothing much wrong with the rooms here, but they seem relatively overpriced at US$10 for a non-s/c double with fan. To get there, follow the main road past the Ghana Commercial Bank and Bach Supermarket, and after the second big tree to your left turn into a vehicle-width track. After perhaps 500m you'll pass a conspicuous, blue water tower, then after another 100m reach a road with the cathedral in front of you – turn right into the road and the guesthouse is immediately on your right.

Even further out of town, the **Tono Guesthouse** is the only accommodation in the vicinity of Lake Tono, an artificial body of water that forms an important source of irrigation for the region, as well as offering good birding for visitors. The problem is that the guesthouse is often full, it's a good 2km from the lake itself, and without private transport you'll need to charter a taxi, or hitch. For those with vehicles, follow the Wa road out of town for roughly 3km, then turn right on to a surfaced turn-off, which after 5km leads directly to the guesthouse. Rooms cost around US$8 and meals can be arranged by advance request.

PAGA

The most frequently used border crossing between Ghana and Burkino Faso, Paga attracts a fair number of visitors owing to the sacred crocodile pool that lies about five minutes' walk from the main road through town. The pool is easy to find from the taxi station: just walk away from the main road through the adjacent market, then follow the footpath running away from the market at a 45° angle to the clearly visible dam wall. Chances are, however, that you'll never find your way past the dragnet of 'guides' and 'caretakers' who hang around the station waiting for custom. Protracted negotiations are the order of the day: you'll be asked a reasonable sum to buy the chicken with which it's customary to feed one of the crocodiles, then about three times more as a guide fee, the purpose of which is unclear, given that the routine is basically to hustle visitors to the pool, throw a chicken to the largest crocodile, take a photo or two, then chase the crocs back into the water, time's up, give us yer money and bugger off! And spare a thought for the crocodiles themselves – for centuries revered and protected as vassals for the ancestral spirits, they now suffer the indignity of being leaped on, prodded about and shooed off with a familiarity that might lead a more sceptical observer than myself to form the conclusion they are preserved solely for the money they generate.

It has to be said that the caretakers at Paga have truly perfected the art of making visitors resent every cedi they've paid – a shame, because it would otherwise be a rare treat to be able to touch and photograph crocodiles at such close quarters. Fortunately, the grasping attitude doesn't appear to extend to the guides. Once show time is over, you'll probably be taken around one of the extended family homesteads that characterise this Burkina Faso border region – fantastic, labyrinthine, almost fortress-like complexes that share much architecturally with the more famous Dogon homesteads in Mali. The homestead we visited, one of the largest in the region and said to be well over a century old, is inhabited by roughly 100 people in ten separate households, each with its own living quarters and courtyard. The flat roofs are used not only for drying crops, but also as a place to sleep in hot weather. Some of the whitewashed mud walls are for some reason covered in labelled paintings of animals, a crocodile with a chicken in its mouth being a particular favourite. The graves of important family members actually lie within the courtyards of their former quarters. If you do visit a house, you'll be expected to make a small donation, but the whole thing is handled with a warmth and dignity that couldn't be more of a contrast to the mood at the crocodile pool down the road!

So far as travel practicalities go, Paga is connected to Navrongo by regular shared taxis, and it's an easy day trip from either Navrongo or Bolgatanga. There's no formal accommodation in the main part of Paga, though doubtless you'd be able to arrange to sleep out on one of the roofs for a small fee. About 4km from town, close to the border, the Paga Hotel has clean doubles for US$8.50.

WA

The unimposing capital of Upper West Region, Wa is one of the oldest cities in the Ghanaian interior, founded in the mid-seventeenth century by an offshoot of the Dagomba state. For several centuries the seat of the Wa-Na (the title given to the chief of Wa), Wa was one of the first parts of the country to adopt the Islamic faith, as evidenced by the extraordinary high number of mosques dotted around the town centre. Of particular interest to tourists are two disused but reasonably well-preserved mud-and-stick mosques in the west Sudanese style situated next to each other behind the modern Great Mosque. The same architectural style has been used to construct the nineteenth-century Wa-Na's palace, a large and striking building close to the main circle. In front of the palace lie the graves of five former Wa-Nas, starting with Pelpua III, who ruled from 1920 to 1935. If the Wa-Na is in town, he will often see visitors – he may not be spoken to directly, but the caretaker outside the palace will put you in the picture.

A worthwhile short excursion from Wa takes you to Nakori, where there's a very striking mud-and-stick mosque, taller than the one at Larabanga and of a similar vintage. The friendly chief of Nakori, to whom you'll probably be required to pay a call of respect, claims that the mosque was constructed in the fifteenth century. Nakori lies within easy walking or cycling distance of Wa, roughly 4km from the town centre along the road passing the Upland Hotel. A taxi charter shouldn't cost more than US$4 for the round trip.

Getting there and away

Coming from the direction of Bolgatanga, the only public transport consists of two bus services run by City Express. Both these services stop at Navrongo, but there are usually no seats left by the time it gets there.

The first service is a direct bus between Bolga and Wa, leaving at 07.00 daily in either direction and arriving ten hours later – be at the station by 05.30 to be sure of getting a seat and take food because little is available along the way. The only scheduled stop is at Tumu, where you can buy chilled soft drinks and (assuming you're brave enough to enter a nominee for the category 'Most Disgusting Toilets that I've seen in Africa') make use of the public conveniences behind the vast and normally empty lorry station.

The second service from the Bolga area is the 'sleeper', so called because it involves an overnight stay in Tumu, 140km from Bolga and 120km from Wa. This trip actually consists of two separate services: a bus leaving Bolga for Tumu at around 14.00 daily and one leaving Tumu for Wa at roughly 12.00 daily. In the opposite direction, the bus from Wa to Tumu leaves at around 07.00 daily, as does the bus from Tumu to Bolga. Should you decide to use this service, there is affordable accommodation in Tumu at Lims Hotel. You might also want to visit the Department of Game and Wildlife office in town to enquire about the possibility of investigating the 565km^2 Gbele Resource Area, which reportedly lies some 15–20km from Tumu along the Walembele road, and is home to significant numbers of roan antelope as well as a wide variety of birds.

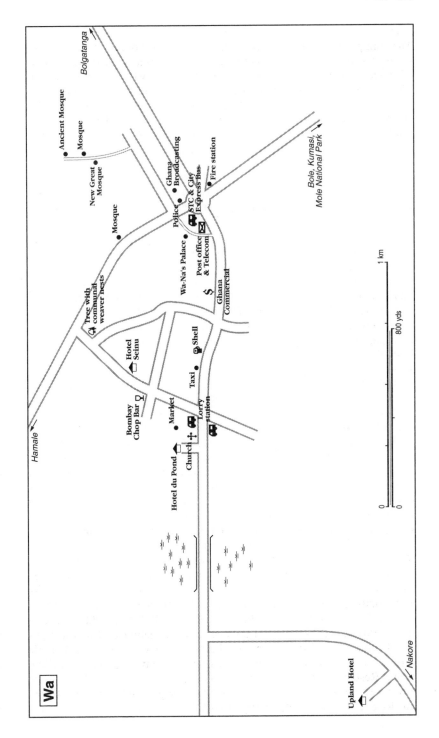

Coming to or from Wa in other directions, plenty of buses run directly between Wa and Kumasi, and the main towns along this route are also connected to each other by localised tro-tro services. Two OSA buses daily run directly between Wa and Tamale, stopping at Larabanga for Moe National Park.

Where to stay and eat

The best budget option is the **Hotel du Pond**, which is very central and close to all the bus and lorry stations. An adequate double room with a fan costs US$3, and the communal showers have running water. It may be noisy on the rare occasions when there's live music, but otherwise it's great value for money. The only other cheap accommodation in the centre appears to be the similarly priced but more run-down **Hotel Seinu**.

In a different league altogether, the **Upland Hotel** lies in attractive grounds some 10–15 minutes' walk from the town centre. Rooms here start at US$10 for a single with fan, US$16 for a s/c double with fan and US$22 for one with air-conditioning.

The restaurant at the Upland Hotel is the best in Wa, serving generously proportioned main dishes for around US$4 per plate. There are several cheaper chop houses and bars scattered in the town centre, and the usual street food is sold around the market.

BOLE

This small town on the main Kumasi–Wa road is of interest primarily for its beautiful mud-and-stick mosque, regarded locally to be the second oldest of its type in the country, but it also boasts some interesting traditional houses. The ancient mosque isn't visible from the main road, but it's easy enough to find, situated about 50m from the modern mosque, a major landmark with its five-storey parapet. A significant attraction of Bole over Larabanga is that the set-up is so much more casual: the Imam seems to be very relaxed about women visitors and photography, and he may well offer to take you inside the mosque and up to the roof. We were asked for a donation, which is only proper – the critical thing is that once we had paid we were left alone to take our time absorbing the atmosphere and photographing the mosque, a far cry from the incessant hassle and chit-chat that characterises the Larabanga experience.

Bole serves as a convenient overnight stop for travellers heading between Kumasi and Mole (see also *Getting there and away* under Mole National Park opposite). The only place to stay in town is the Motel Eureka, a clean, friendly, family-run establishment where a double with fan costs US$3. There's an outdoor bar on the main road, easily recognised by the tell-tale blue-and-white fence, which serves a good selection of refrigerated drinks as well as tasty chop in the evenings. For those with private transport, we were told that there's superior accommodation a few kilometres out of town at the Cocoa Research Centre Guesthouse.

Two further mud-and-stick mosques are clearly visible from the road between Bole and Kumasi, evidence that the modern road approximates a much older Islamic trade route. Both these mosques are fenced, making them less photogenic than the one at Bole. The first mosque is on the east side of the main road through Maluwe, a forest-fringed village which might well hold some interesting walking possibilities. The second mosque, at Banda Nkwanta, lies on the west side of the road, and is notable for having very tall parapets relative to the size of the rest of the building. There's no formal accommodation in either of these villages, but it's unlikely you'd have a problem pitching a tent or finding a room in a private house.

Those with an insatiable desire to see mosques might be interested to know that we were told by everybody we asked in the region that the above (along with the mosques at Larabanga, Bole and Wa) are the only buildings of their sort in Ghana. A few weeks later, in Ho Museum, at the other side of the country, we saw a photograph of a similar mosque at a place called Dondoli, which I can find on no map … so who knows how many other mud-and-stick mosques await discovery by travellers?

MOLE NATIONAL PARK

Established the year after Ghana attained independence, the 4,840km^2 Mole National Park was formally gazetted in 1971 following the controversial resettlement of the relatively few villagers who lived in an area that had formerly been thinly populated due to tsetse flies. Extended to its present size in 1991, Mole conserves an area of relatively flat savannah lying at an average altitude of about 150m above sea level, and broken by the 250m high escarpment on which its only motel accommodation is sited. It is the largest game reserve in Ghana, the most accessible and – at least in terms of general game viewing – the best.

More than 90 mammal and 300 bird species have been recorded in Mole, though several of the larger mammals are thought to be locally extinct or in critical danger of that fate – there has, for instance, been no trace of an African hunting dog noted in more than a decade. In general, however, populations appear to have increased since the last large mammal census was carried out in 1988, and current estimates for the larger herbivores stand at about 800 elephant, more than 1,000 buffalo, and significant populations of hippo, warthog and such antelope species as kob, Defassa waterbuck, bushbuck, roan, hartebeest and grey and red-flanked duiker. Five primate species are present, most visibly the olive baboon, as are 17 carnivores, of which the various mongoose species are most likely to be seen by visitors. Leopard and lion are now mostly known from the occasional spoor, though a pride of three lionesses was sighted at a kill near Lovi in late 1995.

A visit to Mole is easily combined with one to the mosque at Larabanga (see box on page 246), the most famous, frequently visited and reputedly oldest of the half-dozen or so west Sudanese-style mud-and-stick mosques dotted through western Ghana.

Getting there and away

One of Mole's chief attractions for travellers is its accessibility using public transport. The park lies to the north of the reasonably well-travelled dirt road

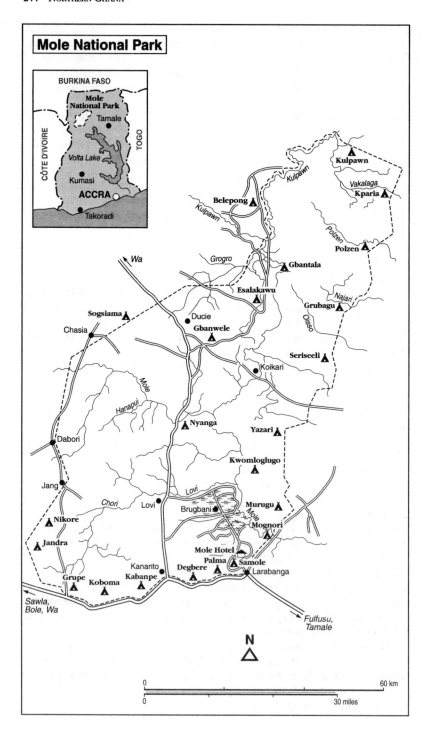

Mole National Park

that connects Sawla on the main Kumasi–Wa road to Fufulsu on the main Kumasi–Tamale road. The turn-off to the park is in Larabanga village, roughly 50km from Sawla, 80km from Fufulsu, and 20km north of Damongo, the district capital of West Gonja. The entrance gate lies 3km along the turn-off from Larabanga and the motel a further 1.5km past the entrance gate.

The most popular approach is directly from Tamale, the terminus for the only bus service that actually goes into the park. This is an OSA bus service which leaves Tamale daily at 14.00, overnights at Mole Motel after arriving there at around nightfall, then begins the return trip at the motel between 05.00 and 06.00, depending on the driver's mood. Anybody who is coming from Kumasi and thinking of boarding this bus at Fufulsu (or, more accurately, at Damongo junction, about 3km north of Fufulsu) should be warned that seats are almost always fully occupied when it leaves Tamale, so you'll probably have to stand as far as Damongo, where most passengers disembark. Travellers who leave Mole for a destination other than Tamale can use this bus service to get to Larabanga (for Wa or Bole) or Damongo junction (for Kumasi).

Aside from the direct service between Tamale and the motel, at least three other buses daily pass through Larabanga. These bus services are particularly useful coming to or from Wa or Bole in the east. Coming from Wa, City Express buses to Tamale leave at around 06.00 and 17.00, taking about three hours to get to Larabanga. Coming from Bole, a City Express bus to Tamale leaves at 06.00 and arrives in Larabanga 2–3 hours later. If you arrive at Larabanga on a bus that doesn't comtinue to Mole, you can either walk to the motel (expect this to take slightly longer than a hour) or else wait for the Tamale–Mole bus to pass through, which will probably be between 17.30 and 18.30.

Leaving Mole in the direction of Bole or Wa, your best bet is to take the Mole–Tamale bus as far as Larabanga, then pick up the first bus heading west, which generally passes through Larabanga before 09.00. If this bus is heading to Wa and you want to go to Bole (or vice versa), disembark at the junction town of Sawla, from where there is plenty of transport in either direction.

If you are heading to Mole as a self-contained excursion from Kumasi on public transport, you'll probably regret trying the most obvious option, changing vehicles at Damongo junction, since no tro-tros run along this road and the buses are nearly always full by the time they get to the junction. Better to take a bus up to Tamale and board the OSA bus to Mole there, or (especially if you are interested in ancient mosques) to catch a Kumasi–Wa bus to Bole, spend the night there, then board the Bole–Tamale bus as far as Larabanga the next morning.

Driving to Mole should be straightforward enough in a good 4x4, even though the stretch of road between Fufulsu and Damongo is poorly maintained. A pick-up truck with good clearance should also see you through, except perhaps after heavy rain, but visiting Mole in any other 2x4 vehicle cannot be recommended.

A NON-HISTORY OF LARABANGA

The mosque at Larabanga may well be the oldest extant building in Ghana. Yet, oddly, nobody seems to agree on just how old it is, or even who built it. Some sources date it to the thirteenth century, which if not impossible is certainly improbable given that Islam had barely infiltrated the region at that time. In Larabanga itself, locals are fixated on the year 1421 and accredit the construction to an Islamic trader called Ayuba. Meanwhile, a display on Larabanga in the National Museum in Accra states that the mosque was built over the period 1643–75 by Imam Bramah, a theory that seems to be based solely on the somewhat negative evidence that the Imam's original illuminated Koran is still preserved in the mosque (but don't get excited, because you won't be allowed inside the mosque, let alone be shown the Koran).

Local tradition has it that the mosque's founder was travelling through the region when he found the so-called mystic stone that lies on the outskirts of Larabanga and decided, for some unexplained reason, that he would throw his spear from there and sleep wherever it landed. This he did, and during the night he had a strange dream about a mosque, the foundations of which were mysteriously in place when he awoke. Ayuba completed the construction of the mosque and settled at Larabanga. How the date 1421 arose is anybody's guess. All the guides at Larabanga could tell me is that the date appears in a book, which means that it must be right (the book in question would appear to be Jojo Cobbinah's German guide to Ghana, a book with a great many merits but no more a work of historical authority than the book you're reading right now!). When pressed on where the book's author got that date, the guides said he had asked around the village – an argument as circular as it is unconvincing. Then again, the early fifteenth century would tie in with dates given by the Imams of other similar mosques, as well as the period that is generally agreed to be when Islam expanded its hold into what is now northern Ghana. And if this is the case, then, yes, visitors to Larabanga are probably looking at the oldest extant building in Ghana, some 50 years old when the Portuguese set about building their first castle at Elmina. But who knows?

Where to stay and eat

The **Mole Motel**, built in 1961 on a cliff overlooking two waterholes, is an attractively situated, surprisingly comfortable complex, marred only by an architectural approach that made no effort to integrate building and environment. Prices at the motel are well within reach of most travellers. Three types of room are available, all with a fan that works only while the generator is running, between 18.00 and 22.00, and a private bathroom with an erratic supply of running water (a bucket is supplied but the onus is on you to keep topping it up). An ordinary double costs US$14, an ordinary triple US$17, and a larger double with a private balcony overlooking the waterhole US$20. It is also possible to camp within the motel grounds at a cost of US$2.50 per person. The communal area of the motel is focused around a swimming pool, empty for many years, but in the process of being repaired and refilled in December 1997. The bar serves sodas, beers and mineral water, the coolness of which depends on whether it was in the fridge while the electricity was running, and the restaurant does a reasonable variety of meals starting at around US$3–4.

In addition to the motel, several **very basic camping sites** are dotted around the reserve, none of them currently used with any frequency by

It is just as difficult to get to the bottom of Larabanga's status as the oldest and most holy of Ghana's mud-and-thatch mosques. People in Larabanga generally deny the existence of similar mosques elsewhere in the country and, if you say that you've actually seen some of them yourself, they turn up their noses at any suggestion that a 'man-made replica' might be of similar antiquity to their divinely created original. In all probability, the mud-and-stick mosques of Ghana *were* built in close succession along a well-established trade route through the west. Larabanga's claim to be the oldest of these mosques is supported by its reported status over several centuries as a surrogate Mecca for Ghanaian Muslims (a status, I hasten to add, about which I was informed for the first and last time in Larabanga itself). It is difficult to verify – and frankly, after the umpteenth occasion on which the date 1421 and phrase 'man-made replica' had been used to stonewall my enquiries, I found myself actively hoping that someday, somehow I'd stumble across a piece of evidence that would shatter the atmosphere of smug consensus that appears to consume the good folk of Larabanga on this subject. Can it be pure coincidence that 'Ghana's oldest mosque' also happens to be the one that lies a mere 5km from the motel in Mole National Park? The sense that the people of Larabanga aren't above a bit of conscious mythologising is heightened when you are taken to the mystic stone, a frankly very ordinary chunk of rock which caused the road towards Bole to be diverted because it 'mysteriously' reappeared overnight every time that it was removed by the road constructors.

Whenever it was built, Larabanga mosque, like others of its ilk, is obviously very old, and a truly strange and inspiring sight. Since 1995, the mosque has also been the cornerstone of a Peace Corps coordinated community tourism project, one of particular importance in that by allowing the villagers to benefit from tourism it has the potential to ease the tension which has marked relations between village and national park ever since the former's traditional hunting grounds were gazetted away without recompense. But it does seem a shame under the circumstances that nobody locally, not even the guides, is able to provide visitors with *any* objective information whatsoever about its history.

tourists. For most travellers, the only realistic way of staying at one of these camps would be to organise an overnight foot safari (see *What to do* page 248). The most accessible camping site, Brugbani, 7km from the motel, has a reliable water supply in the rainy season.

A recently established alternative to sleeping within Mole, a private **house stay at Larabanga** can be organised through the Larabanga tourist centre at a cost of US$2 per person. This is a lot cheaper than staying in a room at the motel, especially as you'll struggle to spend much money on food or drink in Larabanga. The obvious disadvantage is that you'll need to get between Larabanga and the motel early in the day in order to do a morning game walk (one way of doing this would be to hire a bicycle from the tourist centre for US$3 per day). If you want to see Mole at its best but also keep down costs, a good compromise might be to spend your first night at the motel, do an early game walk, then spend a second night at Larabanga. Few travellers stay at Larabanga at present, largely because the house-stay scheme is relatively new and unpublicised, but the village is likely to grow in popularity following the construction of a formal resthouse, hopefully before the end of 1998.

What to do

There would be worse ways to pass a day than sitting on the **viewing platform** at the Mole Motel, cold beer in hand, swimming pool 20 paces away, and two waterholes clearly visible below. In the dry season, even this most passive approach to safari-going should reward you with sightings of elephant, kob antelope, Defassa waterbuck, bushbuck, warthog, olive baboon, green monkey and numerous birds during the course of any given day.

It's far more exciting, however, to head down to the base of the cliff on a **guided game walk** – not that you'll necessarily see a greater variety of mammals, just that you'll get far closer to them, in particular the elephants, which are reasonably habituated to human pedestrians and often allow visitors to approach to within 20m. On foot, you can also be reasonably sure of seeing Nile crocodiles in the dam and of mutually startling a few water monitors – bulky lizards which measure more than 1m long and habitually crash gracelessly to safety when disturbed. A guided walk with an armed ranger costs US$1 per person per hour, regardless of group size, and there are enough rangers for every group to have its own guide. It is customary to tip the ranger. Note that walking in the park without an armed ranger is forbidden, except along the road between the motel and Larabanga.

If the variety of large mammals is limited, the number and variety of **birds** to be seen around the waterholes can be fantastic. Most visitors will notice larger birds such as martial eagle (a pair of which currently nest in the area), white-headed and saddlebill stork, white-backed and palmnut vulture, and various herons and egrets. Colour, too, is not lacking: the noisy but elusive red, black and yellow barbary shrike is something of a speciality, as is the red-throated bee-eater, a colony of which nests in the vicinity. Also worth looking out for are Senegal parrot, Abyssinian roller, green pigeon and violet plantain-eater. All in all, I saw around 60 species in a three-hour walk; a more experienced West African birdwatcher would doubtless have seen more. If birds are of specific interest, ask for a ranger who is especially knowledgeable. The Collins West African bird field guide and binoculars can be rented from the tourist centre in Larabanga at a daily rate respectively of US$1.50 and US$3.

Those wishing to see some of the large mammal species that don't frequent the motel area, or who simply want to experience a genuine wilderness atmosphere, should ask about an **overnight hike** with an armed ranger, using one or more of the many small camping sites scattered through the reserve. This is a thoroughly wonderful prospect, likely to be introduced during the lifespan of this edition at a negotiable rate. By walking deeper into the park, you can be reasonably certain of seeing buffalo, roan antelope and hippo. With outstanding luck, you might even encounter a lion or leopard.

In theory, **game drives** in national park Land Rovers can be organised at the motel. In practice these haven't been operating for some years, nor are they likely to be restarted in the foreseeable future.

Few visitors would want to miss seeing **Larabanga Mosque**, in the village of the same name some 5km from the motel (see box on page 246). If you're going to be bussing directly in and out of Mole from Tamale, then the best way to do this is to walk out from the motel to Larabanga in the mid-afternoon, then either walk back or wait to catch the late afternoon bus coming from Tamale. Otherwise, you'll get a chance to spend time at the mosque while you wait to change vehicles at Larabanga – it's only 50m from the main junction and bus station. The official entrance fee (or more accurately viewing fee since visitors may not enter the mosque) is US$1. In addition to this, you may also be asked to make one donation to the tourist project, another to the Imam for upkeep of the mosque, and another as a tip to the somewhat redundant guide or guides. I can't help but feel that most visitors would be more comfortable with a higher one-off, all-inclusive 'official fee' from which every concerned party could get its cut.

Larabanga village is itself a fascinating place, with perhaps the most southerly accessible examples of traditional flat-roofed mud *kraals* in the country, of particular interest to travellers who are not exploring other parts of northern Ghana. Through the Larabanga tourist centre it is possible to organise a stay in a private house, as well as to take a guided tour of the village and a local farm for US$2 per person.

Bradt Publications
Travel Guides

June 1998

Dear Readers,

You, the readers, can make an incalculable difference to future editions of this guide by writing to me about your trip. The readership of this guide will collectively experience a great many more aspects of Ghana than I ever could - and they'll also test out a far wider selection of hotels, campsites and restaurants.

So, whether you want to make my day with a blow-by-blow account of your off-the-beaten-track adventures, or spoil it by pointing out why I'm wrong about simply *everything*, your time and effort in writing will be greatly appreciated. Every letter will make for a better second edition, which in turn will enhance the travels of those who follow in your footsteps. The more detail the better, but even the smallest snippet will be of use. Bear in mind that information about one good new hotel will be of benefit to the hotel owners, to me, and to all travellers who pass that way in future.

Every correspondent will be acknowledged in the next edition, so do print your name clearly!

Happy travels

Philip Briggs

email: philari@hixnet.co.za

Appendix One

Language

English is the official language of Ghana, widely spoken in those parts of the country likely to be visited by travellers, to a standard that is matched in few other anglophile African countries. This means that there is little need for short-stay travellers to try to familiarise themselves with any local tongues, though as always knowing a few words or greetings in a local language will often help open doors and break through barriers, particularly in rural areas.

Numerous different languages and dialects are spoken in Ghana, but you'll find that most people belonging to one or other of the Akan groups – and that means more than half of the population and practically everybody in southern and central Ghana – will speak Twi (pronounced rather like Chwee) as a first or second language. Twi is the Ghanaian language taught to most Peace Corps and other volunteers spending a lengthy period of time in the country, and it may help travellers to know a few basic words and phrases. Note that pronunciation of the words listed below, as of most place name in Ghana, is phonetic (for example *ache* is pronounced as *ah-chee* rather than the English word *ache*), and that spellings have been simplified to make sense to English speakers (as one example, 'ch' is often spelt 'ky' in Ghana). Note, too, that vowel sounds are closer to the soft French vowels than hard English ones:

a   similar to the 'a' in 'father'
e   as the 'e' in 'wet'
i   as the 'ee' in 'free' but less drawn out
o   somewhere between the 'o' in 'no' and the word 'awe'
u   similar to the 'oo' in 'food'

Basic words and phrases

Do you speak English?	*Wote Borofo ana?*
Good afternoon	*Mma aha* (response *yemu*)
Good evening	*Mma ajo* (response *yemu*)
Good morning	*Mma ache* (response is *yemu*)
Goodbye	*Nanti ye* or *ye ko*
How are you?	*Wo ho te sen?* (response me *ho ye*)
I	*Me*
I'd like... (food)	*Me zi*
I'd like... (not food)	*Me pe*

No	*Dabe*
Please	*Me pawocheo*
Thank you	*Meda ase*
Today	*Enne*
Tomorrow	*Echina*
Water	*Nsuo*
We	*Ye*
Welcome	*Akwaaba*
What's your name? My name is...	*Ye frewo sen?/Ye fre me...*
What is the cost?	*Eyesen?*
Where is ....?	*... wo hin?*
Yes	*Myew or aane*
Yesterday	*Enra*

Numbers

1	*Baako*	30	*Aduasa*
2	*Mienu*	40	*Aduanang*
3	*Miensa*	50	*Aduonum*
4	*Enang*	60	*Aduosia*
5	*Enoum*	70	*Aduosong*
6	*Nsia*	80	*Aduowotwe*
7	*Nsong*	90	*Aduokrong*
8	*Nwotwe*	100	*Oha*
9	*Nkrong*	1,000	*Apem*
10	*Edu*	10,000	*Pemdu*
11, 12 etc	*Dubaako, dumienu etc*	100,000	*Mpemba*
20	*Aduono*	1,000,000	*Opepe*
21	*Aduono baako*		

Appendix Two

Further Reading

HISTORY AND BACKGROUND

I consulted quite a number of books while researching the general and local history sections included in this guide, all of which I was able to buy in Ghana, though I can't guarantee you'll be able to do the same. I've listed them all below, but it would be pushing it to class most of them as recommended further reading. Buah's *History of Ghana* would be the obvious starting point for those seeking deeper insight into the country's historical background; readable, informative and of manageable length, without really propelling you to turn to the next page. More compelling, oddly enough, is Agbodeka's *Economic History*, while Gadzekpo's otherwise rather flimsy *History of Ghana* is especially strong on prehistory. Danzig's *Forts and Castles* offers a good introduction to coastal history, brought to life by the final chapter on living conditions in and around the forts, and it's readily available in Accra and Cape Coast. Best of all in my opinion – certainly the only substantial book in the collection that I could think about reading from start to finish for pleasure – is *A Thousand Years of West African History*, a collection of essays covering most aspects of the region's history, probably a bit dated by now but of great value for the lively, questioning style throughout.

Agbodeka, F *An Economic History of Ghana* (Ghana University Press 1992)
Ajayi, F & Espie, E (eds) *A Thousand Years of East African History* (Thomas Nelson 1965)
Arhin, K (ed) *The Cape Coast and Elmina Handbook* (University of Ghana
Buah, F *West Africa Since AD 1000* (Macmillan 1974)
Buah, F *A History of Ghana* (Macmillan 1980)
Davidson, B *A History of West Africa 1000–1800* (Longman 1977)
Gadzekpo, A *History of Ghana* (Royal Crown Press 1997)
Graham, J *Cape Coast in History* (Anglican Printing Press 1994)
Kwadwo, O *An Outline of Asante History* (O Kwadwo Enterprises 1994)
Kyeremateng, K *The Akans of Ghana* (Sebewie Publishers 1996)
Moxon, J *Volta: Man's Greatest Lake* (Andre Deutsch 1969)
Obeng, E *Ancient Ashanti Chieftaincy* (Ghana Publishing Corporation 1984)
Onwubiko, K *History of West Africa 1000–1800* (Africana FEP 1982)
Onwubiko, K *History of West Africa 1800–Present Day* (Africana FEP 1985)

Packenham, T *The Scramble for Africa* (Jonathan Ball 1991)
Sampson, M *Makers of Modern Ghana Volume One* (Anowuo Publications 1969)
Sarpong, P *Ghana in Retrospective* (Ghana Publishing Corporation 1974)
Tufuo, J & Donkor, C *Ashantis of Ghana* (Anowuo Publications 1989)
van Dantzig, A *Forts and Castles of Ghana* (Sedco 1980)
Ward, W *Short History of Ghana* (Longman 1957)

FIELD GUIDES

The most useful and current all-purpose guide to African mammals is undoubtedly Chris and Tilde Stuart's *Field Guide to the Larger Mammals of Africa* (Struik, South Africa, 1997). If you have difficulty locating this outside South Africa, several other guides are available, most popularly those published by Collins. Alternatively, once in Ghana, you should be able to get hold of Happold's *Large Mammals of West Africa* (Longman 1973) which, despite being rather dated in some respects, is a very handy, lightweight volume with adequate pictures and descriptions.

For bird identification, the most useful title available at present is Serle, Morel and Hatwig's *Field Guide to the Birds of West Africa* (HarperCollins 1977), though it has a great many flaws, most seriously that full descriptions and illustrations are supplied for only half the species recorded in the region, while almost 400 species are relagated to one line each in an appendix. That said, you should be able to positively identify at least 80% of what you might with a more detailed guide. Serious birdwatchers might also want to carry Ber van Perlo's *Illustrated Checklist to the Birds of East Africa* (HarperCollins, 1995), comprehensive for a region which has considerable overlap into West Africa, though you need to be alert to the numerous instances where the two books give different common names (and sometimes even Latin binomials) for the same species.

TRAVEL GUIDES

The only other English-language guide to Ghana is Mylene Remy's *Ghana Today* (Jaguar 1977 & 1992), which has been translated from the French. The best aspect of this 30cm-long hardback book is the photos; the text, while occasionally informative, more often resorts to whimsy and hyperbole. Far better, according to a couple of Germans who we met along the way, is Jojo Cobbinah's *Ghana* (Peter Meyer, 1995), currently only available in German. Definitely recommended for those who are spending a while in the capital is the North American Women's Association's *No Worries: The Indispensable Insiders' Guide to Accra*, an excellent source of advice and contacts in Accra.

Those travelling further afield in West Africa are pointed to one of two guides to the region: Jim Hudgens and Richard Trillo's *West Africa: The Rough Guide* (Rough Guides 1995) and Alex Newton and David Else's *West African Travel Survival Kit* (Lonely Planet 1995). On the basis of the Ghana chapters at least, neither guide inspires great confidence, but for what it's worth, the Lonely Planet guide is generally more accurate regarding accommodation and eating recommendations in Ghana, while the Rough Guide is more engagingly written and tends to push more towards off-the-beaten-track exploration.

FICTION
Ghana has one of the strongest English literary traditions to be found anywhere in Africa, dating back to 1911 and the publication of what is regarded as West Africa's first novel, *Ethiopia Unbound*, by the barrister and nationalist politician Joseph Casely Hayford. A fair selection of local novels are available in most bookshops around the country, generally at very reasonable prices. A few better-known novels include B Kojo Laing's *Search Sweet Country*, Ayi Kwei Armah's *The Beautiful Ones Are Not Yet Born* and *Healers*, Ama Ata Aidoo's *Dilemma of a Ghost* and *Our Sister Killjoy*, and Amma Darko's *Beyond the Horizon*.

BIOGRAPHY
Maya Angelou's *All God's Children Need Travelling Shoes* (Virago 1987) recounts the story of this American author's return to Ghana to search out her roots.

COMPLETE LIST OF GUIDES FROM BRADT PUBLICATIONS

Albania: Guide and Illustrated Journal Peter Dawson/
  Andrea Dawson/Linda White
Amazon, The Roger Harris/Peter Hutchison
Antarctica: A Guide to the Wildlife Tony Soper/Dafila Scott
Australia and New Zealand by Rail Colin Taylor
Belize Alex Bradbury
Brazil Alex Bradbury
Britain, Eccentric see *Eccentric Britain*
Burma Nicholas Greenwood
Canada, North: Yukon, Northwest Territories, Nunavut Geoffrey
  Roy
Cape Verde Islands Aisling Irwin/Colum Wilson
Chile and Argentina: Backpacking and Hiking Tim Burford
China: Yunnan Province Stephen Mansfield
Cuba Stephen Fallon
East and Southern Africa: The Backpacker's Manual
  Philip Briggs
Eccentric Britain Benedict le Vay
Ecuador, Climbing and Hiking in Rob Rachowiecki/
  Mark Thurber
Ecuador, Peru and Bolivia: The Backpacker's Manual
  Kathy Jarvis
Eritrea Edward Paice
Estonia Neil Taylor
Ethiopia Philip Briggs
Galápagos Wildlife David Horwell/Pete Oxford
Georgia Tim Burford
Ghana Philip Briggs
Greece by Rail Zane Katsikis
Haiti and the Dominican Republic Ross Velton
India by Rail Royston Ellis
Laos and Cambodia John R Jones
Latvia Stephen Baister/Chris Patrick
Lithuania Gordon McLachlan *Madagascar* Hilary Bradt
Madagascar Wildlife Hilary Bradt/Derek Schuurman/
  Nick Garbutt

Malawi Philip Briggs
Maldives Royston Ellis
Mali Ross Velton
Mauritius, Rodrigues and Réunion Royston Ellis/
 Derek Schuurman
Mexico, Backpacking in Tim Burford
Mozambique Philip Briggs
Namibia Chris McIntyre
North Cyprus Diana Darke
Palestine, with Jerusalem Henry Stedman
Peru and Bolivia: Backpacking and Trekking Hilary Bradt
Philippines Stephen Mansfield
Poland and Ukraine, Hiking Guide to Tim Burford
Romania, Hiking Guide to Tim Burford
Russia and Central Asia by Road Hazel Barker
Russia by Rail, with Belarus and Ukraine Athol Yates
South Africa Philip Briggs
Southern Africa by Rail Paul Ash
Spitsbergen Andreas Umbreit
Switzerland by Rail Anthony Lambert
Tanzania Philip Briggs
Uganda Philip Briggs
USA by Rail John Pitt
Venezuela Hilary Dunsterville Branch
Vietnam John R Jones
Your Child's Health Abroad Dr Jane Wilson-Howarth/
 Dr Matthew Ellis
Zambia Chris McIntyre
Zanzibar David Else

Bradt guides are available from bookshops or by mail order from:
Bradt Travel Guides
19 High Street, Chalfont St Peter, Bucks SL9 9QE, England
Tel: 01753 893444   Fax: 01753 892333
Email: info@bradt-travelguides.com
www.bradt-travelguides.com

258

PHOTOGRAPHIC TIPS
Ariadne Van Zandbergen
Ghana's colourfully dressed people, varied architecture and tropical scenery have great potential as photographic subjects. In Baobeng-Fiema and Mole, there are also opportunities for wildlife photography, though since most game viewing is done on foot, any lens too heavy to be hand-held will be superfluous for all but the seriously dedicated.

Equipment
The simpler the camera, the less there is to go wrong, since complex electronic gadgetry can be sensitive to rain, dust and heat. For landscapes and portraits, a solidly built manual-focus camera will be adequate and can be bought cheaply secondhand. An autofocus camera will, however, focus with greater precision than any person can hope to on a regular basis, and is particularly useful for capturing moving objects. If you carry only one lens in Ghana, a 28–70 or similar zoom should be ideal for most purposes, but not wildlife photography. A lightweight 80–200 or 70–300 or similar is excellent for wildlife and candid shots.

Film
Print film is the preference of most casual photographers, slide film of professionals and some serious amateurs. You should definitely use slide film if you hope to have anything published. Slide film is more expensive than print film, but this is broadly compensated for by cheaper development costs.

Most serious photographers working outdoors in Africa favour Fujichrome slide film, in particular Sensia 100, Provia 100 (the professional equivalent to Sensia) or Velvia 50. Slow films (ie: those with a low ASA rating) produce less grainy and sharper images than fast films, but can be tricky without a tripod in low light. Velvia 50 is extremely fine-grained and shows stunning colour saturation; it is the film I normally use in soft, even light or overcast weather. Sensia or Provia may be preferable in low light, since 100 ASA allows you to work at a faster shutter speed than 50 ASA. Because 100 ASA is more tolerant of contrast, it is also preferable in harsh light.

For print photography, a combination of 100 or 200 ASA film should be ideal. For the best results it is advisable to stick to recognised brands. Fujicolor produces excellent print films, with the Superia 100 and 200 recommended.

Some basics
The automatic programmes provided with many cameras are limited in the sense that the camera cannot think, but only make calculations. A better investment than any amount of electronic wizardry would be to buy or borrow a photographic manual for beginners and get to grips with such basics as the relationship between aperture and shutter speed.

Beginners should be aware that aperture determines depth of field. At one extreme, an aperture reading of at least 16 is required for a picture in which a close foreground and distant background should both be sharp. At the other extreme, an aperture reading of 2.8 or 4 may enhance the impact of a portrait by blurring the background.

Beginners should also note that a low shutter speed can result in camera shake and therefore a blurred image. For hand-held photographs of static subjects using a low magnification lens (eg: 28–70), select a shutter speed of at least 1/60 of a second. For lenses of higher magnification, the rule of thumb is that the shutter speend should be at least the inverse of the magnification (for instance, a speed of 1/300 or faster on a 300 magnification lens). You can use lower shutter speeds with a tripod.

Most modern cameras include a built-in light meter, and give users the choice of three types of metering: matrix, centre weighted or spot metering. You will need to understand how these different sytems work to make proper use of them. Built-in light meters are reliable in most circumstances, but in uneven light, or where there is a lot of sky, you may want to take your metering selectively, for instance by taking a spot reading on the main subject. The meter will tend to under- or overexpose when pointed at an almost white or black subject. This can be countered by taking a reading against an 18% grey card, or a substitute such as grass or light grey rocks – basically anything that isn't almost black, almost white or highly reflective.

Autofocus is more reliable than manual focus, but can instil a tendency to place the subject at the centre of the frame. A more interesting image will normally be obtained if the subject is at least slightly off-centre; this can be achieved by focussing on the main subject, then holding the focus down while moving the camera to adjust the framing.

Dust and heat

Dust and heat are a problem in parts of Ghana. Keep your equipment in a sealed bag, stow films in an airtight container (such as a small cooler bag), leave used films in your hotel room, and avoid changing film in dusty conditions. On rough roads, I always carry my camera equipment on my lap to protect against vibration and bumps. Never stow camera equipment or film in a car boot (it will bake), or let it stand in direct sunlight.

Light

The light in Africa is much harsher than in Europe or North America, for which reason the most striking outdoor photographs are often taken during the hour or two of 'golden light' after dawn and before sunset. Shooting in low light may enforce the use of very low shutter speeds, in which case a tripod (ideally) or monopod (lighter) will be required to avoid camera shake. Be alert to the the long shadows cast by a low sun; these show up more on photographs than to the naked eye.

With careful handling, sidelighting and backlighting can produce stunning effects, especially in soft light and at sunrise or sunset. Generally, however, it is best to shoot with the sun behind you Because of this, most buildings and landscapes are essentially a 'morning shot' or 'afternoon shot', depending on the direction in which they face. When you spend a couple of nights in one place, you'll improve your results by planning the best time to take pictures of static subjects (a compass can come in handy).

When photographing people or animals in the harsh midday sun, images taken in light but even shade are likely to look nicer than those taken in direct sunlight or patchy shade, since the latter conditions create too much contrast. But do avoid photographing a shaded subject against a sunlit background, which creates severe contrast. Fill-in flash is almost essential if you want to capture facial detail of dark-skinned people in harsh or contrasty light.

Serious photographers should avoid travelling during the harmattan (see page 45).

Protocol

Except in general street or market scenes, it is normally unacceptable to photograph Ghanaians without permission. Some people will refuse to be photographed, some will agree, and others will expect a small payment. Even the most willing subject tends to pose stiffly when a camera is pointed at them; relax them by making a joke, and take a few shots in quick succession to improve the odds of capturing a natural pose.

INDEX

Entries in *italics* indicate maps